W9-ABJ-550

Small Change

Small Change

Money, Political Parties, and Campaign Finance Reform

RAYMOND J. LA RAJA

The University of Michigan Press

Ann Arbor

Copyright © by the University of Michigan 2008

All rights reserved

Published in the United States of America by

The University of Michigan Press

Manufactured in the United States of America

☉ Printed on acid-free paper

2011   2010   2009   2008   4   3   2   1

No part of this publication may be reproduced, stored in a retrieval system, or transmitted in any form or by any means, electronic, mechanical, or otherwise, without the written permission of the publisher.

A CIP catalog record for this book is available from the British Library.

Library of Congress Cataloging-in-Publication Data

La Raja, Raymond J., 1965–

 Small change : money, political parties, and campaign finance
reform / Raymond J. La Raja.

  p. cm.

 Includes bibliographical references and index.

 ISBN-13: 978-0-472-07028-2 (cloth : alk. paper)

 ISBN-10: 0-472-07028-2 (cloth : alk. paper)

 ISBN-13: 978-0-472-05028-4 (pbk. : alk. paper)

 ISBN-10: 0-472-05028-1 (pbk. : alk. paper)

 1. Campaign funds—United States. 2. Campaign funds—Law and
legislation—United States. 3. United States. Bipartisan Campaign
Reform Act of 2002. I. Title.

JK1991.L3 2008

324.7'80973—dc22   2007039068

For Taryn

Contents

Tables

Figures

Acknowledgments

During the several years I worked on this project I benefited from the help of many friends and colleagues. I am especially appreciative of my mentors at the University of California–Berkeley, Bruce Cain and Nelson Polsby. This book grew out of my research as a graduate student under their guidance at the Institute of Governmental Studies (IGS). Thanks to Bruce and Nelson, the IGS was a wonderful place for graduate students to develop their ideas and test them in the broader community of scholars through seminars and informal gatherings. They offered innumerable opportunities for me to engage in fieldwork related to my interests. Most important, and much to my delight, they made the enterprise of scholarship a socially active affair and not a lonesome intellectual pursuit. I will sorely miss my friend Nelson Polsby, who died recently, for his generous spirit and wit. I am also grateful to Judy Gruber, who is sadly no longer with us. She supported me early in my graduate years, and I learned a great deal from her by assisting in her research. She also read and commented on the entire doctoral dissertation, which forms a part of this book.

At the University of Massachusetts, I owe a great debt to Jerry Mileur for reading the entire manuscript. His formidable knowledge of American political parties and consummate editing skills helped me clarify my arguments and place them in proper historical perspective. Other debts were incurred to colleagues and friends who read individual or several chapters and offered their valuable insights, including Herb Alexander (the "dean" of the study of money in politics), Dorie Apollonio, Jonathan Bernstein, Bruce Cain, Jon Cohen, Mike Hannahan, Paul Herrnson, Thad Kousser, Eric McGhee, Sid Milkis, Vin Moscardelli, Bob Mutch, Rob Rodriguez, Richard Skinner, Jennifer Steen, and Craig Thomas.

Some of this work emerged from robust debates, sponsored by organizations such as the Campaign Finance Institute and the *Election Law Journal,* with colleagues who often disagreed with me on particulars but always with goodwill and the spirit of scholarly enterprise. They forced me to think hard about my analysis and opened me to alternative and compelling perspectives on political reform and its consequences. These colleagues include Bob Bauer, Jim

Campbell, Tony Corrado, Diana Dwyre, John Green, Rick Hasen, Robin Kolodny, Jonathan Krasno, Dan Lowenstein, Michael Malbin, Tom Mann, Nate Persily, John Samples, and Clyde Wilcox. Bob Biersack of the Federal Elections Commission provided essential assistance, furnishing campaign finance data and explaining many aspects of regulations on political committees.

I would like to thank my colleagues at the University of Massachusetts, who have been wholly supportive of my research. Their work inspired me to pursue the idea of looking at the historical development of campaign finance regulation, which forms a major part of the book. The leadership in the department, especially M. J. Peterson, George Sulzner, and John Hird, was instrumental in providing me with the resources and supportive environment that allowed me to complete this book. Special thanks to Kate Longley and Nate Kraft, graduate students at the University of Massachusetts, for reading through the entire manuscript, offering helpful edits, and tracking down information. I am also grateful to Jim Reische at the University of Michigan Press for his enthusiastic support of the project and Sarah Remington for her invaluable guidance.

I am grateful to my parents, Ray and Adriana, for encouraging my intellectual pursuits and helping relieve the pinch of graduate school with timely gifts of delicious meals, entertainment, and much more. I can say the same of my in-laws, Bill and Elaine Shea, who have been extraordinarily enthusiastic and supportive of all my pursuits. This book is dedicated to my wife, Taryn, for her unconditional support for all that I do—even in the breathtaking hurly-burly of raising three children—and her inimitable way of helping me appreciate the good and important things in life.

CHAPTER 1

Money and Politics

For at least a century, the nation has struggled with how to reconcile the role of money in politics. Much of the public debate has focused on the potentially corrupting effects of political contributions to candidates and on how to curtail the influence of wealthy donors. Frequently ignored in these debates are the consequences of campaign finance regulations for political organizing and campaigns. These regulations matter not only as a way to prevent influence peddling—the classic quid pro quo—but also because they influence who has power in electoral politics. Campaign finance laws help some political organizations and candidates raise and spend political funds more easily than others. In turn, these laws can influence who gets elected to public office.

Seen from the perspective of electoral engagement, regulating money becomes not merely an issue concerning corruption but also one that raises questions about fairness in a broader sense. Who gains from changing campaign finance rules? How do these rules affect different groups? These are questions this book explores. Rather than focus on candidates or interest groups, as many studies do, this work focuses primarily on political parties. I examine how campaign finance laws affect the two major national party organizations, the Republican National Committee (RNC) and the Democratic National Committee (DNC), which have come to play significant roles in American political campaigns in recent decades. The goal is to understand how rules regulating political money have shaped the activities and influence of party organizations and, more indirectly, the groups and individuals that support these parties. In doing this, a broader purpose is to understand the dynamics of political reform, namely, the underlying motivations for pursuing reform and how rules generate consequences, both intended and unintended. This knowledge is then put to use in a specific context to assess how parties respond to the current configuration of laws under the new Bipartisan Campaign Reform Act (BCRA) of 2002.[1]

The national party organizations have been in existence since the mid-nineteenth century, but they have traditionally been weak institutions in a system of decentralized political parties. Their chief task was to organize the national conventions, after which they virtually disappeared until four years later. Typically, American parties were most influential at the local level among party chieftains who controlled blocs of county or urban voters and the patronage jobs available in the cities and states. The intensely local nature of party politics has changed in the past thirty years. In the 1980s and 1990s national political parties emerged as stronger organizations to help candidates meet the growing expense of campaigns (Aldrich 1995; Cotter et al. 1984; Herrnson 1988; Schlesinger 1984). They came to possess critical electoral resources, giving them the potential to influence outcomes in presidential and congressional races.[2] With permanent headquarters in Washington, staffed with professionals, both major parties became formidable fund-raisers and sources of expertise, controlling vast amounts of voter data. In the 2004 elections, national political committees combined to spend more than $1.2 billion, or more than one-third of the total reported spending in congressional and presidential elections (Federal Election Commission 2005a). Only three decades earlier in 1972 they spent just $11 million, which reflected just 5 percent of total campaign spending for federal races (Alexander 1976, 85–92).

There is wide consensus among political scientists that the emergence of stronger national parties is good for democracy. Parties have proven to be reliable mediating institutions that connect citizens to their government. Through their widely understood labels, parties help voters identify and select among candidates and policies. By contesting elections, parties also bring accountability to governing elites who must face the prospect of being challenged by an opposing party candidate if they are unresponsive to the public. In addition, political parties help to unite various interests through the give-and-take of coalition building necessary for winning elections in a two-party system. In theory, at least, the partisan goal of winning office should give the parties an incentive to mobilize underrepresented groups that lack other institutional bases of support (Key 1942). A strong national presence has the potential to tighten links between different political groups and bring together local, state, and federal candidates behind a common party platform.[3]

While contemporary national parties appear to be thriving, they do so in a campaign environment highly dependent on money. Like other sectors of society—business, media, and nonprofits—politics has shifted from an activity supported by labor resources to one more dependent on technology and capital. Political campaigns compete for the attention of citizens through intense consumer advertising and leisure entertainment. For this reason, politics has turned to techniques of persuasion and mobilization to capture audiences. Modern campaigns now depend on the intensive use of mass media technology, which include the expert services of pollsters, media consultants, and direct mail marketers.

For the past two decades, spending in federal elections has outpaced the rate of inflation, abetted by the huge costs associated with television advertising (Ansolabehere, de Figueiredo, and Snyder 2003, 105–30). The amounts spent in political campaigns seem astonishing to the average American. In 2004, the presidential and congressional elections cost more than $4 billion, which was more than the gross domestic product (GDP) of Haiti (World Bank 2006). The fact that money has become so critical in elections creates fundamental tensions in the democratic system. In theory, the democratic process, at least since the twentieth century, is rooted in the principle of "one-person, one vote." But that principle appears undermined by a campaign finance system that allows unlimited political campaign contributions. Wealthy donors may receive privileged access to lawmakers or have disproportionate influence in electing candidates. Of even greater concern to many is the prospect that politicians could be corrupted by large donations. Rather than pursue policies in the public interest or for their constituents, they might create policies that favor donors in exchange for campaign money.

The potential for political corruption has brought forth numerous calls for reform throughout the twentieth century. A standard response since the Progressive Era at the turn of the twentieth century has been a "prohibitionist" approach that seeks to restrict the flow of money to parties and candidates, either through contribution or spending caps or both. The avowed goal has been to prevent the quid pro quo exchange between wealthy donors and public officials. In trying to prevent the wealthy from having undue influence, Progressives—and those who followed in their path—sought to shore up the legitimacy of the electoral system. In the Supreme Court case *McConnell v. Federal Election Commission* (2003), the majority opinion endorsed Progressive reformer and statesman Elihu Root, who argued that restrictions on political contributions would "strik[e] at a constantly growing evil which has done more to shake the confidence of the plain people of small means of this country in our political institutions than any other practice which has ever obtained since the foundation of our Government." Root's efforts, along with those of other Progressives, led to the first federal ban on contributions from corporations and banks under the Tillman Act of 1907. The rationale behind this act undergirded reforms that came later in the century to ban labor union contributions and cap contributions from wealthy donors.

The historical record at the turn of the twentieth century shows numerous efforts in the American states to regulate money. These efforts were integral to diminishing the influence of traditional party elites. American political parties were seen as antithetical to the Progressive goal of transforming democratic politics from partisan expressions of loyalty into a more individualized, rational, "educational," and nonpartisan form of political participation (McGerr 1986). Campaign finance regulation, while not central to the Progressive reform agenda, was part of a broader strategy to deemphasize the partisan nature of political campaigns, to elevate the quality of debate beyond emotional appeals, and to lessen the importance of material motives (such as patronage) as a reason for supporting candidates. The Progressives, with help from the Populists, passed legislation for direct primaries, initiatives, referendums, and campaign finance regulation, all of which challenged the party bosses who previously controlled nominations as well as significant political resources.

A RESOURCE-BASED MODEL OF POLITICAL REFORM

Seen from the historical perspective, campaign finance reforms have been *party* reforms because the regulations influence the scope of party activity in American elections. While the major thrust of the laws has been to prevent corruption, they have had important consequences on political parties that have yet to be fully explained. Reforms have typically pushed money "outside" the regulated electoral system, reflecting a pattern in which resources seeped away from central political actors, such as party organizations, and toward candidates and interest groups. The decentralizing effects of Progressive-style campaign finance laws have done little to staunch the flow of money in politics but have made it more difficult for broad-based political parties to assume responsibility for elections.

It is not my argument, however, that campaign finance laws *caused* candidate-centered American elections. Many other factors were at work—technological, institutional, and demographic—but the campaign finance laws surely encouraged and reinforced a movement away from political parties toward an individualized politics by shifting the flow of resources away from the formal party organization.

The partisan consequences of campaign finance reforms do not end here. Reform of any kind tends to favor one party or the other because laws enhance or diminish the value of particular electoral resources relative to others.[4] Through their long histories, the Democrats and Republicans have possessed distinctive sets of resources, supplied by their diverse constituencies. Most obviously, the Republicans, as the party of business and middle class, appear to have access to a larger constituency of wealthy donors. Thus, the RNC tends to perform better than the DNC under regulatory regimes that are more laissez-faire. History shows, in fact, that the RNC has consistently raised more money than the DNC. The DNC, however, has relied heavily on labor unions to mobilize supporters, which provides them with a noncash resource to win elections. For this reason, Democrats tend to prefer restrictions on cash resources.

Democrats have also borne the additional burden of holding together a more heterogeneous coalition than Republicans. While having the support of different constituencies confers obvious electoral advantages, this diversity also increases the cost of organizing. The Democratic Party—divided more than Republicans by section, ethnicity, and ideology—finds it especially difficult to have a strong national apparatus. More than Republican campaigning, Democratic campaigning has been guided by local elites with strong ties to different constituencies. The decentralized nature of Democratic campaigning often means that electoral resources are not used in the most efficient manner. But this has not stopped the party from winning elections by keeping its coalition intact. The divided nature of Democrats has also increased the difficulty of raising money centrally through the DNC since party loyalties tend to be local. Given this disadvantage relative to Republicans, Democrats, I will show later, tend to prefer regulatory regimes that encourage dispersed and decentralized financing of politics, whereas Republicans tend to prefer regimes that allow the RNC to amass funds centrally.

Beyond the interparty effects of reform, rule changes also have partisan consequences *within* the party. The laws alter the balance of power within a coalition by giving some groups resource advantages over others. Laws that discourage cash contributions, for example, increase the party's dependency on outside groups that can mobilize their members, campaign on behalf of party candidates, or make endorsements. Party leaders adapt their electoral strategies to new laws, and in the process they become more or less dependent on factions within the party structure that can influence the outcome of political campaigns using their particular set of resources. The new dependencies generated by political reforms thus alter power relations between party factions since each group has bargaining power relative to its access to critical electoral resources (Panebianco 1988; Pfeffer and Salancik 1978).

These intraparty dimensions are rarely, if ever, addressed in research on campaign finance, but they have important implications for how we think about electoral reform. The process is fraught with potential for manipulation of rules for political gain. Partisans fight over rules because they control different configurations of electoral resources, which will be affected by new regulations. Reforms may enhance or diminish the value of resources they control, giving them more or less electoral influence. Individual political entrepreneurs, such as Senator John McCain, gain politically from passing reform. Not only do they garner the mantle of being called "reformers," which brings positive publicity, but they also diminish the power of party leaders, and the dominant factions that support the leaders, by helping to pass laws that curtail party-based resources. These entrepreneurs work with discontented factions in either party that desire to weaken the influence of dominant factions within the party.

In this book I argue that the emergence of new campaign finance laws can be tied to partisan strategies for influencing the value of one faction's resources relative to those of rivals. Most previous studies acknowledge the role of partisan interest in passing reform. The historical record illustrates, for example, how Democrats have tried repeatedly to diminish the cash advantages of Republicans and how Republicans in turn have tried to prevent nonparty groups from helping Democrats with in-kind support. But the story of *intra*party rivalries in shaping reform has not been told. While descriptive accounts of reform allude to factional maneuvering in passing legislation, they fail to elaborate a theory of how this maneuvering results in particular reforms.[5] Progressive Republicans in the early twentieth century, for example, had much to gain from loosening the ties between traditional Republican elites and corporate interests. Similarly, southern Democrats during the New Deal era were champions of reforms to limit the ability of labor unions and federal workers to campaign on behalf of New Deal Democrats. Campaign finance laws were shaped primarily by groups seeking greater electoral influence over rivals, even those within the same party.

There are broader implications to these partisan and intraparty skirmishes over reform. The laws resulting from these political rivalries have made it more difficult for political parties to perform vital integrative functions. Instead of encouraging parties, candidates, and allied groups to campaign collectively in elections, the laws give these groups incentives to campaign independently of each other. This dynamic stimulates a kind of fragmented campaigning that reduces political accountability, allowing candidates to distance themselves from the negative campaigns waged against their opponents by political parties or interest groups. It also allows interest groups, such as Swift Boat Veterans for Truth or MoveOn.org, to influence electoral outcomes in their own right, even though most of the public has no idea what these groups stand for and who supports them.[6] While it is constitutional and perfectly reasonable—indeed vital to democratic politics—for political groups to criticize or show support for government leaders, the electoral system would benefit to the degree that rules encouraged diverse partisans to form coalitions and pool resources under the banner of a political party. Such arrangements would nurture a politics of compromise rather than confrontation, while providing the voters with a relatively clear understanding of the policy differences between the major parties. Instead, we have a system that abets polarization between the parties because political factions—often amorphous and transient—have strong incentives to mobilize adherents on hot-button issues and force candidates to focus on narrowly defined moral agendas.

In contrast, campaign finance laws that privilege political parties are likely to increase the political accountability of officeholders. In most democracies, political parties have meaningful "labels" that the wider public recognizes and draws upon to make choices at the ballot box. Unlike many political committees that come and go quickly, political parties possess a past, present, and future that constrain their behavior to widely accepted political norms. To be sure, in the United States these norms include hard-hitting negative advertisements against opponents, but the party cannot run away from egregious campaign behavior so long as they are closely linked with their candidates running for office. One problem, however, is that existing American campaign finance laws, which limit how much political parties and candidates can work together, have encouraged the parties to institutionalize the practice of "independent" campaigning. Such spending cannot be limited because the Supreme Court finds no evidence that uncoordinated financial activity would lead to corruption.[7] This strategy allows candidates to benefit from party campaigns while claiming they cannot control what the party does. Thus, the bonds of accountability have become more threadbare in the U.S. campaign finance system through laws that limit party and candidate coordination.

The campaign finance laws have also favored politically entrenched incumbents and interest groups. In most democracies, political funds flow through the parties, which have an incentive to recruit candidates, organize campaigns, and develop party-based issues for future elections. As I explain later, in the United States, in contrast, the laws encourage wealthy individuals, institutions, and even small donors to contribute to those who already occupy office. The result is that incumbents possess war chests that enable them to ward off competition in their own races and make contributions to electorally vulnerable colleagues. The latter strategy helps them garner political favors as they move up the congressional hierarchy, a practice that makes money all the more important in the daily life of members of Congress.

This candidate-centered system plays a significant role in shaping the dynamics of campaign contributions, particularly the strategies employed by interest groups. The vast majority of interest groups have a strong incentive to contribute to incumbents rather than challengers through their political action committees (PACs) in order to maximize the potential to influence public policy. Few PACs would risk giving money to challengers because they would not want their sponsoring organization to be punished if the incumbent won. At the same time, these PACs hardly represent an unbiased population of political interests since this population remains relatively small and concentrated among a few types of interest groups. Groups that form PACs tend to have institutional bases of support and legal expertise, such as business corporations and labor unions. Few nonprofits or citizen-based groups have the resources to establish PACs and exploit the strategic advantages of giving campaign contributions to officeholders (Apollonio and La Raja 2004, 1159–79; Gais 1996).

The political parties, in turn, have become reliant on powerful incumbent officeholders and interest groups for their survival. The congressional parties, for example, rely heavily on incumbent officeholders for their funds (Malbin 2004, 177–91), a practice that inhibits their willingness to assume electoral risks by supporting a broad swath of challengers. Instead, they focus on a small percentage of toss-up races and forego the chance to build the party by seriously contesting many districts. Congressional parties face an organizational problem resulting from the fact that incumbent officeholders are central to their fund-raising capacity, yet incumbents are not interested in building the party over the long term; incumbents want to control Congress *now*. Indeed, the 2006 midterms point to how difficult it is even for the DNC to pursue a broad party-building strategy because congressional party leaders demanded that the DNC chair, Howard Dean, pour resources into targeted districts rather than pursue a fifty-state strategy to shore up local party organizations.

In this campaign finance environment, political parties remain weakly institutionalized, behaving frequently like "super PACs" that merely supply campaign resources to the tightest races rather than like transformative associations that might increase political competition and strengthen the party in places where it fares poorly. While the weak condition of American political parties relative to those in other democracies cannot be attributed solely to campaign finance laws, these regulations have played no small part in preventing parties from becoming more robust institutions, mainly by unrealistically limiting the source and size of political contributions. The most recent reforms under the McCain-Feingold Act—which, among other things, restricted the size and source of contributions to political parties by banning so-called soft money—have also made it almost impossible for a strong third-party challenge to the Republicans or Democrats. It is rare for any significant public-oriented institution to emerge without the support of major patrons willing to subsidize the immense costs of launching and sustaining an organization while it pursues broader public support (Olson 1965; Walker 1991).

In economically advanced nations like the United States, political parties require copious resources in order to be strong and electorally competitive. This fact emerges from an economy of modern campaigns that puts a premium on capital-intensive technologies rather than labor. Ideally, the capital resources should come from diverse constituencies; otherwise, the party organization has little incentive to perform the vital integrative functions and coalition building that serve the broader political system. For this reason, there is a weaker argument to privilege congressional campaign committees under campaign finance laws. These committees tend to lack the thick web of partisan relationships with local parties and activists that would compel them to assume broader goals than simply winning targeted congressional races.[8] By contrast, national committees, which derive their authority from local and state party delegations and engage in the cross-national presidential elections, have a greater potential to assume the functions of a strong party.

While winning elections is clearly the primary goal of political parties, a *strong* party organization, as V. O. Key would suggest, is one that has the capacity to pursue this goal across multiple fronts, from the earliest stages of candidate recruitment and nomination to later stages of campaign advertising in the closing days of an election (1956, 1–17). Party strength in elections is not simply the amount of money that the party has in its coffers but also its capacity to shape its political environment at various stages in the electoral process rather than only react to events and serendipitous opportunities. Given sufficient resources, a strong party possesses the institutional capacity for achieving long-range planning, attracting and keeping talented staff, developing grass roots support, and waging effective political campaigns across the party ticket in all the states. As I argue in this book, the national committees have moved in this direction during the past two decades, but recent reforms under the BCRA will make it much more difficult for strongly institutionalized party organizations to emerge. Given the constraints on fund-raising and spending under this law, long-range party building will tend to be sacrificed in order to meet the short-term demands of incumbents running for office. Moreover, much of the campaign activity will continue to be outsourced to consultants, interest groups, and "shadow" party organizations.

REFORM AND ITS CONSEQUENCES

This book challenges previous studies of campaign finance in at least two important ways. First, it challenges the public interest explanation of reform. In these accounts, a small but dedicated cluster of political reformers working against partisan interests develops policies to improve the political system (Corrado 1997, 25–60; Mutch 1988; Zelizer 2002, 73–111). They push an uphill battle to change the system against entrenched interests, gradually piecing together a reform coalition that draws support from moderates or mavericks in both parties. The reform drive, however, stalls unless a scandal occurs that ignites a public reaction. In a tidal wave of indignation, politicians of all stripes sign up for reform. The reform issue becomes so salient that no official can afford to stand in the way of change.

Public interest theory, however, does a poor job explaining most political reforms. Reforms often occur in the absence of scandal. In 1910, for example, the Publicity Acts, which paved the way for disclosure of political funds, came into being several years after major scandals involving the New York insurance industry and legislators in that state and after the Tillman Act had already banned corporate contributions in 1907. In 1940, there were no major scandals pushing forward the campaign finance provisions in the Hatch Acts. And in 1971, Congress passed major legislation—including public funding for presidential elections—in the years *before* the Watergate scandal.

The historical record reveals that reform bills cycle continuously through Congress, punctuated by scandals involving money in politics. But the causal link between reform and scandal appears to be extremely weak. Even more problematic for this theory is the fact that campaign finance reform is rarely, in itself, a salient public issue. In public opinion polls, support for reform issues is often broad but ranks consistently low as a priority among Americans, suggesting that politicians have little to fear by avoiding the issue. The research also suggests that campaign finance reform receives little attention in the news media in the weeks and months leading up to votes for political reform.

In contrast to the public interest explanation, I argue that reform is better explained in a partisan context as a struggle over electoral resources. I define electoral resources in the broadest sense, not only in terms of money but also in the form of labor, expertise, and influential ties to broad segments of American voters. Political reform is more likely to transpire during times of electoral uncertainty about resources for one of the major parties. This uncertainty increases when the rival party appears to have important resource advantages. At this point, the resource-poor party seeks a method to constrain the resource-rich rival. But to pass reform it must form a coalition with a minority faction in the rival party that has something to gain by supporting reforms. One advantage for reformers is that they typically have the support of influential opinion makers—from newspapers, universities, and foundations—who are steeped in a Progressive worldview that participation in politics should be individualistic, nonpartisan, and unblemished by material motives. Reforms that attempt to constrain the role of money in politics tend to enhance the influence of these elite opinion makers at the expense of traditional party elites.

While others have argued against the public interest perspective, none to my knowledge have explained the role of factions in pushing for particular reforms within each of the major parties. Moreover, prominent scholars continue to overstate the importance of scandal as the proximate cause of reform. While I do not dispute that scandal may *sometimes* serve as a catalyst, it is hardly ever sufficient. As I show, reforms often take place without the presence of scandal. Scandals typically serve as a useful backdrop for political entrepreneurs, but it is rarely the scandal itself that motivates policymakers to pass reform.

My findings also challenge a conventional understanding that campaign finance reforms have had little impact on American political parties. This widely accepted view stems, in part, from an unexplored assumption that campaign finance laws had little bite prior to the 1974 amendments to the Federal Election Campaign Act (FECA).[9] While it is true that poor campaign finance disclosure and the absence of strong enforcement made it easy for political groups to evade the law, this does not mean regulations failed to influence behaviors. Legal constraints, however permeable, have significant consequences, affecting, among other things, the relative clout of party factions and the institutional capacity of party organizations. As I show in this book, constraints on party spending since early in the twentieth century induced partisans to establish "independent" committees, funnel money through state-based organizations, and give candidates strong incentives to take greater responsibility over fund-raising for their campaigns. A similar response has emerged since the passage of the BCRA in 2002. Both parties have relied increasingly on nonparty groups and independent but affiliated party organizations to carry out much of the campaigns.

The consensus among political scientists that American parties are highly adaptable supports the minimalist view of the law's impact. To be sure, American parties have survived wars, depressions, technological changes, and rapid demographic shifts. However, a primary reason for this adaptability is that national political parties are, in fact, weakly institutionalized. They have a modest ability to control their environment for the purpose of creating long-term organizational solutions to ongoing challenges and tasks. Run by a cadre of elites, political parties have been able to transform relatively quickly to adapt electoral conditions to meet *short-term* electoral goals since they are less constrained by ideologies and organizational structures than most European parties (Epstein 1986; Panebianco 1988).[10] But these adaptations have come at a cost. In the twentieth century, American parties have typically failed to use organizations to recruit new voters, engage them in meaningful political work, and groom future candidates. Indeed, to the disbelief of many foreign observers, American political candidates go so far as to campaign *against* their own party organizations to win office.

Thus, it is one thing to say parties adapt and survive and another to say they thrive. While addressing the nuances of party strength is necessary for this project, a more central question is whether and in what ways it matters for the electoral system if partisan organizing takes place in formal structures such as the party organization or through an extended partisan network that includes candidates' committees, PACs, consultants, and affiliated interest groups. Some have argued that all of these affiliated groups constitute the party (Bernstein and Dominguez 2003, 165–69; Skinner 2006). While these groups may have shared goals and loyalties, I argue that a dispersed partisan network creates tangible costs for the political system. Indeed, one premise of this study—which is surely contestable—is that a strong formal party organization generates systemwide electoral benefits. These benefits include, but are not limited to, making elections more transparent, accountable, and competitive.

Instead of encouraging these stronger formal party organizations, campaign finance reforms have tended to advance and reinforce a trend toward candidate-centered elections and highly fragmented partisan electoral activity. Partisans adapt to new laws by pushing money outside formal party structure to affiliated committees that are beyond the reach of the law. The result is not only one of less transparency in the electoral process but also one of greater influence for incumbent officeholders, interest groups, and the media. By showing how partisans have attempted to thwart the laws by scattering resources throughout a partisan network, this book casts doubt on the widely held assumption that campaign finance laws had little impact on party organizations before major legislation was passed in the 1970s.[11]

In addition, this book undertakes a close examination of how and why Republicans and Democrats respond differently to campaign finance reforms, moving beyond previous work in this area. While some excellent research has shown key institutional differences between the two major party organizations, these differences have not been linked to stable preferences for, and responses to, campaign finance regimes. Moreover, these previous accounts have not demonstrated how the two parties adapt differently—and yet in predictable ways—to each wave of reform. In the parlance of political science, I argue that the costs of "collective action" have not been uniform across the major parties. Drawing on insights from organizational theory, I explain how the fundamentally different paths toward institutionalization between the two major parties, especially at the national level, impacted their (current) responses to campaign reform law. In particular, this study shows how the distinctive resource dependencies of each party on various allied factions constrained responses and led to particular electoral strategies.[12] In elaborating these differences, this work adds to current understandings about how parties adapt to new environments (Aldrich 1995; Harmel and Janda 1982; Herrnson 1988).

OUTLINE OF BOOK

Chapter 2 begins with a brief history of the origins of campaign finance reform. First, an overview is provided of the political thought of the Mugwumps, who inaugurated the movement to displace politics from partisan roots toward a more individualized and rational model of civic participation. Chapter 2 continues with an examination of the campaign finance laws that emerged in the American states as part of a reform agenda to alter the relationship between citizens and government by weakening the intermediary of the political party. In chapter 3, I take up a history of campaign finance laws at the federal level in the twentieth century and show how a Progressive template for reform was repeated in successive waves of campaign finance laws. Indeed, the template was appropriated by partisans and wielded strategically to seek electoral advantages. Chapter 4 draws on this historical record to develop a theory of partisan reform, which helps explain the BCRA of 2002. One puzzle emerging from passage of the BCRA was why Democrats supported this bill and most Republicans opposed it. The conventional wisdom was that it was a Democratic "suicide bill" because it banned party soft money, which Democrats relied upon heavily. I show that the Democrats' partiality to the BCRA reflected a century-long pattern of support for legislation that played to their electoral strengths as a highly decentralized party. The support for the BCRA among Democratic leaders also reflected factional support for a soft money ban by a core constituency of progressive activists that party leaders could not afford to ignore.

The last three chapters speak more directly to the consequences of campaign finance reforms. In chapter 5, I focus on how parties attempted to raise money under each successive wave of reforms. The law's emphasis on attracting small donors created significant collective action problems for the broad-based, weakly principled American parties. In spite of numerous efforts to raise money from small donors, they consistently came to rely upon large donors to pay election costs. Ultimately, both parties achieved greater success seeking money from small donors in the 1980s and 1990s with the aid of technology, which lowered fund-raising costs. Another important factor, however, was the increasing ideological homogeneity of the parties. With greater policy coherence differentiating the two parties, potential donors came to see national party organizations as organizations through which they could further their policy goals.

Chapter 6 looks at party spending under different campaign finance regimes. It focuses on how the parties have used resources to win presidential elections. My research shows consistent differences between the Republican and Democratic presidential campaign strategies. Republicans tend to use the party organization as a central actor, while Democrats prefer an ad hoc approach, which relies more on nonparty groups. This chapter also explores the role of soft money in strengthening political parties and the ways in which parties adapted to the BCRA ban on soft money in the 2004 and 2006 elections. In chapter 7, I conclude by assessing how political parties will respond to the BCRA over the long term. Though these conclusions must remain speculative, since only one presidential election has taken place under the new law, they are clearly grounded in historical patterns of response based on similar reforms.

The implications of this study seem clear enough. The problem of money in politics will remain with us for the foreseeable future. Undoubtedly there will be future attempts to regulate political money, as soon as political actors appear to have gained the ability to navigate around the current set of regulations. Rather than cast the entire reform project in doubt, this study encourages a reformulation of the problem of money in politics. The historical perspective shows that, while circumstances have changed considerably since the Progressive Era, the basic assumptions about the problems related to money in elections and how to deal with them have not. Progressives pushed for laws limiting the flow of money into politics as a way to eliminate corruption in the form of the quid pro quo. Today, there is a growing consensus among historians and political scientists that quid pro quo corruption is less of a problem than it was in the past.[13] Yet, it is widely noted by experts that the campaign finance system has not directly addressed the issues of fairness. In the current system, political challengers can rarely gather sufficient resources to run meaningful campaigns. Incumbents consistently and overwhelmingly outspend challengers. Moreover, serious third-party candidates are an anomaly unless they can find a wealthy nominee who is willing to self-finance, such as Ross Perot. The unequal distribution of political money is also evident in that it is spent mostly in targeted contests, which tends to dampen voter turnout in other areas. Though my study does not address how financial inequities or depressed voter participation manifests in legislative elections, the findings do suggest that the current focus on prevention of quid pro quo corruption may be misplaced, given other problems with the electoral system, such as the fragmentation of campaigns and the resultant political ills.

This study also raises important questions about the reform process. To some, to suggest that political reform engages partisan interests is to state the obvious. But it is a point that is commonly overlooked, or simply ignored, in complex policy debates that tend to engage only a small cadre of experts in law and elections. In revamping or even tinkering with the rules, some gain advantages over others. It is not always obvious who gains and loses, but it is worth an earnest effort to understand political consequences, acknowledge trade-offs, and seek compromises. When deferring to experts or invoking the public interest to justify political reform, it is wise to recall Madison's dictum in the Federalist No. 10 about the nature of factions—that "the latent causes of faction are thus sown in the nature of man"—and so to maintain a healthy skepticism about human nature as the process unfolds. Let me be clear that the overarching point here is not that reforms are unnecessary or that they spring from base motives but simply that such rule changes alter the contours of political power by altering incentives, behaviors, and institutions. Given these potential consequences, a broad understanding of the consequences of reform appears to be a worthy pursuit.

The project of explaining reform and its consequences is a humbling undertaking. Politics is a messy business. My two subjects—political parties and campaign finance—are conceptually and analytically complex. Given this, my arguments at times may appear to oversimplify causal relationships or ignore important explanations. Surely, some will have good reason to disagree with my conclusions. The book, however, is an invitation for such disagreements, which may enlarge a conversation about the means and ends of political regulation. At the very least, I trust I have not distorted the facts or presented a view that is at odds with fundamental values of democratic politics.

CHAPTER 2

Mugwump Reform and the Decline of Political Parties

The United States possesses one of the more densely regulated campaign finance systems among developed democracies, yet Americans remain intensely disappointed about the results of these regulations. Public opinion polls consistently show that Americans believe the system is flawed and that interest groups have excessive influence through their political contributions. They see candidates amassing war chests as well as a profusion of PACs in Washington and political advertisements sponsored by organizations they have never heard of. Much of this activity is the product of a constitutional system that encourages robust electoral participation among numerous interest groups. At the same time, we have constructed a campaign finance regime that stimulates highly decentralized political activity, favoring incumbent politicians and wealthy interest groups over challengers and political parties. Precisely because laws have made it difficult for party organizations to gather resources and coordinate activity, the American campaign finance system lacks the kind of political accountability that reformers seek and that political parties traditionally provide in elections.

How did we arrive at the current fragmented system of political financing? Part of the answer reflects the profoundly antipartisan character of campaign finance reforms originating during the Mugwump era and the Progressive Era. Statutes regulating money in politics made it difficult for political parties at the national and state level to amass the kind of resources that would enable them to play a robust role in politics, on par with that of political parties in other nations. While the American party system has always been highly decentralized—for reasons related to both structure (federalism, separation of powers) and culture (individualism, diversity)—the campaign finance statutes have reinforced localism and contributed to the weakness of national parties. The laws, in fact, have fractured accountability, moving political funds away from central actors such as political parties and toward interest groups and candidates.

The historical roots of federal campaign finance reforms as well as the political ideas motivating them are the subjects of this chapter. The current regulatory regime emerged from a wave of anticorruption and antipartisan reforms during the Progressive Era. The inspiration for these reforms extends even further back to the Mugwumps of the post–Civil War period. Reviewing this history illustrates why Progressives chose to craft the kind of campaign finance reforms they did. These early Progressive efforts, in turn, influenced subsequent approaches to regulating money in politics. Indeed, the nation has not strayed far from the original Progressive impulse to emphasize an individualist, antiassociational politics through various regulations on political parties, especially those pertaining to campaign finance. The Mugwump-Progressive approach has its roots in the American Romantics such as Thoreau and Emerson. These thinkers spurned organized society and spoke the language of self-sufficiency and moral purity of the independent individual. Their ideas resonated with the educated class of reformers at the end of the nineteenth century. Through political reforms, Progressives sought to maximize enlightened civic participation, provide the means for political self-knowledge (primarily through nonpartisan newspapers), and encourage citizens to interact directly with their government rather than through intermediary organizations such as political parties.

The historical approach to understanding campaign finance reform challenges conventional accounts in several ways. First, historical analysis shows that the path of genuine reform did not begin with the much-heralded post-Watergate reforms of 1974. Rather, previous reforms from earlier periods have shaped the contours of contemporary laws and structured political activities in ways that encourage candidate-centered rather than party-centered campaigns. While most commentators claim early laws—such as the Tillman Act of 1907, which banned corporate donations, or the Publicity Act of 1910, which limited political spending—were completely ineffective, they had important consequences for the development of national political parties and the party system more broadly. The first laws, in fact, have provided a remarkably durable template for our current system. They promulgated the essential features of the contemporary system: requirements to disclose financial activity; constraints on political contributions and expenditures; and an emphasis on small, voluntary donors. Revisiting previous efforts to regulate money in politics reveals strong links between the most recent national reform, the BCRA of 2002, and the dense cluster of statutes passed in the American states roughly a century ago.

A second feature of the historical approach is that it places efforts to regulate campaign finance in the broader context of regulating partisan politics. Indeed, Progressive attempts to regulate money were part of an extensive effort to weaken the grip of political parties and not simply to address the problem of corruption in the narrow sense. Early regulations on political money, which was controlled by political parties, originated in the profoundly antipartisan sentiments of the Mugwumps and Progressives during the nineteenth century. To be sure, many reformers were motivated primarily to combat corruption rather than undermine the parties per se. They shared an understandably deep unease about the new way of financing politics through the emerging colossus of the corporate trusts. That the costs of democracy would be paid for principally through these private, capitalistic institutions raised alarm bells among citizens across the political spectrum. It exposed, in raw form, a fundamental tension between a capitalism that generated great disparities in wealth and a democracy that was predicated on an ideal of political equality.

But however much reformers may have wanted to spare the parties in their quest to minimize the role of money in politics, the effect on parties of their prohibitionist strategies could not be avoided. These laws took away an increasingly vital resource—cash—and encouraged its dispersion into the smaller tributaries of candidate committees, professional "bundlers," and interest groups. While the rhetoric of campaign finance laws has always been about thwarting corruption, a consequential impact of regulations has been their deleterious effect on the political parties. Indeed, campaign finance reforms might be more aptly described as *party* reforms because they altered relationships and activities among partisans. In some instances, party weakening was merely a by-product of anticorruption efforts. But, as I explain later, the efforts to regulate campaign money sprang from a larger movement by Progressives to diminish the influence of political parties in American life. Whether reformers were truly antiparty or not, the effect was the same: an increasingly weaker role for political parties in financing elections throughout the century.

Ironically, as Progressives were trying to wean political parties from financial resources, they were introducing other reforms that elevated the importance of money in elections. The institutions of the direct primary and direct election of U.S. senators, for example, made politics more expensive simply by increasing the number of elections. The Progressive impulse to make politics more "educational" rather than tied to an emotionally based party politics—a legacy that motivates reforms to this day—also contributed to the importance of money. Through reforms, such as the Australian ballot, which made the vote secret, citizens were encouraged to think of voting as an entirely private affair to be performed in the solemnity of a booth rather than as a public display of political identity amid pomp and celebration. As Election Day became less of a social affair for local citizens and as partisan loyalty diminished, candidates and parties had to spend more cash to attract the attention of voters. With partisan attachments of voters weakening and party organizations atrophying, candidates would need greater amounts of cash to mobilize constituencies on their own.

By observing regulation of money in this broader partisan context, it becomes apparent that political parties themselves were important actors in shaping campaign finance legislation. Because money was becoming a more important political resource in the twentieth century the two major parties used campaign finance reform to gain advantages over the rival party. Most proposals for reform that *passed* emerged from a coalition of legislators intent on diminishing resources of a party—or, more typically, a faction within the party—that threatened them. Typically, reforms passed when one faction gained a significant resource advantage over others in presidential elections. Using the rhetoric of reform, a coalition of disadvantaged factions would propose reforms to check the resource advantages of a rival group. As shown in subsequent chapters, this situation accompanied each new set of campaign finance regulations.

The story of campaign finance reform begins with the Mugwumps, whose ideas gained legitimacy after the Civil War during the 1870s. The Mugwumps set in motion a powerful belief that political parties ought to be regulated and, if not eliminated, weakened significantly. Mugwumps were middle-class Republicans like the Progressives, but they were stronger in the Northeast.[1] They were a moving force behind both civil service reform and the Australian ballot that found success in the 1880s (Massachusetts was the first state to adopt the secret ballot in 1888, and all states had it by the end of the century). Some Mugwump ideas found a receptive audience in the Populists, who championed direct forms of democracy and sought an end to the role of political parties as elite institutions that stood between the people and their government. Mugwump-Progressivism and Populism were distinct movements, emanating from different classes and regions of the nation and with different visions of how American democracy should work. While the former emphasized the role of experts in managing democracy, the latter reified the opinions of the common man. They were united, however, in their antipartisan, antiassociational conception of politics.

In the 1890s through 1920s, the Progressives built on antipartisan ideas inherited from the Mugwumps. The Progressive movement was centered in New York City, where it supported governmental efforts to regulate business, and in Chicago, where the focus was more on politics and democracy (blending with the old Populism). Progressives instituted electoral reforms that curtailed party influence in a number of areas, including the nomination of candidates and funding of elections. Campaign finance rules were but one strategy to prevent the accumulation of power by party leaders. While the Mugwumps had crafted the case against partisanship in public life, their followers, the Progressives, were instrumental in passing specific policies that shifted elections away from their party-centered roots. These policies now inform contemporary strategies for regulating partisan politics.

THE MUGWUMP CHALLENGE TO PARTY POWER

It is difficult for the contemporary observer to appreciate the primacy of party organizations in the nation's politics between the 1840s through 1880s. American political parties supported a popular politics that flowed into the smallest tributaries of local civic life. Not only did parties control who would run for public office; they also staged all the events leading up to an election, including the printing and distribution of ballots to voters and the mass entertainment that swirled around the campaigns. The strong consensus among historians and political scientists is that political parties made mass democracy work by organizing the selection of candidates, shaping the campaign agenda, and getting voters to the polls.

But parties were not merely mechanisms to organize the vote. They were important socializing agents in American democracy that educated citizens in politics and nurtured habits of a civic culture that persist to this day. Local parties, for example, created what McGerr calls the "vital democratic theater," which made voting seem like an important and meaningful act. The "spectacle" produced by parties around elections attracted voters to the polls and gave them the emotional pull of being around campaigns (McGerr 1986). Through torchlight parades, mass rallies, and various campaign clubs, parties encouraged an exuberant partisanship that galvanized citizens into paying attention to politics.

To the degree that money was important in elections, it went toward promoting the spectacle of partisan elections. Local elites, as patrons of the parties, would pay for the uniforms of marching clubs and brass bands that paraded the streets in the days preceding elections. These colorful parades—complete with horse-drawn floats of Lady Liberty and symbols of the nation's history—were gripping attractions in a society with vastly fewer leisure options than we enjoy today. Rather than face the quiet darkness of a rural homestead, onlookers could join in the nocturnal fun by lighting off fireworks and walking around town, which was lit up for the occasion with Chinese lanterns (McGerr 1986, 37). Intertwined with this festive atmosphere were partisan speeches by local leaders and the exchange of political invective in local taverns, where betting on electoral outcomes was a common pastime.

A vital by-product of party activity was the integration of citizens across social and geographical boundaries. Through spectacle, average citizens were drawn into a ritual of partisan displays of loyalty that linked them to a wider community. The party parades and gatherings brought together rich and poor, townsman and farmer, much like other post–Civil War civic organizations that recruited members from all ranks in society (Skocpol 2003). While political activities were intensely local affairs, the parties tied themselves to national issues, such as tariff policy, in ways that connected citizens to a national polity. Through the party label and its symbols, local office seekers were linked to presidential candidates at the national level and to heroes of the party's past, such as Jackson or Lincoln. In this way, the American party system brought politics close to home by making it meaningful in the context of citizens' ordinary lives. As Sidney Milkis argues, the political parties made the Constitution workable by cultivating an "active and competent" citizenry and joining them in collective purpose (1999, 6). In this way parties gave citizens an education in politics that appealed to their emotions and motivated them to participate in the nation's civic life.

Even before the Progressives initiated political reforms that would weaken local political parties, these organizations were beginning to lose their clout for other reasons. The last two decades of the century produced dramatic social changes that ultimately transformed American political institutions. The emergence of large enterprises in mining, railroads, and steel created a new set of elites and workers tied to large corporations. Rapid postwar industrialization brought millions of farmworkers and immigrants from overseas to urban-based factories. The country was beginning its inexorable shift from an agricultural to an industrial society. While most of the United States would remain a rural economy well into the twentieth century, millions of Americans at this time were moving away from the tightly woven local communities to work as nonskilled wage earners for large mining and manufacturing firms. The movement of capital and labor was generating considerable wealth but also spawning instability with bank failures, cutthroat competition, job cuts, and a cycle of depressions, as in the mid-1870s and mid-1890s.

The complete reorganization of the economy prodded a relatively small federal government toward an increasingly larger role in regulating commerce. Even though the new economic elites preached laissez-faire capitalism, many were concerned that the federal government was not vigorous enough to grapple with rapid changes (Silbey 1991). As leaders of corporations, they wanted help from the government to avoid disastrous competition and the kind of dislocations that led to severe economic failures. Some believed that the governmental system built on a decentralized party system was inadequate to the task of managing a national economy. The intense localism championed by party bosses, which spurred citizen interest in politics, had a limited vocabulary for grappling with major policy questions. Instead, parties were concerned with distributional politics, which focused on allocating material benefits flowing from the control over patronage and government contracts.

Even when the parties addressed major economic issues, such as the tariff, their stances were tied closely to sectional benefits. The looseness of the party structure allowed coalitions to shift and change on this issue so that a strong party majority could rarely be found. To be sure, the tariff issue or disputes over the gold standard galvanized local parties, especially in the elections of 1896, but it seemed beyond the capacity of a decentralized two-party system to forge competing doctrines of commerce on the scale that would overcome traditional sectionalism. Parties were too prone to the kind of bargaining that would undermine vigorous governmental action. As the historian Joel H. Silbey observes: "In practicing the art of the possible, in putting electoral success first, they sacrificed correct policy" (1991, 227). A rising group of industrial elites believed that pursuing correct policy would require a party system that centralized power in the executive, where decisions would not be subject to the unceasing slings and arrows of congressional compromises.

While some business leaders were pushing in the direction of a Hamiltonian government that would take the lead on economic issues, a different set of elites challenged the emerging institutional order more profoundly with their ideas. In the northeastern cities of Boston, New York, and Philadelphia, these "liberals" would form the vanguard of reform efforts. Others referred to them disparagingly as Mugwumps, a term that has been attributed to an Algonquin word meaning "great chief." Yet it is more likely that the political usage derives from the image of a fence-sitter whose "Mug" is on one side of the fence but whose "Wump" rests on the other, suggesting someone who cannot make up his mind. The label *Mugwump* was widely applied to the liberal Republicans who opposed Grant's reelection in 1872, joining forces temporarily with the Democrats to nominate the aging Horace Greeley for the Democratic ticket. Mugwumps, especially strong in New England, were typically educated men from old stock families, including luminaries like Henry Adams and Charles Eliot, the president of Harvard.[2]

The broad Mugwump agenda included ideas for reforming the civil service, pacifying the South, improving government control over the economy, and purifying political life (Josephson 1938, 159). Early attempts at organizing an independent political movement proved frustrating, given the formidable strength of the two-party system, but the reformers persisted to push their ideas through journals and newspapers. Eventually, this rump Republican group bolted the party again in 1884 to support Grover Cleveland when the Republicans nominated the orthodox James G. Blaine.

From the Mugwump perspective, the emerging industrial order appeared to bring out the worst excesses of Jacksonian democracy. Mugwumps worried about the rising tide of immigrants, especially the Irish, who provided the votes that fed political machines like Tammany Hall. They saw cities as plagued with small-minded plunderers of the municipal purse who gave out railcar and construction contracts to their friends. They were also uncomfortable with the nouveau riche robber barons who increasingly dominated the economic and social life of the nation. Across the country, large corporations or trusts were stripping the nation of its natural resources for personal profit and uprooting men from their families and communities to work at menial jobs with short-term rewards. It can scarcely be doubted that elites from old stock families suffered anxiety about how rapid social changes would alter traditional patterns of deference affecting their own status in society.

For Mugwumps, the essential problem with politics was the localism and self-interested compromises that were inherent in party politics. The party bosses were too concerned with protecting local fiefdoms to appreciate the nature of problems confronting the United States. Instead of relying for policy on the backroom deals of provincial party leaders, Mugwumps envisioned a more powerful national state to address some of the grave social conditions resulting from industrialism. Curiously, the idea of centralizing party power and accountability through stronger national committees did not seem to occur to them. It would be left for future progressives, particularly Woodrow Wilson, to contemplate a stronger role for parties.

The liberals faced an uphill battle taking on the parties, even as these institutions were ebbing. They advertised reformist ideas and their contempt for partisan politics through magazines such as the *Nation, Harper's Weekly,* and *North American Review* (McGerr 1986, 44). But they were writing at a time when strong partisanship remained part of the fabric of the wider culture, not just in politics but in social relationships. As the historian Michael McGerr observes: "Voters who cast independent ballots could expect to lose business and friendships and to suffer attacks on their manhood" (1986, 44). While partisanship thrived, however, rapid social and economic change was undermining the community structure that supported the patterns of deference built into local partisanship.

It was these two distinct groups—business elites and Mugwump reformers—that revived an antipartisan sentiment that was an undercurrent in American political culture ever since George Washington warned citizens in his farewell address to beware "factions." The Mugwumps and their progeny, the Progressives, tapped into historical fears about factions and succeeded in undermining a central tenet of nineteenth-century American democracy, namely, that party loyalty should be the authoritative benchmark for political engagement. Instead, they gave broad legitimacy to the idea that citizens should make political choices based on rational evaluations of individual candidates and their ideas rather than on party loyalty and emotional appeals. In short, Mugwumps revived a civic myth that valued the independent man who stood above politics.

The Mugwumps had some success regulating party resources, even if only indirectly, as in the case of the civil service reforms that attacked the system of party patronage and required prospective officials to take examinations to demonstrate proficiency as administrators or experts. Mugwump lobbying won the passage of the Pendleton Act of 1883, which was the first federal civil service reform. The act created classes of jobs that could only be filled by applicants after passing an examination. Instead of receiving posts through political connections, civil servants would rise through the ranks based on grades in the merit examinations and length of service. Not only did this law make it more difficult for parties to dispense patronage, but it also prohibited party representatives from soliciting political funds from federal employees (those classified in civil service jobs), which was a common practice in the nineteenth century.

The greatest success won by liberals against the parties came through ballot reform, which gave government control over the content of ballots and paved the way for regulation of political parties. Throughout much of the nineteenth century, political parties printed and distributed their own ballots to voters. These ballots usually had distinctive colors to enable party poll watchers to know whether voters "delivered" when they deposited the ballot in the box. To encourage sympathy for the ticket, party officials might treat voters to alcoholic beverages, cigars, and other gratuities before and after they deposited their ballots at polling stations (Altschuler and Blumin 2000). In certain localities, direct cash payments for the vote made electoral mobilization even more efficient. However, once the government took control over the ballot, placing candidates for both parties on the same piece of paper, party workers could not always confirm whether the voter performed his end of the bargain.[3] Even though treating became less prevalent by the time the government began to regulate political funds extensively in the 1890s, the early campaign finance laws focused significantly on preventing parties from doing so (Pollock 1926).[4]

Though the political parties would be able to resist or evade many reforms during the 1880s and 1890s, they had begun to lose the battle of ideas to the Mugwumps. The reformers had etched a regulatory template that would provide legitimacy for future government intervention in party affairs. Such reforms were guided by the Mugwump idea that citizenship is a private act and ought to be based on rational decisions rather than loyalties bound by emotion or self-interest (McGerr 1986). As McGerr argues persuasively, Mugwumps helped move campaigns from party spectacle to a kind of eat-your-oatmeal civic lesson favored by educated elites. An unfortunate consequence of the new politics was that traditional political institutions, especially parties, found it increasingly difficult to mobilize voters across classes. To attract voters, party leaders like Mark Hanna began borrowing expensive practices from the emerging field of business advertising. Indeed, when Hanna began organizing the McKinley presidential campaign in 1896, party donors were shocked at the amount of money he requested for the distribution of campaign literature, posters, and the like (Shannon 1959, 32).

The Hanna method of mass advertising was a response to the weakening of the local partisan culture. New forms of entertainment, such as baseball and horse racing, had emerged that appealed to the tastes of a growing middle class, while the popularity of street fairs sponsored by parties waned in one community after another (McGerr 1986). These new and competing spectacles changed the local character of the party habits and pushed partisan displays of loyalty to the periphery. More and more, those with a predilection for politics—Robert Dahl's *homo politicus*[5]—would become separated from those who were not inclined to follow politics without the added pull of spectacle. Political parties encompassed a smaller mass of citizens in their rituals, and by the end of the century torchlight parades were almost a relic of the past. Sibley believes that 1888 was the last full-bore party campaign with all the pageantry, expressions of partisan loyalty, and "army style" campaigns (1991). To get the attention of voters, party chieftains would have to embrace the style of an emerging mass culture through advertisements, images, and symbols that appealed to respectable middle-class notions of politics nurtured by the Mugwumps. In other words, American society was trending toward mass culture, which could more easily be reached through impersonal advertising. Coupled with Mugwump ideas that put a premium on educating *individual* voters rather than mobilizing them through group loyalties, politics became a very expensive affair.

It seems evident from historical accounts that local parties were already losing influence before Progressives came upon the scene at the turn of the century with reforms to weaken their power. However, since party excesses remained part of local lore and the antithesis of middle-class respectability, the Progressive case against machines did not require a leap of imagination for the general public to believe political parties were corrupt institutions. Indeed, in many places they were. Increasingly, the campaign against parties resonated with members of a growing middle class who did not see their destinies tied to the fortunes of political parties, as did those in lower classes who continued to benefit from various kinds of party favors.

THE PROGRESSIVES

After the Mugwump challenge to politics in the Gilded Age, policy proposals circulated in a milieu receptive to governmental reforms. Starting in the 1890s, Progressives benefited from widespread support for change among elites and the perception among many citizens that traditional forms of partisan politics were outdated. With an emerging elite consensus that political institutions lacked the capacity to address fundamental public concerns, Progressives were able to put into practice many ideas they inherited from the Mugwumps. A group of intellectuals gave voice to the reform agenda through their writing and activism. These included Herbert Croly, Jane Addams, John Dewey, and many others who contributed to liberal journals like the *New Republic*. Their observations impressed on Americans the gap between the promise of American life—as Croly titled his most famous work—and the status quo in political affairs.

While it is difficult to define the core principles of the Progressives, they had an underlying passion to reshape the American political system for a modern era. Like their Mugwump forebears, Progressives believed government could be run more rationally and sought institutional changes to bring this about. In place of the localism championed by parties, they believed policies in the common interest could be implemented through a strong national executive, backed by experts in the bureaucracy. They sought to tackle economic and social problems with facts and analysis and then apply solutions on a national scale, if not by government then by voluntaristic, nonpartisan associations in the private sector. They also emphasized civic participation by well-informed voters who understood the common good. Public education would play a large part in their program for reforming the American polity.

From the Progressive perspective, an informed citizenry would not have to rely on intermediary institutions such as political parties to link citizens with governmental policies and leaders. A more direct and unfiltered connection was possible. Thus, the key to institutional change for Progressives was weakening the party grip on power. Above all, Progressives sought to avoid established party politics that diverted sound decision making from its true course of action, which came from scientific analysis. While party politics may have served a useful purpose earlier in America's transition to mass democracy, these institutions had outlived their usefulness and were now parasites on the body politic (Croly 1910, 1965). Indeed, parties prevented policy experts from using knowledge to pursue the common good.

Building on the intellectual foundations of Mugwumps, the Progressives were successful in transforming party politics through a variety of electoral and administrative reforms. On the administrative side, they pushed for changes that would insulate decision making from the hurly-burly of politics. Toward this end, they created regulatory commissions staffed by experts and administrative reforms that transferred policy-making from elected to appointed officials. On the electoral side, they attempted to sap the power of political parties through a series of institutional reforms emphasizing direct democracy such as the initiative, the recall and direct primary, and the direct election of U.S. senators. They also pushed for nonpartisan elections at the local level, where candidates could not associate themselves with parties on the ballot. Together, these reforms shifted power away from traditional party brokers toward elites who could influence popular opinion through media such as newspapers, magazines, and, later on, radio.

Campaign finance reform was not a primary focus of Progressives, but it was no less a part of the reform agenda to remake American politics. When the government printing office issued Senator Robert Latham Owen's pamphlet *The Code of the People's Rule* (1910), this manifesto "for terminating the abuses of machine politics" linked campaign finance regulation with a host of other progressive reforms, starting with the initiative and referendum. "Will machine men commit suicide," Owen asked, "depriving themselves of the means through which they control elections, to wit, by fraudulent registration, fraudulent voting, the corrupt use of money, the corrupt use of bribery, coercion, intimidation, and every artful practice of machine politics?" (3–4). Owen, a Democratic senator from Oklahoma (1907–25), combined populist and progressive rhetoric. Once "the people" had control of the laws through the initiative and referendum, they could legislate how money could be spent in politics "for the termination of corrupt government and for the overthrow of professional politicians" (4). His *Code* compiled the best reform practices from around the nation, focusing especially on progressive states like Oregon, where laws required publicity of political funds and restricted campaign contributions and expenditures.[6]

Other reformers recognized the importance of clamping down on party money as a way to reform the party. Kansas newspaper editor William Allen White, the "sage of Emporia," was brimming with optimism about the rapid spread of campaign finance laws around the nation, which would reform the party. He saw these laws as part of a package of political regulation that would sap the party and cause it to wither on the vine. He wrote:

> By making the party a legalized state institution, by paying for the party primaries with state taxes, by requiring candidates at primaries to file their expense accounts and a list of their contributors (as is done in some states), but limiting the amount to be spent (as is done in certain states), and by guaranteeing a secret vote and a fair count, the state has broken the power of money in politics. . . . Now, the political machine is in a fair way to be reduced [to] mere political scrap iron by the rise of the people. (White 1910, 47–61)

Political scientists of the time also made this connection between campaign finance reform and the antipartisan movements of the era. James Pollock, who compiled the first comprehensive study of campaign finance in the United States, began his 1926 book by linking ongoing reforms in campaign finance with broader efforts to purify party politics, declaring that the "movement for effective [campaign finance] laws has not ended, as the movement for the secret ballot ended when laws on the subject were passed in the various states" (Pollock 1926, 21). Pollock, like other scholars of the time, understood that campaign finance reforms emanated from the same Progressive spirit to remake partisan politics.[7]

The attention to political money was perfectly consistent with other kinds of Progressive reforms. To weaken parties, Progressives sought to remove critical resources from party leaders—control over nominations, the ballot, and patronage. In seeking to drain party resources, Progressives could not ignore the growing importance of cash for organizing elections and motivating voters. Indeed, reformers feared that greater party wealth at the national level after the 1888 elections was, according to the *Nation,* moving the country "one step nearer to the possibility, which now stares us in the face, of the purchase of the entire Administration from the National Committee of the winning party."[8]

Paradoxically, money had become even more important as a result of previous reforms. Direct primaries, for example, increased the need for cash to pay for an additional election, while civil service reforms diminished the supply of "unpaid" partisans willing to mobilize voters in anticipation of getting a future job. Furthermore, as Mugwump and Progressive notions of "education" politics spread and party spectacle declined, voter tastes inclined toward sophisticated and expensive forms of political persuasion.

The election of 1896 brought all these points home. Mark Hanna, the chair of the RNC, organized the most massive national political campaign the country had known to that point. To carry out his education campaign, Hanna knew he would need huge infusions of cash. He raised money centrally, using the business skills he honed as an entrepreneur in Ohio. According to his biographer Croly, Hanna transformed party politics with his new administrative and marketing approach to campaigning. In raising party funds, Hanna targeted business firms, assessing them for fixed sums based on their total capital. Croly wrote: "Mr Hanna always did his best to convert the practice [of fund-raising] from a matter of political begging on the one side and donating on the other into a matter of systematic assessment according to the means of the individual and the institution" (1965, 220). According to Croly, Hanna's methodical fund-raising scheme allowed the RNC to spend roughly $3.5 million ($68.4 million in 2000 dollars), which was double what Louise Overacker estimated was spent by the Republicans in the previous election (Overacker 1932, 73).[9]

A key to Hanna's success was organizational: a centralized operation in New York from which to coordinate national activities as efficiently as possible. Using a community chest model of fund-raising, he established local Republican finance committees in all the states, each with a set of quotas to raise funds from wealthy elites in the area. Money was passed up to the RNC. These funds were then channeled by the RNC into the important electoral states, like New York or Pennsylvania.[10] Hanna purchased ads in foreign language newspapers, bought millions of lithographs of McKinley, and paid for political cartoons that emphasized pithy slogans (e.g., "A Full Dinner Pail") (Pollock 1926, 64–65). Above all, he focused on advertising the Republican candidate, emphasizing personality over party issues. While this had been done in the past, Hanna raised the level of personalized politics to a new standard. The extent of Hanna's use of business marketing for politics led a future devotee of the new style, Theodore Roosevelt, to exclaim: "He had advertised McKinley as if he were a patent medicine" (Shannon 1959, 33n64).[11]

The Hanna approach to campaigning was a harbinger of change. The advertising style in presidential elections was suited to centralized organization where candidate images could be crafted and publicized to targeted electorates in the nation. Instead of relying wholly on local party organizations to churn out loyal constituencies for the presidential ticket, the Hanna method built more personal support for the candidate McKinley rather than that mediated by the partisan solidarity that had defined elections since the 1830s. As McGerr argues, the new politics accommodated an emerging middle class, which shunned the overt expressions of party loyalty embodied in the old-style campaign, considering it unsophisticated and an affront to idealized self-conceptions of independent-minded voters (1986).

Conceivably, the new campaign style might have increased the strength of national party organizations. Under Hanna, the national committee of the Republican Party emerged as a potentially influential vehicle for running presidential campaigns that relied on cash and exploited the new technologies of persuasion. Previously, the national committees were little more than ad hoc groupings of fund-raisers who collected money from wealthy friends to be sent to state and local party chieftains. The advertising style, in contrast, required greater coordination from the center, not only for fund-raising but also for carrying out campaign activities. Josephson's account of the 1896 campaign cap-tures the spirit of the Hanna enterprise, even if it likely exaggerates the prominence of the national committee during this period. According to Josephson:

> Hanna set up a complete machinery for modern political warfare. The Republican National Committee, which he headed, instead of being a sort of clearinghouse, a kind of central agency (chiefly for receiving appeals for funds from State bosses worried about their districts), became the general staff of the whole army. Its orders were carried out by the State Committees automatically, as if they were the branch offices of one of the modern, centralized industrial Trusts in oil, steel, or sugar. A loose confederation of Republican regional leaders and ward heelers was whipped into the shape of a machinelike army, under a single leader who oversaw everything, who infused all its men, from top to bottom, with his confidence and resolution. (1938, 695)

Hanna was laying the groundwork for a stronger national party organization, but his successors found it hard to institutionalize his practices. Indeed, it would take nearly a century for the RNC to approach anything like this kind of organizational influence again. The Democrats faced far greater obstacles—rooted in their factional diversity—and have barely succeeded at institutionalizing a strong national organization.[12]

Progressives were especially keen to stop the emerging unholy alliance between parties and corporate interests. Two principal concerns were that corporate funding of politics would corrupt politicians and also undermine the basic principle of one person, one vote. But reformers were also fearful that this alliance might create a new kind of party machine—one that was not local but national. Hanna had shown what was possible. The nationalization of the party organization would be particularly troublesome since Progressives aimed to elevate politics to a national stage, where pressing public problems might be attacked more comprehensively. But strong centralized parties jeopardized the Progressive strategy to increase the power of a national executive who stood above politics. The Hanna experiment with a strong national party organization threatened to institutionalize party politics in Washington just when Progressives were achieving some success at undermining it locally. The policy "drift" caused by party politics in the states might simply be reincarnated at the national level.

The hope of most Progressives was to remake politics through a vigorous national government, which would pursue rational policies in the common good and stand up to large corporate trusts that diverted policymaking toward purely private interests. Many Progressives believed, like Roosevelt, that only large public institutions could stand up to the influence of growing private institutions. But if concentrated private wealth was linked permanently with political parties, an opportunity to remake politics was lost. Expressing fears that politics might remain mired in affairs of expediency, Croly called the relationship between corporations and parties "an alliance between two independent and coordinate powers in the kingdom of American practical affairs" (1910, 123).

In highlighting the party-corporate financial relationship, Progressives tapped into populist fears of the two American organizations famously known for dangerous concentrations of power—one political, one economic. As Jerome Mileur observes: "The twin cancers on the body politic were the party bosses with their machines and the robber barons with their trusts, who were united by a mutuality of interests: the machines for money and patronage, the trusts for sympathetic legislatures and courts" (1999, 265). Through campaign finance reforms, Progressives might help slay these two organizational beasts at once.

Regulating money in politics took on an added dimension as political parties changed from an era of partisan spectacle to that of education politics. Capital was becoming an increasingly essential resource relative to manpower in elections. In addition, the cadre structure of American parties—quite unlike their European counterparts with their dues-paying members—meant that they had to rely on corporations or wealthy patrons to sustain the organization, especially as civil service reforms cut back on the routine flow of contributions dunned from public employees.[13] Thus, regulating campaign funds became an important aspect of the Progressive agenda. Reformers, of course, were concerned about the corrupt exchange of political money, but they also harbored fears that political parties would be resurgent through corporate resources, even after they had passed other laws to weaken the machines. With infusions of cash, the new party might have the wherewithal to thrive, even with the new educational style of campaigning.[14]

As for many policy areas, the movement for campaign finance reform began in the American states. During the Progressive Era, a wave of laws for regulating money in politics swept through the nation. While recent scholarship suggests that these early reform efforts were piecemeal, Overacker and other scholars from her period describe a movement that spawned, in her words, "voluminous" statutes in the states. By 1928, with the Progressive Era ended, no fewer than forty-four of the then forty-eight states had laws regulating some aspect of political funds. Only three states—Illinois, Mississippi, and

Rhode Island—failed to mention political funds in their laws. But even these states had statutes prohibiting bribery, intimidation, and other similar abuses (Overacker 1932, 294n6). To be sure, many states had statutes that were rudimentary, and most were enforced poorly.[15] But the idea that political funds should be regulated received broad public support during the Progressive Era, manifested in detailed statutes in almost all of the American states.

A review of state campaign finance regulations during this period reveals remarkable breadth of coverage, with statutes addressing all aspects of campaigns down to the smallest details. Figure 1 shows several dimensions of regulation in state campaign finance laws and the frequency of their inclusion in state laws by 1928.[16] In contrast to the conventional understanding that limits on the source and size of contributions constitute the first line of defense against corruption of candidates, the early state laws reveal extensive concern with how much money was *spent* rather than how it was raised or even where it came from. Overacker reports that only two states in 1926, Massachusetts and Nebraska, had laws limiting the size of contributions from individuals. In contrast, three-quarters of states had limits on the total amount that governors could spend for an election. The focus on political spending reflected anxiety about how parties used money to bribe voters rather than fears about contributors bribing politicians.

To curtail bribery and treating of voters, the laws frequently specified which campaign expenses were legitimate. No less than two-thirds of the American states had regulations about how parties and candidates could spend their political funds. In states like Iowa, Nebraska, Nevada, and Oregon, the regulations aimed at old practices of party treating, expressly forbidding committees from distributing alcoholic beverages, cigars, and other tobacco (Overacker 1932, 305). Massachusetts—perhaps because its western farmers grew tobacco—specifically mentioned in its statute that purchasing cigars and tobacco was permitted, but not "intoxicating liquors." Other states challenged several party practices, stipulating that the local committees could not sponsor betting on the elections. Nor could they pay the naturalization fees or poll taxes of potential voters. Even transporting voters to the polls was forbidden in eleven states.[17] In the most extreme instances, states like Oregon, North Dakota, and Wisconsin banned all "electioneering" on Election Day—meaning they could not use paid workers to get out the vote (Overacker 1932, 307).[18]

These rules governing political spending were intended to prevent corruption of the voter, but they supported a Progressive understanding of how citizens *should* participate in elections. They were intended to promote a certain

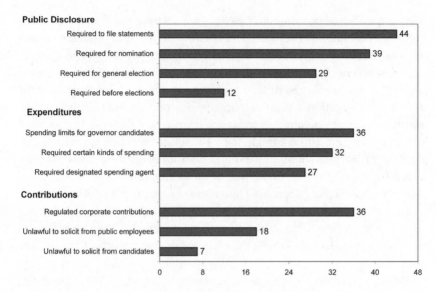

Public Disclosure
- Required to file statements — 44
- Required for nomination — 39
- Required for general election — 29
- Required before elections — 12

Expenditures
- Spending limits for governor candidates — 36
- Required certain kinds of spending — 32
- Required designated spending agent — 27

Contributions
- Regulated corporate contributions — 36
- Unlawful to solicit from public employees — 18
- Unlawful to solicit from candidates — 7

FIG. 1. Campaign finance laws in the forty-eight states, by 1928. (Data from Sikes 1928.)

kind of voting and establish new norms for how citizens made political choices. Nothing could be more anathema to the Progressive spirit than to cast a vote based on some material reward or emotionally laden appeal. The material exchange violated the dignity of the self and foreclosed the possibility that a citizen might contemplate the common good when casting his ballot. Immigrants, the poor, the drunks, the indifferent—all were susceptible to treating by party workers who trolled the neighborhoods with walk-around money.[19] To elevate the quality of discourse in campaigns, some reformers even tried to ban the use of negative advertising. In five states with influential Progressive movements, for example, it was unlawful "to circulate literature reflecting on candidate's character."[20] In contemporary campaign finance laws, we see echoes of these early efforts to shape how citizens make choices in elections through statutes that limit the use of political advertising, which is seen by many as mindless candidate bashing.[21] Recent research indicates, however, that political advertising informs citizens who typically lack an interest in politics and makes them pay attention as elections approach.[22]

Another tenet of Progressive faith was the emphasis on transparency in political finance. It was naturally assumed that, by providing as much information as possible about candidates, voters would have the capacity to make informed and rational decisions. The disclosure of campaign finance reports became central to every aspect of regulating money in politics. During the Progressive Era, only four states did not require statements to be filed by political committees or candidates. At least twelve states stipulated that statements be filed *before* an election, a practice that reformers hoped would encourage candidates to be more circumspect with their finances and diminish the potential for the quid pro quo. Interestingly, there were more states that required disclosure for primary elections (thirty-nine) than for general elections (twenty-nine). No doubt this was a reflection of the circumstance in southern states, where the primary was *the* election. But it was also true that, for individual candidates, money mattered more in the primary than in the general because they were fighting to win the nomination on their own, without the help of party workers. In the general election, the party would cover much of the costs of campaigning.

While most states failed to create regulatory regimes that provided accessible and accurate information to the public, the norm was clearly established during this period that financial reporting of party and candidate activity was a legitimate government function. The failure of states to provide necessary institutional mechanisms for collecting and disseminating reports was no doubt related to the refusal by politicians to give adequate resources or authority to an agency whose efforts might hurt their electoral prospects. Progressives underestimated the cost of providing electoral information, especially given the available technology and relatively weak administrative capacity of most states. Nevertheless, the concept of financial disclosure was embraced across the political spectrum in the United States, even as other democratic nations shunned this aspect of the law.[23] A lasting legacy of the Progressives' focus on transparency is that few nations provide better reporting about political activities than the United States.

The level of detail in disclosure laws affirms that Progressives were interested in more than preventing corruption. Reformers hoped that disclosure would improve accountability and raise the tenor of campaigns. State laws, for example, tried to prevent partisans from disguising their identities during the campaign or passing off political advertisements as news stories in daily papers. In twenty-six states, sponsors of posters and advertisements were required to show the name and address of persons responsible for them. In twenty-two states, laws required political ads in newspapers to be labeled as such to prevent them from masquerading as genuine news or dispassionate commentary.[24] We observe contemporary similarities to these efforts to "out" partisans and improve political discourse in contemporary campaigns through recent reforms, under the BCRA, that require groups to self-identify when they air political advertisements and candidates to announce in their campaign commercials that they "approve this ad."[25]

Regarding political contributions—a topic that receives much attention today—Progressive reforms aimed primarily to restrict the *source* of funds, particularly funds from corporations to parties and candidates.[26] Limits on the size of contributions appear to be a lesser concern, perhaps because Progressives believed individual contributions—detached from group interests—were inherently less corrupting. By the end of the era, three-quarters of the states regulated contributions from corporations. In some states the laws also sought to take away opportunities for parties to draw upon traditional sources of campaign support. For example, eighteen states banned contributions from public employees, and seven banned parties from soliciting them from candidates. These laws were, in part, about protecting individuals from being exploited by parties. Similarly, some have argued that the ban on corporate contributions was intended as a way to protect shareholders from misuse of corporate funds (Winkler 2004, 871–940; Joo 2002, 361–72). These bans, however, were also rooted in a profound distrust of organizations and an abiding Progressive faith that civically minded individuals would support the costs of democracy through voluntary political contributions. In chapter 5, I discuss the faulty premises of this faith and the consequences for party financing.

THE LONG-TERM EFFECTS OF EARLY CAMPAIGN FINANCE LAWS

What is germane to this study is that the Mugwump-Progressive approach to politics established the foundations for our current system of regulating money in politics. These preliminary approaches to regulating money in politics marked future boundaries for reforms and inaugurated patterns of response from the regulated community. After a century of politics under a regulatory regime mapped out mostly during the Progressive Era, political actors adapted in ways that are now institutionalized through candidate campaign committees, political action committees, and party structures.

Delving into political history shows that attempts at comprehensive regulation of campaign money did not begin with the FECA in 1974. The scope and breadth of laws in the states suggest that there were serious efforts to address concerns about money in politics at the turn of the century. The Tillman Act of 1907, which contemporary reformers cite as a benchmark in the progress to regulate political funds, was but one element in a dense thread of laws emerging in the states to control both the sources *and* uses of money. At the federal level, only a few years after the Tillman Act additional regulations would be passed regulating disclosure and campaign spending, which I cover in the next chapter.

Contemporary understandings of the earliest laws tend to view them as narrowly concerned with preventing corruption, particularly via regulation of corporate wealth in politics.[27] But these laws, in fact, reflected a broader agenda to limit the power of traditional partisan elites and remake American politics. While regulating campaign finance laws was but a minor tributary in the Progressives' reform agenda, it was no less fashioned by the sentiments and philosophical underpinnings of this movement. Beyond combating corruption, the earliest campaign finance laws expressed strong normative claims about how politics should be practiced. The earlier laws placed constraints on how money should be spent, elevating some kinds of campaigning over others.

To be sure, preventing bribery was a principal concern, but the laws sought to discourage other kinds of attempts to manipulate voters, including the use of emotive electoral appeals. For this reason, some Progressive states, such as Oregon, subsidized a portion of expenses for the publication of government-distributed pamphlets reflecting the party platforms. The parties rarely took advantage of the partial subsidy because they did not see it as an effective means of attracting voters (Pollock 1926, 104–6).[28] With an emphasis on public disclosure of party finances, Progressives sought to elevate the importance of transparency in the practice of politics. The new politics required diffusion of political knowledge, including financial reports about partisan activity. Such knowledge would help the impartial, responsible citizen evaluate politicians and make independent judgments. The overriding logic of laws was to put an emphasis on policy-based appeals. The most receptive audience for this campaign style would be educated, middle-class voters.

By diminishing traditional sources of party funding, by downplaying partisan appeals to emotion, and by placing so much faith in individual donors, these reforms erected obstacles for political parties in making the transition to the emerging cash-based economy of campaigning. At a time when other kinds of organizations during the twentieth century—business firms, advocacy groups, news organizations—were becoming nationalized and bureaucratized, the party committees remained acutely localized and weakly institutionalized.

To be sure, the constitutional design of federalism and separation of powers makes central organizing difficult, but the political parties were able to overcome these obstacles later in the century. As Paul Herrnson illustrates in *Party Campaigning in the 1980s* (1988), national political parties eventually adapted to this changing electoral system, taking advantage of new technologies to build a strong organizational apparatus at the center.

Campaign finance laws, which grew from antipartisan roots, have been one reason why national parties were slow to emerge as stable campaign organizations. Even as other kinds of political organizations were developing a strong national presence, the national party organizations remained stunted for reasons that cannot be explained entirely by the constitutional system. Writing about the critical years of partisan transformation at the turn of the century, Robert Marcus observes that "the increased bureaucratization and centralization of American life was almost completely thwarted in party politics" (1971, 252). The campaign finance laws disrupted the transition from a decentralized to a centralized form of campaigning. Hanna, as party leader of the Republicans, had pointed the way, though his methods obviously lacked legitimacy. Dunning corporate robber barons a percentage of their profits was clearly an unacceptable way to pay for politics.

The campaign finance laws, of course, were but one minor thread in the larger fabric of Progressivism's influence on American institutions and public attitudes. As James Q. Wilson (1962) points out, other reforms put forth by Progressives came quickly after the Hanna period—for example, nonpartisan elections and the direct primary—all of these reducing the possibility of strong state or national party organizations. The regulation of party funds was an additional constraint that hurt national organizations precisely at the time when money was an increasingly important resource and when national politics was becoming more relevant in the lives of Americans.

As will be shown later, partisans responded to Progressive laws by channeling contributions through numerous local party committees or setting up "independent" nonparty committees. After each new reform, they also attempted, in vain, to collect numerous small contributions to support their activities. Political parties withered as cash from voluntary donors became an increasingly essential resource in the campaign environment. Not only did laws make it difficult for them to raise and spend money to compete in the new-style education campaigns, but these organizations had structural disadvantages relative to candidates and interest groups, as I discuss in subsequent chapters.

It is nearly impossible to disentangle the independent effect of campaign finance laws in pushing the campaign focus away from parties to candidates. However, England's regulation of political money is instructive here. At the turn of the century, campaigns in England shifted from a candidate-centered system in place in the nineteenth century to party-centered campaigns, in which the party organizations controlled almost all the political funds. In the British model, the central parties were left almost completely unregulated with respect to campaign money. They could raise and spend funds even as candidates faced strict caps on the amount they could raise and spend. Nor were British parties required to report their financial activity. Paradoxically, American states and Congress drew on the British Corrupt Practices Act of 1883 as a model to craft their own campaign finance systems during the Progressive period, except that American political parties were typically heavily regulated while the British parties were not. In the British model, regulations applied to candidates rather than parties.

The heavy regulation of American parties has rendered them weak relative to their European counterparts even though a consensus exists among scholars that American parties are highly adaptable. When Leon Epstein claims, for example, that the "porous" nature of American parties allows them to adjust successfully to changing electoral environments, he also acknowledges that parties are weakly institutionalized (1986). Campaign finance laws contributed to keeping national parties weakly institutionalized by cutting off potential sources of money. At the local level, machines in some cities managed to survive by locating new sources of patronage to retain constituencies and win elections (Erie 1988). The political parties, however, atrophied to such a point by midcentury that their status brought forth a unique appeal from political scientists in 1950 to stimulate stronger party organizations (APSA. Committee on Political Parties 1950). Among the recommendations they urged were the deregulation of party finances and more opportunities for parties at the national level to raise and spend money. These recommendations went largely unheeded among a public imbued with a Progressive mind-set about the pernicious effects of money in politics and the nefarious role of political parties.

Operating within a political culture distrustful of money in politics, party leaders since the Mugwump era and the Progressive Era have exploited campaign finance reform periodically as a strategic tool to gain advantages over the rival party. They have sought laws that improve the prospects of their party relative to the other. Indeed, each major party has played a game of ambush, trying to make it more difficult for the other to raise and spend money. The ongoing skirmishes between the parties over campaign finance reforms—usually in the pursuit of short-term gains—have had harmful consequences over the long term for party building at all levels. The next chapter takes up the story of how partisan-inspired regulations have suffused the Progressive template for controlling money in elections, with important consequences for the party system.

CHAPTER 3

A History of Federal Campaign Finance Laws

The previous chapter provided historical perspective on how anti-corruption reforms emerged early in the twentieth century as part of a broader agenda to weaken the influence of political parties and give a new direction to modern politics. Progressives wanted to recalibrate the standards for political legitimacy and transform the political culture. In the new millennium, partisan politics would no longer be the benchmark for assessing the worthiness of policies or candidates. Instead, Progressives sought an emphasis on the public interest, as defined by experts and supported by free-thinking, informed citizens. This effort to move from a politics based on partisanship to one based on public interest would shift power to a different set of elites. Progressive reforms reduced the influence of traditional party bosses and elected officials and shifted power toward an intelligentsia based in universities, foundations, news organizations, and government bureaucracies.

Campaign finance regulation was one element in a wider strategy to curtail partisan politics. The flow of money into politics challenged Progressive goals, not only because it threatened to corrupt in the narrow sense but also because easy access to capital might reinvigorate parties. As campaigns changed from partisan spectacle to educational electioneering, money would give parties the wherewithal to make the transition to modern politics. The new politics put a premium on advertising candidates through various forms of mass media. In the broader sense, money "corrupted" political parties because these organizations might use it to expand machine politics on a national scale, enabling them to compete with muckraking newspapers, journals, and other nonpartisan sources of information. Progressives helped transform American political culture to the point where citizens began to support radical antiparty reforms such as direct primaries, nonpartisan municipal elections, and so forth. The Progressive makeover cleared the way for reforming the campaign finance system as well.

Partisans, however, were hardly bystanders in efforts to reform political finance. They did not allow regulations to wash over them without bending them to partisan purpose. Acknowledging the force of Progressive culture, members of Congress could not ignore external pressure for political reform—pressure that came from neo-Progressive factions in both parties. Instead, members reacted to the reformist impulse emerging in the twentieth century by supporting regulations strategically to advance partisan and factional interests. Party leaders in Congress recognized that they needed the legitimacy that came with being "the party of reform," but they also sought reforms that favored their side. While campaign finance laws were pursued in the name of public interest, partisan goals were integral to the design and motives for legislation.

In pursuing reform, incumbent officeholders tended to embrace a self-interested version of the Hippocratic oath: "First, do no harm to myself." Most assuredly, members of Congress were not about to pass reforms that would hurt their own reelection prospects. Instead, they called for federal campaign finance reforms that appeared to limit the flow of money in politics but were actually easy to circumvent. To be sure, the new regulations would make the campaigning more complicated and costly. But these additional costs would typically be harder for challengers to overcome than for incumbents. Indeed, incumbents might gain from making it harder for challengers to raise and spend money against them.[1]

But my argument is that reforms are not simply about incumbents protecting their own positions. The reform dynamic is multilayered, since individuals are also motivated to advance the position of their political party and the *influence of their particular faction within the party*. Each major party possesses unique electoral resources derived from the different constellation of constituencies that support them. Party leaders must ensure that these resources are protected from "harmful" reforms, while foisting regulations that typically impair the resources of the other major party. This partisan explanation of reform has been made by others in various contexts,[2] but I also believe it falls well short of explaining how and why reforms have been passed.

What these previous accounts leave out is the *intra*partisan struggles over reform. Given the coalitional nature of the major American parties, the reform battles take place within the major parties as factions compete for influence over the direction of the political party. Intraparty rivalries drive preferences for different approaches to reform, since some approaches to reform supply advantages to one faction or another. This is particularly true in presidential elections, which require enormous amounts of resources from several constituencies. Partisan factions maneuver to gain the best outcome from reforms that elevate the value of their unique resources over those of others. This advantage gives them greater influence in elections and hence greater influence within the Democratic or Republican Party.

One important consequence of the partisan and factional maneuvering is that campaign finance reforms tend to reinforce a trend toward fragmented political campaigns, especially in presidential elections. The strategic use of regulations to neutralize the electoral advantages of rivals makes it extremely difficult to organize coherent national campaigns. Instead, the dense overlay of restrictions on political contributions and spending, especially for party committees, has made it all but impossible to run a campaign through the national party committees the way it is done in other democracies. Instead, the unintended consequence of many federal campaign finance laws has been the dispersion of money and activities among candidates and "shadow" party groups, who are legally distinct, if not separate, from the official national party committees.

I elaborate this theory in greater depth in the subsequent chapter. In this chapter I lay the groundwork for this theory by giving a history of campaign reforms during the past century. The narrative fleshes out the legislative actors, partisan contexts, and underlying motives for reform. It is by no means a comprehensive account of the legislative record in Congress, but, unlike previous histories, it charts the growth of federal regulation, starting in the nineteenth century. Most studies simply choose to begin discussions with the FECA of 1971 and 1974 and merely salute the first early effort to ban corporate donations under the Tillman Act of 1907. More informed accounts provide some cursory mentions of previous "failed" reform efforts without examining the context in which reforms were discussed or the real consequences of these supposedly failed efforts. By starting with the FECA they argue or imply that these were the first laws "with any teeth." The evidence gathered here indicates otherwise. Reforms that date from the early twentieth century may have been ineffective in the sense that they did little to staunch the flow of money into politics or make political contributions more transparent to the public, but they certainly influenced behavior, as I will explain in chapters 5 and 6.

In this chapter, I seek to map periods of reform marked by distinct patterns of partisan and factional-inspired legislation. Outside of partisan accounts of reform, the orthodox explanation for reform focuses on the role of public interest groups. In such accounts, public interest groups are instrumental in forging coalitions in the wake of scandal to pass tougher campaign finance laws (Corrado 1997, 25–60; Mutch 1988; Theriault 2005; Zelizer 2002, 73–111). My argument, however, is that partisans drew on the language of Progressives— and the public interest groups that followed in their wake—to push for rules that favored their electoral interests at the expense of rivals. The design of the BCRA of 2002 was no less partisan than previous reforms. Indeed, the two parties championed different approaches that map clearly onto previous reform efforts.

There are three distinct periods of campaign finance reform in the twentieth century. The first period began with the Progressives, ending in roughly 1925. During this time, the project to regulate political financing emerged from a broader movement to reform political parties. Democrats latched onto the reform movement as a way to attack Republican advantages of raising money. In the next period, from 1939 to 1947, Republicans championed regulations to weaken the labor movement, which had emerged as the strongest electoral force of the New Deal coalition. With the help of antilabor southerners, Republicans passed laws restricting union contributions and making it more difficult for a burgeoning federal workforce to participate fully in campaigns to elect New Deal Democrats. Finally, in the 1960s, Democrats once again became the party of reform as the costs of television advertisements increased rapidly, exposing, once again, the party's structural weakness in raising money relative to the Republicans.

During each reform period, the major parties tended to pursue reforms that cut into the strengths of the rival party: the Republicans sought reforms to minimize in-kind sources of support available to Democrats, and the Democrats pursued reforms to reduce Republican advantages of raising cash. Factions *within* each party were instrumental in designing reforms that gave them leverage over other factions in the party. I refine these arguments in the subsequent chapter when I explain this theory of political reform.

PROGRESSIVE PERIOD, 1907–25

When Teddy Roosevelt, a champion of many Progressive reforms, ran for election in 1904 he had the financial backing of men who ran the corporate trusts.

A few months before Election Day, he called for E. H. Harriman, a Wall Street financier of trusts, to help raise additional funds for the campaign (Morris 2001, 359–60). As the campaign approached its final weeks, the Democratic candidate, Alton B. Parker, who himself benefited from large donations, charged that Roosevelt had been bought by the trusts. The *New York Times* and other newspapers picked up on the charges in their editorials and kept the issue in the news for several months after the election. The story about political money received renewed attention by the New York papers in 1905 when a state senate investigating committee revealed how large insurance companies routinely made payments to politicians with the expectation that they would attain policy benefits in return.[3]

Roosevelt believed the "muckrakers" were overselling the problem of financing campaigns, but he did not hesitate to call for reform once he was elected (Corrado 1997; Mutch 1988). He was sensitive to public perceptions about corruption, particularly since he needed credibility to wage his public campaign for national economic reforms. By being associated too closely with the barons of industry and finance, Roosevelt risked losing his image as protector of the little guy. His bully pulpit style would lack legitimacy unless he was perceived as a man who stood above politics. In speaking out against corporate political contributions Roosevelt hoped to neutralize populist Democrats like Senator Ben "Pitchfork" Tillman, who were holding up legislation that Roosevelt wanted.

In his first message to Congress after the 1904 election Roosevelt urged that it pass a law to disclose the sources and uses of campaign funds by political committees and candidates.[4] The Republican-dominated Congress resisted. In the following year, he called for a prohibition of political contribution by corporations.[5] Again, there was no response from Congress. Finally, in 1907, he went further, calling for the radical measure of supporting political parties with public funds.[6] Roosevelt was actually quite skeptical about the feasibility of enforcing regulations on money in politics. Indeed, his call for public funds to support the major parties reflected his concern that the "unscrupulous" could easily evade disclosure or that the "man of unlimited means" could buy his way into office if others did not have adequate access to campaign money. His call for public funds also reflected his belief that politics was costly; one could not skimp "to meet the necessity for thorough organization and machinery" of the "great national parties" (Roosevelt 1907). In contrast to most Progressive reformers who wanted to cap political spending, Roosevelt supported a supply-side solution, meaning he believed the costs of democracy required robust expenditures that could be supported through the public treasury.

Roosevelt, however, was not successful in his calls to change the system. Even the scandals in New York and the charges against Roosevelt during the campaign could not get congressional Republicans to support campaign finance reform. While the GOP was home to a neo-Wugmump faction calling for reform, party stalwarts were not prepared to give away a growing financial advantage, particularly when the emerging political environment emphasized expensive education-style campaigns over local spectacle. Starting with the 1896 elections, Mark Hanna, as chair of the RNC, perfected an elaborate system of assessing American corporations a percentage of their profits for the campaign. He was scrupulous in staying within these guidelines, writing letters to firms that did not pay their "fair share" and even returning funds to corporations that gave too much (Croly 1965, 326). Hanna, a product of the emerging corporate elite, believed the level of corporate contributions should reflect returns these firms received from Republican policies that supported national prosperity. The Hanna method of taking a cut from corporate profits emulated a previous party method of dunning government workers a percentage of their salaries. The underlying premise of the party solicitation was the same: those who benefit from the party should support its reelection efforts.

Hanna was adapting to a new political environment in which campaigns were becoming more expensive and traditional sources of funding were ebbing because of civil service reforms. The first federal legislation on money in politics was passed in 1867, covering workers at navy dockyards during the Civil War. The law protected them from being assessed for political donations. This became a principle extended to all federal employees under the Pendleton Act of 1883. In turn, the Pendleton Act set the standard for future Mugwump and Progressive efforts to reform civil service, advancing the merit system, in part to weaken patronage politics. Many states pursued similar reforms aimed at preventing state and local parties from tapping their dense network of government patronage for money.

While Republicans had been accepting corporate gifts long before 1896, Hanna's efforts in the first McKinley-Bryan election surpassed all previous financial efforts to centralize fund-raising and strategy under the RNC. Indeed, the election of 1896 marked the end of an earlier era of campaigning that relied on local campaign spectacle. In its place Hanna inaugurated the mass education campaign with which we are familiar today. Hanna recognized that voters were less interested in traditional party pageantry of local parades and treating when they had alternative leisure activities to pursue. Ballot reforms also compelled parties to sell their candidates retail—on a one-by-one basis for each elective office—rather than wholesale through the party-distributed ballot.[7] It was the beginning of the candidate-centered campaign.

Mark Hanna appeared to understand the new politics. He certainly recognized that it required previously unheard of amounts of cash. Republican industrialists were open to Hanna's appeals for money, even though some were shocked by the size and insistent nature of the requests (Shannon 1959, 32). Herbert Croly, his biographer, estimated the sum raised at roughly $3.5 million (1912, 219). Subsequent RNC chairs would imitate Hanna's strategy, though not quite on the same scale as the critical election of 1896, when the electorate realigned to provide reliable Republican majorities over the next several decades. Roosevelt's pick for party chair in 1904, George Cortelyou, used Hanna's methods to support Roosevelt's candidacy but managed to raise only $2 million, according to a study by Louise Overacker (1932, 73). This was still a considerable sum by historical standards and almost three times the amount that the Democrats raised for their nominee, Judge Alton Parker.

With Roosevelt in office, the Democrats were worried going into the 1908 elections. The Republicans looked unbeatable in the presidential contest, especially with their access to a steady supply of corporate funds.[8] The challenge to the Republican money machine came from two wings of the Democratic Party: the agrarian southern wing represented by Ben Tillman, a senator from South Carolina, and the northern establishment wing represented by Perry Belmont, a New Yorker with close ties to the DNC.

The Democrats were helped by the Progressives in the Republican Party who bucked party leaders to support campaign finance reform. Banning corporate contributions had been a long-standing goal of many Progressive Republicans, including statesman Elihu Root, who urged adoption of a ban on corporate political contributions as early as 1894 at the New York state constitutional convention. "Great moneyed interests," Root declared, "are more and more necessary to the support of political parties, and political parties are every year contracting greater debts to the men who can furnish the money to perform the necessary functions of party warfare. The object of this amendment [to ban corporate political contributions] is by laying down a simple rule to put an end, if possible, to that great crying evil of American politics" (Jessup 1964, 172–79).[9] Root was supported in his various reform efforts by leading muckraking newspapers and prominent New Yorkers, including Dr. C. H. Parkhurst and Seth Low, the president of Columbia University (Jessup 1964, 192–93).

In Congress, the leading Republican on the issue was Senator William E. Chandler (R-NH), who had been trying to pass a ban on corporate funding of elections since 1901, but he received almost no attention from the press and limited support from his colleagues. He had introduced his 1901 bill as a lame duck, soon after losing an election in the state legislature, which chose U.S. senators at that time.[10] His bill called for banning all corporations engaged in interstate commerce or chartered by the federal government from contributing to election campaigns at any level (Mutch 1988, 5). As chair of the Senate Committee on Privileges and Elections, he had little difficultly reporting the bill from committee, but it was never voted upon on the floor of the Senate. Chandler's bill may have reflected an act of retribution against the New England railroad interests, which had engineered his departure from the Senate through their influence in the New Hampshire legislature. In pushing his bill, Chandler argued he was trying to protect stockholders from having their funds embezzled by corporation officers to pay for politics (Shannon 1959, 38; Winkler 2004).[11]

Since Chandler could not get any of his Republican colleagues to reintroduce his bill after he left the Senate, he went to his unlikely ally, Ben Tillman (Mutch 1988). Incongruously, Tillman's interest was stirred by Chandler, who was a former "radical" Republican.[12] Tillman was an improbable reformer even though he was a self-proclaimed champion of the common man against the corporations and bankers. In his earlier political career, he was instrumental in disenfranchising black voters, a strategy that helped him win the gubernatorial race in 1890. In his classic account of southern politics V. O. Key refers to Tillman as a "demagogue" and "negro-baiter" (1984, 142–44). It seems self-evident that his interest in campaign finance reform was hardly in the tradition of the good-government Progressives.

Tillman saw an opportunity to embarrass Republicans, capitalize on popular anticorporate sentiments, and undermine Roosevelt's broader legislative agenda (Epstein 1968; Mutch 2002; Sikes 1928; Simkins 1944, 408–18). He was a fervent antagonist of Roosevelt across a range of issues, clashing with him most ferociously on the "Negro question." Tillman was also a constant critic of Roosevelt's efforts to pursue trust busting, pointing out that members of the president's administration frequently left government to work for the very corporations they had been regulating. Alton Parker's allegation that Roosevelt's reelection campaign was furnished by corporate contributions gave Tillman the opportunity to introduce resolutions asking the treasury secretary to look into political contributions by national banks. When nothing turned up, Tillman asserted the reports were fraudulent and pressed for an investigation by the Senate Committee on Privileges and Elections. At the hearing, he had done little homework to prove his case (though subsequent investigations found evidence of large contributions). He expressed frustration, however, that though the "crime" of campaign contributions "was acknowledged by everybody," the Senate committee "seemed to pooh-pooh the idea of an investigation" (Simkins 1944, 413–14).

As a rural southerner, Tillman had little to lose by railing against northern corporate and banking interests. Moreover, the Democratic Party, even in the North, had little to fear from his proposal since the ban would not apply to state-based party committees. While Republicans tended to raise their funds centrally at the RNC from corporations (Hanna style), Democrats tended to raise their money through local and state committees. These committees relied heavily on contributions from government employees and local business firms trying to get municipal contracts. To be sure, the DNC also received a portion of funds from corporations. But these donors were less likely to be from the inner circle of big business. Indeed, corporate donations to the DNC appeared to be based more on personal relationships and local ties rather than on "pro-business" policies, which were the natural domain of Republicans.[13] Research by James Pollack also shows that it was wealthy individuals rather than corporations per se that gave to the DNC.[14]

Through Tillman's efforts, the Senate Committee on Privileges and Elections reported a bill in April 1906 that would ban corporate political contributions. The committee report revealed little investigative work on the issue, claiming that the nature of the problem was self-evident. Expressing the committee's wholesome motive for supporting the measure, the report commented:

> The evils of the use of money in connection with political elections are so generally recognized that the committee deemed it unnecessary to make any argument in favor of the general purpose of this measure. It is in the interest of good government and calculated to promote purity in the election of public officials.[15]

Congressional Republicans argued successfully against the original bill and weakened it so that the legislation would apply only to the national party committees. The original version declared that Congress had the right to ban corporate contributions in *any* election, including state and local elections, based on arguments derived from the interstate commerce clause. Before the bill reached the floor for a vote, the chairman of the Senate Committee on Privileges and Elections, Joseph E. Foraker (R-OH), made sure that the bill did not permit Congress to regulate state elections. Foraker also insisted that the bill could not regulate state-chartered corporations, even those engaged in interstate commerce. Congress, he argued, possessed only the power to regulate federal-chartered corporations with respect to congressional elections.

No doubt he and other Republicans were mindful that corporations could continue making contributions to state and local parties for state legislative elections, in which senators were elected. They probably also understood that there was nothing to prevent surrogates of the national committees from setting up committees within a single state to raise corporate money in elections. Moreover, individual business executives could still give money to the national committees and be reimbursed by the corporation. With these revisions, both the Senate and House passed the 1907 bill with little debate or opposition.[16] Republicans apparently felt it was more important to get corporate political contributions off the pages of editorials than to fight this battle (Mutch 2002, 10). Given their centralized fund-raising apparatus, Republicans would need to adjust more than Democrats to the new law. They appeared to accept this reality since the bill passed easily. The unintended result of this early campaign finance law, however, was to decentralize party fund-raising, especially for Republicans.[17] I discuss this consequence at greater length in chapter 5 on fund-raising.

While Tillman was pushing for the ban on corporate contributions, the other wing of the Democratic Party was pushing for laws to promote publicity of campaign finance legislation. This, too, would have the effect of scattering funds into numerous state party and independent committees, since many wealthy donors preferred to be anonymous. The reform was sponsored by a group called the National Publicity Law Organization (NPLO), a forerunner of contemporary public interest groups such as Common Cause. While the membership of the NPLO appeared bipartisan, it was founded by a former treasurer of the DNC, Perry Belmont.[18]

Belmont took up the cause of campaign finance reform after the 1904 election, writing an article about money in politics for the *North American Review* (Pollock 1926, 10). He may have been sincerely convinced that disclosure of campaign funds would fix many of the problems associated with raising money for politics, but as a loyal Democrat, he was surely concerned that the RNC outspent the Democrats by a three-to-one ratio in the 1904 elections. Belmont possibly hoped a publicity bill would curtail corporate contributions once shareholders and the public saw who was funding elections. He apparently had little problem with large contributions from wealthy individuals, which included his own brother, August, a New York financier, who contributed $250,000 to the DNC in the 1904 election, roughly one-third of the national committee funds (Overacker 1932, 141).

The Federal Corrupt Practices Act (FCPA), also known as the Publicity Act of 1910, passed with the full support of Democrats and insurgent Republicans who had recently challenged the iron-fisted rule of House Speaker Joe Cannon (R-IL) (Milkis and Young 2003).[19] The Old Guard of the Republican Party joined in the final vote after they had watered down the bill considerably. It was the first law regulating disclosure of contributions made for the purpose of influencing U.S. House elections. The 1910 law defined the term *political committee* as one that operated in two or more states and required a committee treasurer to keep a record of receipts and expenditures to be filed with the clerk of the House of Representatives within thirty days after an election.[20] Most important, the 1910 law did not require publicity before the election, which might have compelled campaigners to avoid the kind of large contributions that attracted negative publicity (Overacker 1932, 238).

Democrats had another opportunity to tighten the regulations when they took control of the House in the 1910 elections. They pushed for amendments to the Publicity Act in 1911 that would require political committees to disclose funds at least ten days *before* an election and extended reporting requirements from political committees to all candidates (including Senate candidates who were still elected by state legislatures). Candidates, however, were exempt from reporting many types of campaign expenditures.[21] More important, other groups could spend money on behalf of the candidates, so long as it was done without the candidate's knowledge. The Republicans tried to kill the new publicity bill by requesting that publicity requirements extend to primaries, which would make southern Democrats balk at passing these amendments. Southern Democrats tried to keep this provision out of the package, but they could not beat back an alliance between Republicans and northern Democrats to pass it (Mutch 1988).

The most significant and controversial aspect of the law was a proposal by a House Democrat to limit the amount of campaign expenditures for House candidates to five thousand dollars per election (one hundred thousand dollars in 2004 dollars). According to Robert Mutch, this part of the law was affixed to the legislation hastily by Senator James Reed (D-MO), who penciled it in during the floor debate (1988, 14).[22] Even the *New York Times,* which was not quite the pro-reform newspaper it is today, said the expenditure cap was "sweeping and severe" (*New York Times* 1911). For most campaigns at the time, the five thousand dollar cap posed little difficulty since congressional elections remained rather inexpensive. But in larger states, incumbents complained that the limit was unrealistically low.

After 1911, Congress considered various reform proposals to further regulate money in politics, but the next set of reforms would not come until 1925. Some proposals before then called for extending regulations to state and local committees, since national committees could easily evade the new laws by funneling money through state and local parties. In 1913, the Seventeenth Amendment raised constitutional issues about the scope of congressional authority in regulating Senate elections, particularly primaries. These issues were finally addressed in *Newberry v. United States* (1921).

Newberry involved a Senate primary contest for the Republican nomination in Michigan in which automobile tycoon Henry Ford competed against the party favorite, Truman H. Newberry, who had served in the Roosevelt administration. Ford lost the primary to Newberry, though he would later receive the Democratic nomination and face Newberry in the general election. Ford accused his primary rival of violating the federal campaign finance laws by receiving and spending funds in excess of the rules established by the 1910 and 1911 laws. Newberry admitted to spending nearly $180,000, much of it contributed by his family (Mutch 1988, 16).

The district court ruled in favor of Ford, but Newberry appealed to the Supreme Court, which reversed the ruling. At issue was whether Congress had the power to regulate primaries. In a highly complex decision, the judges held that Congress had no power to extend the 1910 and 1911 laws—which predated the Seventeenth Amendment—to the regulation of senatorial primaries. This did not mean, however, that it was unconstitutional to pass a new law, taking the Seventeenth Amendment into consideration.[23]

As legislative proposals circulated to address the *Newberry* case, the Teapot Dome scandal in 1924 temporarily publicized the need for further reform.[24] The Senate investigations into the leasing of oil reserves to the Sinclair Oil Corporation revealed evidence of bribes to government official and suggested that Harry Sinclair himself had covered the debts of the RNC in the 1920 elections with a loan.[25] A parallel investigation conducted by William E. Borah (R-ID) looked closely at campaign financing in the 1924 elections. A staunch Progressive, Borah was bitterly opposed to the Republican Party's return to "normalcy" under the presidencies of Harding and Coolidge. The Progressives had once again broken with the party in 1924 to support Robert La Follette's third-party bid for the White House. The Borah committee released a blistering report against the Coolidge campaign weeks before the election, accusing them of using slush funds to buy voters and turning the Republican Party into the "rich man's club" (*New York Times* 1924b). Democrats, of course, were enthusiastic about Borah's investigations, which were ongoing during the 1924 campaign.[26] They were once again being thoroughly outspent in the presidential elections and hoped his report would hurt the Coolidge campaign. After the election Progressives and Democrats teamed up to push for changes to the federal campaign finance laws under the Borah bill.

Borah introduced a bill in 1925 to revise the FCPA of 1910, attaching it as a rider, Title III, to the Postal Salary Increase Act before the latter was headed to conference committee.[27] The Democratic leadership in the House was eager to join with Progressives in approving this rider, but Speaker Nicholas Longworth (R-OH) replaced it with a watered-down substitute sponsored by Representative John Cable (R-OH) (*New York Times* 1924a). House conferees were then instructed not to approve the postal rates and salaries bill unless the Cable rider was included. The decisions surrounding the substitution of the Cable amendment for that of the Borah bill are unclear because there is nothing in the *Congressional Record* to explain what happened. But Borah was obviously displeased with the changes because he was one of only eight senators who voted against the final version of the FCPA.[28]

The 1925 act consolidated previous federal laws relating to campaigns and modified provisions in three important ways. First, laws would apply only to general elections, to take account of the *Newberry* decision. Southerners were pleased about this change; they had fought off all attempts by Republicans to include primaries. The act also improved financial disclosure requirements by laying out a calendar of dates when reports had to be filed with the House clerk.[29] Finally, the act increased limits on the amount of money that Senate candidates could spend in the general election, giving some flexibility to candidates in larger states. Under the revised law, they could spend up to $25,000 ($270,000 in 2004 dollars), depending on the size of their state, rather than the previous limit of $10,000. House candidate spending remained the same at $5,000.[30]

The 1925 FCPA would be the basic law of the land for regulating money in politics for the next five decades until the passage of the FECA in 1971. The 1925 act encapsulated the Progressive approach to reforms that would follow in the future with its emphasis on publicity through disclosure and limits on the amount of money in politics. The law was weakly enforced, since there was no institutionalized method for submitting, maintaining, and providing public access to reports. Nevertheless, the threat of sanction compelled candidates, parties, and interest groups to adapt to its provisions. In many instances, adaptations involved forming shadow committees to campaign on behalf of candidates to avoid exceeding the spending limits or reporting electoral activity.

Given the attention that historical accounts of reform give to the Teapot Dome scandal, it is surprising that the FCPA of 1925 was buried in a rider on a major bill to increase postal rates and salaries. Congressional debate was curiously absent, and the *New York Times* barely mentioned the passage of corrupt practices legislation. In contrast to conventional accounts of reform, it appears that scandal played a modest role in moving the 1925 act. Indeed, partisan motives were more important in the push for this bill, including both Progressives seeking to undermine the conservative wing of the Republican Party and Democrats still reeling from another loss in presidential elections.[31]

The FCPA closed the first period of federal campaign finance reform. The following list summarizes key elements of legislation during this period.

Key Provisions of Campaign Finance Laws, 1907–25

1. Ban contributions from national banks and corporations to any committees operating in two or more states (1907).
2. Public disclosure
   - Required for political committees helping to elect federal candidates in two or more states.
   - Treasurer of committee must submit detailed reports of receipts and expenditures with clerk of House of Representatives.
   - Reports must be filed ten to fifteen days before election and within thirty days after election.
   - Must contain name, address, and amount of each contributor of one hundred dollars or more.
   - Must contain name and address of each person to whom sums of ten dollars are given.
   - Reports kept on file as public records for fifteen months after election.
3. Expenditure limits
   - Expenditures limited to amounts permitted by laws of state.
   - Five thousand dollars is upper limit (regardless of state laws) for nomination and election for U.S. House; twenty thousand dollars is limit for Senate candidate.
   - Exemption of limit for expenses incurred for personal traveling, subsis-

tence, stationary, postage, printing, (other than newspapers), distribution of letters, and telegraph and telephone.

- Punishment for violation; fine of not more than one thousand dollars and imprisonment for not more than one year or both.

REPUBLICAN REFORMS, 1939–47

Changes to campaign finance laws in the 1930s and 1940s grew from the same template as previous reforms but were rooted in partisan battles centered on the New Deal. While the first federal campaign finance laws were inspired by the Progressive movement, changes between 1939 and 1947 were driven by Republican and southern Democrat fears about the growing power of the labor movement in the Democratic Party. The policies of the Roosevelt administration were remaking the role of the federal government and consequentially shifting power among political factions. As FDR approached his election for a third term, political rivals sought to weaken the ability of labor unions to support him. To this end, a coalition of anti–New Deal lawmakers crafted three separate laws during this period to minimize the electoral clout of the labor movement and prevent the administration from using its burgeoning federal workforce to campaign against politicians opposed to the New Deal.[32]

The Hatch Acts (1939, 1940), the Smith-Connally Act (1943), and the Taft-Hartley Act (1947) were part of the same agenda. The goal was to limit resources flowing to New Deal Democrats. Just as Democrats at the turn of the century feared the Mark Hanna juggernaut—a Republican Party flush with corporate funds—so too did Republicans fret about the revival of Democratic organizations supported by federal relief workers and labor unions. In the 1930s, labor organizations increasingly tied themselves to the Democrats through political contributions and impressive get-out-the-vote operations. Prior to the 1930s, many labor leaders had avoided electoral politics, especially overtly partisan campaigning. If they gave money, it was primarily to the Labor's Non-Partisan League, which spent money on postage, leaflets, and the expenses of speakers (Overacker 1946, 50–51). The nation's largest labor organization in the early decades of the twentieth century, the American Federation of Labor (AFL), explicitly pursued a nonpartisan political strategy under its leader, Samuel Gompers. Gompers believed that government should stay out of business-labor relations.

The interventionist policies of the Roosevelt administration, however, began tilting power away from management toward unions. The more militant unions recognized the benefits of keeping FDR in office and began to discard nonpartisan strategies in favor of open support of New Deal Democrats. In the 1930s, a new breed of union leaders, such as Sidney Hillman of Amalgamated Clothing Workers of America and John Lewis of the United Mine Workers, pushed aggressively into partisan politics through their industrial unions. While the AFL leadership remained cautious about engaging in electoral politics, the industrial unions did not shy from it. In 1936, for example, John Lewis appeared eagerly at the White House with a photographer and a check made out to the DNC for $250,000 (Kennedy 1999).[33] Leaders from the industrial unions wanted to advertise the fact that they were a vital part of an ascendant Democratic coalition.[34] Before 1936 labor's political contributions were "small and sporadic," according to Louise Overacker. Then they started to rise quickly. Labor union expenditures in campaigns almost doubled between 1936 and 1944, from roughly $770,000 to $1,300,000 ($14.1 million in 2004 dollars) (Overacker 1946, 59). It is likely that these figures did not include significant amounts of in-kind support from labor unions to mobilize voters through union-based get-out-the-vote campaigns.

While Republicans became restive over the growing closeness of labor unions with the Democratic Party, conservative southern Democrats were no more happy. Labor unions represented a serious threat to traditional elites who controlled politics in the South. Looking back on this era, V. O. Key observed how labor occasionally had played a decisive role in factional struggles in states like Florida and Texas. Labor's muscle might nurture antiestablishment factions to challenge the power of party bosses and other local elites. Conservative Democrats in Dixie and elsewhere may also have been concerned that the leftward tilt of the national party would jeopardize their relationships with business elites who supported Democrats in their states (Key 1984, 673–74). Surely, many conservative Democrats in Congress did not appreciate how Roosevelt was changing the locus of political and government authority through ties to powerful independent organizations and federal workers. New Deal critics saw in labor unions and government workers the makings of a modern Tammany that would operate on a national scale, independently of state and local party organizations (Milkis and Young 2003, 50–51). Like in the previous period of reform, a restive faction in the majority party—in this instance, conservative Democrats—provided an opportunity for the minority party to mount a drive to chip away at resource advantages of the core group in the majority.

Even some northern Democrats who were tied to urban machines felt threatened by the growing influence of labor unions. Northern party bosses

still organized themselves around securing jobs and contracts for loyal supporters. Political patronage remained their bread and butter. An independent
labor movement, however, presented a challenge to local machine influence.
Labor leaders in the 1930s were not averse to throwing their electoral weight
behind liberal Republicans instead of unsupportive Democrats or even to making attempts to create their own political party. Fears of labor union power and
the possibility of labor forging its own party prompted Tammany Democrats to
introduce a bill in 1938 in the New York state legislature to prevent union contributions to political parties (*New York Times* 1938a). Roosevelt was able to
attenuate these tensions between labor and northern city machines by building
a coalition through his New Deal programs that provided important benefits to
both groups (Milkis 1993).

It is unsurprising that traditional party elites in both parties tried to undermine the influence of New Deal supporters. They feared New Deal policies
were creating a personal federal machine for FDR through relief programs that
put thousands of voters into federally sponsored jobs. And New Dealers
appeared increasingly confident to challenge the status quo using tough political tactics. Perhaps the most controversial were the "purge" campaigns, which
sought to unseat the Democrats whom FDR called Copperheads: southerners
who blocked the administration policies.[35] A series of articles in the Hearst
newspapers stoked southern fears by claiming that workers from the Works
Progress Administration (WPA) and Civil Works Administration (CWA) were
helping White House favorites win reelection through political contributions
and political leafleting in support of New Deal candidates.[36] Roosevelt's refer-
ence to events of the Civil War, coupled with his political challenge to Democratic elites in the South, inspired a countermobilization (Milkis 1999, 91). The
Hatch Act, passed in 1939, emerged from outrage over FDR's intrusion into
southern politics and Republican fears about the influence of the labor movement in the Democratic Party.

The Hatch Acts of 1939 and 1940

Senator Carl A. Hatch (D-NM) was largely an unknown legislator except for his
sponsorship of an act that would make federal workers lose their jobs if they
participated in politics.[37] In many policy matters he was conservative, though
he seemed sympathetic to the New Deal approach. He supported a federal minimum wage and pushed for the expansion of the national parks system. On the
other hand, his support of trade liberalization was not popular with labor
unions. Many suspected, however, that Vice President John Nance Garner was

the force behind the Hatch Act (Alsop and Kintner 1939). Garner, a rural Texan and former Speaker of the House, was a likely rival of FDR for the 1940 nomination. He was not a loyal New Dealer, believing federal programs to be a temporary remedy for unemployment (Kennedy 1999, 60–61, 124). The Hatch Act was the only piece of legislation Garner endorsed publicly as vice president, predicting from the steps of the White House that Congress would not adjourn in 1939 without passing it (Krock 1939). One aspect of the Hatch bill that would surely help Garner was a provision that prevented federal jobholders from attending party conventions. This obscure detail in the bill would weaken Roosevelt's ability to be nominated for an unprecedented third term.[38]

The overarching purpose of the Hatch Act, however, was to limit partisan political involvement by federal workers.[39] The formal title was the Act to Prevent Pernicious Political Activities, implying in no uncertain terms that political action could be separated clearly into good and evil. It prohibited any kind of federal worker from participating in or contributing to presidential or congressional nominations and elections. Thus, officials of the WPA could not coerce campaign contributions or political support from workers by promising jobs, promotion, financial assistance, contracts, or any other benefit.[40]

New Dealers in Congress challenged the bill by offering outlandish amendments, which highlighted the partisan nature of the legislation. Representative Claude Parsons (D-IL), floor leader for the opposition, pushed an amendment to prohibit newspapers from accepting paid advertising of candidates and banning editors or reporters from expressing their opinions on political subjects and candidates (Dorris 1939). Another "kidding" amendment was proposed by Representative Leon Sacks (D-PA) to make it unlawful for a political party to offer a platform that "promised anything to anybody." In the same mocking spirit, Representative Richard Duncan (D-MO) proposed to make it unlawful for candidates to make "audible speeches, or gestures, or other such efforts to affect an election" (Dorris 1939, 4).

In spite of efforts of loyal New Dealers to block the Hatch Act, it passed both houses and was signed reluctantly by Roosevelt on August 2, 1939, after he made the unprecedented move of conferring with the sponsor, Senator Hatch, and the attorney general over the details of the bill (Krock 1939). In particular, Roosevelt wanted assurances from both of them that this bill did not violate the Bill of Rights. FDR may have wanted this meeting to be part of the legislative record, in anticipation of court challenges, and perhaps as a way of finding safe harbors to organize future political activity not mentioned in the bill. Many New Dealers in the administration urged Roosevelt to veto the legislation.

White House aides apparently drafted a veto message criticizing the bill for not banning all private contributions and appropriating public funds for the use of political parties (Milkis and Young 2003, 54).

Reformers were not done yet. The Hatch Act was followed one year later by a "clean state politics bill," known as the Hatch Act II. These additions to the Hatch Act extended the ban on political activity to state and local workers who were paid, in part, through federal programs. Republicans wanted to prevent Democrats from getting around Hatch I by using workers on state payrolls to help Democrats win elections. They were joined by a moderate faction of Democrats, especially senators who feared that Hatch I tilted power to state officials with their control over nonfederal government employees. Several Democratic senators had argued during debates over Hatch I that a bill barring activity of federal workers would give governors greater leverage in state party politics because state workers were not covered.[41]

Roosevelt's advisers conferred long and hard over a strategy to kill or substantially weaken Hatch II. Harold Ickes, for example, drafted a veto message that called for more stringent measures aimed at hurting Republicans and southern Democrats. He proposed setting a cap on party expenditures at $3 million and limiting individual contributions to five thousand dollars (Ickes 1953–54, 226). Since the RNC typically outspent the DNC, this ceiling would hurt Republicans more. Democrats, in comparison, relied more than Republicans on local activities of parties and labor unions to mobilize voters. Most of these organizations would not be affected by the Hatch bill.[42] In an attempt to get southern Democrats to fight the bill, the administration encouraged Hatch to extend the FCPA to primary elections, which set off a firestorm of protest in the Senate.

Ickes acknowledged in his memoirs that his plan was also part of a short-term campaign strategy to highlight differences between the parties in the 1940 elections. He believed that a push for legislation to limit national party expenditures and cap contributions at five thousand dollars would highlight Wendell Willkie's (the Republican presidential nominee) ties to Wall Street and show how much more money the Republicans were spending than Democrats.[43]

The administration's strategy to introduce poison pill amendments to derail Hatch II did not work. Legislative gamesmanship in both chambers was extraordinary—attesting to the political stakes. In the House the hard-fought battle included calls for secret committee balloting, as well as a discharge petition among bill sponsors to get the bill out of the Judiciary Committee. Meanwhile, in the Senate a series of filibusters ensued to prevent a vote on the bill.

Majority leader Alben Barkley (D-KY) even threatened to resign his post because of the bitter fights within Democratic ranks (Hurd 1940b; *New York Times* 1940c; Hurd 1940a). Speaking for southerners, Senator Josiah Bailey (D-NC) called the bill "vicious" and an assault on federalism. He charged that the bill "would turn Jim Farley [DNC chair] loose while restraining the Sheriff of my county from making a public speech," adding that the "Republicans were playing a shrewd game, for which they should be commended" (*New York Times* 1940a). In the end, the Republicans triumphed over a divided Democratic Party: 89 Democrats supported the Republicans (120 Democrats were opposed), while only 1 Republican voted against it (*New York Times* 1940b). FDR signed the bill on July 19, 1940 (*Congressional Record* 1940c).

Since Republicans had compromised by accepting many of the Democratic amendments, the final version of the Hatch Act was more consequential for political parties than imagined. While not intended by reformers, the provisions in this act accelerated the dispersion of political funds to nominally independent political committees (Overacker 1946, 25–48). Congress, for the first time, imposed a contribution limit to political committees of five thousand dollars (sixty-five thousand dollars in 2004 dollars).[44] The limit, however, was evaded easily by wealthy donors who were encouraged to split their donations among several committees. Moreover, federal contribution limits did not apply to state and local parties or independent committees, so donors might easily give as much as they wanted at a more local level. The decentralizing effects of these limits hurt the Republicans more than the Democrats, given that Republicans relied heavily on a national committee apparatus to collect and distribute funds to states. Consequently, the Hatch Act forced Republicans to create additional committees in the states, which would be legally separate from the RNC.

In agreeing to the five thousand dollar limit, Republicans believed this cap would apply to contributions by labor unions as well. Indeed, this was the express goal of conservative Maryland Democrat Millard Tydings, who proposed targeting labor unions in response to his being a target of Roosevelt's purge campaign (Milkis and Young 2003, 56). When the five thousand dollar cap was first inserted by the House Judiciary Committee, Republicans pushed for a broad interpretation of the word *person* to include "an individual, partnership, committee, association, corporation, and any other organization or group of persons."[45] In practice, this definition would mean that a labor union like the United Mine Workers would be restricted to a five thousand dollar contribution *total* to committees and candidates. In subsequent legislative battles,

Democrats clarified the language to ensure that labor unions and other donors could give five thousand dollars to each of any number of candidates and political committees. This revision preserved labor's ability to give money but discouraged them from giving lump sums to the national political party as in the past. Thus, labor unions could target their contributions, giving them additional leverage over individual candidates and bypassing the filter of political parties. Unions could also give unlimited amounts to state and local committees that were exempt from the bill.

There is little doubt that the Hatch Acts enhanced the influence of labor unions and other nonparty groups relative to party organizations. The most devastating blow to the national political parties was the $3 million cap, first proposed by Ickes as a way to bury the bill. The cap was absurdly low. Both national committees had been spending substantially more than this amount in every election since 1928; indeed, Republicans had spent as much in the elections of 1896 and 1900 (Overacker 1932, 73). Even at the height of the Depression in 1936, the combined expenditures of the two national parties exceeded $14 million (Overacker 1946, 17). The Hatch Act also came at a time when the increasing use of radio in campaigns was rapidly escalating electioneering costs. Overacker argued that adoption of this provision did more than any other to encourage the growth of outside spending in campaigns by numerous interest groups and party surrogates (1946, 25–48).

The Republicans had only acquiesced reluctantly to the cap because they recognized that it applied only to the national committees and not to state and nonparty committees. The cap hurt them more than the Democrats, given that the RNC had organized and centralized fund-raising for presidential elections. But apparently they believed they would be able to adapt by using partisan organizations outside the formal party structure.

It is also worth keeping in mind that the national parties were more consequential for the presidential wing of the party than the congressional wing. Members of Congress relied heavily on their state and local organizations (if they relied on them at all). Thus, the $3 million cap might hurt a future presidential nominee for the Republican Party, but it would do little to affect reelection prospects of members of Congress. Thus, self-interest, narrowly defined, made it easier to swallow the so-called poison pills that Ickes and the New Deal Democrats foisted in the Hatch Act against Republicans. Congressional Republicans were more concerned with keeping New Deal workers from campaigning against them in their own races than with guarding the resources of the RNC. The same could also be said about anti–New Deal southern Democrats.

The Hatch Acts, like the various FCPAs before them, were implemented as a partisan war of attrition. Each party sought short- and long-term strategic advantages against the other. Columnists of the day acknowledged the partisan nature of the legislation. According to Frank Kent of the *Wall Street Journal*, "there was about the solidity of [Republican] support a gloating and hypocritical smugness which sufficiently revealed that their attitude was inspired more by thoughts of political advantage than inherent virtue" (1940, 4). Republicans had exploited a split in the Democratic Party to pass legislation that appeared to benefit their own party. However, the Hatch bill seriously hindered the development of national organizations for both parties, even if this response was unintended by the original reformers. The provisions made it more difficult for party organizations to control financial resources in presidential elections and spurred the proliferation of nonparty groups.

The Smith-Connally Act of 1943

Two subsequent pieces of legislation during this period had important consequences for election financing. The primary aim of both was to curtail the influence of labor unions. Thus, the consequences were more harmful for the Democratic Party, which relied heavily on this constituency for both election money and in-kind campaign support. As in the past, the goal of legislative sponsors was to undermine critical campaign resources of a leading faction in the party. They exploited timely events to push for reforms.

When miners struck in 1943, Congress reacted quickly with the Smith-Connally bill, known also as the War Labor Disputes Act, a measure providing for seizure of war plants disrupted by striking workers.[46] The sponsors claimed the act would prevent labor unions from taking advantage of a war situation to increase their bargaining power through strikes. Antilabor groups had argued that the union push to increase wages was harming the war effort. In 1942, Roosevelt had called for a freeze on wage increases that was vehemently opposed by both the AFL and the Congress of Industrial Organizations (CIO). The Smith-Connally Act gave the president the authority to seize war facilities and prosecute strikers, even though Roosevelt claimed he already had this authority under executive order of proclamation (Peters and Woolley 2006). In arguing against the act, FDR claimed that the legislation would actually induce more strikes.

The Smith-Connally bill went further than government intervention in work stoppages. The bill was amended in the Committee of the Whole by Representative Forest Harness (R-IN) to ban labor organizations from making political contributions through union dues they collected from members. Congressman Gerald Landis (R-IN), a coauthor of the measure, said the bill would "put labor unions on exactly the same basis, insofar as their financial activities are concerned, as corporations have been on for many years."[47] Landis's view was that labor unions reflected a concentration of economic power, just like corporations. For this reason, the Tillman Act ban could be extended to unions as well.

The Smith-Connally Act passed over the objections of New Deal Democrats, who claimed that the bill discriminated against workers and that the comparison to business firms was inappropriate since unions, unlike corporations, were associations of individuals.[48] FDR remanded the bill to Congress without his signature in June 1943, whereupon both houses passed it with two-thirds majorities, making it law over the president's veto. As a consequence of the Smith-Connally Act, the CIO formed the first PAC in 1944 to raise money for the reelection of Roosevelt. Because PAC money came from voluntary contributions of union members rather than the general funds of unions, it was not prohibited by the Smith-Connally Act. Of course, the CIO and other unions also continued to campaign on behalf of Democratic candidates outside the party structure. The capacity of unions to adapt in elections raised fears among Republicans that no campaign finance law could prevent labor's influence. Republicans went so far as to consider legislation to make it illegal for unions to spend *any* money in elections. A House report in 1944 posed the following rhetorical question: "Of what avail would a law be to prohibit the contributing direct to a candidate and yet permit the expenditure of large sums in his behalf?"[49] Prodded by Senator Robert Taft (R-OH), a special Committee on Campaign Expenditures investigated the role of the CIO's PAC in the 1944 elections. Taft was infuriated by how the CIO distributed pamphlets to oppose his reelection. Labor leaders argued that the expenditures were an exercise of free speech and therefore protected by the First Amendment. In response, Republican senators sought unsuccessfully to broaden the scope of the law beyond what they believed was a narrow judicial construction of political contributions.

The Taft-Hartley Act of 1947

After the 1946 congressional elections swept Republicans into power, Congress passed the Taft-Hartley labor bill to make the temporary wartime legislation of the Smith-Connally Act permanent and amend the Wagner Act of 1935.[50] Once again, Republicans sought to change Section 313 of the FCPA to construe certain kinds of expenditures as contributions in support of candidates. The Taft-Hartley Act was pushed forcefully by its sponsor, Senator Taft, who cited a familiar refrain of campaign reformers: "all we are doing is plugging the holes."[51] The Republican-controlled Congress easily passed the Taft-Hartley bill and then overrode President Harry Truman's veto. The labor unions challenged the Taft-Hartley bill in court, but the courts upheld the statutes provisions, without addressing fundamental constitutional issues related to rights of association and freedom of speech.[52]

In the final analysis, the campaign finance reforms passed during the New Deal reflected the heightened partisanship of the era. Roosevelt had laid the groundwork for a formidable Democratic coalition, but one that was rife with internal power struggles. The civil service reforms and antilabor laws, of which campaign finance statutes were only a part, were put into place by an alliance of Republicans and southern Democrats.

Ironically, these laws made the Democrats even more dependent on labor unions for electoral support. They made it harder for labor unions to contribute money to the party and encouraged labor organizations to develop their infrastructure for mobilizing voters. The Democratic Party would become inescapably dependent on labor's electoral muscle, an arrangement that would weaken incentives for the party organization itself to strengthen its own electoral machinery. The Hatch Act with its party spending cap ensured that national committees would need to decentralize their activity, whereas the Smith-Connally and Taft-Hartley Acts inadvertently laid the groundwork for the future campaign system in which PACs would play an important role. Labor unions were the first to develop these committees, but business interests would learn how to exploit these organizational forms as well.

To summarize, the Republican period of reform achieved the following significant changes in campaign finance rules.

Key Provisions of Campaign Finance Laws, 1939–47

Ban federal government employees and nonfederal workers paid partially with federal funds from engaging in electioneering activity (Hatch Act).

Ban contributions from individuals and businesses working for the federal government (Hatch Act).

Limit contributions of five thousand dollars per year for individuals to a federal candidate or political committee (Hatch Act).

Limit spending to $3 million for political committees operating in two or more states (Hatch Act).

Ban political contributions from labor unions (Smith-Connally Act and Taft-Hartley Act).

DEMOCRATIC REFORMS, 1971–2002

The quest to reform the campaign finance system continued among a small group of progressive legislators through midcentury. But neither party had strong interest in putting together a coalition for comprehensive reform until the 1960s when Democrats realized they were losing the money chase in presidential elections to Republicans. As they did in 1907 with the Tillman Act, Democrats once again decided they needed to restrain Republican fund-raising through regulations on political contributions. At the same time, they sought to expand the supply of funds available to Democrats through public subsidies.

Prior to the 1960s, the campaign finance system appears to have achieved an equilibrium in which both major parties felt they could raise the necessary resources to compete against each other. Despite numerous congressional investigations during the 1940s and 1950s and widespread recognition that the existing laws discouraged genuine public disclosure and accountability of political money, there were few serious efforts to change the campaign finance system. In 1951, a special committee report stated that it was "patently impossible for a candidate to conduct a Congressional or Senatorial campaign" within the existing limits and that the "present unrealistic limitations on campaign contributions and expenditures are an invitation to criminal violation" (quoted in Alexander 1972, 201).[53]

So long as Sam Rayburn (D-TX) was Speaker of the House, however, campaign finance reform would not be a serious issue. His acolyte in the Senate, Lyndon Johnson (D-TX), was hardly more enthusiastic about reform. Both Texans had learned that easy access to campaign cash was a valuable resource to help them scale the leadership ladder in Congress.[54] Certainly, neither of them would entertain any bills that regulated primaries, and few bills of any sort were allowed out of committee in either chamber. The attitude in Congress was typified by the Senate's response to a scandal in 1956 in which Senator Francis Case (R-SD) was offered twenty-five hundred dollars in campaign money to vote for a gas bill (Morris 1956). Indignant senators prodded leaders Lyndon Johnson and William Knowland (R-CA) to introduce a reform bill that would eventually include eighty-three cosponsors. Yet this proposal never reached a vote in the Senate. Campaign finance expert Herbert Alexander noted wryly, "of the several views about the reason for its demise, the favorite was that, with so many sponsors, the bill would have to be passed if it reached the floor" (1972, 202).

The 1960 elections prodded Democrats to take reform seriously. The presidential election had been enormously expensive. The immediate concern among Democrats was the party debt, which had ballooned to almost $4 million ($27 million in 2004 dollars) after the election (Alexander 1962, 13). Democrats feared they could not keep pace with rising election costs in presidential elections, particularly because of the dramatic shift toward television advertising. Money spent on radio and television broadcasting in the final two months of the election by both parties was estimated at $14.2 million, or 44 percent more than in 1956 (Alexander 1962, 34).

Though the Republicans found it somewhat easier to raise money, they were also worried about having enough funds to change their status as the minority party in Congress. The proposals put forth during the early 1960s were largely about finding legitimate means of expanding access to funds in order to pay for the increasing use of television. The focus on enhancing the supply of campaign money marked an important shift from previous supply-restricting strategies in campaign finance reform debates.

President Kennedy established the Commission on Election Costs soon after he got into office. The last time a president had seized the initiative on campaign finance reform was more than a half century earlier, under Theodore Roosevelt. Ironically, both were wealthy men, and perhaps they were sensitive to charges that they bought their elections. They were also presidents who relied heavily on public popularity to gain influence in Washington. The taint of money might easily undermine their ability to connect with the public if it was widely believed they routinely courted big money.

The commission, which was led by two political scientists, tried to steer away from the previous emphasis on reforms to reduce the amount of campaign money through contribution and spending limits.[55] Instead, the final report focused on enhancing the supply of funds through public subsidies such as tax credits, deductions, and matching funds to encourage small donations.[56] In an unconventional move, the commission recommended that political parties receive these public funds and proposed that all limits on party spending be removed. It believed this would bolster national party influence and increase party integration in campaigns. Another important innovation called for an independent agency, called the Registry of Election Finance, to be responsible for dealing with disclosure. The commission submitted its recommendations to Congress in 1962, but reform languished after Kennedy's death.[57] Alexander reports that the only serious lobbying was from the broadcasting industry, which did not like proposed changes to the Federal Communications Act.[58] More than a decade later, however, many ideas set forth by the commission came to fruition under the FECA of 1971 and its amendments in 1974.

The factions of the Democratic Party may have been united in their desire for public subsidies, but they were fatally split over how public funds would be allocated. Labor leaders opposed the Kennedy commission's recommendation that funds be channeled to national party committees and one committee in each state (designated by the national committee). Instead, they argued that subsidies should be available to nonparty organizations and were averse to the possibility that public money would be given to state party committees controlled by antilabor factions. Labor unions also objected to the use of tax deductions for political contributions because this scheme favored wealthy contributors. Instead, they wanted a tax credit, which would apply to contributions for all political organizations, including labor unions. Political scientist Alexander Heard believed the reluctance of labor leaders to support the reforms was linked directly to a strategic concern, namely, that these reforms might strengthen the Democratic Party and make it less reliant on union support to win elections.[59] Less reliance would mean less influence for the labor faction in the party.[60]

After Johnson's election in 1964, two scandals stirred public attention, encouraging him and congressional leaders to test the waters of reform. The first scandal involved Bobby Baker, a young Senate majority secretary, whose career rose swiftly while serving under Johnson in the Senate. Washingtonians wondered how a man living on a meager Senate salary could have an estimated net worth in excess of $2.5 million. During Senate investigations, it became apparent Baker was using his access to Johnson and other power brokers to spur business investments. According to the *New York Times,* Baker had "built a business and financial empire" that included motels and restaurants, a vending machine company, real estate holdings, and a mortgage insurance company.[61] The other scandal involved Senator Thomas J. Dodd (D-CT), who used his campaign funds for personal use (*New York Times* 1966a).

Republicans exploited these Democratic scandals to push for rules aimed at undermining Democratic congressional fund-raising, which was based primarily on an annual dinner. In 1966, Congress passed the Williams amendment to limit corporate advertising in party program books that were handed out at party gatherings. Senator John Williams (R-DE), a member of the Senate Finance Committee, wrote legislation that would eliminate tax deductions for corporations that bought advertising in any party publications. In 1965, the Democrats had raised more than $1 million by selling advertising to corporations for a party magazine. The Democrats said the magazine was for "voter education" though it was simply a yearbook of bland tributes to Democratic members of the Eighty-ninth Congress (Morris 1966). Williams said the parties were involved in a "shakedown" of corporations that did business with the federal government (Herbers 1966). The amendment was in place a little over a year before it was rescinded by a Democratic-dominated Congress just in advance of the 1968 elections.

Despite eliminating the Williams amendment, the Democrats remained in a financial bind as election costs vastly exceeded the funds they were accustomed to raising. Given the heterogeneity of the party, Democrats lacked a national constituency of donors (a topic I take up in chapter 5). They could no longer rely on old tactics for raising money, especially in the wake of recent Democratic scandals. Even though the Republicans had been beaten soundly in 1964, the RNC and the Goldwater election committee had managed to raise an astonishing $18.5 million from ardent conservatives. Herbert Alexander estimates they raised much of this in small sums from approximately 651,000 citizens (1966, 70). With this in mind, President Johnson may have encouraged Russell Long (D-LA), his old Senate friend, to sponsor a bold proposal for public funding of presidential elections. Long had not previously expressed an interest in campaign finance reform, nor was he a participant in earlier congressional debates over public financing. In 1966, he simply attached his amendment to a major tax bill. His proposal cut through earlier partisan debates over whether the government should use tax deductions and credits by employing a characteristically populist solution: the government would simply pay the cost of campaigning from the public treasury. His reform ignored long-brewing discussions over financing congressional elections, as well as proposals to set up an independent agency for monitoring financial activity. For these reasons, some of the strongest opposition to the Long proposal came from liberals in the Senate, led by the senior Albert Gore (D-TN). Senator Gore had toiled at length on this subject and was hoping for comprehensive reform (*New York Times* 1966b). He argued that Long's bill did not go far enough in holding down campaign costs and providing for public disclosure. Even the liberal *New York Times* and *Washington Post* were opposed to Long's plan. In an editorial, the *New York Times* complained that Long's proposal would cost more than $20 million each fiscal year but would do nothing to diminish election costs (*New York Times* 1966b). These criticisms reflected a long-standing Progressive-inspired bias for reforms to curtail campaign spending, which would give more influence to institutions such as the news media.

Long's response to his critics was that at least he was doing *something*, while others only talked about reform (Mann 1992, 247–54). Whether Gore's opposition to the Long bill was based on policy differences or jealousy (after all, campaign finance reform was *his* turf), the disagreements over this bill led to monumental showdowns on the Senate floor between them. They each did their part to hold up an important vote on the tax bill, with Senate leader Mike Mansfield (D-MT) pleading with them to arrive at some compromise so the Senate could conduct other business. Long refused to give in, using parliamentary techniques to keep the bill alive, all the time quietly encouraged by President Johnson (Alexander 1972, 218). There was more than a month of debate with five inconclusive votes. Long tested the patience of his colleagues by prolonging the issue, but Alexander suggests the lengthy public debates opened the campaign finance issue to a wider audience and stirred a broader movement for reform (1972, 221).

Long's tenacious support raised publicity for the campaign finance issues and gave legitimacy to Theodore Roosevelt's idea that public funds should be used in elections. His amendment proposed that every taxpayer who filed a federal income tax return could designate that one dollar be paid into the Presidential Election Campaign Fund. In each presidential year, the treasury would then pay major and minor parties according to a formula based on their performance in the previous election. The bill would have provided $30 million ($177 million in 2004 dollars) to each of the major political parties.

Senator Long wanted public funds to go directly to the political parties, which would have enhanced their position in the electoral process. But factional divisions within the Democratic Party prevented this from happening. Gore believed the Long bill would foreclose the opportunity to pass more comprehensive campaign finance reforms (proposed in his own bill) that might include constraints on political contributions and expenditures, free broadcast time, timely disclosure, and regulatory oversight. Other liberals, like Senator Robert Kennedy, did not want public funds to be placed in the hands of Johnson loyalists at the DNC, and he argued for a system in which funds would be given directly to a candidate.[62] Johnson favored the Long bill because it would provide his campaign with an easy infusion of resources (Mann 1992, 247–54).[63] Johnson may have also hoped this legislation would take the pressure off him to support reforms to regulate primaries and improve campaign finance disclosure, two policies that would have roiled his colleagues from the South. Some southerners, who at first balked at Long's proposal, joined in support once they understood that the bill promised favorable treatment for the independent candidate, Alabama governor George Wallace.[64]

In the end, Long compromised on the direct subsidy to the political parties.

The money would go directly to candidate committees, which satisfied liberals who did not want to enhance the power of traditional party leaders. To supplicate Republicans, Long included a measure allowing tax deductions of up to one hundred dollars on political contributions, in addition to the one dollar checkoff on tax returns. In the end, however, not a single Republican voted for the Long bill. Some liberal Democrats refused to support the bill because it did not include money for congressional campaigns. Long was masterful in pushing his bill through Congress, but he never really created a solid coalition to support his plan. Only one year after it was signed into law, liberal Democrats and Republicans, led by Senators Gore and Williams, repealed the Long Act.[65]

Even though the Long Act was discarded, congressional interest in campaign finance issues broadened, extending beyond the progressive core of reformers. Southern Democrats, who had a long history of blocking reform, were now warming to it as they faced the threat of real general elections. Republicans in the South were beginning to mount isolated offensives and winning key statewide elections. Under the leadership of Ray C. Bliss at the RNC, Republicans had undertaken a nuts-and-bolts strategy of building state organizations by training local operatives, purchasing voter files, and helping with fund-raising (Green 1994). With the prospect of facing a strong challenger, southerners may have been thinking that imposing constraints on Republican money was not such a bad idea. Though Goldwater had lost badly, he had raised a lot of money, much of it from the South.

Republicans had reasons for wanting to change the laws as well. Notwithstanding a few successful incursions in the South, they were reeling from the 1964 elections. Not only did Goldwater lose the presidential election in a landslide, but Democrats picked up thirty-six seats in the House, giving them a two-thirds majority. With this loss fresh in their minds, Republicans sought reforms that would ensure they had access to funds for rebuilding the party. The Hatch Act, with its $3 million cap on national party spending, put serious constraints on party development.

A conservative coalition of Republicans and southern Democrats, united in their opposition to the influence of labor organizations in elections, pushed for a bill in 1967. The Ashmore-Goodell bill, named after Robert T. Ashmore (D-SC) and Charles Goodell (R-NY), was thoroughly antiunion. One provision barred trade associations, unions, and corporations from using their treasury funds to support staff and administrative expenses on any partisan activities. Of course, union organizations were in the vanguard of electioneering activities, so the bill would have hurt them more than trade associations or corporations, which were not yet involved in such activities. Union leaders accused Republicans of trying to put the AFL-CIO's Committee on Political Education (COPE) "out of business" (Morris 1967). But Republicans had something else to gain in the Ashmore-Goodell bill besides weakening labor union influence. The bill would abandon the spending ceilings that were adopted under the Hatch Act. If Republicans wanted to compete for control of Congress they needed a strong party organization to raise and spend money.

In the end, the Ashmore-Goodell bill failed because it offended too many Democratic interests. Not only did the bill undermine the power of labor unions (Landauer 1968), but it also included the regulation of primaries, which limited support among many southern Democrats. However, this bill would eventually shape the contours of the FECA of 1971, especially its proposal to create the Federal Election Commission (FEC), which would receive, analyze, and audit public spending reports by all candidates and committees in federal elections.[66]

Even as ideas and bills churned through Congress, stalemate continued. By the start of the 1968 elections, it could be argued that nothing new had taken place in the realm of campaign finance reform since 1947. Not only had the Long Act been rescinded, but Democrats had successfully weakened the Williams amendment to help them raise money in time for the upcoming congressional elections.

Passing the FECA of 1971

The 1968 elections once again exposed Democratic weaknesses in competing with Republicans for political money in presidential campaigns. Richard Nixon broke all fund-raising records in 1968.[67] Meanwhile, Democrats emerged from the campaign with a record $9.3 million debt (Franklin 1971).[68] The party was badly divided over the Vietnam War and civil rights; funds would not be easy to find to pay back debts and prepare for the 1972 election. With Nixon in the White House, Democrats considered grimly that this president—a formidable fund-raiser by any standard—would have even more opportunities to obtain campaign money from corporate interests. Much like Mark Hanna at the turn of the century, Nixon's campaign team established contribution quotas for different industries and firms (Alexander 1992, 18). The subsequent Watergate scandal would reveal the full extent of these successful, if unethical, fund-raising strategies.

With fears brimming about being swamped by Republican money, Democratic leaders met during the summer of 1970 to plot a strategy for leveling the playing field through campaign finance reforms (Weaver 1971a).[69] They decided to push for a bill that would inject public funds into Democratic Party coffers for the convention and provide money to presidential candidates. Presidential candidates who accepted roughly $20 million in public funds would have to agree to limit spending to the amount of the grant. Democrats knew, of course, that they could also continue to rely on outside support from labor unions. The public funding plan called for a tax checkoff system—introduced previously with the Long Act, which had subsequently been repealed. Tax deductions and credits for political contributions were also introduced.[70] Tom Wicker of the *New York Times* described the plan as a "terrific windfall for the Democratic Party" (1971, 47).

The bill would also help Democrats in congressional races. The bill proposed spending limits on media buys for all federal candidates.[71] A senator running for office in New York in 1972, for example, would not be allowed to exceed $490,000 in media spending, almost half of what had been typically spent in these Senate races (Finney 1970). As the incumbent party, Democrats had less to fear from scaling back media expenditures, since incumbents generally have greater name recognition than challengers. Even more important from the perspective of Democrats, these limits would prevent an arms race in media spending that gave advantages to the wealthier Republicans. A separate bill was also being introduced to make media purchases cheaper. The measure required broadcasters to give deep discounts to candidates for purchasing air time (Peabody et al. 1972, 36).[72]

The Democrats pursued a legislative strategy that appeared to catch the Republicans off guard (Weaver 1971a). They introduced the reform bill in the Senate at the last minute as an attachment to a tax bill favored by the president (the Revenue Act of 1971). A bitter partisan fight ensued, but Democratic leaders kept the party together, losing only five southern Democrats and passing the measure by a vote of fifty-two to forty-seven. Only two Republicans supported it. John Tower (R-TX), chair of the National Republican Senatorial Committee, had sent a letter to colleagues arguing the bill was "against the best interests of our party" (Finney 1970). In conference, this measure was attached to the tax bill, already approved by the House. As soon as the bill was introduced, the Nixon administration said the president would veto the campaign finance provision. While Republicans labeled the plan a "slush fund" for politicians and a "raid on the federal treasury," Nixon's greater concern may have been the provisions requiring him to disclose all his donors (Weaver 1971b, 1971e).

Democrats were confident they would prevail in conference committee, keeping the campaign finance bill attached to the tax bill. Democratic leaders were willing to compromise on the tax measures to keep the campaign bill part of the package or at least force a showdown with the president. But the Democratic strategy failed when Wilbur Mills, chair of the Appropriations Committee, offered a compromise to Nixon to the effect that public funding of the presidential election would be put off until the 1976 elections. Party leaders were furious at Mills for capitulating to pressure from the administration, but the Arkansas Democrat claimed he did not have the votes in the House to override the president's veto (Weaver 1971a).

President Nixon signed the tax bill into law on February 7, 1972, with little attention given to the campaign finance statutes. At the time, the public seemed unconcerned about reform. There were no scandals to mobilize public opinion—the Watergate episode was still to come. But a new style of politics was emerging that would stimulate greater public awareness as the problems of Watergate unfolded. Public interest organizations such as the National Committee for an Effective Congress and Common Cause were developing a constituency for reform with their highly publicized lawsuits, lobbying, and direct mail campaigns. In January 1971, Common Cause, which had only been around for a year and claimed just over fifty-three thousand members, filed a class action suit against political parties in New York, claiming they violated or conspired to violate the FCPA of 1925.[73] By moving campaign finance issue to the courts, public interest groups intensified the pressure on authorities to enforce laws that had never been enforced. At the same time these lawsuits exposed the inadequacy of the laws on the books that were so easy to evade.

The FECA of 1971 was clearly a partisan bill. Democrats used their majorities in Congress to pass legislation to benefit their party. There were no scandals to motivate Republicans to vote for reform, though they were undoubtedly concerned about being perceived as antireform by their constituents. Nixon's continued threat of a veto gave them cover to vote in favor of reform. The fact that public funding of congressional elections was not part of the deal made it that much easier for them to go along with the bill. Republicans did win some battles: they were able to remove all preexisting contribution and spending limits for candidates. The act also imposed limits on how much candidates could contribute to their own campaigns, which would deter the wealthy from funding their own campaigns.[74] The cash-strapped Democrats were typically more open to finding wealthy candidates who would not drain resources from party coffers.

Republicans had demanded an independent agency to monitor election spending because they felt Democrats would use the internal reporting system in the House selectively against them in campaigns. But Democrats were lukewarm about creating an independent agency. Wayne Hays (D-OH), chairman of the House Administration Committee, which considered the legislation, had eliminated a provision for an independent FEC. Instead, the reports would continue to go to the clerk of House or secretary of Senate, with both houses controlled by Democratic leadership. Republicans forced a compromise to require presidential candidate filing with the General Accounting Office, even though congressional candidates would still file with the House and Senate clerks. The provisions requiring greater disclosure would expose the nefarious campaign practices of President Nixon's reelection committee and establish the evidence to impeach him. It also laid the groundwork for amendments to the FECA.

The FECA of 1974 Amendments

If ever scandal proved decisive in campaign finance reform, it was the events surrounding the Watergate burglary that was linked to President Nixon's reelection committee. A bill amending the FECA passed with bipartisan support even though the Republican leadership believed the new law was awful for the Republican Party. But Republicans had little ground to defend themselves since it was their own party leader, the president, embroiled in the scandal. Democrats were freshly triumphant in the 1974 congressional elections based significantly on promises to clean up politics.

As investigations uncovered both illegal and tawdry practices, Congress began considering tightening the campaign finance laws. The Senate contemplated legislation that was far broader and tougher than anything proposed in the House. Liberals like Ted Kennedy (D-MA) sought public funds for congressional elections and an independent oversight agency with significant powers to investigate campaign activities.[75] They earned favorable publicity generated by Common Cause, the public interest organization founded by neo-Progressive John Gardner (Peabody et al. 1972; Rosenbaum 1974). Labor unions pushed for rules that constrained candidate spending, while permitting organizations to contribute money through PACs. At the time, few other groups exploited such committees in federal elections.

Despite a strong liberal-labor alliance and favorable public opinion on reform, it was not easy passing amendments to the FECA. Democratic leaders in the Senate had to contend with lengthy filibusters from southern Democrats and Republicans before they could get a bill to conference. Moreover, in the House, Wayne Hays, chair of the Ways and Means Committee (which would review policies for allocating public funds for elections), repeatedly rebuffed Senate-inspired reforms. Many House Democrats did not want an independent agency to oversee congressional campaigns. Hays, in particular, refused to entertain the possibility that campaign reports of congressional candidates would not be kept with the clerk of the House, who was appointed by the majority Democrats. The House bills were also crafted with an eye toward preserving Democratic majorities by exploiting the advantages of incumbency, as I explain shortly.

In conference committee, a deadlock ensued over public financing of congressional elections. The Senate conference members dropped this part of the bill after they won concessions from House members to support higher spending limits in congressional campaigns and a strong independent electoral commission to enforce the law.[76] The new agency would assume administrative functions previously divided between congressional officers and the General Accounting Office. It also was given jurisdiction in civil enforcement matters, authority to write regulations, and responsibility for monitoring compliance with the law.[77]

Before he resigned, Nixon had threatened to veto most bills circulating in Congress. He was especially adamant against using treasury funds for federal elections through the tax form checkoff.[78] His stance protected congressional Republicans, who could vote for campaign finance reform knowing that the president would veto legislation that contained a public funding provision. In the end, the House overwhelmingly approved the bill (355–48), only hours before Nixon announced on August 8 that he intended to resign (*CQ Almanac* 1974, 612). Republican support for the bill did not prevent Minority Leader John Rhodes (R-AZ) from recommending a presidential veto on grounds that the legislation was strongly biased and would "preserve the Democratic majority" (*CQ Almanac* 1974, 627). Nixon's successor, Gerald Ford, signed the bill reluctantly on October 15, observing that "the times demand this legislation" (Herbers 1974).[79]

The final bill appeared to strengthen the Democrats' position considerably. By providing generous public funds to presidential candidates, the law addressed the quadrennial Democratic predicament of finding money to keep up with the Republican presidential nominee. Further, the bill protected the incumbent party through its limits on campaign contributions and spending.[80] Not only would restrictions on individual giving cut back on large pro-Republican donations from businessmen, but such constraints would typically help incumbents who possess nonmonetary advantages such as experience and name recognition.[81]

The mandate that interest groups make contributions only through PACs was believed to be a boon to Democrats and labor unions. Republicans, in fact, had proposed banning PAC contributions in favor of permitting individual contributions only. Neither party could foresee that business firms and associations would adapt to dominate the PAC system—a change that would ultimately benefit Republicans. Finally, though it was hardly noted in the publicity over novel features of the law, the Democrats managed to rescind Hatch Act restrictions on voluntary activities by state and local employees in federal campaigns, opening up opportunities for a growing constituency of public employees to help them in elections.

The attention given to candidate committees and PACs revealed the marginalized position of American political parties. Regulating parties appeared as an afterthought (Sorauf 1992). In a late version of the House bill, parties were treated the same as PACs, with the same contribution limit of five thousand dollars, until Bill Frenzel (R-MN) spoke up to argue that parties should be strengthened by allowing contributions of ten thousand dollars. There were no objections, even though it appeared to be an important concession to Republicans, who relied more on party organizations.[82]

The FECA enshrined the candidate-centered system by institutionalizing the role of candidates and PACs in statute. Paradoxically, in ignoring political parties, the law opened opportunities for parties to adapt to the new campaign environment. Favorable court rulings would later grant parties more protection from government regulation, and parties would press the FEC for lenient interpretations of statutes that applied to political parties.

The 1974 amendments would not be the last word. Senators James Buckley (R-NY) and Eugene McCarthy (D-MN) immediately joined in a suit against the law, charging primarily that the spending provisions violated the First Amendment. The Supreme Court handed down its ruling on January 30, 1976, in *Buckley v. Valeo*,[83] which upheld contribution limits because they served a vital public interest in protecting against corruption but overturned the expenditure limits because they imposed greater restrictions on free speech and the potential for corruption was less clear. At the same time, restrictions on candidates who accepted public funds were deemed constitutional because candidates were free to reject public financing and use private funds.[84]

Congress responded to the Supreme Court decision with amendments, passed May 11, 1976, that repealed expenditure limits, except for those presidential candidates receiving public funds. Congress also restricted the scope of PAC fund-raising by corporations and labor unions. This action was in response to a FEC advisory opinion that would allow corporations to solicit political contributions from not only stockholders but also rank-and-file employees.[85] In the 1979 amendments Democrats pushed for tighter rules that prevented corporations and unions from operating multiple PACs. They were clearly concerned about the expansion of corporate PAC activity. Unions, however, were permitted to continue giving through locals and at the national level as well. The 1979 amendments also attempted to ease the regulatory burden by simplifying reporting requirements.[86]

Democrats had wanted to pass amendment to the FECA in 1978 that would curtail party contributions and coordinated expenditures and provide more public funding of campaigns in an effort to delay Republican rebuilding efforts (Kolodny 1998, 134). The question that eventually led to the most controversy was whether to allow state and local political parties to spend unrestricted sums for targeted party-building efforts, which were not directly related to the election of federal candidates. There were frequent complaints from party officials in the states where FECA had made it more difficult for them to engage in grass roots campaigning because of restrictions on providing assistance to presidential candidates who received public funds. In response to these complaints, the 1979 amendments declared that grass roots activities—such as registering and contacting voters, putting up lawn signs, and handing out palm cards—would be exempt from the FECA limits. At the same time, the FEC had issued advisory opinions to several state parties allowing them to use nonfederal funds—soft money—to finance campaign portions of activities they claimed were related to state elections. In other words, they could mix soft money with federal "hard" money when conducting joint federal-state campaign activities. In most instances, the constraints on nonfederal fund-raising were fewer. In some states, for example, there were no restrictions on the source and size of contributions to a political party. The state parties exploited this opportunity to raise and spend as much soft money as they could in elections, even when federal races were on the ballot. The national parties argued successfully with the FEC that they should have access to soft money because they were engaged in state elections as well. These adaptations to the FEC advisory opinions marked the beginning of the so-called soft money loophole.

Key Provisions of Campaign Finance Laws, 1966–79

Establish FEC (1974).
Create public funding system for presidential elections (1966, 1971, 1974).
Allow public funds for party conventions (1971, 1974).
Set limits on expenditures (1974, repealed 1976).

Set limit of one thousand dollar contributions to candidate committee per election; aggregate limit of twenty-five thousand dollars (1974).

Allow corporations and unions with federal contracts to establish and operate PACs to make political contributions (1974, 1976).

Limit individuals to a five thousand dollar contribution to a PAC and a twenty thousand dollar contribution to a national committee (1976).

Limit PACs to five thousand dollars per union or corporate election committee; no aggregate limit.

Limit political parties to ten thousand dollar contributions, with ceilings (adjusted for inflation) for expenditures on behalf of candidates.

Allow state and local parties to spend nonfederal funds (soft money) for party building and grass roots (1979).

Improve disclosure and enforcement; heavy fines for not reporting; commission may enforce criminal violations.

But reformers were not thinking about soft money yet. Instead, in the 1980s progressive factions of the Democratic Party continued to press for reforms to constrain the growing population of PACs. These PACs tilted heavily toward business interests, and progressives were dismayed that Democratic Party leaders, such as Democratic Congressional Campaign Committee chair Tony Coelho, were trying to woo probusiness PAC money (Sorauf 1992, 117, 173; Kolodny 1998, 147–52).

It was not until the 1990s that attention turned from PACs to the issue of soft money, which both parties had been using increasingly to support their candidates through targeted voter mobilization. As will be elaborated in the next chapter, a proreform coalition of Democrats pushed to ban soft money, getting a boost when they gained the support of neo-Progressive senator John McCain (R-AZ), who ran a populist campaign for president based on the need to reform the campaign system. McCain had been tarnished in 1988 by the Keating Five scandal involving a large soft money donor seeking regulatory relief, and some have suggested his turn toward reform was an attempt to clear his name (Dwyre and Farrar-Myers 2001, 36).

These efforts culminated with the McCain-Feingold bill, which passed in 2002 as the Bipartisan Campaign Reform Act. The McCain-Feingold bill was rooted in century-long Progressive conceptions about the problem of money in politics, as advertised by Progressive-inspired public interest organizations lobbying for reform. The stated goal of BCRA supporters was to prevent corruption and its appearance. It is my argument, however, that strong partisan and factional interests motivated reform. The final vote on the BCRA was nudged by scandal involving the much-reviled Enron Corporation, which gave significant amounts of soft money to members of both parties. But the story of the BCRA, as with previous reforms, is as much about strategic choices. In this case, the Democrats exploited the campaign finance issue for short-term campaign advantages, casting themselves as reformers against the majority party. Democrats also believed their party was well suited to pursuing campaigns outside the party structure. They knew they could rely on labor union support and campaigning by other groups to keep the party competitive in the next presidential election. Republicans, however, preferred to operate campaigns through the formal party structure. In contrast to the conventional wisdom that the BCRA was a Democratic "suicide bill," the soft money ban for parties—the central feature of the bill—might end up hurting Republicans more than Democrats. In the 2004 election, the first one under the McCain-Feingold bill, Democrats demonstrated they could organize a formidable campaign—with the help of labor unions and other partisan groups—using soft money outside the party structure. Unluckily for them, however, Republicans were able to mount an effective party-based voter mobilization campaign even without soft money.

The next chapter introduces a theory of reform that makes use of this narrative about factional struggles and party resources to explain the design and timing of federal campaign finance reforms, including the BCRA of 2002. My argument is that partisans sought to gain electoral advantages by pursuing certain kinds of campaign finance reforms over others. Democrats, who always lagged behind Republicans in fund-raising for presidential elections, tended to desire reforms that made it difficult for Republicans to gather resources centrally at the RNC. Republicans, in contrast, supported reforms that would make it harder for outside groups, especially labor unions, to help the Democratic Party through in-kind campaign efforts on behalf of the party ticket. Moreover, factions within each party determined their support for particular reforms based upon whether these proposals would give them resource advantages— and hence *influence* within the party—relative to other factions. By encouraging the flow of money outside the party structure and into the hands of candidates and interest groups, most reform proposals unintentionally reinforced the fragmented nature of American political campaigns.

CHAPTER 4

Explaining Campaign Finance Reform and the BCRA

One puzzle about political reform is why it happens in the first place. Why would incumbents, for example, tamper with a campaign finance system under which they are clear winners? Some changes sought by reformers might help challengers compete more effectively against incumbents. Even minor reforms impose unwanted costs because politicians may have to spend more time raising money or simply learning new rules. And why would politicians pass campaign finance reforms in the midst of lukewarm public interest and weak preferences for any such kind of reform? In this chapter I consider two competing theories—public interest theory and partisan theory—to explain the puzzle of reform.

Previous accounts of campaign finance reform stress the importance of scandal as it forces politicians to shake up the status quo and pass laws that reflect the public interest (Corrado 1997, 25–60; Mutch 1988; Theriault 2005; Zelizer 2002, 73–111). The assumption in this public interest theory of reform is that politicians would not voluntarily alter the electoral rules that give them a competitive advantage. They need to be forced into passing reform through fear—fear that their constituents will punish them at the polls if they vote against campaign finance reforms precisely at a time when scandal exposes how "corrupt" the system actually is.

In truth, however, scandal plays a modest role in shaping political reforms. Rather, the motivation underlying reform is partisanship or, more specifically, strategic partisanship in pursuit of electoral advantage. American political parties—and factions within them—have sought campaign finance reform when it is in their interest to do so. Scandal occasionally provides a useful catalyst to win over wavering legislators to pass reform, but it is not a sufficient or necessary condition. Building on the historical narrative in the previous chapter, the following account develops a theory of *partisan* reform in the context of campaign finance regulation. I explain how the major parties pressed for reforms at different periods when they believed the rival party possessed resource advantages to win elections, particularly presidential elections. An important goal of reform for the resource-poor party has been to level the playing field by reducing the advantages of their rivals. The role of scandal is to cast the rival party as "corrupt," thus allowing the "reforming" party to gain the first-mover advantage of proposing a raft of reforms that are better suited for their own organization. This partisan theory of reform explains the timing and design of reforms better than public interest theory.

My account does not deny an important role for a "nonpartisan" reform constituency, who are the inheritors of the Progressive Era traditions. This constituency is typically led by experts, think tanks, philanthropists, foundations, public interest groups, and a core group of legislators seeking reform. They are backed by a significant portion of middle- and upper middle-class voters, typically professionals, with an orientation to politics reminiscent of the Progressives. Although political reformers have policy proposals at the ready, they are frustrated in their efforts until party leaders believe particular reforms will provide electoral advantages (Kingdon 1984). The reform proposals are then slashed and shaped to suit specific partisan needs.

To this point, my argument parallels that of Julian Zelizer, who, in explaining the campaign finance reforms of the 1970s, argues that legislation fails until strong political interest develops (2002). His account, however, places the reform community itself outside the sphere of partisanship, presenting it as an exogenous force pushing for reform. According to Zelizer, the reform constituency patiently patches together a legislative coalition, exploiting the moments when raw political interests might induce groups to join the coalition. But his analytical argument may, in fact, have it backwards. It is possible that party leaders use reform movements to pursue partisan ends. First, party leaders may view reform as a short-term strategy to undermine the rival party's electoral advantages. They reach for particulars in circulating reform proposals to constrain the other party from raising and spending campaign money. Second, party leaders may also respond to elite pressure from *within* their own partisan coalition. The reform constituency was an important constituency within one or the other party at different times during the twentieth century.

Party leaders must accommodate the demands of the reform constituency precisely because they possess the kind of intellectual, financial, and "moral" resources parties need to win elections. Thus, reform helps a party in elections by restraining the resource advantages of the rival party and simultaneously shoring up support from an important proreform faction within party ranks.

When party leaders consider various reforms, the way in which a new law will advantage their party relative to the other is foremost in their minds. Laws such as the Taft-Hartley Act, which attempted to restrict labor union political activity, obviously favored the Republicans, who voted unanimously for the bill against New Deal Democrats. Similarly, the FECA of 1971 and its amendments provided presidential public financing, a measure the Democrats sorely needed to keep up with the Republicans in presidential elections. This bill was an easy choice for Democrats particularly since labor unions, an essential electoral ally, could give money through PACs. At the time, business firms had not begun to exploit this organizational form. The 1971 law also sought to limit campaign spending, which would help the majority congressional party (Democrats), since challengers typically need to spend more to introduce themselves to voters (Samples 2006).

When the electoral consequences of reform are not so obvious, party leaders may feel pressure to pursue reform because of an ongoing internal struggle over goals and values within the coalition. To simply ignore a faction risks losing the loyalty—and resources—of elites who support particular policies.[1] When Republicans at the turn of the century refused to bend to Progressive demands for economic and political reforms, the latter threatened to leave the party. When they eventually bolted in 1912, it cost the Republicans the election. In recent times, liberal progressives have existed within the Democratic Party and were the most vocal supporters of campaign finance reform during the 1990s, pitting themselves against both labor union and probusiness factions in the party. Given the size and influence of this constituency, Democratic Party leaders could not easily ignore them. Like the Republicans at the turn of the century, the Democrats believed the safest strategy was to pursue reforms that party leaders knew could be circumvented more easily by their own party than by the rival party. Before the McCain-Feingold Act went into effect banning soft money for political parties, Democratic strategists were already planning to use "527" organizations, which could raise and spend soft money, even as party leaders pushed members to vote for reform (Edsall 2002; Eilperin 2002). These 527 organizations, named because of their tax status with the IRS, were political committees set up by partisans to influence the presidential election. Their tax status prevented them from expressly asking citizens to vote for or against a federal candidate, as that would bring them under the more restrictive regulations of the McCain-Feingold Act. By seizing the mantle of reform, the party accommodated a powerful faction and was able to fashion provisions that minimized Republican strategic advantages.

Partisan inspiration for political reform during the twentieth century has been more prevalent than acknowledged in previous accounts. Most research emphasizes a narrative describing nonpartisan reformers pitted against entrenched interests, which obstruct changes in the status quo. However, the reality is more complex, and theories need to account for this. Reform constituencies are typically seen as standing above and outside politics—an assumption rooted in the Progressive worldview—but they are part of the partisan calculus in pursuing reform. In the remainder of the chapter I contrast two basic theories of reform: public interest versus partisan. This is followed by evidence that partisanship motivated most successful efforts to change the campaign finance system at various points in history, including many of the changes brought about by the BCRA of 2002.

COMPETING THEORIES OF REFORM

Two distinct theories have been used to explain the reform of campaign finance. One is a theory of public interest, a narrative that emerges directly from the language of Progressives, in which government acts to redress a dilemma or crisis that harms the commonweal. Public interest theory emphasizes that scandal pushes members of government to put aside selfish interests in order to pursue policies that are widely perceived as fair and just. Partisan theory, in contrast, assumes that reforms are self-interested and pursued for private gain. Partisan narratives tend to reflect Madisonian understandings about the nature of factions and, more fundamentally, about human behavior. In this perspective, political actors approach policy—including reforms—with a view to their interests.

Public Interest Theory

In public interest theory, campaign finance reform results from an emerging national consensus that the status quo should be changed for the benefit of the public. There are typically two strands of this theory. The first is the straightforward argument that reform emerges from public outrage over a situation that seems unjust or undemocratic. Scandal plays the decisive role in educating citizens and rousing public opinion against the status quo. Politicians who have been against reform are then forced to act, sometimes against their selfish interests. The analytical focus of this theory is on the demand side: government responds to an angry electorate to reform the system. Most conventional accounts of reform rely on this populist narrative to explain reform.

The second strand of public interest theory is more nuanced and focuses on supply-induced reform. In this version a small but dedicated elite perceive a failing of the system, develop a solution, and lobby to convince the public and policymakers of the necessity for change. Reform bills languish unless circumstances arise that make the policy issue more salient among the public or broader group of political elites (Kingdon 1984). Typically, a "focusing event" that attracts wide attention provides a window of opportunity for political entrepreneurs to offer their solution. The focusing event is likely a scandal that highlights the appearance of corrupt behavior. This scandal motivates a wider circle of elites to join the cause of reform. Long-brewing policies finally get passed because the reform coalition expands to include otherwise reluctant participants who have joined to avoid the fallout of negative public opinion (Zelizer 2002). Like the demand-side version of this theory, scandal and public reaction to it play a vital role in passing reform.

This second version of public interest theory is the classic Progressive perspective on reform. The process depends on expert elites who educate the citizenry and engage them in the drive to change the system for the benefit of the public interest. This theory of the policy process dominates contemporary explanations of campaign finance reform and political reform more generally (Corrado 1997; Mutch 1988; Sorauf 1992; Zelizer 2002).[2]

Critique of Public Interest Theory

The problem with public interest theory is that it fails to robustly explain the passage of many campaign finance laws throughout the century. Here are three weaknesses with the theory.

1. Public interest theory fails to explain reforms in the absence of scandal. The public interest narrative has been used to explain the BCRA of 2002 and, before that, the FECA amendments in 1974. But the emphasis on scandal-generated reform fails to account for occasions when reforms pass without wide public attention. For example, the 1974 reforms, which followed Watergate, were amendments to the FECA that passed in 1971. How do we account for the fact that Congress acted to pass major legislation *before* the scandal? To be sure, the 1971 act was not as significant as what followed with the post-Watergate amendments, but the original, pre-Watergate legislation made major changes to the campaign finance system.[3] We can ask the same question about reforms passing in 1939 and 1940 as part of the Hatch Acts; in 1947 as part of the Taft-Hartley Act; and in 1966 with the Long Act, which made public funds available to political parties. A review of major newspapers reveals no discussion of scandals during deliberations over these laws. Even the Teapot Dome scandal, which preceded the Corrupt Practices Act in 1925, is barely mentioned by the *New York Times* in the months preceding passage of the law. The salience of the corruption issue was so minimal that the Corrupt Practices Act passed as a mere rider attached to legislation on postal rate increases (*New York Times* 1924a).

2. *Public interest theory overpredicts reform.* Another problem with public interest theory is that it is not helpful in predicting when reforms will pass. Scandals appear, but reforms do not always follow. Why do we see no reforms in the 1950s after the widely reported Case scandal, in which Senator Francis Case announced he was offered a bribe to change his vote?[4] Why the absence of reforms in 1990 after the Keating Five scandal exposed that senators intervened with federal regulators on behalf of a large soft money donor? In both the 1950s and the 1980s, comprehensive reform proposals had been circulating among progressive legislators, but none made it through the gate. To explain reform—or its absence—in the aftermath of scandal, we need a better understanding of the conditions that lead to reform coalitions. Public interest theory, which is rooted in the scandal thesis, needs to account for when the likelihood of reform increases. The link between scandal and policy change appears too random when viewed through a historical lens.

3. *Public interest theory fails to account for weak public opinion.* This is the most serious charge against the public interest thesis. The theory assumes an important role for public opinion, namely, that public outrage over scandal will push legislators to enact reform. But the historical record fails to indicate that the public has been greatly concerned about issues of corruption from political contributions. A study by David Primo suggests there is no obvious link between public opinion and campaign finance reform. The general public does not care much about the issue (Primo 2002, 207–19). As I show later in this chapter, even in the immediate aftermath of scandal, the public does not place corruption at the top of the list of issues they are concerned with. The nature of public opinion on campaign finance thus suggests that reform is an elite-driven phenomenon. Elites are the ones primarily concerned with reform, and the role of scandal is limited and indirect.

PARTISAN THEORY

A basic premise of partisan theory is that reform is pursued primarily for private gain. While dialogue about reform reflects the language of public interest, an underlying motive for changing the rules is to gain advantages over competitors. Since rules matter for political outcomes, partisans want to ensure that the rules favor their side. Such it is with campaign finance. Because campaign finance regulations allocate costs and benefits among various groups, partisans have an incentive to push for rules that minimize their costs while maximizing their benefits. Thus, partisans compete to pass reform legislation that favors their side. Sometimes, the major parties may agree on regulatory policies that keep out third parties.[5] On other occasions, partisans seek rules that distinctly favor their party against the rival. Or a subset of partisans may prefer rules that give them leverage *within* the party.

Partisan theory assumes that the rules of the game constitute a contestable domain for political action. These rules are subject to political gamesmanship as much as legislative policy-making. Indeed, because these rules affect the "electoral connection," which is the primary concern of lawmakers, they are all the more subject to such behaviors.[6] The reluctance to change regulations stems primarily from the fact that existing rules appear good to those fortunate few who have earned a seat in Congress. For this reason, incumbents—and especially members of the incumbent party, which desires to stay in power—have little incentive to change the system. Given that the electoral rules are made by incumbents, it is highly unlikely that reforms will be passed, since the status quo should be preferred by those who have already succeeded under the system. Indeed, it is more likely that any changes in the system, should they occur, will have the effect of helping incumbents stay in office (Samples 2006).

The probability of reform increases, however, when electoral uncertainty increases for one party or a subset within a party. Politicians seek reforms when they perceive that their party or faction appears to be losing influence or competitiveness relative to other groups. In the two-party system, this happens when one party recognizes that the other party possesses resources that give them significant advantages. The "weaker" party seeks to level the playing field through government intervention.[7] The great difficulty for would-be reformers is that incumbents, even if they are members of the minority party, are reluctant to pursue reforms because altering rules could affect their own electoral prospects. Thus, the reforming party has to convince enough of its members that the new rules will hurt them less than incumbents in the rival party.[8]

Typically, most reforms that pass are incumbency enhancing for members of Congress (Samples 2006). Self-interested members of Congress have a solid reason to support the new rules, even though the party collectively might be hurt by reform, particularly in presidential elections. It is no coincidence that federal laws during the first three-quarters of the twentieth century rarely impinged seriously on the ability of congressional candidates to raise and spend money. Even caps on political spending had exemptions that were easy to exploit, and when spending caps were hit, candidates simply established multiple committees to finance their campaigns (Kolodny 1998, 124–25). When crafting federal reforms, the first rule of thumb has always been to "do no harm to my reelection."

A member's willingness to support reform is conditioned by second-level concerns, beyond his or her own reelection. These include the collective interests of the party or faction he or she supports. The member might ask: do the new rules help my *party* pursue or maintain control of government? Can these laws help my *faction* gain influence within the party, for example, by giving my faction greater leverage in selecting the next party nominee for president?

Since the costs of congressional elections were typically small prior to the 1970s, most reform battles to that point had been fought primarily for strategic advantages in presidential contests. Since the 1970s, however, congressional elections have been considerably more expensive, which raises the stakes for members in choosing among various proposals to reform the campaign finance system. Unsurprisingly, policy discussions in Congress about campaign finance issues have became increasingly intense and partisan because rules affect the flow of critical resources to win control of the legislative branch as much as the executive.

Under partisan theory, the push for reform is not broad based but limited to parties and factions that might gain advantages in the political process. Groups will lobby for reform based on their own interests. Organizations with nonmonetary resources, for example, will seek reforms that curtail the role of cash in politics. These organizations include labor unions or groups with large memberships that they can mobilize for electoral goals. The American Association of Retired Persons (AARP), for example, used its grass roots lobbying to help pass the BCRA (McSweeney 2005). According to *Fortune* magazine, AARP is the largest membership organization and second-most influential lobbying group in Washington, even though it does not make political contributions or engage in electioneering spending. From the AARP's perspective, laws that restrict spending on political contributions and electioneering spending will tend to enhance the value of its noncash resources, such as access to a pool of members willing to place phone calls and write letters to members of Congress. Proreform groups may also include those who compete with political parties as rival institutions that mediate between the public and officeholders. Such institutions include news organizations, universities, think tanks, public advocacy groups, and single-issue activists. By reducing the availability of money to political parties and politicians, these groups elevate the importance of their institutions as political intermediaries. However much reform groups may claim to speak for the public interest, they are simultaneously factions vying for power in the political system. By diminishing the importance of political contributions and party-based resources through reforms such as the BCRA, reformers enhance their own influence in the policy process relative to political parties.

PARTY FACTIONALISM AND CAMPAIGN FINANCE REFORM

Most partisan explanations of political reform are parsimonious to the point of oversimplification, particularly those rooted in economic theories (Abrams and Settle 1978, 245–57; Regens and Gaddie 1995). They take the parties as a monolithic set of interests with uniform resources. In truth, the parties are composed of various factions that control highly differentiated electoral resources. Campaign finance laws affect factions differently precisely because they wield different kinds of resources. For this reason, reforms that constrain money or regulate a particular electoral activity alter political influence *within* party coalitions, as well as between the two major parties. Indeed, subgroups within party coalitions are wary about any reform that cuts into their strategic resources, even if a proposed reform might help the party they support. As the previous chapter illustrated, labor unions blocked many campaign finance reforms championed by Democratic partisans in the 1960s and 1970s, for example, public funds for party organizations, precisely because these laws would weaken the influence of labor interests relative to other elements of the Democratic coalition.

In this pluralist understanding of political parties, subgroups compete for influence within the party, with political reform reflecting one of many contested domains. A key to having influence over the party's goals and strategies is the degree to which a subgroup has access to essential resources for the party's electoral success.[9] In contemporary politics, cash is vital for winning elections, which gives individuals or groups with access to cash a prominent role in party politics. But cash is not the only resource that matters. Parties also need workers, experts, and ideas that help the organization succeed. In acquiring these resources, party leaders inevitably give up some autonomy to groups that supply them. The power of particular factions comes from their capacity to withdraw vital electoral resources if they are dissatisfied with the direction of the party. This power is enhanced if few other groups provide the same resource or if the party cannot find substitutes for it.

Party leaders seek resources from subgroups in the coalition but want to avoid overreliance on any single subgroup that might jeopardize electoral success. Overreliance on a subgroup is risky, not only because immediate withdrawal of this group's resources could devastate the party but also because the subgroup is in a position to make narrowly based claims on the leadership that might limit the party's appeal to a broader electorate (Pfeffer and Salancik 1978). In an ideal world, party leaders prefer complete independence to choose goals and strategies for winning elections. However, no organization is self-sufficient, so leaders must bargain and negotiate with external and internal groups to ensure the continued flow of resources. This exchange process reflects a trade-off between autonomy and survival.

Campaign finance regulations have the potential to confer advantages on some partisan factions over others, giving them greater influence in party affairs. Since these laws determine the limits and kinds of resources allowed in elections, they affect the degree to which organizations are able to contribute their particular resources to political parties. For several groups with large memberships, such as labor unions or advocacy organizations, key resources might include campaign workers and activists willing to mobilize voters. For other subgroups, such as business firms, what matters primarily is access to financial resources for political contributions. And still for others, what matters is their capacity to shape or influence public opinion, through their status as professionals at universities, think tanks, and foundations and in the media. Organizations do not have the capacity to substitute resources easily, if at all, so campaign finance laws that alter the value of particular kinds of resources may enhance or diminish their influence within the party.

One example of factional power within a party organization is the role of labor union activists in the Democratic Party since the 1930s. Labor organizations have power over other subgroups within the party to the degree that the labor movement maintains its formidable machinery to mobilize potential Democratic voters. The fact that labor unions are critical for generating party votes makes them part of the "dominant coalition" guiding the Democratic

Party (Abrams and Settle 1978, 245–57; Regens and Gaddie 1995). While Democratic Party leaders value the contributions of labor leaders, they also try to hedge against labor union dominance by seeking resources from other groups as well, such as environmentalists, feminist organizations, or business interests.

When considering how to design campaign finance rules (or any set of political rules, for that matter), party leaders have an incentive to seek regulations that increase their probability of winning elections. Since the two major parties are compositionally different, it is no surprise that they each prefer campaign finance regimes that benefit subgroups in their coalitions. The party as a whole benefits when its subgroups can thrive under particular campaign finance regimes.

Democrats, for example, tend to prefer regimes that devalue the importance of cash versus labor as a political resource. This is because Democrats possess a natural constituency—labor unions—to help mobilize voters. The cash-poor Democrats also prefer a system that subsidizes political campaigns—cash grants and free broadcasting—or minimizes the advantages of wealth through contribution and spending limits. More broadly, Democrats favor campaign finance regimes that decentralize partisan activity. The reasons for this are rooted in the heterogeneous nature of the partisan coalition. Given the party's diversity and strong sectionalism, it has been difficult for them to centralize activities in Washington among the national committees. Instead, the party tends to perform better when candidates, interest groups, and state-based parties manage campaigns locally, with minimal intervention from the national committees. In subsequent chapters on fund-raising and campaigning I explain this behavior in greater detail. Suffice it to say, at this point, that Democrats are a looser coalition of interests than Republicans.[10] This fact makes them relatively more comfortable managing campaigns outside the formal party structure.

Republicans, in contrast, have been more united ideologically, which makes it easier for them to centralize campaign operations. Ideological homogeneity tends to permit greater concentration of power at the center, since followers are more willing to defer to authority to the extent they agree. Additionally, greater ideological homogeneity has allowed the Republicans to benefit significantly from the cash-based economy of modern campaigns. The explanation for the traditional Republican advantage in raising money is more complex than the conventional understanding that they are the "rich" person's party. As I discuss in the next chapter, it is easier for the RNC to solicit contributions from small donors because the party has a more coherent ideological message.

Given the nature of the Republican coalition it is not surprising they prefer laissez-faire campaign finance regimes. Their ideological coherence and affinities with citizens of greater wealth give them a broader base of contributors than Democrats. Their preference for the laissez-faire approach to campaign finance, while consistent with the conservative philosophy, has the virtue of being in the best interests of the Republican Party.

Fortunately for the Democrats, the laissez-faire approach preferred by Republicans was discredited by the Progressive movement early in the century. Democrats—and occasionally Republicans—have been able to draw on a well of public sentiment, steeped in a Mugwump-inspired political culture, to push for reforms that regulate money in politics. As described in the previous chapter, during the Progressive Era Democrats teamed with Republican Progressives, who were trying to beat back conservatives in their own party, to pass reforms that would rein in Republican advantages with corporate donors. In midcentury, during the New Deal era, Republicans lashed back at the Democrats. As the party out of power in the executive branch, Republicans provided the momentum to pass laws, such as the Hatch and Taft-Hartley Acts, to hamper the ability of the Democrats to benefit from electoral resources provided by government employees and labor organizations.[11] This time, Republicans had support from the southern Democrat faction, which feared the rise of labor influence in the Democratic Party and the increasingly federal-centered, liberal tilt of the party. During the third era of reform, starting in the 1960s, the Democrats once again launched an attack on Republican financial advantages by restricting contributions and expenditures and voting for public subsidies in presidential elections. A dominant liberal, progressive faction within the Democratic Party pursued many of these reforms, in part, to increase its influence in the party at the expense of traditional party elites, who included labor union activists and southern conservative Democrats.

As this summary suggests, reforms reflect not only actions against the opposing party but also factional struggles within parties. Among Republicans, the fights were between Progressives and conservatives, especially early in the first quarter of the century. Progressives did not want the party to rely on business contributions because such support tilted the party away from the market intervention policies they supported. Instead, Progressives sought a system in which candidates relied on individual contributions from the professional and middle classes, whose sentiments they shared. Like their Mugwump forebears, these middle-class, mainline Protestant constituents disliked the partisan politics of "robber barons" in the Republican Party, as well as the Catholic and immigrant-based Democratic Party. These groups threatened their elite status in the community. Antipartisan political reforms—not just in the area of campaign finance—served their interests because the changes they wrought capitalized on their strengths as educated elites capable of engaging in politics without parties serving as intermediaries.

On the Democratic side, the struggles over party direction were fiercer later in the century as the New Deal coalition was breaking up, pitting liberals, conservatives, and union activists against one another for party influence. These battle lines were clearly relevant in arguments over Russell Long's proposal for public financing. As I discussed in the previous chapter, Long's bill gave public funds directly to the political parties at the national and state levels. Union activists opposed this because they did not want to see money in the hands of antiunion state parties, particularly in the South. Instead, they proposed subsidies that would be available to labor unions as well. Liberals, like Robert Kennedy, argued for subsidies to go directly to candidates rather than party organizations, which were controlled by traditional party elites.

As in other areas of political reform, the Democratic intraparty feuds over campaign finance typically pitted professionals against amateurs.[12] The incentives motivating professionals have been primarily material: jobs, patronage, contracts, and other perks.[13] Winning office helps secure these benefits, and ideology plays a minor role in being an active member of the party. The icon of the Democratic professional is the machine boss, who dominated northern American cities at the turn of the century. The modern versions of machine-era bosses and workers are the professional consultants—the "hired guns"—whose chief goal is to win elections. To be sure, consultants are partisans because they stick with one team (just like the boss and his precinct workers), but their incentives to participate are primarily material. And like those who worked for the machine, contemporary professionals want maximum autonomy to win campaigns, which means they favor "minimalist" campaign finance regimes and strategies that allow the party to move to the center, if necessary.

In contrast, amateurs in the Democratic Party prefer a campaign finance system with stringent regulations on political money because these augment the importance of resources they have to offer the party. As laws make it difficult to raise and spend money, the value of other resources becomes more significant. These resources include interest group electioneering, campaign endorsements, access to the news media, and elite opinion emanating from universities, foundations, and advocacy organizations. Democratic amateurs are the inheritors of the Progressive faith in education politics, which puts a premium on expertise and the dispassionate interest of virtuous citizens. They seek reforms that minimize the importance of material incentives relative to *purposive* incentives for attracting followers to the party. Laws that restrict campaign money, for example, give amateurs greater influence in party circles because the party becomes more reliant on activists motivated by purposive incentives, that is, motives tied to ideology and policy.

Republicans may soon be facing similar tensions between amateurs and professionals now that they have attracted a committed core of conservative activists, especially among evangelicals, with strong purposive goals. Similar to the New Left Democrats, these groups have sought to take over state and local organizations to gain influence in selecting and supporting favored candidates. It is too soon to tell if factional disputes within the Republican Party will spill over into policy disagreements about political reform, such as campaign finance. Under the BCRA, however, more of these activist "amateur" groups might be encouraged to establish 527 organizations to push their issues and candidates. Most true believers tend to lose interest in participating in the formal party organization—except during party caucuses—because it forces too many compromises on them in comparison with narrow, issue-based organizations. Powerful nonparty organizations that support conservative Republicans include the Club for Growth (a probusiness, antitax organization) and the Christian Coalition. It is no coincidence that Republican Party stalwarts are interested in clamping down on 527 organizations (Nelson 2005; Pershing 2005). One obvious reason is to prevent Democratic-leaning organizations from attacking Republican candidates, but another reason may be intraparty factionalism. Conservative organizations have been willing to campaign vigorously for favored candidates in primaries, even challenging party incumbents.[14] In 2006, for example, the Club for Growth helped insurgent Republican Steve Laffey in the primary for U.S. Senate against centrist Lincoln Chafee. Though Chafee won, the hard-fought primary battle depleted much of Chafee's campaign treasury and weakened him in the general election, which he eventually lost. Such examples warm mainstream Republicans to the idea of restraining spending by outside groups.

Typically, proreform constituencies have much to gain, in terms of intraparty influence, the more tightly they constrain traditional sources of electoral support. For this reason, Progressive Republicans early in the century teamed with Democrats to weaken Mark Hanna Republicans. Similarly, southern Democrats teamed with Republicans at midcentury to weaken New Deal Democrats. Much later in the century, when the parties became more cohesive ideologically, campaign finance reforms tended to benefit one party or the other. Nonetheless, rules continue to enhance or diminish the influence of factions within each party, depending on how these rules affect the relative value of resources possessed by a faction.

In summary, campaign finance reform is about gaining partisan electoral advantages. It is most likely to succeed when one party faces heightened uncertainty about gathering sufficient resources to win presidential elections. Trying to alter rules that impact congressional incumbency—which indirectly helps the minority party—is far more difficult and unlikely to happen. The history of successful reform, however, shows that the party that does not control the White House typically supports changes. The one exception to this was the Long Act in 1966, which passed during President Johnson's tenure. But the Democratic Party was justifiably concerned about being able to wage an effective presidential campaign in 1968. The party was still reeling from a record debt held over from previous elections, and LBJ was concerned that Republicans would match or exceed their phenomenal fund-raising for the Goldwater campaign in 1964.

Another condition for successful reform is that it must clearly enhance the influence of an important faction in one party that feels threatened by the status quo. Typically, this faction is the inheritor of the Progressive tradition, which desires nonmaterial resources (education, status, ideology) to play a greater role in elections relative to cash-based resources. To pass reform, the party out of power will team with a "reform" faction in the rival party. In this way, the minority party has a substantial influence on a policy outcome. Bipartisanship is enhanced to the degree that the new rules do not substantially affect the reelection of incumbent legislators. Eric Schickler, in his discussion of rule making in the U.S. House, has used the term *common carrier* to suggest how a particular rule wins support for different reasons (2001). The rule change may generate a collective good for a party or faction, while others may support the rule for private interests, in this case their individual chances for reelection.

Scandal, however, is rarely the reason for greater bipartisanship. In the history of campaign finance reform, only Watergate provided momentum to win *broad* bipartisan support for amendments to the FECA in 1974. No other campaign finance reforms generated widespread support because of scandal—not even Teapot Dome. In 2002, the Enron scandal encouraged the most vulnerable Republican candidates—those who were from highly competitive districts—to cast their votes with a handful of Progressive Republicans led by John McCain. But four out of five Republicans in the House and Senate did not support reform (*CQ Weekly* 2002).

To lend support for this theory of partisan reform, I look historically at the timing of reform, sponsorship, and roll call votes on campaign finance reforms. Subsequent chapters build on this evidence by showing how parties and factions exploited new rules to gain favorable advantages in presidential campaigns.

PARTISANSHIP AND TIMING OF REFORM

The partisan model of reform suggests that campaign finance reforms should occur during periods of heightened electoral uncertainty for one party in presidential elections. Electoral uncertainty occurs when party leaders fear they lack resources to compete effectively against the rival party. When partisans perceive a growing resource gap, they will invoke the morality play about political corruption as one strategy to change campaign finance laws. They will appropriate aspects of reform proposals in circulation, trying to build a winning coalition with a proreform faction in the rival party. The reform proposals are sweetened typically with measures that aim to protect incumbent legislators (Samples 2006). From the perspective of party leaders, however, the main goal is to improve the party's electoral prospects either by forcing a redistribution of resources or by making it harder for opponents to campaign effectively. In short, the disadvantaged party presses for rule changes that favor their side.

One measure of uncertainty is to compare the gap in cash resources between parties. We should expect the resource-poor party to seek reforms when this gap widens significantly. To explore this hypothesis, I assembled data on election spending by the national parties and their affiliated national committees during presidential election years. These data have been gathered periodically by political scientists in studies of campaign finance.[15] They relied chiefly on figures retrieved through Senate committee investigations for presidential elections since the Publicity Act of 1911.[16] To be sure, we should be skeptical about the reliability of these figures, given the primitive nature of campaign reporting. But these figures were widely reported in partisan circles, giving the impression—if not the reality—of partisan resources advantages. Researchers on campaign finance—for example, Pollock, Overacker, Heard, and Alexander—backed up their financial reporting with anecdotal accounts from insiders about how the parties fared in raising and spending money.[17]

Figure 2 shows the ratio of Republican versus Democratic spending set against a time line of campaign finance legislation. The data point to an important historical fact about American political parties. Republicans consistently

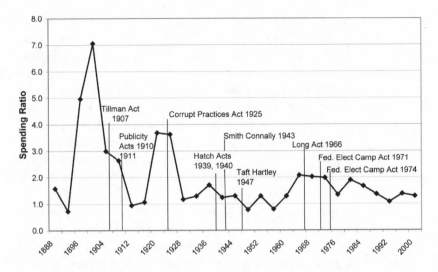

FIG. 2. Republican/Democratic ratio of spending in presidential elections. (Data from Pollock 1926; Overacker 1932; Heard 1960; Alexander 1962, 1966, 1971, 1976, 1979, 1983; Alexander and Haggerty 1987; Alexander and Bauer 1991; Alexander and Corrado 1995; Green 1999; Magleby 2002.)

outspend Democrats. On only six occasions since 1888 have the Democrats been able to achieve parity or spend slightly more that Republicans.[18] This finding supports the argument that Republicans made the transition from labor to cash campaigns more easily than Democrats. Democrats, of course, have possessed important nonmonetary advantages that do not show up in financial figures. For example, they were more likely to have strong urban machines, and they received critical in-kind support from labor unions beginning with the New Deal. The Republican cash advantage is particularly important in the era of "education politics" that emerged during the Progressive Era and remains to this day. As I explained in chapter 2, the candidate-centered politics of the twentieth century depends more on capital for mass media persuasion methods than did the party-based campaigning of the nineteenth century.

The time line shows a correlation between periods of heightened Republican advantage and campaign finance reform. After an election in which Republicans outspend Democrats by roughly two to one, reforms follow. This occurred during the Progressive Era with reforms in 1907, 1910, and 1925 and then later in the century with reforms in 1966, 1971, and 1974. In contrast, during the midcentury, when the gap between parties was less significant, Republicans sponsored reforms like the Hatch Acts (1939, 1940), the Smith-Connally Act (1943), and the Taft-Hartley Act (1947). Despite closer financial parity between the parties, Republicans apparently believed Democrats possessed nonmonetary advantages in the form of electoral support from labor unions and government employees. Recall that the labor union movement swelled during the New Deal era; unions became highly active in electoral politics, especially on the side of New Deal Democrats. At the same time, the number of government employees surged under the Roosevelt administration. It is no surprise, then, that Republicans pushed for reforms during the New Deal era to restrict electioneering by these groups.

The data in figure 2 suggest that partisan reform may achieve the intended effect of closing financial disparities, at least among the national party committees. In election cycles after Democratic reforms, which imposed financial constraints on political parties, the spending gaps between parties narrowed temporarily.[19] There is little doubt that political parties conceived new methods to spend money outside the party structure so funds did not have to be reported. But such adaptations are not without costs to the political parties. Creating splinter committees to spend campaign money makes it more difficult to coordinate partisan activity. Democrats typically benefit from reforms that push activities outside the party structure because they rely more on alliances with nonparty groups to mobilize Democratic voters.

PARTISANSHIP AND THE DESIGN OF REFORM

The previous section focused on instances when political parties have an incentive to pass reform. It will be shown here that the nature of the reform—the proposed remedies—coincides with partisan interests. Specifically, partisans want to pass rules that help their side. The rules they propose reflect the relative organizational strengths of the parties and the factions within those parties.

The Democratic Party, for example, possesses organizational characteristics that encourage party leaders to seek reforms that decentralize partisan activity. Through much of the century the Democrats represented a heterogeneous coalition of farmers, unskilled workers, union members, ethnics, minorities, and elderly. Until the 1970s, it had also been the party of white southerners, whose ideology was more conservative than other elements of party. Given the size and scope of the Democratic coalition it has been harder for them to develop strong centers of power. Through much of their history party leaders have rarely tried to impose order on this fractious coalition because of the political costs it might incur.[20] They have been content to let local parties and politicians address the needs of campaigning, which are tailored to distinct political cultures. Thus, Democrats prefer campaign finance regimes that tend to decentralize political activity.

The second characteristic of the Democratic Party is that key constituencies possess organizational structures at the local level that can be exploited for campaigning. The infamous political machines run by Irish party bosses helped Democrats win voting majorities among ethnics in major urban centers (Erie 1988). These machines exploited local patronage to control city politics. They used dense ward-based networks in multiple neighborhoods to capture city hall and generate votes for presidential candidates. Similarly, since the 1930s labor interests have helped Democrats through their get-out-the-vote operations run by local unions. And after the Voting Rights Act of 1965, African American churches mobilized pro-Democrat voters. These Democratic constituencies—urban machines, labor unions, and African American churches—all possess, or possessed at one time, institutionalized ties to masses of citizens who could be exploited for electioneering. The Republicans, in contrast, have typically lacked connections to organizations that mediate politics for large blocs of voters, although the Christian Right in recent decades has assumed the role.

Traditionally, the Republican Party's strength has been that they are more cohesive ideologically and culturally than Democrats. They have drawn activists from the ranks of upper income groups, business professionals, white-collar workers, and mainline Protestant denominations. The narrower ideological and cultural range has made it easier for them to centralize operations without incurring as many political costs for various factions within the party. Progressives, of course, bolted the party earlier in the century, but they also shared a social status with the conservative wing of the party. These elites circulated in the same schools, clubs, and neighborhoods, which made political compromise and accommodation somewhat easier for them than for Democrats. Contemporary surveys of political elites suggest that the Republicans remain more culturally homogeneous and ideologically consistent than Democrats (Jackson, Bigelow, and Green 2007, 51–74).

Furthermore, as the party of business, Republicans have adopted a businesslike approach to political organizing. Many party chairs, such as Mark Hanna, have been businessmen who bring to the job the same organizing principles of business administration. Thus, scholars have observed that Republican political committees are more rationally organized than Democratic groups (Cotter et al. 1984; Heard 1960; Herrnson 1988). They show clear patterns of hierarchy and authority and draw on professional practices for tasks such as advertising candidates (Bibby 2002, 19–46). They also borrow practices from their experiences as business civic leaders, such as raising money for community chest organizations and other philanthropic groups.[21] As the party in minority during much of the twentieth century, Republicans have also had a strong incentive to build an organization that can recruit and fund candidates to beat incumbents.

Given their unique organizational characteristics and the nature of their factions, the two major parties have sought different kinds of campaign finance regimes. Democrats, with their nonmonetary advantages and decentralized structure, favor a system that (a) minimizes the importance of private cash resources and (b) discourages concentration of resources. Thus, they consistently seek regulations, such as contribution and spending limits, that tend to scatter resources locally and enhance the value of noncash strategies. Being cash poor relative to Republicans, they also tend to favor public subsidies in presidential elections.

Republicans, in contrast, prefer campaign finance regimes that give them maximum flexibility to use money. Raising money is easier for Republicans, not only because their constituents are wealthier but also because the party's unity makes impersonal appeals for donations (through direct mail, for example) more successful. As I discuss at length in the next chapter, the Republican donors are more likely to "trust" the national party leaders since they are less divided by sectionalism and ethnic identity than members of the Democratic Party. Given these features, Republicans want to avoid campaign finance reforms that restrict cash-based electioneering. If they pursue reforms at all, they are aimed at minimizing Democratic strengths by trying to prevent labor organizations or public employees from helping in elections.

Typically, Democrats favor laws that encourage public disclosure of campaign funds. Since Republicans raise more money, publicity laws give Democrats the opportunity to make funding a campaign issue. They can point to the Republicans as the party of the rich.[22] Meanwhile, Democratic campaigning can continue "under the radar" through nonparty organizations that do not disclose their activity. But the publicity strategy is a double-edged sword, particularly when Democrats control the majority. Republicans can use the same tactics against Democrats to show that they are "bought and sold" by interest groups. During the 1960s and 1970s, for example, Democrats resisted greater publicity while they held majorities in Congress. Democratic leaders like Wayne Hays insisted that reports be sent to the clerk of the House, which they controlled, rather than an independent election commission. Republicans, of course, preferred the outside commission because they felt the manipulation of reports could be used against them in campaigns.

One indication that party preferences exist for campaign finance rules is the legislative record. Table 1 shows chronologically when Congress enacted specific remedies for fixing the campaign finance system. It shows bills that inaugurated key features of contemporary U.S. campaign laws. Those have been sponsored by members of the party that stands to benefit. As the cash-poor party, Democrats clearly had a greater incentive to regulate the campaign finance system. Democratic members of Congress have been responsible for introducing reforms that tend to limit the use of financial resources. For example, Senator Tillman, a Democrat, introduced a successful bill to ban corporate contributions (1907). Similarly, Democrats introduced measures that would cap contributions (1940, 1966, 1971, 1974), limit candidate spending (1911, 1971, 1974), or limit party spending (1940, 1971, 1974).

In contrast, Republicans tend to sponsor reforms that limit nonmonetary advantages (restricting union electioneering) or reduce the electoral influence of strong factions in the Democratic Party. A Republican, for example, proposed that financial disclosure be extended to primaries (1911) as a way to counter Democrats in the South, where primaries selected officeholders. And they introduced a measure to limit labor union electioneering under the

TABLE 1. Emergence of Key Features of U.S. Campaign Finance Law: Party Affiliation of Member Introducing Bill or Amendment

	Democrat	Republican
Corporate ban on contributions	1907 (S)	
Public disclosure of election funds	1910 (S)	1910 (H)
Extending regulations to primary[a]		1911 (S)
Spending limits on candidates	1911 (S)	
Government employee restrictions	1939 (S)	
Contribution limits	1940 (S)	
Spending limits on national parties	1940 (H)	
Labor union ban on contributions		1943 (S)
Public financing	1966 (S)	

Source: Mutch 1988; and various reports in *Congressional Record*, 1910–66.
Note: S = originated in Senate; H = originated in House. In 1910 a publicity bill was simultaneously introduced.
[a]Struck down by *Newberry v. U. S.* (1921).

Smith-Connally Act (1943). Somewhat surprisingly, a Democratic senator from New Mexico, Carl Hatch, submitted a bill to prevent government employees from participating in federal elections. He was encouraged to do this by southerners in the Democratic Party, who opposed a third term for FDR; they sought to cut off the president's support from federal employees. The Republicans, of course, supported the bill almost unanimously. The "common carrier" for both Republicans and conservative Democrats was to pass reform that curtailed the electoral resources of Roosevelt and the New Deal Democrats.

The BCRA was exceptional in the sense that the bill had bipartisan sponsorship, unlike most previous reform legislation. The sponsors, however, clearly represented factions in each party that stood to gain from imposing a particular design for reform, in this case a ban on soft money. Senator McCain and Representative Christopher Shays (R-CT), both Republicans in the Progressive tradition and both mavericks who challenged party leadership frequently, sought to weaken the power of traditional party leaders by taking away soft money controlled by these leaders. Similarly, on the Democratic side, the bill was sponsored by two very liberal members, Senator Russ Feingold (D-WI) and Representative Marty Meehan (D-MA), who understood that the liberal faction of the party benefited by making candidates more reliant on liberal activist networks rather than corporations and unions that supplied soft money, a fact I will elaborate on in subsequent chapters.

PARTISAN SUPPORT IN CONGRESS FOR REFORM

Whether partisan motives generate partisan roll call votes on final passage of a bill is far from clear. The historical record shows, in fact, that reforms in the early part of the century passed easily by voice vote or with strong support from both parties. One obvious reason for this is that the early laws were but minor harassments to the congressional candidates, though they had long-term effects on how partisans organized themselves to finance presidential elections. Most proposals would have minimal effect on the ability of congressional incumbents to finance their reelections. Throughout most of the twentieth century, political fund-raising was not institutionalized to the point where changes in the law would require major adjustments. It was clear to most observers that the laws could be circumvented by setting up numerous independent committees or rerouting funds through local and state parties.

Fear of public backlash from scandal seems an unlikely cause of bipartisan voting, except in the case of the 1974 post-Watergate reforms. For previous reform legislation, there was hardly a mention of scandal in the pages of the *New York Times* in the weeks and months leading up to final passage of a bill. Indeed, the *New York Times* gave little space to campaign finance reform legislation at all until the 1960s. Prior to then, the articles were buried deep in the paper or mentioned in a laundry list of legislative issues taken up by Congress. Moreover, Congress did not give prominence to reforms by voting on them as a unique piece of legislation. The FCPA of 1925, the Long Act of 1966, and the Revenue Act of 1971 (which provided public funding for presidential elections) were passed merely as riders to large budget and tax bills.

During the Progressive Era, bipartisanship resulted from a coalition of Progressive Republican and Democrats. Conservative Republicans reluctantly went along with campaign finance reforms, weakening provisions where they could, just as Senator Foraker (R-OH) did when he amended the Tillman Act to limit the corporate ban to federal-chartered corporations and federal elections. Republican leaders did not typically fight hard against Progressives on this issue, even though the new campaign finance rules would make it more difficult for the party to organize campaigns. The ongoing threat by Progressives to bolt the party on the issue of political reform may have been sufficient to convince enough Republicans to vote in favor of it (Shannon 1959, 39). Keeping the Progressive wing of the party satisfied was important, at least concerning reform issues, where party leaders did not see changes as crippling to their interests. The Progressives, after all, provided important resources to the party, being a fount of ideas, talent, and legitimacy.

More intense partisan differences on campaign finance reform emerged during the New Deal era. As table 2 shows, only 38 percent of House Democrats voted for the Hatch Act I and 43 percent voted for the Hatch Act II; the Republican votes were near unanimous. Later, in 1943, the percentage of Democrats voting for the antilabor Smith-Connally Act increased to 61 percent with the help of the southern faction of the Democratic Party. To be sure, these bills touched on more than campaign finance issues. However, the provisions related to campaign finance reform were clearly partisan. Republicans pushed for campaign finance reforms to limit the power of government employees and labor unions. In roll call votes they were able to peel away Democrats from the South and some western Progressives. Southern Democrats, of course, supported antilabor laws that buttressed their traditional positions of power, and they were angered by FDR's "purge" campaigns in 1938, which exploited the campaign labor of federal employees. It was mostly the northern New Dealers who stood by Roosevelt against campaign finance reforms that sought to weaken the national party and its growing alliance with federal employees and union members. Legislation such as the Hatch Acts, the Smith-Connally Act, and the Taft-Hartley Act reflected not just battles between the two major parties but intraparty skirmishes among Democratic constituencies. Republicans successfully exploited rifts in the Democratic coalition to weaken FDR and his New Deal supporters by removing access to important campaign resources.

In the 1960s and 1970s, Democrats mounted surprise attacks to pass bills designed to help the party compete in presidential elections with Republicans. No one expected Russell Long to submit a bill for public financing in 1966—not even the ardent proreform, progressive faction in Congress led by Senator Gore. The 1971 FECA, which *preceded* Watergate, was passed with similar legislative tactics. Once again, after the failed effort by Russell Long four years earlier, Democratic strategists sought to inject public funds into party coffers and constrain presidential election spending by Republicans (Weaver 1971a). Indeed, much of the momentum and design for the bill came from the National Committee for an Effective Congress (NCEC), a self-proclaimed public interest group whose major function was to raise campaign funds primarily for liberal

TABLE 2. Roll Call Votes on Campaign Finance Reform

	House Democrats (% yea)	House Republicans (% yea)	Senate Democrats (% yea)	Senate Republicans (% yea)	Party in White House
Tillman Act (1907)[a]	Voice vote	Voice vote	NA	NA	Rep
Publicity Act I (1910)	NA	NA	100	80	Rep
Publicity Act II (1911)	86	100	71	100	Rep
FCPA Act (1925)[b]	NA	NA	100	92	Rep
Hatch I (1939)	38	100	NA	NA	Dem
Hatch II (1940)	43	100	71	100	Dem
Smith-Connally Act (1943)	61	95	53	95	Dem
Long Act (1966)[c]	81	73	22	96	Dem
FECA I (1971)	95	93	100	95	Rep
FECA II (1974)	99	75	80	41	Rep
BCRA (2002)	94	19	96	21	Rep

Note: NA = no data available.
[a]Officially known as An Act to Prohibit Corporations from Making Contributions in Connection with Political Elections.
[b]Attached as rider to the Postal Services Act of 1925; vote is on the attached rider.
[c]The Long Act, H.R. 13103, was included in the Foreign Investors Tax Act of 1966. The Senate party percentages reflect the vote to strike Title III (Presidential Campaign Election Fund). A "Nay" vote means the member wants public funds to remain part of the bill. In the House, members did not vote on a separate bill but only on the conference report, which included provisions for both presidential public funds and significant tax legislation.

Democratic congressional candidates (Berry and Goldman 1971).[23] Senate Republicans were caught off guard when Democrats introduced an amendment to include public financing of presidential elections (among other reforms) at the last minute to a tax reduction bill the Nixon administration wanted very badly. The amendment passed on a partisan vote (Weaver 1971d). In conference, Democrats threatened to sink the entire tax bill unless the campaign finance measures were included (Weaver 1971b). Nixon, in turn, called their bluff, saying he would veto the tax bill if the campaign finance measure was included. This tactic gave cover to Republicans to vote for the bill, while Nixon then negotiated a compromise with conference chairman Wilbur Mills (D-AR) to put off public funding until the 1976 elections. Democratic leaders were furious at Mills for backing down (Weaver 1971c).

In the aftermath of the Watergate scandal, Congress passed amendments to the FECA in 1974. Indeed, the changes were such that the 1974 version could be considered an entirely different law, including the creation of an independent agency for enforcement. As I described in the previous chapter, the law was tailor-made for Democrats: full presidential campaign funding in the general election, contribution and spending limits (which helps the incumbent party in Congress), campaign finance disclosure, and a system in which groups could give through PACs. Until that point, pro-Democrat unions had been the primary users of PACs. Few Republicans felt they could vote against the bill, even though they believed it was entirely against the interests of the party (Rosenbaum 1974). About 75 percent of House Republicans voted for it, and only 41 percent of Senate Republicans did so. Even before the final vote in the Senate, Hugh Scott of Pennsylvania, the Republican floor leader, announced he would recommend that the president veto the entire package (Weaver 1971d).

If ever scandal induced reform, the FECA of 1974 was it. The reforms, however, were hardly bipartisan. They clearly shored up Democratic weaknesses—for example, lack of funding for presidential elections—and exploited Democratic advantages over Republicans—for example, labor union PACs.[24] The 1974 amendments were also pushed by the progressive faction of the Democratic Party, which stood to gain by encouraging political contributions from small donors (who were likely to be educated professionals sympathetic to progressive goals) and by limiting political spending.

The next and most recent set of reforms came with the BCRA of 2002. Paradoxically, it was the most partisan vote ever taken on campaign finance reform in U.S. history. It garnered the support of 94 percent of House Democrats but only 19 percent of House Republicans. Similarly, in the Senate, only one in five

Republicans voted for it. Why was the vote on this bill so partisan, and why did it succeed?

EXPLAINING THE BCRA

First, some background on the BCRA is necessary. The two key provisions of the BCRA are (1) a ban on soft money fund-raising and spending by national parties and (2) a prohibition on using soft money, by *any* organization, on broadcast communications thirty days before a primary and sixty days before a general election in which a federal candidate is on the ballot (see the following box for a complete listing of major provisions). Soft money are funds raised in amounts greater than federal contribution limits and from sources banned under the Tillman Act (corporations) and the Taft-Hartley Act (unions). In the 1980s, the national committees exploited state laws allowing soft money, arguing that they could use these funds because they engaged in state elections as well. Taking advantage of favorable regulatory rulings by the FEC, they claimed to spend all the soft money on broad-based party building to enhance grass roots participation. In truth, a good portion of the money was targeted for thinly disguised "issue ads," which were campaign commercials for federal candidates.

When the BCRA was passed, some political commentators likened it to a Democratic suicide bill (Gitell 2003). The reasoning behind this was that the Democrats had benefited considerably from soft money. In the 2000 election, more than half their funds were soft money compared to 43 percent for Republicans. Republicans, as usual, had been more successful raising hard money, topping $213 million compared to the Democrats' $137 million. But the soft money gap between the parties was smaller: Democrats raised $136 million compared to $166 million for Republicans. Why would Democrats give up an important source of income that gave them greater parity with Republicans?

Democrats had two motives to push for reforms, one involving factional rivalries within the party and the other involving an effort to gain advantages over the Republican Party. First, a powerful constituency within the Democratic Party was calling for reform. This constituency bore a striking resemblance to early-century Progressives who fought for reforms within the Republican Party. They were progressives with roots in the New Left and the social movements of the 1960s. They included citizens with ties to environmental and social welfare organizations; mainstream and liberal Protestant churches; good government groups like the League of Women Voters; foundation executives; and, of course, newspaper editors who came of age during Vietnam and Water-

Major Provisions of the BCRA

Soft Money

Prohibition on any soft money financing (contributions and expenditures) for national political parties.

Federal candidates and officeholders prohibited from accepting, soliciting, or spending soft money.

Prohibition on soft money expenditures by state and local parties for any "federal election activity," defined to include the following:

- Voter registration within 120 days of a federal election.
- Voter identification, "Get out the vote" (GOTV), or generic campaign activity in connection with a federal election.
- Work by state or local party employees who spend more than 25 percent of their time on activities in connection with a federal election.
- Federal candidate-specific ads that promote or attack a candidate. ("Promote or attack" is not defined by the bill.)
- State parties must use hard money for all of these activities or, where applicable, Levin Amendment soft money (soft money from contributions of less than ten thousand dollars).

Political parties must choose between making coordinated expenditures on behalf of their candidate or independent expenditures on behalf of their candidate, but not both (ruled unconstitutional in McConnell v. FEC).

Other Contribution Restrictions

Hard money legal limits raised:

- Limit for individual contributions per candidate per election increased from one thousand dollars to two thousand dollars.
- Limit for individual contributions to national party committees increased from twenty thousand dollars to twenty-five thousand dollars per year.
- Limit for individual contributions to state and local party committees increased from five thousand dollars to ten thousand dollars.

Aggregate limits of ninety-five thousand dollars per election cycle on how much individuals may give to candidates, parties, and PACs, with maximum sublimits for each of these committees.

Indexing for inflation of contributions to candidates and parties and individual aggregate and coordinated spending limits are indexed for inflation (but not for PACs).

Millionaire Opponent Provision increases contribution limits for congressional candidates facing self-financed candidates on sliding scale.

Political Advertising

A ban on issue ads funded by soft money from any organization if the ads refer to candidates for federal election in the sixty days prior to a general election or thirty days prior to a primary election.

Disclosure of sources of financing for "electioneering communications" in excess of ten thousand dollars per year.

gate. Over the course of the century, the core Mugwump principles of participatory democracy—untainted by material motives—have migrated from being
primarily in the Republican Party to lodging firmly in the Democratic Party.
The neo-Mugwumps in the Democratic Party have been opposed to traditional
party power brokers: labor unions, southerners, and New Dealers. And like
their Progressive forebears, progressives have been most adamantly opposed to
corporate influence within the party, which is manifested transparently
through corporate soft money contributions.

Neo-Mugwumps in the Democratic Party lobbied hard through the 1980s
and 1990s for campaign finance reform. But Democratic leaders were not
enthusiastic so long as some parity existed with Republicans over electoral
resources, particularly for congressional races. Anxiety increased sharply in
1994 when Republicans took control of Congress and in 2000 when they won
the White House. Having power meant Republicans could significantly
increase their fund-raising advantages. After 1994 and again in 2000, Democrats pushed hard on the reform issue. They were supported by the news media,
foundations, and liberal progressive organizations that were members of the
Democratic coalition (Dwyre and Farrar-Myers 2001, 176–81). In 2001, no fewer
than thirty-seven editorials calling for campaign finance reform were published by the *New York Times,* the paper widely read by progressive activists
throughout the nation (McSweeney 2005, 513). There is little doubt that newspapers like the *New York Times* behaved like advocacy interest groups for the
BCRA reforms, labeling all other reforms as "sham bills" or "pseudo-reform" in
their editorials (*New York Times* 1998, 2000).

Perhaps the continued emphasis by the *New York Times* and other liberal-
leaning papers, such as the *Washington Post,* explains why more Democrats
than Republicans thought this was an important issue. In early 2001, more than
one year before the BCRA passed, only one in five Americans ranked campaign
finance reform as a "highest priority" for federal policymakers. Democratic
voters were more inclined to rank it as a "highest priority" at 24 percent compared with just 14 percent among Republican voters (*Washington Post*/ABC
News 2001).

Even though reform did not rank as a "highest priority" with most Americans, a clear majority supported significant changes in the methods of campaign finance. Voters who considered themselves "strong Democrats" favored
major reform more than others. Table 3 shows that in 2002, when the reform
issue was most salient, 71 percent of strong Democrats wanted an overhaul or
major changes, while 59 percent of strong Republicans favored significant

changes and 63 percent of voters overall wanted major change. Support among weak or independent Democrats was very similar to the national average.[25] A recent study on campaign finance reform shows that ideology and partisanship are strong predictors of support for reform, with liberals and Democrats much more likely to support constraints on political money than conservatives and Republicans (Grant and Rudolph 2004).

In choosing whether to pursue campaign finance reform, leaders in the Democrat Party faced a dilemma similar to the one Republicans experienced at the turn of the century. Neo-Mugwumps in the party wanted reforms that might hurt the electoral prospects of the party. The party, however, could not lightly ignore a powerful constituency. The reform community could easily discredit the party and undermine its legitimacy among party activists. Indeed, the proreformers represented the views of the most passionately committed partisans; among them were activists who sponsored fund-raisers, knocked on neighbors' doors, and motivated others to support Democrats. These activists tended to be professionals and "idea" elites who shaped public opinion through the news media and advocacy organizations (Judis and Teixeira 2002). To them, soft money, which came increasingly from corporations, challenged their influence within the party, making Democratic leaders more sympathetic to business interests at the expense of progressive causes.

More worrisome for Democratic leaders was the fact that even *their own individual donors* were overwhelmingly in support of reform. Table 4 shows that, among self-identified partisans in the 2002 elections, 90 percent of Democratic donors favored overhauling the campaign finance system, compared with 65 percent for all Democrats. Republican donors were less enthusiastic

TABLE 3. Partisanship and Support for Major Campaign Finance Reform

	2000	N	2002	N
Strong Democrat	66%	286	71%	206
Weak Democrat	52%	217	61%	229
Independent-lean Democrat	56%	216	63%	178
Independent-pure	51%	158	80%	88
Independent-lean Republican	48%	202	60%	173
Weak Republican	47%	184	57%	211
Strong Republican	52%	205	59%	215
Total	54%	1,468	63%	1,300

Source: American National Election Studies 2000 and 2002 (weighted).
Note: Percentages show respondents who believe campaign finance system should be completely overhauled or undergo major changes. The alternative response was minor changes or the status quo.

about reform, with 64 percent wanting significant changes. Previous research on major donors in congressional elections—those who give at least two hundred dollars—demonstrated that Democratic donors look favorably on increased regulation and public subsidies of one kind or another (Francia et al. 2003). Major Republican donors, in contrast, are more supportive of deregulation.

The neo-Mugwump faction within the Democratic Party had much to gain by pushing for a ban on soft money. A soft money ban would weaken the influence of large firms and labor organizations relative to individuals who gave hard money and supported progressive causes through advocacy organizations.[26] At the same time, a ban on soft money ads had the potential to increase the importance of newspaper endorsements, since politicians would need to rely more on free media to gain supporters. The BCRA prohibition on issue advertising was an attempt to diminish the importance of political ads (though it did not work), which are often criticized by progressives for empty messages and emotive appeal. In this criticism they are echoing the disapproval of the Mugwumps in the nineteenth century, who disdained the party spectacles that generated enthusiasm for candidates.[27]

Many party professionals on the Democratic side warned against reforms that might undercut the party's opportunities. They disdained calls to ban soft money because they believed a system with only hard money would favor the Republicans with their broader fund-raising base. Anticipating that Congress might pass the BCRA, Democratic professionals launched a secret effort to channel soft money to nonparty groups even as their elected leaders publicly supported efforts to ban soft money. One Democratic operative admitted, "We would laugh bitterly when we saw Democratic senators on the floor saying, 'Let's get big money out of politics and go back to grass-roots politics'" (Grimaldi and Edsall 2004). Party professionals, like Harold Ickes Jr., realized the Democrats would need to pursue strategies outside the party structure,

TABLE 4. Party Donors and Support for Major Campaign Finance Reform, 2002

	Party Donors	N	All Party Identifiers	N
Democrats	90%	49	65%	612
Republicans	64%	71	59%	599

Source: American National Election Studies 2002 (weighted).

using soft money that would be banned under the BCRA. (Ickes's father, coincidentally, had organized independent campaign operations in support of FDR in the 1930s.) In subsequent chapters, I show that the "outside" strategy was hardly novel for Democrats.

DEMOCRATIC CAMPAIGN ADVANTAGES OF THE BCRA

The second factor pushing Democrats to support the BCRA was for purely partisan advantage. No doubt that the BCRA was a gamble for Democrats because the party benefited from soft money as much as Republicans, but the prohibitionist approach to reform was entirely consistent with its electoral strengths. The laws would encourage the kind of decentralized campaigning that traditionally suited the Democratic Party. This is a theme I take up in greater detail in subsequent chapters. For present purposes, it is sufficient to point out that the Democratic Party has long been reliant on labor unions and other advocacy groups for electioneering. Moreover, the sectional, ethnic, and ideological division in the party has traditionally encouraged congressional candidates to campaign independently from the national party, certainly more so than Republicans. While the soft money ban would take away party funds, it would not prevent the wealthy from donating millions to nonparty committees that could support presidential or congressional candidates.

As the out party in 2004, Democrats knew that an incumbent president and a Republican-led Congress could raise more soft money than they could. The soft money gap would likely grow in 2004 relative to previous years, since the vast majority of soft money contributors were business firms (Apollonio and La Raja 2004, 1134–54). What particularly scared congressional Democrats was the fact that Republicans received roughly 70 percent of all soft money given by corporations in the 1998 elections. In that same year, corporate soft money accounted for three-quarters of Republican soft money, while it provided just under half for Democrats (in 2002, it accounted for more than two-thirds of Republican soft money but only one-third of Democratic soft money).[28] Democrats received more soft money than Republicans from individuals and labor unions. Even though individual labor unions typically gave more soft money than corporations, there were many more corporations than labor unions to give soft money. It was not unrealistic, then, for Democrats to fear that the income gap between the parties would expand if corporate soft money donations became institutionalized. It was believed that a soft money ban would turn off the corporate spigot, but not necessarily the soft money that came from Democratic groups. The latter were less risk averse and more ideologically motivated than corporations; they would find ways to push their money into the system even if party soft money was banned. As it turned out, Democratic strategists were right. Corporations did not try to push soft money into the political system in the 2004 elections after the party ban. Instead, it was mainly pro-Democratic groups such as labor unions, environmental organizations, and other progressive organizations.

Since corporations are typically interested in using donations to gain access to legislators, they would be more reluctant than electorally oriented groups to funnel money outside the party structure for campaign purposes. For an access-oriented donor, the value of giving a contribution to an outside group is considerably lower, since the act is several steps removed from the candidate who ultimately benefits. Ideological partisans, on the other hand, are willing to invest for electoral outcomes. Thus, they have an incentive to contribute soft money to outside groups when asked. Among policy-oriented and ideological partisans, Democrats have greater parity with Republicans. The fact that these contributors can give unlimited amounts to nonparty groups is an advantage for Democrats, with their narrower base of donors (Gais 1996). By banning soft money donations, Democrats understood that corporations—being more risk averse in campaigns than ideological organizations—would avoid trying to reroute money through Republican-leaning 527 organizations. In fact, corporate soft money did dry up, while ideological organizations, particularly on the Democratic side, found alternative nonparty outlets for their money.[29]

Some Democratic consultants and strategists warned party leaders Representative Dick Gephardt (D-MO) and Senator Tom Daschle (D-SD) to avoid passing this bill because it would hurt party prospects. As aspiring presidential candidates, Gephardt and Daschle may have had personal reasons for championing reform, particularly if they understood they could rely on nonparty organizations, such as labor unions, to support them in presidential primaries.[30] But the party leaders also had collective interests at stake. One Democratic insider described Gephardt's basic argument: "We cannot compete any more on soft money. With George Bush in office, Republicans are going to pull away from us and bury us. So Shays-Meehan is critical to us as a party" (Eilperin and Edsall 2001).

As the party out of power, Democrats might also use reform as a campaign issue, putting forth a populist message that the incumbent party is corrupt and building on traditional Democratic campaign themes that Republicans are the party of the rich. In this way, the partisan strategy behind the BCRA was a replay of the Tillman Act of 1907, when Democrats like Tillman were trying to weaken Roosevelt and divide the Republican Party. To be sure, passing the BCRA was a gamble for Democrats in 2002. But like 1907, Democratic leaders understood their party was less reliant on the party organization than Republicans. Pushing for reform was a calculated risk that would not prevent them from mounting effective presidential and congressional campaigns. At the time, the party was making significant gains building up a national constituency of hard money donors, and they could simultaneously exploit soft money through nonparty groups.

From the Democrats' perspective, the ban on soft money might be a larger blow to the cash-dependent Republicans, who rely more heavily on party-based organizing. Since the 1970s the Republicans had assiduously pursued a party-building strategy to grow their state organizations through fund-raising and voter identification projects. As described previously (and demonstrated in subsequent chapters), the campaign operations used by Republicans are typically more hierarchical and centralized than Democratic campaigns. The Republican organization-building strategy is feasible because the party is more cohesive ideologically and culturally than the Democrats (Klinkner 1994; Mayer 1996; Polsby 1983), with shared understandings of party, greater levels of trust, and greater willingness to defer to authority.

Republicans strongly opposed the BCRA precisely because the party had proven to be a successful instrument in regaining majorities. The BCRA, with its constraints on party finances, posed a greater threat to the Republican party-based strategy than the Democratic strategy of "outsourcing." According to one participant in a closed-door GOP meeting a few days before the floor vote, Speaker Dennis Hastert warned his colleagues, "Six people wouldn't be here now if it weren't for soft money" (Eilperin and Dewar 2002). Apparently, the Enron scandal was not sufficient to motivate most Republicans to join in passing a bipartisan bill, even though Enron appeared linked more closely to the Republican administration. President Bush had strong ties with corporate executives such as Ken Lay at the Houston-based company. In order to widen support among Republicans, the BCRA's sponsors offered to increase the individual hard money contribution limits from one thousand dollars to two thousand dollars. Most insiders believed higher hard money limits would benefit Republicans, and indeed an academic study suggested major Republican donors were more willing to increase their contributions if the limits were raised (Brown, Powell, and Wilcox 1995). But the increased hard money limits did not appear to change the position of most Republicans. Indeed, the fact that the vast majority of Republicans refused to support the BCRA, even with the Enron debacle linked to them, suggests further that the scandal theory of reform does not adequately explain how reform occurs.

In reality, there is little evidence that the Enron scandal fueled a strong public groundswell to push members of Congress to support campaign finance reform. Most Americans, in fact, viewed the Enron situation as a debacle for American workers rather than a political scandal. When asked what bothered them most about Enron, 63 percent of Americans said they were most concerned about the financial toll on Enron employees who lost their jobs and retirement savings. At the same time, 13 percent were concerned that executives of a large firm abetted its collapse. Only 9 percent appeared most concerned about the possible favoritism received by Enron through its political contributions to elected officials (*Gallup Poll* Editorial Staff 2002).

To be sure, Americans have overwhelmingly favored new laws to restrict political donations, with a clear majority supporting "campaign finance reform" when asked in the abstract. There is little doubt from public opinion polls that voters generally believe the campaign finance system is corrupt. Indeed, proreform factions can always count on public opinion to be predisposed toward "reform" even in the absence of scandal. But a Gallup Poll several months after the Enron debacle broke shows only a modest increase in support for campaign finance reform. During February 2002, when the Enron scandal dominated the news, support for passing such laws increased slightly from 65 percent in July 2001 (before the scandal broke) to 72 percent (Jones 2002). Paradoxically, support for restricting soft money declined slightly from 76 percent favoring limits in March 2001 to 69 percent after the scandal.

It is also worth pointing out that, while voter support for practically anything labeled "reform" is high, Americans rarely give the campaign finance issue top priority, even in the aftermath of scandal. When asked, "What are the two most important issues that Congress and the President should deal with?" the issue of campaign finance has never exceeded 1 percent in any given year since the question was asked starting in 1998 (*Gallup Poll* 1998–2007). A more sobering finding is that, even as Americans desire reform, they are skeptical that changes in laws would make much of a difference. While the reform debate continued in the shadow of the Enron scandal, more than two-thirds of voters replied that special interests would maintain power in Washington regardless of changes to the campaign finance laws (Public Opinion Online 2002b).

One irony about the passage of the BCRA is that public approval of Congress was increasing *before* reform passed, and it began a steady decline one year

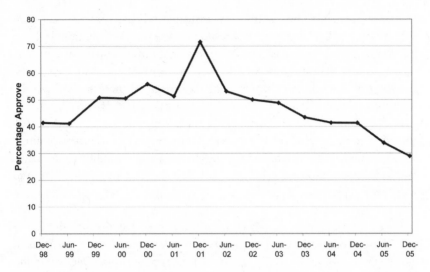

FIG. 3. Do you approve or disapprove of the way Congress is handling its job? (Data from Gallup Polls, various years, "Congress and the Public.")

after reform passed, suggesting that passing a reform law did little to improve American's faith in its governing institutions. As figure 3 shows, both parties achieved a peak in public approval in April 2002, which was six months after the Enron scandal broke and six months before the BCRA was signed into law. After this point, approval declined steeply to its lowest levels during the period under study. This finding suggests that neither scandal nor reform drives public opinion about Congress. Another study by Persily and Lammie uses forty years of survey data to show that trends in public perception of corruption may have little to do with the campaign finance system. In this study, the share of the population describing government as corrupt declined, even as soft money contributions skyrocketed. Instead, it appears that individuals' perceptions of corruption are tied to their socioeconomic status, their opinion of the president, and the performance of the economy (Persily and Lammie 2004, 119–80).

The purpose of showing ambivalent and inconsistent attitudes about reform is not to assert that reform is not necessary or that reform fails to have an effect on reducing corrupt behaviors. There may, in fact, be very good reasons to change the law as a means to reduce opportunities and incentives for elected officials to favor one set of interests over others because of money. While corruption is hard to prove—particularly on roll call votes—a study by

Hall and Wayman shows, at the very least, that moneyed interests can gain helpful access to key lawmakers who respond to political contributions by helping donors in the committee markup process and through their extra involvement in legislation (1990, 797–820). In short, money matters in some instances. But the key point in this chapter is that reform is not necessarily driven by eruptions of public outrage over scandal and incidences of corruption. The public opinion data suggest that there is widespread consensus among Americans that some kind of reform is needed with respect to money in politics, which means that politicians cannot completely ignore the public on this issue. Political insiders, however, can use the broad, if shallow, support for reform to work toward partisan advantage.

In the end, the BCRA was voted along partisan lines, in spite of the title of the bill. The Enron scandal did not compel Republican members of Congress to change their minds. The BCRA passed with the support of the Democrats and a Republican faction of vulnerable incumbents who had few incentives to support strong Republican Party leadership (Moscardelli and Haspel 2007, 79–102). Who were these Republicans, and why did they vote for reform? They were mostly from the Northeast, where the national Republican Party was viewed with skepticism because of its increasing hold by the southern conservative wing of the party (Samples 2006). The northeastern Republicans were fighting to save their own elections in tightly contested districts where liberal Republicans and independent voters—who were especially sensitive to the reform issue—might decide the outcome. Indeed, one of the chief sponsors of the BCRA, Christopher Shays, was typical of this near-extinct breed of Republicans who try to distance themselves from the national party in order to get reelected. Shays received tremendously favorable local press throughout the period he was pressing for reform, being portrayed as David against Goliath in his battles with the Republican Party leadership. His home state newspapers depicted him as a cartoon superhero, calling him "Super Shays," a crusader for reform (Dwyre and Farrar-Myers 2001, 126). Shays's credentials as a reformer who bucked the Republican leadership may have saved him from a national tide against Republicans in the 2006 elections. He is now the lone New England Republican in the U.S. House.

On the Senate side, the party maverick and policy entrepreneur behind reform was John McCain. He promised to help vulnerable Republicans by campaigning in their districts. McCain, of course, was the icon of a Progressive tradition and was popular among independent voters. His efforts to change the campaign finance system would weaken the power of central party leaders and give him greater opportunities to pursue the presidency through his own brand of neo-Progressive politics. At the very least, his championing of reform made him extremely popular in the press, which bolstered his stature and influence in the Senate.

In retrospect, the campaign of 2004 revealed two miscalculations by Democrats in pursing a partisan reform strategy. On the negative side, they underestimated the strength of the Republican organization—even without soft money—in mobilizing voters through party-based networks. The RNC and its state affiliates carried out an intensive precinct-by-precinct GOTV strategy combining volunteers with information technology to produce a modern version of the ward-based canvassing of the machine era. Their efforts outgunned the Democrats in an area that is traditionally a Democratic strength. I say more about this in chapter 6. Meanwhile, Democrats pursued a dual strategy of using both state parties and outside 527 organizations to get out the vote. The BCRA restricted coordination between these two sets of groups, which hurt partisan efforts to get their voters to the polls. According to strategists, efforts were duplicated wastefully in some areas but not pursued at all in places where the partisans failed disastrously to lure Democratic voters to the polls (Lindenfeld 2006).

However, Democrats underestimated how well they would do raising hard money. As I discuss in subsequent chapters, they were able to capitalize on a highly partisan environment to attract additional small donors. For the first time in its history, perhaps, the DNC raised slightly more money than the RNC. It appears that Democrats potentially possess a national constituency of donors as committed as the Republicans. It remains to be seen whether future elections will generate the kind of partisan polarization that mobilizes small party donors. The war in Iraq and the intense dislike that many Democrats have for George W. Bush certainly helped boost contributions to the party in 2004.

In subsequent chapters I show how parties are affected by these back-and-forth partisan efforts to alter campaign finance rules. The thickening of regulations inevitably makes it harder for national committees, candidates, and allied organizations to organize partisans collectively in political campaigns. Instead, parties have incentives to campaign independently from their candidates, while money is simultaneously channeled to less accountable shadow parties called 527 organizations (as I will explain in chapter 6). To be sure, political parties adapt and survive, but the Byzantine regulatory structure weakens parties relative to other groups by imposing costly regulatory burdens uniquely on parties, while providing incentives for wealthy nonparty groups to enter the fray of campaigns. In the end, Democratic leaders who supported reform in 2002— much like Republicans in 1907—calculated that the party could appease an important constituency while possibly gaining electoral advantages. They reluctantly supported reform to shore up legitimacy with an important pro-reform faction in the coalition. Maintaining legitimacy with this constituency was, in fact, a form of guarding an important party resource.

But the Democrats, in supporting reform, inflicted harm on party organizations. This was a choice they made because they understood that Republicans relied more heavily on such organizations. Democrats believed they had a better chance to compete with Republicans under institutional rules that devalued the party committee as a central organizing mechanism. For this reason, they drew on the antipartisan template of Mugwump and Progressive reforms—supplied, of course, by the good government factions that inherited this tradition—which sought to limit the flow of resources to party committees. Subsequent chapters will explain why the two major parties prefer unique institutional rules when it comes to campaign finance and how they adapt differently to such rules.

CHAPTER 5

Consequences of Reform for Party Fund-raising

How have national party committees responded to campaign finance reforms? For most of the twentieth century, national parties were in a weak position to capitalize on the small, voluntary donor system rooted in Progressive-style laws. American parties, which reflect loose coalitions of sectional, ethnic, and class factions, could not generate a national constituency of donors. Hampered further by a confederative structure that kept party power at the subnational level, the national committees remained organizationally weak until late in the twentieth century. The campaign finance laws encouraged and reinforced a decentralized campaign environment in which candidates and interest groups thrived.

To meet the growing financial needs of national campaigns, national party leaders devised ways around campaign finance laws, continuing their reliance on large donors. Presidential candidates were supported by a proliferation of nonparty committees and took greater control over their electoral destinies through personal campaign committees. It was not until much later in the century—in the 1970s—that parties began to attract large numbers of voluntary donors through ideological appeals. At this point, they gained a strong and stable foothold in political campaigns, building organizational influence during the 1990s through soft money contributions and attracting additional hard money supporters in a polarized electoral environment.

Even so, the BCRA in 2002, with prohibitionist constraints on party activity, generated a similar organizational response. As in the past, parties reinvigorated efforts to attract small donors and simultaneously used shadow party groups to supply money from large donors. The national committees have never been in such a strong position to adapt to campaign finance reform. Yet the new law, like previous ones, appears to institutionalize a new campaign vehicle called 527 organizations (so-called because of their tax status under the Internal Revenue Service), which will be in a position to compete with party committees in the future.

The challenge of raising money through the national committees earlier in the century may be explained by classical theory on collective action and incentives for citizens to participate in politics. Though American national parties ultimately succeeded in acquiring sufficient resources from voluntary, small donors, the collective action quandary helps explain why they initially failed to acquire these resources. Parties are well positioned to draw contributions from ideological contributors in the coming years. At the same time, partisans will have strong incentives to pursue electoral goals through nonparty organizations such as 527s.

POLITICAL PARTIES AND THE COLLECTIVE ACTION PROBLEM

Organizations need to attract resources from the surrounding environment to pursue objectives. They seek support from potential members who agree with their objectives by asking them to contribute money, time, or expertise. In return, members expect to benefit from the successful achievement of group goals. Getting individuals to contribute, however, is problematic. Even if individuals share the group's objectives, they may understand that their single contribution to the cause will make little difference on the overall outcome. So long as others contribute, they will receive the benefits of a collective good, which, by definition, cannot be excluded from them. Under these circumstances rational individuals should choose to be free riders and let others pay the costs of collective action. Of course, if all individuals behaved like this, the organization would fail to obtain the necessary resources to provide the collective good.

Mancur Olson (1965) applied the free-rider problem to an analysis of pressure groups, challenging the widely held pluralist assumption among political scientists that common interests among citizens will naturally lead them to organize. Olson explained the difficulty of forming and maintaining groups because rational citizens should choose to avoid making organizational contributions. He noted also that smaller groups tend to have fewer difficulties organizing than larger groups. Not only do large groups face relatively high costs when attempting to organize compared with small groups, but individuals in large groups gain relatively less per capita from successful collective action. Thus, they have fewer incentives to contribute. As a result, large groups are less able to pursue a collective good than small ones because incentives to act are so diffuse among large groups compared to smaller ones. Olson's conclusion that small groups would find it easier to become pressure groups presented an impressive challenge to conventional understandings of majoritarian democracy.

Pushing his analysis further, Olson argued that groups in which members have different levels of resources are more likely to pursue collective action than those that are equal in resources. In small groups with roughly the same number of members, each member has the same incentive to free ride since she or he derives a relatively small benefit from collective action. Among groups with members of mixed sizes, however, there is a strong incentive for the wealthiest or largest members to cover most or all of the costs of organizing, since they accrue the most benefits.[1] In this manner, collective action is achieved even though the smaller, less wealthy members may easily free ride off the large members. Olson calls this arrangement the "exploitation of great by the small" (1965, 29). As the size of the group gets larger, however, it becomes harder for large members to cover all the costs.

Olson offered potential solutions to the collective action problem. First, collective action is typically accompanied by selective incentives to reward contributors or punish noncontributors. With regard to the latter, some organizations possess coercive mechanisms that prevent members from free riding. Trade associations, for example, that confer professional licenses might deny professional standing to those who fail to contribute. Similarly, labor unions have pushed for state laws requiring "closed shops" so that all workers must join the union to get a job. Other, less rigorous, forms of coercion include social pressure to ostracize those who do not contribute. Typically, social pressure works best in small groups, where members can readily observe who gives and who does not, which is one reason why small groups are easier to form.

Without recourse to coercive strategies, group action depends on selective rewards to join because most potential members will not join to achieve the benefit of a collective goal. These selective rewards might include discounts on travel, free car-towing service, or wide access to recreational facilities. Americans, for example, may join the AARP because they want discount drugs or may join the National Rifle Association (NRA) because they will receive free access to gun-related events. By offering selective incentives, groups attract supporters who enable them to pursue a collective mission. This mission, however, is achieved as a *by-product* of offering these selective or particularized incentives, which may be unrelated to the main objectives of the organization.

Political scientist James Q. Wilson suggests there are three kinds of incentives available to induce organizational commitment (1962). The first is the *material* incentive, in which organizational leaders offer individuals money, jobs, or some cash-value benefit in exchange for supporting the party. An alternative way to attract individuals is through *solidary* incentives, which appeal to those who enjoy the social life of an organization or take intrinsic pleasure in the organization's work. Finally, the third kind of incentive is *purposive*. In this case, individuals are attracted to the organization for its ideology or policy goals. These "purists" want to pursue the collective goals of the organization for their own sake. Their strongly held beliefs motivate them to support an organization seeking like-minded goals.

In sum, the collective action problem is significant. It cannot be assumed that citizens will organize even if they have shared interests. Citizens typically require selective incentives to induce them to participate. Otherwise, the organization needs a major patron to bear the costs of collective action. Successful achievement of collective action is easier for small groups, especially when such groups contain a wealthy member willing to bear the majority of costs. This theory of collective action suggests that American political parties—given their large, heterogeneous structure—face formidable tasks when raising campaign money in a system that requires small, voluntary donors.

PARTY RESPONSE TO CAMPAIGN FINANCE LAWS

Parties are not pressure groups, but they face similar obstacles to collective action. They need resources to maintain themselves and run election campaigns. How they acquire resources is a central question for this chapter. Party financial strategies reflect changes in technology, political competition, and societal norms about campaigning. They have also been shaped, in part, by campaign finance laws passed by Congress over the years. Campaign finance laws influence the size and source of contributions to the organization, as well as how parties may spend resources. With each new law, parties begin experimenting with methods to raise and spend money under the new constraints.

In practical terms, parties grapple with the problem of overcoming the free-rider problem in the context of the regulatory environment. Campaign finance laws affect directly or indirectly the quantity and kind of incentives parties might offer to potential contributors. *By regulating the flow of incentives, campaign finance laws influence which groups parties come to rely upon for organizational support.*

Throughout much of the nineteenth century, parties relied financially on local elites to pay for the minimal expenses of staging spectacles around Election Day, such as uniforms, political banners, and decorations (McGerr 1986,12–41). As elections became more expensive over the course of the century, party leaders sought regularized means of acquiring funds. They turned to patronage as a chief source of revenue. In return for receiving a government job from the party, individuals had to contribute funds to the organization. This practice became systematic in parts of the country where party officials automatically dunned a portion of government worker salaries. The "two percent" rule operated famously in places like Philadelphia, where it was estimated in 1913 that 95 percent of the public employees paid an assessment (Pollock 1926, 119; Overacker 1932, 106).

Under the patronage system, the party had few problems acquiring campaign funds. Observed through the lens of Olson's theory, American parties overcame the collective action problem by rewarding followers with material incentives in the form of jobs. Given the local nature of the patronage system, it was relatively easy for party leaders to monitor whether rank-and-file activists helped the party through cash contributions or door-to-door campaigning.

Then came Mugwump civil service reforms in the 1880s. At the federal level, the Pendleton Act of 1883 began a merit system for civil service whose expansion limited the availability of political spoils for ardent party supporters. Similar reforms spread to states and municipalities around the same time. Party leaders could no longer rely chiefly on patronage to encourage the rank and file to help the organization and its candidates. Parties looked elsewhere for resources. The problem was made more acute because election costs were escalating as campaigns relied less on local spectacle and more on expensive mass advertising. As described in chapter 2, Mugwumps successfully established a norm against ritual displays of party pageantry, which put a premium on campaigning through newspapers, leaflets, and other forms of mass persuasion. The transition proved expensive: national parties needed large literary bureaus and had to pay for advertising for newspapers and billboards.[2]

Paradoxically, the good government ideas promulgated by Mugwumps encouraged parties to turn toward a strategy of seeking money from wealthy patrons. These patrons were affiliated with the corporate trusts, or they were individuals made wealthy by the new industrial economy. Such patrons, according to Mancur Olson, were willing to bear significant costs of organizing because they expected a larger share of benefits. In 1896, the new corporate elite expected much from having their favored party control office. Mark Hanna, chair of the RNC and architect of the McKinley campaign, raised money by exploiting fears in the manufacturing and banking sectors that Democrats would remove tariffs under William Jennings Bryan.

Party reliance on corporate patrons lasted several elections until the Tillman Act of 1907. The Tillman Act prevented parties from accepting funds from the corporate treasury, but wealthy donors could continue to make contributions. A few years later, publicity laws championed by Progressives discouraged large donations from wealthy individuals.[3] The publicity laws were a classic Progressive solution to the problems of money in politics: provide the public with information to assess the relationship between parties and political contributors. Once "sunshine" revealed improper behavior to impartial observers, the perpetrators would be punished at the ballot box or shamed into changing their practices to fit societal norms of decency.

The publicity laws were the first steps toward institutionalizing the role of the small, voluntary donor. Public disclosure made wealthy contributors reluctant to give large sums directly to parties and encouraged parties to turn toward a broader audience for financial support. This behavior is precisely what Progressives desired. Financial disclosure policies furthered the Progressive ideal of participationist democracy through incentives for political actors to seek small donations. The iconic citizen for Progressives was the disinterested individual of modest means willing to support causes that merited his esteem.

American political parties, however, were not well suited to a new norm that emphasized small, voluntary donors. From their origins, they had been skeletal organizations controlled by a small, established leadership. As cadre parties, and unlike European parties, they lacked mass memberships that might pay regular dues. Rather than rely on ideological members or affiliated organizations, such as labor unions, American parties used their control over nominations and material benefits to attract contributions. To be sure, the two major American parties have always been ideologically distinct (Gerring 1998), but policy differences were not the firmest basis for establishing partisan loyalties in the electorate or among elites. The fact that contributors were motivated to give for reasons other than ideology gave party leaders considerable discretion in policy matters. As their access to patronage shrank and their ability to control nominations declined (due to the direct primary), party leaders lost control over the traditional incentives they offered followers.

The alternative for American parties was to follow the European model and pursue mass memberships as a way of supporting themselves. Party scholar Maurice Duverger predicted this would happen (1954). The European model, however, required that parties be more ideological than American parties had ever been. American parties have traditionally focused on broad governing principles rather than issue-specific agendas that attract ideological supporters. From their inception, American parties exploited the presence of local elite networks rather than attempt to create a strong organization at the national level. Thus, parochial issues and personalities dominated the earliest local parties, even as their supporters campaigned for national personalities in presidential elections. The presidential elections provided the ever malleable but sticky glue that ultimately held the parties together.

In addition to localism, strong sectionalism divided major parties, making it difficult to pursue a coherent national program. Democrats from the South have been more conservative than their northern counterparts. Cultural and economic differences among Republicans in the East and West have also been difficult to bridge. Nonetheless, parties survived as grand coalitions. Success depended on muting ideological components and rallying constituencies around historically important issues. Rather than focus on a particular set of national issues, local party leaders might mobilize partisans through unique appeals to social identities of ethnicity, class, and region. During presidential nominations, state-based party leaders brokered deals among locally based factions and nationally recognizable social groups. In this way, American parties were successful institutions for creating grand compromises. But they were poorly suited for raising money from a mass membership base.

Democrats especially have struggled to acquire a national constituency of donors. Traditionally they have been more fragmented and diverse than Republicans. Indeed, the Democratic Party—or, more precisely, parties— thrived on the local character of politics, from its urban machines to its personality-driven factions in the South. As politics became less local, less an emotionally charged spectacle, their rivals, the Republicans, the party of the middle class, benefited. Not only were the Republicans less divided ideologically, but culturally the Republican organization was infused with a no-nonsense business style amenable to raising money efficiently.

In the wake of Progressive laws, there have been two characteristic responses by both major political parties. First, they have made earnest efforts to cultivate small donors to compensate for the loss of patrons and to ensure their legitimacy among a burgeoning middle class. Second, parties have consistently complemented these efforts with loophole strategies to get money from large donors as Election Day approached. The most common approach was to decentralize fund-raising through shadow party organizations. Instead of giving to the national committees, the wealthy could contribute to numerous political committees set up by party leaders, which were exempt from the Tillman Act; publicity laws; and, much later, laws such as the BCRA of 2002. Both parties also relied heavily on debt financing. I will elaborate on these strategies later.

In parallel with campaign finance laws, other Progressive-based laws at the turn of the century accelerated fragmented campaigning, which helped institutionalize a candidate-centered system. The direct primary and the long ballot gave candidates the incentive to create their own donor networks and run campaigns apart from the party. Personal appeals for contributions from the candidate were more successful than impersonal party letters requesting a donation, particularly as party loyalties waned. Interest groups were well suited to the task of recruiting small donors in this environment. They were smaller and more homogenous than parties. Consequently, it was easier for them to coerce contributions (through social pressure) and appeal to members based on material or ideological goals. These groups preferred to give directly to the candidates as a way of building personal relationships and bypassing the filter of the party organization. Thus, the small donor system has encouraged greater pluralism and organizational fragmentation in the financing of politics.

The national parties were not in a strong position to develop viable small donor operations until later in the twentieth century. American parties could not take advantage of the nationalizing of politics—they were too loosely structured, given federalism and local party traditions. Campaign finance laws were an additional impediment holding them back. The regulations made it difficult to centralize operations nationally and created opportunities for individual candidates and other groups to prospect for donors. Indeed, one prominent study in the early 1960s was doubtful that parties could ever raise money from small donors, explaining that "the primitiveness of party organization in America, the lack of communication and sanctions, the absence of emotional appeal and tax incentives for the giver, plus the likelihood that other and easier (if less theoretically pure) money-raising techniques are available to the parties— given all these facts, the national committees cannot hope to be supported soon, or perhaps ever, entirely by small contributions" (Cotter and Hennessy 1964, 186).

Paradoxically, about the time this was written parties began to improve their capacity to raise money from small donors. They benefited from the sifting out of party ideologies, abetted by the civil rights movement and domestic migration to the South and West. They also possessed new technologies, such as computers and direct mail, to identify and reach potential donors. As Democratic supporters became more liberal across policy issues and Republicans more conservative, the party organizations could make successful ideological appeals to a wider national audience. Impersonal appeals—through direct mail, advertising, and telephones—are most successful with ideological donors (Brown, Powell, and Wilcox 1995; Francia et al. 2003). Ironically, the "nonpartisan" Progressive-style reforms made parties increasingly reliant on ideologically based fund-raising. The Progressive-style regulatory emphasis on small, voluntary donors puts a premium on attracting members through purposive, policy-driven incentives. In the next section, I explain more specifically how parties responded to periodic bursts of campaign finance reforms.

PARTY FUND-RAISING, 1907–74

The Publicity Acts passed in 1910 and 1911 had the effect of encouraging parties to seek small, voluntary donors for the first time. The acts required treasurers of all political committees trying to influence the presidential election in two or more states to submit financial reports to the clerk of the House after the election. In practice, this statute applied only to national party committees. As a consequence, in the election of 1912, the RNC and DNC submitted reports with the names and addresses of all contributors who gave more than $100 ($1,750 in 2004 dollars).[4] The glare of publicity made several traditional major donors shun the party. In response, party officials created new committees that allowed donors to divide their donations among them, making it look as if they gave less to the national committees. By 1916, this practice became common, with nearly $1 million raised and spent by shadow party committees to support Woodrow Wilson or Charles Evan Hughes. These committees included the Woodrow Wilson Independent League; the Wilson Business Men's Alliance League; the National Hughes Alliance; and, the largest one, the Republican National Publicity Committee, which, as its name implies, was intended to finance campaign advertising (Pollock 1926, 56).

While parties continued to rely on large donors, they inaugurated small donor drives. Both the RNC and DNC started "membership" fees ranging from $1 to $10, which was a strategy that may have been borrowed from European parties (Pollock 1926, 67–69). Membership fees brought in little money, and both the major parties ended up in debt, even though election spending in 1912 was low compared to previous elections. Ironically, the Progressive candidate for the Republican nomination, Robert La Follette, learned firsthand the difficulties of mounting a campaign by simply passing the hat during speeches. Even "Fighting Bob" had to rely on large donors. More than 80 percent of his funds came from just four men, all of whom gave more than $185,000 (in 2004 dollars) (Overacker 1932, 123).

In the 1916 election, Democrats, under the leadership of DNC chair William D. Jamieson, began an unprecedented letter-writing campaign to gather small donors. The "Jamieson Plan" may have been the first direct mail effort in American campaigns. The DNC compiled names and addresses of potential donors on 400,000 index cards, including suggested amounts to solicit from each individual (Pollock 1926, 69–70). The party fell well short of its goal to obtain one million contributors. Even worse, the DNC had spent as much on letter writing as they took in. The expensive project required 150 clerks, taking up three floors of a Washington office building, using 125 state-of-the-art typewriters over a four-month period preceding the election. Under the Jamieson Plan, the party ended up critically short of funds for Wilson's reelection campaign. In the end, the president relied on last-minute contributions from his old Princeton roommates (Shannon 1959, 40–41). These friends also paid off the party debt of $650,000 at the end of the campaign.

The Publicity Acts encouraged Democrats to rely on debt financing in subsequent elections as well. Since the party was not capable of acquiring sufficient campaign funds through relatively small donors, they took out large loans to finance much of the campaign. These loans were paid off postelection by major party donors. Under the Publicity Acts, parties did not have to disclose the names of those who made loans or financed their debts, which allowed them to continue relying primarily on large contributions.

If the direct mail strategy seemed untenable for gathering small donors (at least at this point in time), the RNC developed an alternative in 1920 that held greater promise, though it did not fill party coffers. From their experiences during World War I raising funds for the Red Cross and Liberty Loans, Republican leaders recognized the effectiveness of the *personal* solicitation and went about building an infrastructure that would make it feasible. Applying their civic model to politics, they established a layered network of "ways and means committees" to raise money outside the formal party structure.[5] Republican finance committees were set up in each state under the aegis of the national party. Below the state level were county and city committees, run by a chairman and vice chairman (always a woman), who identified and solicited donors through personal networks. Money from these finance committees would flow up to the national party, where officials would allocate a negotiated amount to state and local organizations. The RNC strategy required extraordinary coordination among different levels of the party and a degree of deference toward the national party leadership, which appeared completely absent in the Democratic Party. Indeed, chroniclers of party finance over the years report fierce resistance by local Democratic parties to any nationally based strategies for raising money (Heard 1960; Overacker 1932).

RNC chair Will Hays made the fateful promise in 1920 that all contributions to the Republican Party would be held to under $1,000 ($8,600 in 2004 dollars). The consequence of holding the line at $1,000 meant that the RNC did not raise sufficient funds for the election and generated the largest debt in its history of $1.5 million ($13 million in 2004 dollars). The party ended up turning to megadonors to defray the loans. One of these megadonors was Henry S. Sinclair, an oil operator, who gave the party $360,000 to pay off debts. Sinclair established dummy contributors and devised a convoluted scheme of selling bonds to hide that the contributions came from him. He also made large personal "loans" to the secretary of the interior, Albert Fall. One of the biggest scandals in presidential history ensued when the public learned that the Harding administration, through the Department of Interior, had leased federal oil reserves in Teapot Dome, Wyoming, to Sinclair without a competitive bid. The scandal appeared to motivate Congress to pass the FCPA of 1925, which did not change election accounting practices substantially.

In 1924, the RNC relied less on local ways and means committees but continued to support a centrally controlled finance apparatus that operated in parallel with state and local party organizations. To complement locally raised funds, Republicans tapped business executives in various industries to seek funds from colleagues (Pollock 1926, 77–78). This business sector approach allowed Republican businessmen to use their social and financial ties to pressure fellow corporate executives for political contributions. The sector strategy was a harbinger of future PACs, through which companies or trade associations raised political funds from individuals.

Democrats struggled unsuccessfully through the 1910s and 1920s to raise money in small amounts. Convinced that they were the party of the common man, they tried reaching voters through newspaper ads and radio appeals. While parties gained additional small donors with every subsequent election cycle, they continued to rely on super donors to pay off the large debts at the end of the campaign. As table 5 shows, indebtedness at the close of the campaign was common for the Democrats.[6] In 1916 their debts soared to almost $11 million (in 2004 dollars) even though Overacker reports that the DNC more than doubled the number of contributors to 170,000 from the previous election. In 1928, they faced an unprecedented deficit of $17.5 million (in 2004 dollars).

In addition to debt financing, the Publicity Acts and the FCPA encouraged the proliferation of nonparty committees. The campaign finance laws did not apply to political committees established in only one state. In practice, this meant that the national parties were the only committees, excepting congressional candidates, that were regulated under the law.[7] Although the FCPA of 1925 altered the Publicity Acts to require state affiliates of national associations to file reports, most political committees simply ignored or refused to report their finances, claiming their activities were "educational" rather than electioneering. Churches claimed exemptions from the FCPA, as well as Prohibition associations such as the Anti-Saloon League, which had close ties to church organizations. The FCPA also turned a blind eye toward committees that spent money on behalf of congressional candidates. Under the rules, House candidates were allowed to spend five thousand dollars and Senate candidates twenty-five thousand dollars. Not only could candidates easily exploit legal exemptions on broad categories of spending to get around these limits, but they benefited from unrestricted in-kind expenditures by outside groups and individuals. Candidates were not liable for outside spending if it was done without their knowledge. This interpretation of the FCPA had a lasting legacy called "independent" expenditures, enshrined by the Supreme Court decision *Buckley v. Valeo* (1976) and subsequent rulings, which permitted noncandidate committees to spend unlimited amounts to support or oppose candidates so long as they did not coordinate activity with the candidate.

TABLE 5. DNC Debts at End of Presidential Campaign, 1912–28

	Total Debt (nominal dollars)	Total Debt (2004 dollars)
1912	48,000	905,660
1916	632,000	10,896,552
1920	272,364	2,569,472
1924	261,938	2,878,440
1928	1,600,000	17,582,418

Source: Data from Overacker 1932.

The weakness of the FCPA was highlighted in the first election after its implementation. The 1928 Democratic candidate, Al Smith, the first Catholic presidential candidate and a "wet," stimulated strong opposition from Protestant groups and Prohibition supporters. These nonparty groups spent heavily to oppose Smith's candidacy. A sampling of these organizations and their expenditures was compiled by Louise Overacker and is shown in table 6 (Overacker 1932, 165).

The polarized campaign of 1928 also encouraged a record number of small contributions to the parties. But even so, the RNC and DNC continued to rely on a few large donors. To ensure ample funds from the wealthy for the Democrats, Al Smith tapped several millionaires to serve on the DNC finance committee, including its chair, a top executive at General Motors (Shannon 1959, 51). In the end, just four men financed most of the Democratic candidate's election and helped pay the $1.6 million postelection debt.[8]

The two Hatch Acts in 1940 and 1941 were the most influential pieces of legislation affecting the national committees. Hatch I prohibited federal administrative officials from engaging in elections or nominating efforts for the president. Along with the Ramspeck Act of 1940, which brought unclassified federal workers (those not under civil service or competitive exam positions) under civil service provisions forbidding partisan activity, the anti–New Deal coalition in Congress effectively tried to thwart the emergence of a national political machine under Roosevelt. Thus, it prohibited any kind of federal worker from participating in or contributing to presidential or congressional nominations and elections (see Milkis 1993, 133–40).[9] In this way, Democrats—President Roosevelt, in particular—were prevented from exploiting new sources of fed-

TABLE 6. Outside Spending in the 1928 Presidential Campaign

	Millions of 2004 Dollars
Campaign Committee of the Anti-Saloon League	1.90
Hoover for President Engineers Committee	1.10
National Democratic Constitutional Committee (anti-Smith)	0.90
Anti-Smith Democrats	0.40
National Women's Committee for Hoover	0.90
Association against Prohibition Amendment	5.20
Citizens Committee of Illinois (pro-Smith)	2.80
Independent Citizens Committee	3.30

Source: Data from Overacker 1932.

eral patronage through burgeoning agencies created by the New Deal. Hatch II extended the ban on political activity to state and local workers who were paid, in part, through federal programs. As a ploy to kill the legislation, Democrats proposed caps on party expenditures at $3 million and limits on individual contributions of five thousand dollars (sixty-five thousand dollars in 2004 dollars) to political committees engaged in presidential elections (Overacker 1946, 27). Since Democrats relied less on a national fund-raising apparatus than Republicans, they believed these measures would inflict greater harm on Republicans. Indeed, Democrats were fortunate in benefiting considerably from the organizational muscle of labor unions to mobilize voters on their behalf. In the end, the Republicans called the Democrats' bluff and accepted the poison pills.

The RNC and DNC paid dearly for the Hatch Acts. Louise Overacker believed the Hatch Acts were disastrous for the parties and for promoting public disclosure of political money. The $3 million cap was unrealistically low, as both parties had spent well over this ceiling in previous campaigns. This was also a period in which campaigns turned increasingly to expensive radio broadcasts in campaigns, which meant that parties would need even more money than in previous decades.

The party spending caps spurred the rapid growth of outside spending in campaigns by interest groups and party surrogates. According to Overacker, "[u]ntil 1940 . . . the national party committees were assuming more responsibility for the collection and distribution of funds, a trend toward centralization which greatly facilitated the assembling of pertinent information." She lamented that reformers chose to emphasize impracticable prohibitions backed by criminal sanctions rather than emphasize requirements for better public disclosure of political financing (Overacker 1946, 25–48). The decentralizing consequences of this strategy were predictable.

The $5,000 contribution limit could be easily evaded by wealthy donors who chose to split contributions among several committees and use the names of other family members to make contributions. The Pew family—the very same family that established a charitable trust that would eventually finance much of the campaign reform efforts in the 1990s—listed a total of $164,000 ($2.2 million in 2004 dollars) from a dozen different members. The Rockefellers did likewise (Overacker 1946, 35).[10] Since federal contribution limits did not apply to state parties or independent committees, donors could give unlimited amounts to these organizations.

The Hatch Act forced the RNC to abandon joint fund-raising committees with state organizations. Instead, Republican leaders established state finance committees that were legally detached from the national parties. In practice these organizations were still controlled by national leaders, but the legal separation undoubtedly complicated campaign coordination. With less coordination and fund-raising by national committees, state political parties turned increasingly to large fund-raising dinners. Among Democrats, Jefferson-Jackson dinners for state parties assumed a new level of prominence (Heard 1960, 233–45). Because national parties lacked sufficient funds, some state parties began to operate like national parties by funneling money to targeted swing states. The North Carolina Democratic Party, for example, transferred $100,000 to the New Jersey Democratic Party in the final days of the 1944 campaign to pay for radio ads in support of FDR. Previously, transfers of this amount were typically discharged through the national committees.

The appropriately named Hatch Act also spawned a profusion of organizations dedicated solely to presidential candidates, anticipating a future in which candidates rather than parties would dominate campaigns. According to Overacker, Willkie groups in 1940 "sprang up like mushrooms," and similar groups emerged to support Roosevelt (1946, 33). The trend toward independent groups intensified in the subsequent 1944 election. Overacker estimated that Dewey benefited from $13 million ($140 million in 2004 dollars) in campaign support, yet just $3 million ($32 million in 2004 dollars) came directly from the RNC, as required by law. The balance came from an assorted list of state parties, party-sponsored finance committees, and independent groups. Dewey, for example, received support from new organizations with opaque names such as the People's Committee to Defend Life Insurance and Savings or strongly conservative groups such as the National Association of Pro-America.

Prior to the Hatch Act, Roosevelt had nurtured a personal constituency of major donors through the "One Thousand Club," whose members gave at least one thousand dollars to his reelection. This presidential fund-raising committee became especially important because the DNC could no longer raise money by selling advertisements in the profitable book of the Democratic convention. The Hatch Act banned political committees at the national level from selling goods or advertisements to corporations or persons. More than half of funds raised by Roosevelt through the One Thousand Club paid for radio ads.

The One Thousand Club flourished because it was based on a *personal* appeal from the president of the United States. Members had opportunities to meet with FDR or attend White House–sponsored functions. Decades later, the Clinton administration would be harshly criticized for inviting major donors to White House teas and Lincoln bedroom sleepovers. Then, as now, donors were made to feel as if they belonged to an inner coterie of advisers. The incentive to contribute was based mostly on *solidary* motives—the sense of being important and taking pleasure in the activity itself. Under FDR, the White House also sought to exploit material or purposive incentives, depending on the nature of the constituency. Campaign advisers such as Harold Ickes helped organize occupation-based political committees, particularly among groups reflecting the New Deal coalition.[11] These included the Social Workers Non-Partisan Committee for Roosevelt and the Serviceman's Wives to Re-elect Roosevelt (Overacker 1946). Members of the Hollywood Democratic Committee, who were often entertainers and artists, were more likely motivated by purposive rather than material motives.

At this time, the groups that mattered most for Democrats were labor unions. The Hatch Act strengthened their position in the New Deal coalition by making Democrats more reliant on labor union electioneering. New Deal policies had made economic cleavages more salient, putting labor interests firmly in the Democratic Party. Led by the militant unionists, such as United Mine Workers president John L. Lewis and Amalgamated Clothing Workers president Sidney Hillman, labor unions were eager to help Democrats get elected. Occasionally, they were even willing in primaries to challenge anti–New Deal Democrats who might oppose prolabor policies. While labor groups typically focused on congressional elections where efforts might easily tip the electoral balance, they also helped the Roosevelt campaign. In 1936, they made large political contributions to advertise their support for Democrats. In subsequent elections, they invested more heavily in mobilizing members for the presidential contests (Overacker 1946; Heard 1960).

A strengthening labor movement operating outside the party structure created lasting tensions within the Democratic coalition and stirred support among Republicans for campaign reforms (Heard 1960, 186). In 1943, Congress passed the Smith-Connally Act to challenge labor union power. The act was ostensibly aimed at preventing strikes during wartime, but it also prevented labor unions from making political contributions in federal elections. Labor unions adapted quickly. Their unique organizational structure allowed them to raise "voluntary" contributions easily for a separate PAC. Applying old-fashioned social pressure, local leaders and shop stewards pressed members to give one dollar contributions to the new PAC by posting names of donors at union halls or publicly shaming those who refused to contribute (Heard 1960).

The first official PAC began in July 1943, sponsored by the CIO. It was funded by contributions of members from seven unions.[12] Sidney Hillman, who ran the PAC, was masterful at taking advantage of campaign finance laws. Since primaries were not covered under the FCPA, he used general treasury funds during this period to support the Roosevelt-Truman ticket. In the general election, he switched to PAC money. The CIO PAC, however, continued to use general treasury funds for political canvassing and fund-raising. Hillman claimed—like leaders of nonparty groups before and after him—that this kind of spending should not be covered by campaign finance laws. These activities were said to be either administrative or educational. Furthermore, he argued, to the degree that union spending was *political*—and did not *directly* finance a candidate's election campaign—it should be protected under the First Amendment (Hillman 1944, 5–58). Hillman's strategies are remarkably similar to those employed in contemporary elections under the BCRA. In recent elections, interest groups have changed the sources and uses of funding depending on the timing of an activity before an election and the nature of electoral activities.[13]

Members of Congress who opposed labor did not accept Hillman's argument that his activities did not directly support candidates, particularly Senator Robert Taft, who felt the strong bite of labor union organizing against him in his reelection. Taft argued that it was only fair that labor unions operate under the same rules as corporations (Mutch 1988, 155–57). Ignoring the constitutional principle regarding associational rights, his reasoning appeared based on a weak "equality" syllogism: corporations have been regulated because they are powerful institutions; labor unions are now powerful institutions; therefore, labor unions should be treated like corporations. But unlike corporations, which are not necessarily constituted by members, labor unions *are* associations of individuals. Members of labor unions pool their individual resources in the union treasury to pursue common objectives; thus, it makes little sense that labor unions should be forced to set up separate PACs to engage in political activities when members have already chosen to give the union a portion of their income to achieve mutual goals.

Nonetheless, after the war Congress passed the Taft-Hartley Labor Management Relations Act (1947), which made the Smith-Connally ban on labor union contributions permanent and extended the prohibition to political expenditures. As a result, labor unions institutionalized their PAC strategies. Since PAC contributions were legally distinct from labor union funds, they could be used for contributions to federal candidates or any *direct* campaign activity in federal elections. At the same time, labor unions continued spending general treasury funds (collected through union dues) on activities that only *indirectly*—

but substantially—affected elections, such as "educational" expenditures to sponsor registration drives, GOTV campaigns, and printing of the voting records of legislators. One effect of using PACs as intermediaries was to further discourage unions from funding political parties directly, as had been done in Great Britain and other democracies. Instead, labor unions were encouraged to make political contributions to individual candidates through their PACs, while spending greater sums independently on "indirect" election activity to help favored candidates. Over the long term, the PAC innovation became institutionalized as a permanent vehicle to give money to candidates. Much to the chagrin of the labor movement, business interests exploited the use of PACs in the 1970s to make political contributions. In the past three decades, the sum of political contributions made by business-related PACs to congressional candidates has far outstripped that of labor union PACs.[14]

The series of campaign finance laws between 1940 and 1947—Hatch, Smith-Connally, and Taft-Hartley—helped consign national committees to the periphery of campaigns in the 1950s and 1960s. National committees were poor vehicles for amassing and coordinating campaign resources in presidential elections, while "voluntary" committees organized around presidential candidates became prominent. Eisenhower was the ideal candidate to take advantage of voluntary committees in 1952 and 1956. As a centrist from outside party ranks, he was attractive to those in the rapidly growing middle class who shunned traditional partisan appeals. Voluntary organizations for Eisenhower raised and spent the majority of funds in his campaigns. To be sure, Republican Party leaders controlled many of these groups. This was demonstrated by the frequency and patterns of transfers among Republican Party organizations and voluntary groups (Heard 1960, 299). But the coordination costs were high, and many voluntary amateur groups fiercely resisted taking orders from the RNC (Lawrence 1952). Not surprisingly, coordination between voluntary groups was less apparent among Democratic partisans. Committees in support of Adlai Stevenson (the Illinois governor who headed the Democratic ticket in 1952 and again in 1956) appeared much more independent from the local, state, and national party organizations. Unlike the Republicans, they rarely received funds from the party and only occasionally made contributions to the party.[15]

The postwar patterns of party response to tightening campaign finance restrictions were becoming increasingly clear. The Democrats, as the more heterogeneous party, organized around their candidates and operated in an environment in which partisans were loosely connected. Not only did Democratic presidential candidates rely more heavily on organizations outside the party structure, such as labor unions, but these organizations were less well integrated into the formal party structure than were their Republican counterparts. Republican partisans tended to work together more closely with efforts coordinated by the national party committee.

The difference between the two parties in their pursuit of campaign dollars could not have been starker. Taking advantage of greater unity, Republicans established dense networks of finance committees in the states, which supported activities for all levels of the party. At the national level, congressional and national party committees shared fund-raising files, a practice that continues to this day. Republicans also borrowed strategies from philanthropic organizations, classifying prospects by occupation or residency and according to their ability to pay. Alexander Heard observed that "a visitor to the headquarters of a well-organized Republican finance committee senses the same atmosphere that pervades a giant philanthropic drive" (1960, 222). These adaptations could only be possible in a milieu in which activists and leaders shared beliefs, experiences, and norms.

In contrast, Democratic fund-raising for national elections was more informal, ad hoc, and even "frenzied" (Alexander 1972). Local Democratic Party leaders would not tolerate separate finance committees established by higher echelons of the party. They were reluctant to allow national party elites to solicit among potential local donors. As a result, the DNC became more reliant on the generosity of the state parties to contribute to the national fund. The results were akin to the national government's experience under the Articles of Confederation. The DNC was reduced to begging for state parties to fill their quotas (Heard 1960, 282–317; Cotter and Hennessy 1964, 173–91).

National committeemen from the states were expected to raise funds for the DNC, but, surprisingly, many of these members did not have strong ties to party fund-raisers back home (Heard 1960, 289). Instead, the DNC tended to appoint treasurers who used personal friendships to establish a core group of major donors. This nucleus changed from cycle to cycle because of turnover in the party leadership. Indeed, the disorganization was such that major donors and solicitors appeared unsure whether they were part of the DNC team from year to year. According to Alexander Heard, "A loose kind of Democratic national finance committee of 75 to 100 donors and solicitors has usually existed on paper, though, when queried, some of the listed members have not been sure whether they were on the committee or not, and what they were supposed to do if they were" (1960, 227).

Scholars studying campaign finance, like Heard, Overacker, and Alexander, were mystified by the Democratic failure to improve and stabilize fund-raising. Heard attributed the failure primarily to the party not having a business constituency. But the Democratic weakness stemmed less from lacking a unique cash constituency and more from simply having too many constituencies. Democratic coalitions have been too unwieldy to sustain a national constituency of regular donors that could support a strong national organization. Given the ideological and cultural gulf among Democratic groups throughout much of the twentieth century—southerners, ethnics, farmers, and union members—the party could not hope to attract enthusiasm for contributing to a national-level committee. Instead loyalties remained local and changed depending on the attractiveness of particular presidential candidates to these various groups. Consequently, political resources remained at the local level, with a machine organization that might rely on patronage and social ties to ensure adequate campaign resources. Pace Democratic Speaker Thomas "Tip" O'Neil, money in politics was local, especially so for Democrats. The ideological constituencies that might support the party organization instead gave money to like-minded groups, such as the National Committee for an Effective Congress. Overcoming the collective action problem to attract voluntary donors at the national level required a degree of internal organizational consistency that eluded Democrats during much of their history.

For this reason, the DNC often turned to ad hoc gimmicks to raise money. These included last-minute appeals for cash from wealthy donors and expensive dinners when state parties failed to fill their quotas. The political dinner became an essential fund-raising vehicle for Democrats in the post–New Deal era. While dinners had always been social affairs for party elites, they expanded outside this core to attract donor constituencies. The success of dinners depended on the personal appeal of candidates and social pressure to support the organization, much like raising money for philanthropic associations.[16] In combination with dinners, Democrats relied on selling advertisements in the party convention books that were sold at dinners and other events. Indeed, a major portion of party funds came from selling corporate advertising through the book of the Democratic convention.

The Democrats had not given up entirely on finding small donors. The party made occasional, if futile, attempts to generate small donors throughout the mid-twentieth century. In 1952, for example, they tried the "Ruml Plan." Beardsley Ruml, DNC finance chair, wanted to reach people who had never been asked to give or had never considered giving.[17] Ruml inaugurated a "Five-Dollar Certificate Plan" that asked local party workers to sell certificates of membership for the Democratic Party. The DNC anticipated receiving 60 percent on sales of $12.5 million. In the end, the party netted only $218,000 from sales of $600,000, providing just 10 percent of total DNC receipts. Heard attributed failure to lack of technical staff to carry the plan out and disagreement among local and national party officials about who would receive most of the revenues.

The Ruml Plan, however, revealed concretely the difficulty in raising money directly for the DNC. Local party officials were never invested in the plan since they did not want a rival operation cutting into their own fund-raising. The most successful promoters of the plan were, in fact, the amateur volunteers rather than the party professionals (Heard 1960, 250–56). The certificate plan was dropped in subsequent years, though the DNC followed up with the less ambitious "Dollars for Democrats" in 1956, and, like the RNC and successful state parties, it developed a "Sustaining Fund" to attract dues-paying membership of major donors (Epstein 1958).

Republicans began using direct mail programs after Eisenhower's first election. Initially, however, they did not raise much money through these impersonal solicitations. The turning point came during the Goldwater campaign of 1964, when the RNC experienced a sharp rise in small donors. Goldwater was an ideological candidate who attracted strong support among conservative partisans. These donors preferred giving to Goldwater or the RNC because they did not trust local Republican parties, which might support more moderate candidates (Alexander 1972). Direct mail fund-raising from the more ideological members of the party was such a success that the RNC had surplus funds after the election. Learning from this experience, the new RNC chair, Ray C. Bliss, institutionalized a direct mail program that would grow over the years, nurtured by subsequent chairs. He also increased the party's emphasis on the Republican Sustaining Fund (contributors who gave ten dollars per year), which covered daily costs of running the RNC outside of election periods. Bliss wanted the party to have a steady source of funds year-round to run the organization. Rather than have the RNC rely on the generosity of state parties, he turned to a national constituency of small and medium donors that grew out of the conservative movement in the Republican Party.[18]

Unlike their counterparts, Democrats did not institutionalize fund-raising during a period in which they dominated government. Presidents John Kennedy and Lyndon Johnson continued to rely on large donors through the President's Club, which was the old Roosevelt strategy to rope in major donors through personal appeals. Kennedy, of course, benefited from his family wealth during his election campaign. Nevertheless, he was sufficiently concerned about political financing to establish a presidential commission on campaign finance.[19] This commission, however, withered under LBJ. As president, Johnson may have assumed that his method of personal solicitation from wealthy Texans during his Senate leadership would carry over to the White House. But this strategy became untenable in the wake of media scrutiny on Bobby Baker, a former Johnson staffer who created a business empire through his political connections.[20]

In 1968, the DNC took out a large loan to finance direct mail appeals for donors. But the effort to imitate Republicans was poorly timed. The party was split by the Vietnam War and the civil rights movement, and partisans looked to individual candidates to champion their causes. Ad hoc fund-raising appeared unavoidable for Democrats.

Regrettably for Democrats, they were operating in a milieu in which campaign cash appeared increasingly valuable relative to traditional "shoe leather" GOTV efforts organized by labor unions. Starting in the 1960s election costs soared with the increased emphasis on television advertising. Unsurprisingly, Democrats began calling for public funding of presidential elections, as they were drowning in debt. But all too characteristically, the Democrats had difficulty crafting a public financing law that satisfied all of the party constituencies. They fought especially over the question of who should receive the public funds. Senator Russell Long's plan in 1966 gave subsidies to the parties, which President Johnson favored. Senator Robert Kennedy and others, including labor union leaders, refused to go in this direction. Kennedy did not want to strengthen an organization that was under the control of his rival, Johnson. Labor unions did not like that Long's plan gave subsidies to state parties, particularly those parties in the South, many of which were controlled by antilabor factions. Labor leaders also recognized that the bill might make the party less dependent on them for electioneering, which would reduce their political influence in the party coalition.

Senator Long's legislation passed after a tumultuous legislative battle but was rescinded only one year later by a coalition of Republicans and liberal Democrats (see chap. 3). The Democratic Congress, however, continued to push for public funding in presidential elections because members recognized the party's structural problem. The DNC was asking donors to pay off debts from the previous cycle while Democratic presidential hopefuls were trying to raise money for the upcoming contest. Public funds might dig the party out of this deepening hole.

In 1971, Democrats proposed subsidies for presidential elections as part of a larger reform package entitled the Federal Election Campaign Act.[21] The FECA set limits on the ability of candidates to use their personal wealth for campaigns, limited the amount of media spending, and required all candidates to disclose their campaign funds. Congress inserted a provision to subsidize presidential elections as part of the Revenue Act of 1971.[22] While Nixon clearly wanted this tax package, he threatened to veto the entire bill if public funding was included. He eventually acquiesced to public funds on the condition that the program did not begin until the 1976 elections. Unlike the 1966 Long Act, the public funds would go directly to the candidates rather than the political parties.

Without the benefit of public subsidies, the Democrats were left with a gaping debt in the presidential election of 1972. They tried to relieve this debt with a series of telethons in 1974 and 1975, combining entertainment by nationally known performers and appearances by political figures with appeals for contributions. The party hoped to build on its recent procedural reforms, which encouraged participatory democracy in the presidential nominating process, by broadening its base of donors. These telethons raised some cash, but they were high-cost, low-yield affairs. Moreover, the effort to reach new donors did not broaden the demographic profile of typical party contributors. Donors remained overwhelmingly male, wealthy, white, and older (Ellwood and Spitzer 1979, 828–64).

FUND-RAISING, 1976–PRESENT

The Watergate break-in and ensuing scandal opened wider possibilities to reform of the campaign finance system. Progressive Democrats were swept into office in 1974, giving greater influence to those who championed earlier reform efforts. This faction conceived a plan that was stronger than the original FECA of 1971. The legislation to amend the 1971 FECA included a ceiling on campaign spending in congressional campaigns (later declared unconstitutional), limited individual contributions, and created the independent FEC to enforce the laws. While the overriding goal of the FECA was anticorruption, the new laws coincidentally gave strategic advantages to Democrats.[23] Spending caps, for example, would make it more difficult for challengers to mount effective campaigns against incumbents and would protect Democratic majorities in Congress (Samples 2006). More broadly, the system institutionalized candidate-centered campaigning, which suited a party composed of diverse ethnic, sectional, and ideological groups. Democrats also believed that requiring interest groups to give money through PACs would favor their party. To this point, PACs had only been established by labor unions. But corporations would soon take advantage of PACs after the *SunPAC* decision allowing executives to contribute to a corporate-sponsored PAC.[24] In the 1980s, because of this decision, corporate PACs would outnumber labor union PACs substantially.

The FECA was fashioned on the century-long template of Progressive reforms that conceived of politics as an activity to be engaged in by disinterested individuals rather than by partisan organizations and factions. It was also a product of its times. Crafted during the height of candidate-centered campaigning, the laws institutionalized patterns that had developed in midcentury. With candidates managing their own campaigns and supported by personal constituencies rather than the party leadership, the FECA placed responsibility for financial reporting squarely on candidate committees. Other political committees—parties and PACs—would also be required to report finances. But it was assumed that candidates would have independent control over their own campaigns, with noncandidate committees providing limited resources. The vast majority of funds would come from individual donations that went directly to the candidate committee.

Parties appeared half forgotten in the initial design of the FECA of 1974. Since the overriding goal was to get rid of the "fat cat," the sponsors of the FECA saw little threat from the national parties. After all, they had been capped at $3 million in spending since the Hatch Act, and even with this constraint, they were chronically in debt. Initially, parties were treated just like PACs, with the requirement that they could only contribute five thousand dollars to candidates. Republicans argued that the limit on party contributions should be higher, and the final bill resulted in a ten thousand dollar cap and an agreement that parties could make limited "coordinated" expenditures on behalf of their candidates.

While the public funding program increased the candidate-centered nature of presidential campaigns, it may also have freed parties to pursue party building rather than simply raising money for presidential candidates. The provision of public money for party conventions also unburdened party leaders from fund-raising obligations for these costly affairs, at least temporarily. In the early 1980s, the conventions were not quite the festive gatherings and expensive advertising extravaganzas they were to become in the 1990s.

In spite of constraints imposed on political parties, the 1971 FECA and its 1974 amendments were an improvement over previous reforms. Simply by removing the Hatch Act cap of $3 million, RNC spending increased to $6 million in 1972 and then $26.6 million in 1976. Similarly, DNC expenditures went up to $4.5 million in 1972 and to $14.3 million in 1976 (Alexander 1979, 1976). More indirectly, the laws carved out a permanent role for political parties by setting limits on nonparty committees. Across the board contribution caps for *any* political committee ensured that all money did not simply flow through nonparty groups. Candidates could receive no more than one thousand dollars per election from individual donors (two thousand dollars for the cycle of primary and general elections) and five thousand dollars from PACs per election (ten thousand dollars per cycle). Parties, in contrast, could give ten thousand dollars to candidates per election *and* an additional ten thousand dollars through in-kind support—called "coordinated expenditures"—that was adjusted each cycle for inflation. Since the FECA's other contribution limits were not indexed to inflation, coordinated expenditures became increasingly valuable relative to other kinds of support.

Going into the 1990s, political parties capitalized on the changing nature of political campaigns and exploited the FECA to enlarge their electoral role. In the next chapter, I describe these shifts in detail. Here, I will only explain how party fund-raising benefited significantly from emerging partisan polarization. Republicans and Democrats were becoming ideologically "purer" in the 1970s and 1980s. With the disappearance of conservative southern Democrats, each major party became more distinctive and cohesive around policy issues. To be sure, differences within the party coalitions remained, especially for the Democrats. Shifting partisan loyalties, however, established a firmer foundation to develop national donor constituencies. Rather than rely excessively on dinners and assorted gimmicks like selling ads in programs, parties gradually exploited technologies to reach voters through impassioned, yet impersonal appeals for funds. Direct mail fund-raising began to provide parties with a stable source of revenue.

The parties also benefited in the 1980s and 1990s from a deregulatory environment that gave them greater financial autonomy than previously envisioned in the initial design of FECA. Congress passed an amendment to FECA in 1979 granting permission for state and local parties to spend unlimited money on grass roots campaigning, which would be exempt from restrictions under the presidential public funding program. State parties argued successfully with the FEC, the regulatory agency, that they should be able to spend a portion of funds raised under state campaign laws, since grass roots activities also involved campaigning for state-level candidates. State laws were typically more permissive than federal rules. The FEC agreed to allow partial funding of state party campaigns with these funds, which became known infamously as soft money (Corrado 2005, 32). By the 1990s the national parties were also using it for paying overhead expenses and for transferring funds to state parties for advertising (national party operatives argued that their organizations were also supporting state-level candidates).

The parties also received help from the courts. In 1996 the Supreme Court declared, in *Colorado Republican Party v. FEC,* that the government could not limit how much political parties spent supporting candidates, so long as parties made these expenditures *independently.* This decision rested on a prior ruling in *Buckley v. Valeo* (1976), which affirmed that political spending was tied directly to free speech. Thus, spending could not be abridged without violating the First Amendment, absent a compelling anticorruption rationale. Since *spending* money was not corrupt, per se, political parties, as private associations, were guaranteed First Amendment privileges just like any other group or individual. So long as candidates did not *knowingly* benefit from party spending, the corruption rationale did not appear to apply. The argument that candidate "ignorance" of campaign activity makes independent spending permissible has historical antecedents in the Publicity Acts of 1910 and 1911, as described in chapter 3.

In the post-FECA era, party organizations had considerable potential to make themselves valuable to candidates. One important obstacle to raising party money, however, was that individual donors could not give more than twenty-five thousand dollars *total* in a given year (fifty thousand dollars for the two-year election cycle) to candidates, PACs, and parties. Donors were also constrained by sublimits on different kinds of committees; they could not contribute more than twenty thousand dollars per year to federal candidates (forty thousand dollars per two-year cycle). The scheme of aggregate limits created a competition for political funds among committees. A major donor who gave the maximum amount of twenty thousand dollars to federal candidates, for example, was only permitted to give five thousand dollars to a political party. In this way, aggregate limits made it difficult for either party to rely on major donors. It created a necessity to seek small, voluntary donors who would not bump up against these limits.

In competing for campaign dollars in a candidate-centered system, the national parties were in a relatively weak position. By the 1970s, Progressive norms—individualist, voluntary, and antipartisan—were woven into the electoral fabric. Donors preferred contributing to favored candidates and issue groups rather than political parties. National parties possessed relatively few incentives—material, solidary, or purposive—to attract prospective donors. Thanks to the Pendleton Act, patronage for federal office was limited. To be sure, winning candidates appointed favorites to ambassadorships and executive positions in the bureaucracy, but these actions were controlled by the candidate's top advisers rather than the political party.[25] As for solidary incentives, national parties were far removed from the kind of grass roots politics that attracts personal devotion through social interactions. While large dinners might lure major donors who enjoy "being part of the team," these fund-raising strategies are a poor way to build long-term financial stability. The only incentive available to national parties was a policy-oriented, purposive approach. The ongoing nationalization of politics and the presidential focus of the media made it increasingly easier for national committees to appeal to policy-oriented donors. But political parties in the 1970s continued to be at a competitive disadvantage relative to candidate committees and interest groups.

That donors have more incentives to give to nonparty committees is evident in a study of civic participation by Sidney Verba, Kay Schlozman, and Henry Brady. In their wide-ranging 1995 survey of political participation, they asked donors why they gave money to political causes. Table 7 shows the results, demonstrating that donors find it more gratifying or beneficial to contribute to nonparty groups. Only 8 percent of donors *to parties* claim to be motivated by material benefits, 5 percent by social gratifications, and 37 percent by policy motivations. While 86 percent said they gave to parties for civic gratifications, this motive was widely reported for donors across all political committees, suggesting that parties possess no competitive advantage here. Moreover, civic-mindedness appears to work only when paired with other kinds of incentives.[26] In contrast, donors report more reasons for giving to candidate committees: 18 percent say they give for material reasons, 22 percent for social gratifications, 80

TABLE 7. Gratifications Reported by Campaign Donors (percentage mentioning gratification among activists)

Contributed to:	Material Benefits	Social Gratifications	Civic Gratifications	Policy Gratifications
Candidate	18	22	80	46
Party organization	8	5	86	37
Work-related PAC	46	14	63	64
Issue organization	1	6	88	84

Source: Excerpt from Verba, Schlozman, and Brady 1995, table 4.1, 115.

percent for civic gratification, and 46 percent for policy interests. Donors also report more reasons for giving to work-related PACs, with a heavier emphasis on material benefits (46 percent) and policy motives (64 percent).

The gratifications reported by campaign donors for contributing to "issue organizations" appear closest to the pattern for political parties. But the percentage of donors who give to issue organizations for policy gratifications (84 percent) is much higher than for parties (37 percent). Thus, issue PACs—the party's chief competitor for ideologically motivated donors—are more attractive to policy-motivated donors than parties. In fact, the percentage of party donors who mention policy motives as a reason to contribute is considerably lower compared to *all* the other groups. On the whole, parties appear to provide fewer gratifications for donors than other kinds of political committees.

THE EFFECT OF PARTISAN POLARIZATION ON POLITICAL CONTRIBUTIONS

Despite these disadvantages relative to other political committees, political parties had at least one natural constituency for donors. Strong partisans tend to be activists, participating in a variety of campaign activities, including donating money to parties and candidates (Verba, Schlozman, and Brady 1995; Francia et al. 2003). In the 1990s the national committees had greater success attracting partisan donors because voters began to perceive greater policy differences between the two major parties. Since 1960, the National Election Studies (NES) has been asking respondents in every presidential election cycle, "Do you think there are any major differences between the major parties?" Until 1980, roughly half the electorate responded "yes," but, as figure 4 shows, this percentage increased substantially after this point among both partisan activists and nonactivists. In the 1980s, the upward trend leveled and then began increasing again after the 1992 elections. The fact that more voters see genuine differences between the major parties suggests that parties should find it easier to present themselves as policy-oriented organizations. For this reason, they have been able to attract additional policy-motivated donors.

The most relevant point is that the people who are most likely to give money—the activists in either party—recognize policy differences and act on them. It is also likely that activists stimulate the increasing distinctiveness between the parties. Strong partisans are moving toward the ideological extremes in each party, even though the ideology of the average American voter has not changed much in the past four decades; it has become slightly more

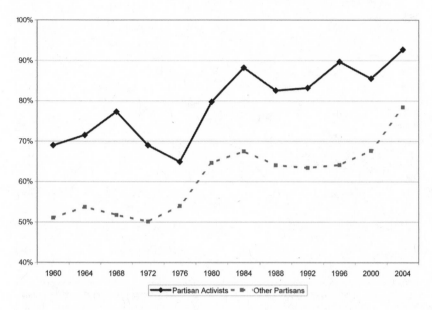

FIG. 4. Any important differences between major parties? Response from activist versus nonactivist partisans, 1960–2004. (Data from the American National Election Studies 2005.)

conservative (Nye, Zelikow, and King 1997). Thus, partisans spur the growing distance between the parties. At the same time, they respond to these differences when they make decisions to contribute. The effect, according to Mark Brewer, is a "closed loop or circuit" (2005, 219–30). As polarization rises among critical party constituencies, party elites respond with partisan rhetoric, issue stands, and policies.

To measure whether strong partisans have been responding to party appeals for money in recent years, I observe trends in political contributions among strong, weak, and independent-leaning partisans. Figures 5 and 6 look at NES data starting in 1980, when the survey began asking respondents whether they made party contributions. Among both parties, it is clear that strong partisans are most likely to make contributions to the party and that this percentage rose during the 1990s. For Republicans, this is especially true. In the 2004 election, only 10 percent of the population claimed to have made a party contribution. Figure 5, however, shows that 25 percent of strong Republicans made a contribution. Meanwhile, the percentage of weak or leaning Republi-

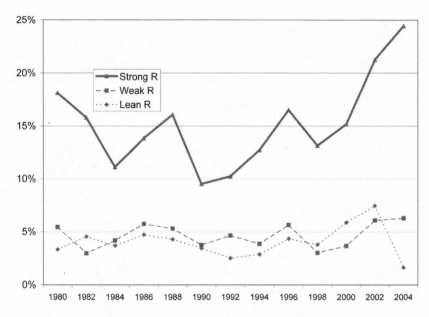

FIG. 5. Percentage donating to party by strength of Republican Party identification. (Data from the American National Election Studies 2005.)

cans choosing to make a party contribution has not changed substantially, fluctuating between 3 and 6 percent. Fortunately for the Republican Party, the number of Americans who consider themselves strong Republicans has increased from 9 percent in 1980 to 16 percent in 2004, which means that strong Republicans constitute an increasing share of all donors. In the 2004 elections, 40 percent of donors nationwide were strong Republicans, compared with just 15 percent in 1980.

The picture is not so rosy for Democrats, although the situation has improved in recent years. Figure 6 shows that 13 percent of strong Democrats claimed to have made a party contribution in 2004, a substantial increase since 1980, when only 2 percent made contributions to the party. But the portion of strong Democrats in the population has not increased from 18 percent in 1980. Thus, even though more strong Democrats are giving, they still only constitute 23 percent of all who gave money to political parties in 2004, compared with 40 percent for strong Republicans. Remarkably, party contributions have increased sharply for Democratic leaners since 1998 (and somewhat less so for weak Democrats). These independent leaners may be motivated to contribute

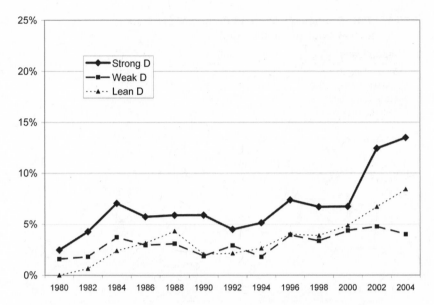

FIG. 6. Percentage donating to party by strength of Democratic Party identification. (Data from the American National Election Studies 2005.)

either for ideological reasons or because of personal dislike of George W. Bush. One study suggests that personal dislike of George W. Bush and his policies was a strong motivator for donors to give to the Kerry campaign and the Democratic Party (Graf et al. 2006).

As discussed earlier, the Democratic Party has struggled throughout its history to create loyal partisan donors to the party organization. Consistent with my earlier argument about a divided Democratic Party, self-described Democrats are simply more likely than Republicans to give to favored candidates and causes rather than to the party itself. As partisan polarization intensifies, however, the Democratic Party should be able to attract ideologically motivated donors, even if these donors are weakly attached to the party. Republicans, however, will continue to receive support from both ideologically conservative and partisan donors.

To test these assumptions I regressed ideology and partisanship on party contributions using NES data from 1980 through 2004. I included other variables from civic voluntarism that predict political contributions. The results of the pooled model are shown in table 8.[27] They support the theory that strength

TABLE 8. Predicted Donors in Presidential Election Years, 1980–2004 (pooled model)

Republicans	Coeff.	SE
Party strength	0.56**	0.10
Liberal-conservative	0.22**	0.07
Interest in elections	0.87**	0.13
Education	0.11*	0.05
Age	0.38**	0.04
Family income	0.48**	0.08
dum84	− 0.15	0.28
dum88	0.28	0.27
dum92	− 0.36	0.27
dum96	0.00	0.28
dum00	− 0.40	0.36
dum04	0.13	0.28
_cons	− 10.57	0.65

Logit estimates		Number of observations	3,063
		Likelihood ratio chi^2(12)	325.4
		Prob > chi^2	0
Log likelihood =	− 750.79	Pseudo R^2	0.1781

Democrats	Coeff.	SE
Party strength	0.18	0.10
Liberal-conservative	− 0.25**	0.07
Interest in elections	0.89**	0.15
Education	0.36**	0.06
Age	0.26**	0.05
Family income	0.19*	0.08
dum84	1.32**	0.43
dum88	1.46**	0.43
dum92	0.65	0.43
dum96	1.34	0.43
dum00	0.85	0.49
dum04	1.52	0.43
_cons	− 9.00	0.75

Logit estimates		Number of observations	3,400
		Likelihood ratio chi^2(12)	233.54
		Prob > chi^2	0
Log likelihood =	− 624.33	Pseudo R^2	0.1576

Source: American National Election Studies 2005.
Note: The data are restricted to self-identified partisans. Party strength: strong = 3, weak = 2, lean = 1. SE = standard error.
*Significant at 5%   **Significant at 1%

of partisanship *and* being conservative predict Republican contributions. This is not true for the Democrats. Instead, ideology, not partisanship, predicts donations to Democratic parties. The implications seem clear for Democrats— to raise money they must present themselves as an ideological party, a strategy that may lose them moderate voters. Alternatively, they might attract additional donors if the Republican Party moves more to the right, which would attract Democrats who perceive a greater threat from having conservatives control government (Miller, Krosnick, and Lowe 2002).

PARTY FUND-RAISING IMPROVES

The growing polarization of the parties accounts, in part, for the surge in party fund-raising. After campaign finance rules that passed in 1974 gave parties a firmer financial footing, the parties expanded the size of their donor pool. Table 9 shows, however, that the DNC consistently trailed the RNC in total receipts until 2004. For the RNC, after a phenomenal surge in 1976 and lasting through the Reagan presidency, fund-raising trailed off considerably in real dollars in 1988 and 1992. One reason may be that President George H. W. Bush, a moderate, did not excite partisans enough for them to increase their donations to the party, even though the number of contributors giving more than two hundred dollars more than doubled during his reelection campaign.[28]

In the 1990s, parties capitalized on the growing polarization and awareness of policy differences to raise more money. Federal receipts to the DNC increased impressively throughout the FECA era, especially from 1992 forward. RNC fund-raising was even more impressive in the 1990s. Between 1992 and 1996, the Republican Party more than doubled its hard money receipts from $115 million to $232 million in real dollars. They also built up a significant lead over the Democrats for hard money receipts, which was one reason Democrats turned increasingly to soft money. Lacking the breadth of donors loyal to the Republican Party, the Democrats tried to close the gap through a core group of major soft money donors, primarily labor unions and wealthy liberals in New York and California.

SOFT MONEY

The most controversial aspect of party fund-raising has been soft money. The rise of soft money appeared to mark the return of "fat cats" and the evisceration of the long-standing ban on corporate funds under the Tillman Act of 1907 and on labor union contributions under the Smith-Connally Act of 1943. National committees had raised soft money since at least 1980, after the FEC ruling that permitted them to spend soft money for party building. Concerns about party soft money escalated in the 1996 elections, when the parties began to use it to pay for campaign ads. Previously, it supported administrative expenses and voter mobilization activities. Once parties learned to exploit it for broadcast advertising, the value of soft money soared and they sought more of it.

Paradoxically, the incentive to use soft money for ads was triggered by the presidential public funding system. Under that system, presidential candidates seeking the party nomination receive public matching dollars up to $250 for each private political contribution. In the general election, however, presidential candidates receive a lump-sum public grant, which may *not* be supplemented with private contributions. In accepting public funds for either the primary or general election, candidates agree not to exceed the spending limits established in each of these contests.

But the campaign finance system proved too inflexible to adapt to these new campaign dynamics. Presidential campaigns had become longer and more expensive due to the front-loading of primaries and the increasing costs of television advertising. Primary contestants were starting their electioneering ear-

TABLE 9. National Committee Fund-raising, 1972–2004 (in millions of 2004 dollars)

	1972	1976	1980	1984	1988	1992	1996	2000	200
DNC									
Receipts—federal (hard)	20	20	28	85	84	89	130	136	39
Receipts—nonfederal (soft)	0	0	9	11	37	42	123	150	
Total receipts	20	20	37	96	120	131	253	286	39
Count of contributions >$200									
(hard only)	NA	NA	5,539	4,212	11,071	32,832	26,618	46,477	151,23
RNC									
Receipts—federal (hard)	27	68	84	193	145	115	232	233	39
Receipts—nonfederal (soft)	0	0	35	28	35	48	136	182	
Total receipts	27	68	118	221	180	163	368	416	39
Count of contributions >$200									
(hard only)	NA	NA	13,903	13,201	10,964	26,021	62,191	92,307	153,38

Source: Federal Elections Commission 2005a. Data for 1972 from Alexander 1976. Data for 1984 from Alexander and Hagerty 1987, 99. Data for soft money in 1980, 1984, 1988 from Alexander and Bauer 1991, 37. Count data from Political Money Line, available at http://moneyline.cq.com.
Note: NA = not available.

lier than before, and a party nominee emerged clearly several months before the party convention. The unofficial winner of the party nomination had an enormous incentive to begin campaigning in earnest against the nominee in the rival party during this "interregnum" period, which lasted until the party officially bestowed its nomination on the candidate at the party convention.[29] After the official candidate had been nominated, the FEC was authorized to release public funds for the general election. Rather than waiting for these public funds and losing an opportunity to define the opposition candidate, the national parties became the vehicle to wage campaigns during the interregnum. The Clinton reelection team in 1996 initiated this process by using DNC soft money to broadcast campaign ads against Bob Dole, the likely Republican nominee. The RNC quickly responded with its own ads.

Beyond the presidential public funding system, the FECA was outmoded in other ways that encouraged end runs around the system. Most critically, the law failed to index contribution limits to inflation. Thus, a $1,000 contribution limit in 1976 was worth only $363 in 1996, and the $250 match for presidential campaigns was worth just $79. With diminishing returns from major donors (those who typically gave the maximum), partisans sought alternative ways of funding campaigns. The soft money "loophole" presented a viable option. With no limits on sources or the size of contributions, soft money reduced competition among political committees for hard dollars. Donors would not bump up against the aggregate limits on how much money they could contribute to all federal committees. Indeed, the two-currency system encouraged parties and candidates to work closely together. A joint fund-raising event might produce a hard money check for the candidate and a soft money check for the party. This kind of coordination, of course, is exactly what concerned people about the emerging soft money system. Candidates appeared to be benefiting from soft money checks earmarked for their campaigns rather than for party building.

Party excesses in raising soft money—such as invitations for donors to stay in the White House Lincoln bedroom, lavish black-tie dinners, and White House teas—drew deserved attention to the potential for quid pro quo between donors and candidates. On the other hand, charges of corruption were thrown about rather loosely in the editorial pages of the nation's newspapers, accompanied by calls to ban soft money (*New York Times* 1991). Concerns about corruption and legitimacy in the electoral system should not be taken lightly, but lost in the populist cries for reform were basic facts about soft money fundraising. The situation was a far cry from almost a century earlier, when it was typical for four donors to supply the vast majority of dollars to either the RNC or DNC. In 2000, the ten largest soft money donors accounted for *just 1.5 percent of total party funds.*

The media's focus on an exclusive group of megadonors obscured the fact that the vast majority of soft money donors were actually small contributors. In a study conducted after the 1998 elections, I estimated that 90 percent of soft money contributors gave less than $25,000 and that the average contribution was only $8,750 (La Raja and Hoffman 2000, 14). These figures do not even include the significant number of donors who gave less than $200 but were not required to report their contributions. Most of these organizations were local hotels, funeral homes, construction companies, towing services, dental offices, hardware stores, landscape services, legal offices, accounting firms, and retail food outlets.[30] Not surprisingly, these local firms gave predominantly to Republicans, which suggests another reason why Democrats favored a ban. Even though Democrats relied heavily on soft money donors, they recognized that with a little effort Republicans could significantly outpace them in soft money receipts.

Another misconception about soft money was that the typical "big donor" was much more likely to donate hard money rather than soft money. In 1998, for example, the median hard money contribution for 2,777 PACs was $10,112. In comparison, the median soft money contribution of the 11,383 groups that gave only soft money was just $375. The focus of the media, however, was on an exclusive group of 870 donors (just 6 percent of all groups) that gave *both* hard and soft money to parties. This same select group provided parties with almost 60 percent of the soft money they received from organizations (25 percent of all soft money contributions came from individuals). And yet this select group appeared more invested in the hard money system: their median soft money contribution was $25,750, while their median hard money contribution was $78,295. In fact, this same group of donors provided more than 60 percent of all the hard money that parties received from PACs.[31] In short, the same set of interests that dominated the soft money system dominated the hard money system. One important difference is that the soft money system had many more donors for parties to rely upon. Starting in 2004, most of these donors disappeared completely with the ban on soft money under the BCRA. But the large business firms that previously gave both soft and hard money had other options. They could increase their hard money giving, increase their expenditures on lobbying, and still make soft money donations for the national conventions, which many of them did in 2004.

Despite the inability to raise soft money in the 2004 presidential elections under the BCRA, the national committees did extraordinarily well raising campaign funds. The Iraq War and strong dislike of President Bush by Democratic partisans and independents boosted DNC receipts to levels well beyond what it had raised in both hard and soft money in previous elections. Unsurprisingly, the RNC also did well, although it did not exceed its totals from the 2000 elections. There is little doubt that if soft money were permitted, both committees would have raised substantially more money. Instead these sums went to outside organizations.

Looking toward the 2008 elections, the political parties will be at a disadvantage raising and spending money compared to 2004 for two reasons. First, unlike in the past, none of the top-tier presidential candidates will participate in the presidential public funding system, which means they will all compete with political parties for campaign dollars. Second, the Supreme Court ruled in *Wisconsin Right to Life v. FEC* (2007) that the government may not prohibit groups from broadcasting issue ads with soft money in the days before an election. This ruling breaks down a significant component of the BCRA, namely, that the government may bar broadcast ads funded with soft money that mention a federal candidate's name in the sixty days before a general election. It is likely that wealthy donors who might have contributed soft money to political parties in previous elections will instead give their money to 527 or 501(c)(4) organizations. These organizations will compete with candidates and political parties for the attention of voters.

SUMMARY

During much of the twentieth century, the national political committees faced a considerable collective action problem in raising money for presidential campaigns and other organizational activity. Inspired by the Progressive worldview, the campaign finance system at the federal level has been consistently unrealistic about the necessity and difficulty of raising money, particularly for large, heterogeneous party organizations. The Progressive laws have, in many ways, failed to acknowledge the importance of election spending to rouse and inform citizens in a large, complex, and diverse democracy. These laws, which emphasize dependence on voluntary donors, have encouraged political money to flow outside the formal party structure to candidates and interest groups, which reduces accountability, competition, and fairness. Party organizations, as well-known entities and with established "brand names," cannot easily escape the scrutiny of the press if they accepted large amounts of money from particular donors or placed nasty television ads on the air. To be sure, the political parties may still do these things, but it is far easier for the public to know who is responsible when they do it. Moreover, the parties have a strong incentive to help challengers win elections, since they want to control government rather than simply support incumbents, like most interest groups seeking access to policymakers.

The most recent reforms (BCRA of 2002) fall within the same regulatory pattern of previous reforms, even if they are not animated by the antipartisan spirit of the Progressives. BCRA stresses a renewed emphasis on the voluntaristic model. Typically, the reliance on the small donor produces "small change" for political parties, though ongoing advances in information technology, such as the Internet, may allow political parties to finally make small donors the most essential component of their fund-raising.

But fund-raising success among small donors depends considerably on a highly polarized environment that motivates ardent partisans to give money. In the 1990s the RNC's and the DNC's success in attracting highly ideological, small donors suggests that American party finance has begun to move toward the European model. The national committees appear to have developed dues-paying members who are committed to distinctive policies. For the first time in American history, the heightened polarization and cohesiveness of partisan elites permit the parties to sustain national constituencies of donors. Aided by vast quantities of demographic and personal data about citizens, party organizations can hone their targeting of policy-oriented donors.

In appealing to donors, parties advertise their differences, while donors simultaneously exert pressure on party leaders to tow the line on policy issues. This feedback loop should intensify as parties rely more heavily on purposive-driven donors who tend to make contributions through impersonal but highly charged appeals. These appeals tend to demonize the policies of the rival party while promising the donor that the "good" party will deliver on policies crafted especially with the donor's interest in mind. Given these dynamics, the middle ground of American politics should become increasingly difficult to locate, as parties refuse to compromise for fear of losing the support of the key ideological factions that provide them with small donations in bulk.

But even if parties successfully build their small donor constituencies, they cannot rely solely on them in the future. History suggests that the demand for electoral resources will eventually bump up against Progressive-style constraints imposed by the campaign finance system. The current legal limits and prohibitions on political parties will generate the same kind of fragmented campaign activity we have seen in the past. Indeed, as in the past, parties will be compelled to solicit large patrons to fund new or additional campaign activities through wink-and-nod arrangements with friendly interest groups. Indeed, this trend already began in the first election after the reforms of 2002. Even given their success at raising hard money in 2004, both parties had already shifted to a strategy of funneling soft money through 527 organizations to pursue electoral goals. These organizations, while legal, were wholly unfamiliar to voters and made the elections less transparent and accountable. In the next chapters, I explain how the major parties exploited various strategies in the 2004 elections to get around impractical limits created by the BCRA and the ways in which campaigning by nonparty groups will likely become institutionalized in future elections.

CHAPTER 6

Consequences of Reform for Party Campaigning

In the past several election cycles parties have enriched themselves through prodigious fund-raising. Now that parties are financially strong it is appropriate to ask, what have they done with this wealth? Are they vast fund-raising enterprises that funnel cash to individual candidates, much like an outsized PAC? To what extent do parties invest their cash—including much-reviled soft money—to strengthen the formal organization so that it might perform traditional party functions like recruiting candidates or registering voters? Do the national committees confine their political spending to just a few battleground states, so that few Americans outside these states experience a presidential election? These questions are central to contemporary debates about campaign finance reform since regulations on money shape how party organizations and affiliated partisan groups engage in elections. Addressing these questions illustrates the impact of campaign finance laws on political organizations and simultaneously illuminates the contemporary role of political parties in American politics.

Some scholars have argued that parties have largely abandoned their collective function and simply serve the interests of candidates. It follows from this argument that parties do not merit a privileged position in the campaign finance system, which would allow them to raise more money than other groups. According to Jonathan Krasno and Frank Sorauf, the increased wealth of political parties has had little effect in terms of strengthening the parties as organizations. They argue that "[n]o one can help but be impressed by the vast amounts of money flowing through the parties, but the money has passed through them without leaving behind anything of lasting benefit" (2003, 54). Another expert on parties and campaign finance, Tom Mann, has suggested that party soft money "has created as many or more problems for parties and done little to nurture grass roots participation or electoral competition" (2003, 32).

I argue that these criticisms are apt for the congressional campaign committees—the National Republican Senatorial Committee (NRSC), the Democratic Senatorial Campaign Committee (DSCC), the National Republican Campaign Committee (NRCC), and the Democratic Congressional Campaign Committee (DCCC)—which tend to have more narrow interests than the national committees, but not for the national committees and many state central committees. Congressional campaign committees focus single-mindedly on helping candidates win in targeted races. The same is true of the party caucus in state legislatures. These legislative campaign committees (LCCs) frequently behave like independent consulting firms rather than party organizations. They provide professional services to candidates, without involving themselves in the broader aspects of party work, such as providing grass roots electioneering with local parties and building sustained campaign coalitions with local interest groups (Shea 1995).[1] Money raised by the congressional campaign committees tends to support a small fraction of party candidates for Congress since these committees simply invest resources in the thirty to fifty races where the outcome is deemed uncertain by nationally recognized political pollsters. Moreover, outside these few closely contested races, the LCCs have few incentives to work with local and state party committees to recruit and nurture future party candidates.

In contrast, the presidential wings of the parties—manifested through the RNC and DNC—have been from their beginnings intimately connected with state and local party organizations. Indeed, members of the RNC and DNC are, in fact, state and local party officials and activists. As early as the elections of 1828, the national leaders worked through local organizations to mobilize voters for the presidential ticket (Aldrich 1995). The cooperation of local and state bosses was essential to building a coalition that might win the presidency. The network of partisan ties was strengthened through a quadrennial national convention, organized by the national committee. During conventions, local party leaders developed personal relationships and brokered institutional commitments to help win the presidency (Polsby and Wildavsky 2000, 219–53). Bonds of loyalty were stitched together by benefits that flowed from patronage and other perks of winning office.

In discussing political parties and their role in financing elections, analysts frequently fail to make distinctions between national and legislative committees. As a result, they overgeneralize when they make assertions about how parties raise and spend money. Since much of the recent research in academic journals has been about LCCs, my focus here is on the national committees.[2] I present evidence that contradicts assertions that national party committees are merely extensions of candidates or that they are akin to large consulting firms. To be sure, national parties spend a great deal of funds directly on candidate support. As pragmatic organizations, the parties' main goal is to win elections and help candidates win by financing costly television ads. The majority of funds, however, are spent internally to maintain robust organizations in Washington and in the states. These funds are spent to strengthen ties with voters through direct mail, telephoning, and canvassing. The party's push to carve a bigger role for itself—a role that is independent of candidates—has roots in a changing political environment that has made the parties increasingly important in contemporary elections. The new campaign environment favors both a strong organizational approach that mobilizes voters "on the ground" and a candidate-targeted strategy that helps presidential nominees broadcast messages on television and radio.

My argument is that the national and state committees are well positioned to assume features of traditional strong parties if campaign finance laws do not starve them for resources. Such features include recruiting local candidates, organizing activists, and nurturing partisan support in the electorate by identifying and contacting voters. Moreover, with generous access to campaign funds, these committees have the potential to exercise an independent influence on campaigns and elections rather than simply be passive "service" organizations or "bank accounts" for individual candidates. What separates them from congressional campaign committees and LCCs is that they have a broader constituency that places demands on them. They are not beholden solely to elected officials in the legislature. As in the past, the institution of the Electoral College provides a sturdy incentive for local, state, and national groups to work together under the party label. Additionally, the broad-based governing structure of the national and central committees encourages these party organizations to make decisions that reflect the interests of multiple constituencies. I turn now to the reasons why national and state parties have emerged since the 1980s as potentially important players in the electoral landscape.

WHY PARTY ORGANIZATIONS BECAME MORE IMPORTANT

The 1950s through the 1970s were the heyday of candidate-centered elections. The presence of volatile public opinion, ticket splitting, and intense focus on candidate personalities revealed the depth of party decay that had been ongoing for decades (Wattenberg 1991). Demographic and technological changes, coupled with institutional reforms, made the traditional nineteenth-century party system based on the power of local bosses less relevant. By the 1970s, self-selected candidates in congressional and presidential contests fought to win the party label in primaries, aided by expensive technology that helped them connect directly with voters through targeted mail and television. The campaign finance system, under the FECA, supported a candidate-centered system by making candidate committees rather than parties the locus of accountability and institutionalizing the role of PACs, which could give funds directly to candidates. At the presidential level, the public financing system further supported this trend by granting public funds to candidates rather than parties.

The pure form of the candidate-centered system, however, began to erode in the 1980s. Several trends were afoot that made national parties more viable as electoral organizations. Ironically, the campaign finance system under the FECA, which envisioned a quite limited role for parties, helped spur this party renewal, though it was not the prime factor in moving the parties in this direction. Ambitious office seekers and activists turned to the party organizations to reduce growing uncertainties in the electoral environment, which had their roots in political, technological, and institutional changes.[3] These uncertainties emerged chiefly in the following three areas.

Increasing difficulty of identifying electoral support. Voter loyalties to the parties began to decline significantly starting in the 1960s. Martin Wattenberg (1991), for example, shows that public attitudes toward parties changed considerably at this time, with fewer people having a positive attitude toward parties than in the previous era. More voters were refusing to vote the party line, choosing instead to split their ticket between candidates of different parties for Congress and the presidency. When asked by pollsters about party affiliation, fewer voters identified as partisans. As figure 7 shows, the percentage of self-identified Democrats in the electorate declined from 47 percent in 1952 to 34 percent in 2000. Most of the change occurred in the 1960s and 1970s with the full flowering of candidate-centered elections. The Republicans, however, did

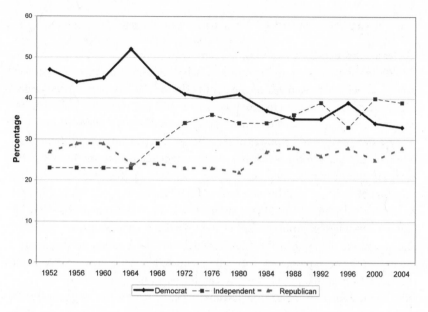

FIG. 7. Party affiliation, 1952–2004. (Data from the American National Election Studies 2005.)

not benefit from the Democratic losses. The percentage of self-identified Republican voters was no more than 28 percent of the electorate in 2004. Meanwhile, the portion of the electorate self-identifying as independents has grown from 23 percent to 40 percent. Presently, the decline in partisanship appears to have stalled, and there is evidence that party attachments have rebounded slightly (Hershey 2007, 107).

The shift by voters away from parties as an important referent made campaigning increasingly difficult for candidates. When voters decline to identify with a party, candidates lose an important source of knowledge about who is likely to support them. To be sure, even voters who fail to declare partisan allegiances frequently lean toward one party or the other in their voting habits (Keith et al. 1992). But identifying these self-declared independent voters and winning them over requires greater investments than candidates can bear on their own.

Rising campaign costs. Spending in presidential elections by candidates has been growing above the rate of inflation for many years. While spending in presidential elections has risen steadily for generations, it burgeoned in the 1960s with the growing use of television broadcasting. Previous to the FECA regime with its strict limits on contributions, presidential candidates sought out large donors, which made it easier for them to raise money for television ads. This practice was shielded from the public as candidates used a variety of campaign committees to hide the origin of their funds. In the aftermath of the 1972 elections, for example, it was revealed through the Watergate investigations that President Nixon's reelection campaign committee had been dunning corporate leaders for support—Mark Hanna style—and hiding funds in various slush fund accounts. President Johnson had also been known for his questionable practices of raising funds from Texas businessmen while he was in the Senate and during his time as president (Caro 2002).

Political reforms passed in 1974 aimed to prevent candidates from relying on large donors. Under the FECA, presidential candidates were eligible for public matching funds in the primaries and a lump subsidy in the general election. Although the public funding program seemed generous at the time, campaign costs escalated beyond its capacity. As figure 8 shows, the amount spent by presidential contenders in primaries and the general election continues to outpace payouts in public funds, which are pegged to the cost of living increases.

The spiraling costs could be attributed to ongoing technological change in running campaigns. In addition to broadcast advertising, candidates took advantage of frequent polling and direct mail to identify and persuade voters. These technologies require high-priced experts, whom candidates have come to rely upon, particularly in places where local party organizations are weak. The 1960s marked the culmination of an extended transition for American campaigns, as they moved inexorably from a labor-intensive to a cash-based economy in which candidates hired consultants to burnish their image rather than rely on party workers to mobilize the electorate (Ware 1985). Even as candidates adapted to the new marketing style of campaigning, they faced competition from commercial marketers for the attention of voters. The cost of reaching voters continued to increase with the widespread use of cable television.

Institutional reforms that failed to accommodate the lengthening campaign season. Institutional changes in federal elections added to the cost of campaigning and limited the capacity of candidates to raise money to meet growing costs. The McGovern-Fraser Commission reforms sponsored by the DNC led both parties in many states to adopt direct primaries in lieu of caucuses for selecting delegates to the party convention. To win the nomination, candidates

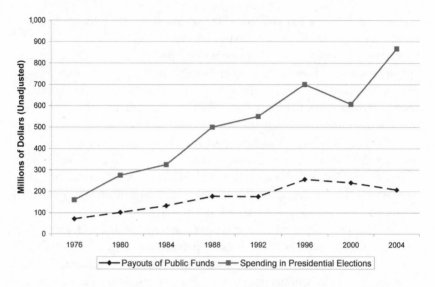

FIG. 8. Spending in presidential campaigns. (Data from Federal Election Commission, various years.)

organized their own campaign organizations for primary elections in order to secure *pledged* delegates well before the nominating convention. (Under the caucus system, delegates were not necessarily pledged to any particular candidate and were controlled by local party leaders at the national convention.) These personal campaign organizations carried over into the general election. Candidates for the presidency, in effect, had to wage two separate campaigns, which added greatly to the length and cost of elections.

Although candidates received public funds for the nomination and general election, these funds were tied to constraints on spending. More critically, the public funding system in presidential elections had not accommodated the lengthening of the general election season, which now begins well before the nominating conventions. The front-loading of primaries has led to an intense period of campaigning in early primary states. A nominee emerges in March, well before the conventions in July or August. At this point, candidates face a prisoner's dilemma: if both refrain from attacking one another, campaign costs are contained. But if one candidate attacks, he or she holds an advantage because it allows him or her to define the opposition and frame the debate. Given these conditions, both candidates have a strong incentive to begin campaigning as soon as the two nominees emerge. Since public funds for the general election are not released until the summer, candidates must seek other ways to campaign during the interregnum, which lasts from the point at which the candidate has enough delegates to win the party nomination until the party convention marks the official start of the general election.

Direct primaries have a less visible cost. They fragment the party, pitting candidates representing different factions against one another. Candidates win by mobilizing factions, appealing to their preferences on issues and downplaying others (Polsby 1983).[4] Hard-fought campaigns for the nomination have the potential to create lasting animosities that spill over into the general election. Disappointed factions whose candidate lost the primary may fail to rally around the party's nominee. The winning candidate also faces the daunting task of reinvigorating his or her campaign organization for a completely different task—taking on the opposition party. The general election presents the winning candidate with a new set of challenges: new states, new voters, and a very short time frame to organize. To say the least, it is an expensive undertaking.

The uncertainties facing candidates in the political environment created an opportunity for entrepreneurial party leaders to strengthen the electoral apparatus of the party. A stronger party infrastructure had the potential to reduce uncertainties related to political, technological, and institutional changes. National committees, for example, have developed into stable institutions that bridge a critical period between elections and prepare for the general election, regardless of who the nominee turns out to be. By relying on national constituencies to raise money (see previous chapter), party leaders have built an organization capable of pursuing essential off-year election work: identifying donors, collecting data on voters, and coordinating the work of consultants and affiliated partisan groups. Early in the campaign process, party organizations sponsor polls, convene meetings with party activists, and monitor the progress of campaign organizations throughout the country. Occasionally, they develop and test campaign strategies in gubernatorial and midterm elections in anticipation of the presidential contest.[5]

In short, electoral contingencies in the 1980s and 1990s have made partisan organizing less ad hoc than previously. The wealth of national committees gives them leverage to convene groups and coordinate the use of campaign resources among state parties and affiliated interest groups (Bibby 2002, 111–15). Indeed, the resources that national parties bring to the table resolve an important collective action problem. Local candidates, parties, and interest groups in the states are willing to invest in cooperative ventures when the national party pledges a large investment in statewide campaigns. The national committees convene members of the coalition to share information, minimize redundant efforts, and learn from past practices.

Organizing for campaigns is also a way of minimizing factionalism. To counter divisiveness generated in primaries, party leaders had to consider ways of bringing unity to the party. One traditional method is through the party conventions. Party conventions, of course, are now four-day advertisements for the party nominee (Bartels and Vavreck 2002). But they also serve the purpose of inspiring and generating loyalty among delegates and activists in the states, many of whom worked for different candidates or causes during the primaries. It should be no surprise that conventions have become lavish affairs, intended to entertain delegates from the states. The pampering that takes place within and outside the convention halls has the effect of inspiring goodwill among party activists, even those who did not support the party nominee.

Party leaders also promote unity by ensuring that state party organizations enjoy a privileged place in the general election campaign. Giving state parties a key role in running campaigns reduces antagonisms between state party activists and campaign staff working for the party nominee. Democratic state party officials have been rankled by the invasion of young staffers telling them how to organize their own states. By centering the statewide campaigns within the state organization, the national party has lessened the likelihood that local party activists would be turned off.

Organizing general election campaigns in states now precedes the selection of the party nominee, with the national party taking the lead as coordinator. The RNC has tried to work more closely with state organizations since the early 1960s. The Democrats did not adopt this strategy until the 1990s. Ron Brown, the DNC chair during the 1992 campaign, pushed for coordinated efforts after the Democrats failed to mount an effective campaign following the party convention in 1988. He declared that the party "had to do more than nominate a candidate. We had to elect a president" (Jaffe 1992; Moss 1992). The Dukakis campaign in 1988 apparently shunned the help of the DNC chair, Paul G. Kirk, who decamped to Cape Cod after the nominating convention (Moss 1992). From Brown's perspective, early organizing in states provided parties with better information about voters as the general election approached, helping to avoid the scramble to identify voters in the closing months before Election Day.

To be sure, party building has not forged ahead in all the states. National parties are rational—they focus on states where they can make a difference, as the subsequent analysis will make clear. But even in Republican strongholds like Idaho, the Democratic state party will receive some funds from the national party. Making small grants to state organizations is part of a coalition-building process. The national committees do not expect an electoral payoff from investments in noncompetitive states, but they feel compelled to give some funds out of a sense of fairness and because local party activists and elected officials may pressure them to help out.

While parties have built a permanent organizational infrastructure, they have also spent money directly to support targeted federal candidates. Campaign finance laws limit the amount of cash and in-kind contributions parties can provide to candidates. But parties have found other, less direct methods of helping their candidates. Their incentive to find loopholes is especially strong in presidential elections, given that their nominees face spending limits if they take public funds. The public funding system has become too inflexible and ungenerous to wage robust campaigns without the use of private funds. As a result, party spending is critical. Indeed, in recent elections parties have outspent the presidential candidates on broadcast advertising in many states (Franz, Rivlin, and Goldstein 2006).

American elections have entered a period in which national party organizations are poised between serving candidate-based interests and assuming broader-based party tasks. These are not necessarily incompatible strategies in the contemporary political environment.[6] The electoral system remains candidate centered in the sense that party labels are rarely invoked during campaigns and candidates assemble their own campaign organization rather than turn over the campaign to the formal party organization. But to win presidential elections requires sustained organization building that no candidate—particularly nonincumbents—can create from scratch. The party organization provides the permanent infrastructure that any nominee might exploit once they earn the nomination. Parties, then, are not simply bank accounts for candidates, as some have argued, because cash for advertising is not what wins presidential elections. Winning the White House now requires robust campaign organizations in the states that can identify voters and implement a mobilization strategy *early* in the process, well before an election year.

DIFFERENCES BETWEEN REPUBLICANS AND DEMOCRATS

Both parties have moved toward strengthening their campaign organizations, but they pursue their strategies in ways that reflect unique political resources and cultures. Along a spectrum between the candidate-centered and party-centered approach to organizing, the Republicans are closer to the party-centered strategy than Democrats, for reasons that were discussed in the previous chapter. Republican behavior results from being a more homogenous party than Democrats, which gives them a greater sense of unity and allows for greater trust in the leadership.[7] Activists in the Republican Party tend to be deferential to party leadership, allowing the organization to assume a more formal, hierarchical structure.[8] The culture of deference gives Republican leadership a degree of insulation to make decisions that is not available to their counterparts and allows them to focus on the nuts and bolts of electoral machinery (Bibby 1998). For this reason, Republican organizations have an advantage pursuing pragmatic electoral goals through the party organization.[9]

Democrats, in contrast, have always been a more heterogeneous party than Republicans, which forces upon them a greater need to spend resources simply trying to maintain their broad coalition (Mayer 1996; Freeman 1986; Klinkner 1994). As a result, Democrats frequently emphasize procedural reforms, caucus meetings, and the day-to-day tending of diverse constituencies, which leaves the party with fewer resources to devote to electoral goals (Polsby 1983). The fact that Democrats have relied heavily on labor organizations since the 1930s to win elections has also dampened incentives for the party to develop its electoral apparatus.[10] The party has always counted on labor organizations to get members of union households to the polls.

Given the heterogeneous nature of the Democratic coalition, its party organizations tend to be weaker than Republicans (Aldrich 1995; Cotter et al. 1984; Herrnson 1988). Democrats are more candidate-centered than Republicans because concentrating power centrally is less tenable in an alliance as disparate as conservative southerners, liberal secularists, and midwestern union members. A winning strategy for local Democrats in the South or the Rocky Mountain states often means running against the national party.[11] An appropriate organizational response to sectionalism and local diversity is to decentralize party activity, allowing candidates to manage their own campaigns with the party in the background.

The differences between Democratic and Republican organizations have important consequences for party campaigning. Republicans tend to invest more heavily in party infrastructure than Democrats. As a result, they have stronger electoral organizations because their political culture supports electoral activity managed by party leaders. The Democrats, in contrast, have pursued a more decentralized strategy that emphasizes candidate-centered support in the form of broadcast advertising and the outside help of affiliated partisan groups in mobilizing voters. Both parties want to win, but their electoral coalitions—which provide diverse resources to achieve this goal—impose different kinds of constraints on party strategy. These constraints influence how parties balance their campaigns between candidate-centered and organizational activities.

HOW PARTIES CAMPAIGN IN PRESIDENTIAL ELECTIONS BEFORE AND AFTER THE BCRA

Presidential campaigns are no longer simply contests managed by candidate committees. During the 1990s, political parties became fully integrated into presidential campaigns at the national and state levels. Wealth has allowed parties to supplement candidate campaign communications with party-sponsored ads (the candidate-centered strategy) while simultaneously expanding traditional party activities such as voter mobilization (the party-centered strategy). The dual-candidate and party-centered strategy has become critical in the contemporary political environment.

To demonstrate that parties engage in dual strategies I observe patterns of party spending at the national and state levels between 1992 and 2004. Reliable data on party spending first became available in 1992 through the FEC.[12] I coded expenditures into three categories: (1) candidate-targeted activity, (2) mobilization and grass roots, and (3) administrative. The last two categories are considered party-centered activity because they tend to provide collective benefits to all party candidates and supporters. The first category, in contrast, contains activities that provide little in the way of lasting benefits to the party. Amounts have been adjusted for inflation in constant 2004 dollars.

Candidate-targeted activity includes funds that support primarily the party nominee rather than the broader party ticket. The vast majority of these funds are for broadcast advertising, including any soft or hard money spending on television and radio to help the party nominee, whether or not the advertisement actually used electioneering words, such as *vote for.* Prior to the BCRA, party soft money, which had no limits, was supposed to be used for broad-based party activity aimed at boosting volunteer efforts and voter turnout. Parties, however, sponsored so-called issue ads that purportedly sought to advertise party positions on issues but were actually aimed at helping elect the party candidate (Krasno and Seltz 2000; Krasno and Goldstein 2002).

This category also includes coordinated and independent expenditures for the presidential nominee. Coordinated expenditures are limited under the FECA. In 2004, each political party was permitted to make $16.2 million in coordinated expenditures.[13] Independent expenditures, which are not coordinated with candidates, have no limits, but all the funds must be raised under the hard money limits (groups may only donate through PACs up to a maximum of fifteen thousand dollars per calendar year, and individuals may give up to twenty-five thousand dollars per election, adjusted for inflation).

Mobilization and grass roots are expenditures for registering and getting voters to the polls. This category includes spending on phone banks, field activities, direct mail, and grass roots paraphernalia such as lawn signs and bumper stickers. While this activity helps the presidential nominee, it also supports candidates lower on the ticket. In addition, such spending should help build the party long term by generating local enthusiasm for the party candidates and generating valuable lists of voters, donors, and volunteers.

Administrative expenditures are related to party staff, office equipment, travel, and any other related operational expenses. This form of spending has potential long-term benefits for the party when used to maintain party headquarters and allow party workers to engage in partisan activities throughout the year.

The following analysis provides a comprehensive portrait of party campaigning by including spending by national, state, and local committees in federal elections, as reported to the FEC.[14] Table 10 shows that both Republican and Democratic committees have increased their spending extraordinarily in presidential elections between 1992 and 2004. During this period, party spend-

TABLE 10. Party Spending, 1992–2004 (in millions of 2004 dollars)

	1992	1996	2000	2004
Republicans				
Candidate targeted (TV ads)	10	56	117	129
Mobilization and grass roots	10	23	49	181
Administration[a]	58	96	159	263
Total	78	175	326	572
Democrats				
Candidate targeted (TV ads)	18	71	144	190
Mobilization and grass roots	12	16	47	133
Administration[a]	49	83	186	215
Total	79	170	377	538

Source: Data from Federal Election Commission.
[a]National and state parties (combined and adjusted for 2004 dollars). Administration includes "unidentified" spending.

ing increased roughly sevenfold, with parties keeping pace with one another. Republican Party spending rose from $78 million in 1992 to $572 million in 2004, while Democratic Party spending increased from $79 million to $538 million. In comparison, presidential candidate spending in primaries and the general election during this time rose 58 percent from about $550 million to just over $867 million.[15]

Significantly, as parties raised more money during this period, their spending increased across each of the three categories with each passing cycle. For Republicans, candidate-targeted spending increased from just $10 million in 1992 to $129 million in 2004, mobilization and grass roots spending from $10 million to $181 million, and administrative spending from $58 million to $263 million. For Democrats, the changes are similarly striking. Candidate-targeted spending increased from $18 million in 1992 to $190 million in 2004, mobilization and grass roots spending from $12 million to $133 million, and administrative spending from $49 million to $215 million. These figures belie claims widely reported by public interest groups and major newspapers that the parties were simply funneling cash (including soft money) into television ads. Instead, the parties appeared to have a balanced campaign approach, spending money not only on broadcasting but also on grass roots work and operation of the party headquarters.

Given the structural and cultural differences between the parties, it is not surprising that they tend to spend their campaign money somewhat differently. While each spends roughly the same total in a given year, Democrats tend to allocate more for candidate-targeted activity (television ads) than Republicans. Republicans, in contrast, have invested more money in the organization itself. As expected, Republican organizations are better staffed, and, as I show later, they pursue a greater variety of electoral work. Republicans in 2004 also pulled ahead of Democrats with investments in voter mobilization, after being even with them in previous years. One reason they leapfrogged Democrats is due to changes in the campaign finance laws, which banned party soft money. This reform encouraged Democrats to pursue a dual strategy in 2004 of dividing mobilization efforts between the formal party organization, which could no longer use soft money, and outside groups, which could.[16] Democratic partisans set up 527 organizations (named after their tax code status), which could accept soft money for a variety of political activities, including voter mobilization. One prominent group, America Coming Together (ACT), spent an estimated $84 million on GOTV efforts in battleground states.[17] If 527 organizations are included in the count when calculating Democratic spending, the

Democrats may have outspent Republicans in 2004. The Democratic response to campaign finance reform is characteristic of a party that depends on a diverse coalition of interest groups. Republicans, in contrast, chose to spend almost all their funds within the formal party structure.

The largest category of party spending is administrative expenditures, suggesting that parties are *not* merely "pass through" conduits to pay for candidate communications. In 2004, for example, Republican Party organizations spent $263 million for administrative and overhead expenses, which reflects almost *half* of their total spending. Similarly, Democrats spent roughly $215 million, or 40 percent of their budget, on administration. A detailed breakdown reveals that, in a typical cycle, half of these expenditures are for staff salaries and benefits. For Democrats, staff costs diminished in 2004 by $20 million from a previous high of $73 million in 2000. Republican staff costs grew slightly to $68 million from a previous high of $65 million. Again, these differences reflect the alternative strategies of Republicans choosing to work within the formal party structure and Democrats hedging their bets under the new campaign finance law by redeploying resources to 527 groups.

In peeling back the layers of administrative costs, it appears that both parties are investing more in expensive new technologies and data bases. In 2004, for example, office-related expenditures (rent, utilities, computers, etc.) surged ahead of staff-related spending. For Republicans, this sum increased from $60 million to $160 million between 2000 and 2004. For Democrats, it increased from $46 million to $127 million over the same period. Republicans apparently exploited commercial data bases that identified consumer buying patterns that were correlated with Republican-leaning voters. According to Republican officials, for example, Coors beer and bourbon drinkers skewed Republican; brandy and cognac drinkers tilted Democrat; homes with caller ID tended to be Republican; people interested in gambling, fashion, and theater tended to be Democratic (Edsall and Grimaldi 2004).[18] The Democrats also had their own expensive version of a new voter data base they called "Demzilla," but postelection analysis suggested that they were not able to exploit the new technology as well as Republicans for identifying likely Kerry voters (Clymer 2005; Edsall 2006b).

After administrative costs, parties spend the next largest amount on candidate-targeted funds. As expected, Democrats spend proportionally more of their funds on candidate-targeted activity than Republicans. In 2004, for example, they spent more than 35 percent of their money on candidate support, in comparison with Republicans, who spent only 22 percent. This difference was apparent in previous elections but more so in 2004. The vast majority of these funds are not political contributions to candidates (which are capped by law) but party-sponsored advertising on network and cable television. These data show clearly that the party has become an essential venue for producing and airing ads in support of presidential candidates, a practice that has been encouraged by caps on candidate spending under the public financing provisions of the FECA. Since presidential candidates cannot exceed spending limits if they accept public funds, they must rely on parties to sponsor a large amount of communications.

Significantly, the BCRA did not curtail the amount that parties spent on candidate-targeted activity, even though some who supported reform had hoped that the absence of party soft money would lead to fewer television ads. On the contrary, direct support of the major party candidates increased from a prereform level of $261 million in 2000 to a postreform amount of $319 million in 2004. A notable difference in 2004 was that parties switched from expenditures for issue ads, funded with soft money, to independent expenditures, funded entirely with hard money. Parties cannot be capped from spending money in elections "independently" so long as they do not coordinate their activity with candidates. In this manner, parties spent a combined $140 million to help their candidates (Corrado 2006), running a completely parallel campaign and one that was formally cordoned off from other party activity to prevent the appearance of coordination with candidates.

The Republicans, however, discovered a way to increase the level of coordination with candidates by running so-called hybrid ads, which permitted them to consult with the candidate.[19] These ads combined a message of support for the president with a generic party message, which enabled the Republicans to divide the cost between the presidential campaign and the party committee. The Democrats quickly imitated the Republican model with their own hybrid ads.

The new campaign finance law achieved one of its major goals, however. It effectively shut down party-based issue advertising that was paid for with soft money. Previous to 2004, the parties had used soft money to air television ads, which were thinly veiled campaign commercials for the presidential nominees. By avoiding electioneering phrases such as *vote for*, parties could claim that these commercials qualified as issue ads that supported broad-based party mobilization. As such, the ads could be funded with soft money, which was designated for party-building activities. Parties exploited this loophole starting in 1996 when the Clinton reelection team used the DNC to run issue ads during the interregnum before the party conventions, which traditionally mark the official start of the general election. By statute, public funds did not become available to nominees until after the convention, which was four months after a candidate had clearly won the party nomination by amassing delegates in early primaries. Parties bridged this period before the start of the general election by airing issue ads, mostly through state parties, where laws allowed greater use of soft money. These early party ads were used to set the campaign agenda and try to define the opposing candidate during the interregnum.

The BCRA, which banned soft money in federal elections, encouraged parties to use alternative strategies to get around their candidate contribution limits. In 2004, the Democrats spent $120 million on independent advertising and an additional $18.6 million on hybrid advertising. These amounts are the same as the money they spent on ads in the previous 2000 election, when they allocated roughly $140 for advertising through issue ads paid for, in part, by soft money. Similarly, in 2004 Republicans spent $18 million on independent ads and $45.8 million on hybrid spending. These amounts were less than in 2000, when they spent about $97 million on issue ads in support of George W. Bush. The differences across both election cycles show that Democrats tend to be more of a candidate-centered party. Not only did they use a greater portion of soft money in the past to run issue ads for Al Gore, but they also spent their hard money post-BCRA for independent expenditures to help John Kerry in 2004. Additional advertising in support of party candidates was sponsored by partisan 527 organizations, with the most being spent by a Democratic-leaning group called the Media Fund (which spent an estimated $58 million).[20]

The third and final category of party spending is for mobilization and grass roots activity. While this is the smallest spending category, mobilization and grass roots activity has experienced the largest spending increases since 1992. The "ground game" has become increasingly important relative to television advertising in presidential elections.[21] The trend began before the new campaign finance law, so it is unclear how much the BCRA may have contributed to a greater emphasis on voter mobilization. In 1992, the parties combined spent just $0.12 per eligible voter on mobilization and grass roots activity. In subsequent years, this figure rose exponentially to $0.20 in 1996, $0.50 in 2000, and $1.50 in 2004.[22] It seems clear that the accumulation of party wealth supports political activities that potentially increase voter turnout.

Much of the additional spending in 2004 was for direct mail. Since direct mail is frequently used for fund-raising as well as for GOTV appeals, these increases suggest that parties responded to the BCRA (which banned soft money) by trying to grow the number of hard money donors. Republican direct mail costs went from a relatively small base of $4 million in 1992 to more than $100 million in 2004.[23] Postage alone in 2004 cost the GOP $44 million, up from $6 million in 2000. In 2004, Democrats experienced a less dramatic rise in direct mail costs than Republicans, but they experienced a significant shift over 2000. In that year, the party spent only $14 million, but they spent $46 million in 2004. Aside from direct mail, Democrats used the Internet to raise money, learning from the success of insurgent candidate Howard Dean in the primaries. Their success with this strategy likely offset fund-raising costs considerably, which may explain why the DNC achieved parity with the RNC in fund-raising even though they invested less than Republicans in direct mail. Even though direct mail will remain important for Republicans—especially for communicating with older party donors who do not use the Internet—they will try to imitate the DNC strategy in the future.

The BCRA also appears to have stimulated voter contact by telephone for Republicans. Phone bank expenses increased from roughly $4 million in 2000 to almost $30 million in 2004. Like direct mail, phone calls are used for GOTV efforts but may also be part of a strategy to raise cash. Instead of investing more in phone banks, Democrats augmented field operations by spending additional sums on canvassing to register voters and to get out the vote. They increased spending from about $12 million to $49 million in this subcategory. Republicans nearly doubled their field operations, from $13 million to $25 million. Anecdotal reports suggest that Republicans relied more heavily than Democrats on volunteers for field activities (Balz and Edsall 2004). Working through state and local parties, Republicans organized and motivated volunteers to contact friends and neighbors to vote for George W. Bush. This strategy appeared very successful—and cost effective. Democrats may attempt to imitate it in 2008, relying less on paid field workers than they did in 2004.

Overall, the spending data demonstrate two important findings. First, greater wealth has allowed party organizations to augment their presence in presidential campaigns, both as financial supporters of candidates and as agents of broader mobilization efforts. While parties have helped candidates get around public financing spending caps by airing party-based communications, they have spent most of their funds maintaining robust campaign organizations, which raise money from small donors and mobilize the electorate through grass roots efforts. In short, parties have not been mere conduits to funnel cash into television ads, as many proreform groups argued before the BCRA passed. The fact that parties continue to invest hard money, post-BCRA, in party-based work rather than merely advertising underscores the importance of a strong organizational strategy in contemporary campaigns.[24]

Not surprisingly, however, the BCRA failed to diminish the incentive for parties to spend money on television ads, even when they lacked soft money. In reality, parties spent more on television in 2004 than in 2000, but through a different tactic of using independent and hybrid expenditures. Party-based advertising was also supplemented by communications delivered through partisan-inspired 527 organizations. According to the Center for Responsive Politics, 527 groups spent at least $160 million on television advertising in the presidential campaign.[25] All told, advertising in presidential elections increased significantly in 2004 even though the reforms were intended, in part, to emphasize grass roots activity. The increases came from interest groups, which, unlike the parties, could continue to use soft money. In the nation's top seventy-five media markets, the number of ads aired by interest groups went up, from 23,850 in 2000 to 124,290 in 2004 (Franz, Rivlin, and Goldstein 2006). Much of this was financed by soft money. The BCRA provides a classic case in which legal constraints on the party activity do little to reduce demand for money but simply push it outside the system toward shadow party organizations and interest groups.

The second major finding—rooted in a theory about divergent party structure and culture—is that the Republican and Democratic Parties emphasize different campaign strategies and respond to reforms differently. Democrats tend to focus more on candidate-targeted activities than Republicans because Democratic candidates often need to distance themselves from the national party to win in the Midwest or the Rocky Mountain states. As evidence, the Democrats continue to spend more money than Republicans on candidate-targeted advertising (through independent expenditures, as they did previously through soft money issue ads). Moreover, in the wake of reform Democrats are more likely to campaign outside the formal party structure through the use of 527 groups. This is hardly surprising, given the looser, heterogeneous nature of the Democratic coalition. The outside strategy, traditionally exploited by pro-Democrat labor unions, has expanded since the 1970s to include environmental, women, and minority organizations. Pursuing an "open" organizational strategy in 2004 was risky for Democrats because of coordination problems but entirely consistent with their political culture. Democratic groups tend to be populated with issue-oriented activists, who are less deferential to party leadership. With divided loyalties between policy groups and the party, Democratic partisans have been more willing to work outside the formal party structure to accomplish political goals.

In contrast, we observe the Republicans investing a greater proportion of resources than the Democrats on party infrastructure, particularly to increase hard money fund-raising through direct mail and telephone solicitations. In 2004, Republicans ramped up their field operations considerably, once again showing a heavier reliance than Democrats on the party infrastructure to organize political campaigns. The spending patterns of both parties were well established before the BCRA. If anything, the BCRA appears to have intensified essential differences between the parties.

THE NATIONALIZATION OF PARTY FINANCE

To provide further evidence that the national committees have used their wealth to increase their influence in elections, I observe the relationship between national and state parties. In the past two decades, party financing of elections has become nationalized, with the DNC and RNC raising most of the funds for presidential elections and managing the flow of resources—both money and electoral data—to political campaigns in the states. State parties, meanwhile, concentrate on field operations with significant oversight from the national parties.

The rational division of labor between national and state parties, with the national parties taking the lead, is relatively new to American politics. When political scientist Alexander Heard was studying campaign finance in 1960, he noted the extremely weak position of the RNC and DNC: "the national organization of neither American party in the mid-twentieth century possessed a sufficient financial constituency of its own so organized as to free it from financial dependence on the state and local leadership" (289). Heard had predicted that national party control over funds would change the loci of power within the party and bring some cohesiveness to party operations.

What Heard was suggesting has come to pass. Since the 1980s national party money has flowed to state parties, which is a complete reversal of how party financing worked in previous eras when the DNC and RNC had to practically beg the state parties to contribute to the national organization. Figure 9 shows that national parties have been passing on millions of dollars in hard and soft money to state parties during the past several election cycles. The control over funds gives the national parties leverage in forcing state parties to accommodate national party strategies in presidential campaigns. Until 1996, most of these funds were for organizing voter mobilization campaigns. In that year, however, transfers rose sharply because parties exploited a loophole to use soft money for campaign ads sponsored nominally by the state parties. This tactic

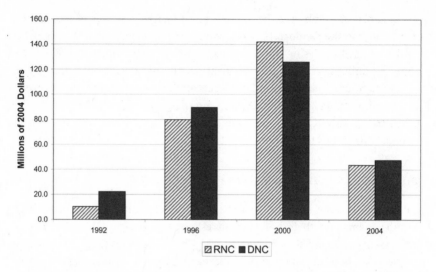

FIG. 9. National committee (RNC, DNC) transfers to state parties. (Data from Federal Election Commission, various years.)

was used intensely in the 2000 elections when Republicans transferred $118 million and Democrats $105 million to their state parties.

The amount of soft money raised by national parties and spent by state parties for campaign ads stoked public attention for reforms championed by presidential candidate John McCain. The chief goals of the BCRA of 2002 were to ban party soft money and sham issue ads before an election. Under the BCRA, national committees could not raise or spend soft money and state parties were limited to small increments of soft money to pay for grass roots activity.

Even though they lacked soft money in the 2004 elections, national committees continued to transfer funds to state parties because mobilizing voters remained an important element in the presidential campaign. In 2004, national committee transfers made up more than a quarter of total state party funds spent in federal elections. Most funds were concentrated in a few large states, though every state received some money. Table 11 shows that in 2004 the RNC sent 69 percent of its transfers to battleground states (fifteen of them), while the Democrats sent 76 percent to these same states. The new campaign finance law, which increased the value of hard money by eliminating soft money, appears to accelerate a trend of parties concentrating money in battleground states much more than previously. One possible explanation is that national parties would rather not use precious hard dollars in noncompetitive states, whereas soft money was less difficult to dispense simply because it was easier to raise. Some of the imbalance in 2004 might also be explained by the fact that national committees no longer swap hard and soft dollars with states parties, which was a common practice before the BCRA.[26]

Whatever the reasons, table 11 illustrates a potentially alarming trend. Voters in noncompetitive states are being increasingly ignored by the national committees. In 2000, the parties transferred a combined $1.14 for each voter in a noncompetitive state. In 2004, party transfers declined to just $0.17 in these states. The last time national parties transferred so little to noncompetitive states was in 1992, when parties had one-third the amount of money in its coffers than they did in 2004. One consequence of the heavily biased distribution of resources is that voters in noncompetitive states do not get mobilized—certainly not in the way voters are mobilized in traditional battleground states like Michigan or Ohio, as I show later in this chapter.

It is routine for parties to allocate resources strategically to win the Electoral College, with a focus on swing states containing the most electoral votes.[27] According to John Aldrich, selective party building of this nature by national elites has been typical since the earliest days of the mass party during the Jack-

TABLE 11. Allocation of Party Transfers in Battleground States, 1992–2004

	Battleground			Nonbattleground			% Transfers Allocated to Battleground
	Total Transfers[a]	Per Eligible Voter	N	Total Transfers[a]	Per Eligible Voter	N	
RNC							
1992	3.4	0.11	10	6.8	0.05	40	33
1996	16.3	0.52	8	63.5	0.43	42	20
2000	67.5	1.14	13	74.0	0.56	37	48
2004	30.2	0.51	15	13.3	0.09	35	69
DNC							
1992	3.5	0.11	10	18.7	0.13	40	16
1996	20.7	0.66	8	68.8	0.46	42	23
2000	61.9	1.04	13	63.8	0.48	37	49
2004	36.3	0.61	15	11.3	0.08	35	76

Source: Federal Election Commission 2005a.
Note: Data on battleground states derived from state polls reported by The Hotline 2004 two months prior to Election Day; battleground states are those with a predicted difference of five points or less between the two major party candidates.
[a]Total transfers given in millions of 2004 dollars.

sonian era. Party leaders, such as Martin Van Buren, focused on states where the cost of organizing was cheapest and where the contest was likely to be competitive.[28] With a short-term electoral orientation, which is encouraged by a decentralized, confederative party structure, national committees have few incentives to invest in underperforming states, where the electoral payoff might be many years away (see Aldrich 1995; Herrnson 1988). The congressional parties, especially, have a short-term view and invest almost exclusively in marginal contests where the payoff is immediate (Cantor and Herrnson 1997; Damore and Hansford 1999).[29] Since the governing structure of congressional committees is such that they lack formal ties to state and local parties, they lack strong incentives (through local pressure) to support party building in states, particularly in districts with no competitive races.

While many close observers of elections have argued that the national committees pursue an Electoral College strategy, to my knowledge there have been no systematic studies conducted that would prove this empirically. More important, research has failed to test whether other factors—in addition to winning the Electoral College—motivate how national parties allocate resources to states. Are national parties interested in shoring up support in states where they are organizationally weak? Are they planning strategically to build support in states with rapidly increasing populations or burgeoning numbers of newly immigrated Latino voters, who are still "up for grabs"?

To explore these questions, I analyzed the pattern of national party investments in the American states. I regressed national party transfers for the DNC and RNC on explanatory variables that measure Electoral College strategies and efforts to invest where the party is weak or where there is future potential to win support, such as Rocky Mountain states. Table 12 presents the OLS regression estimates for each election cycle from 1992 though 2004, predicting national committee transfers to their state parties.[30] The dependent variable comes from data on national party transfers to their fifty state organizations.[31]

The results, which are highly robust across a range of different model specifications, demonstrate the conventional wisdom that national committees pursue an efficient Electoral College strategy, controlling for other factors. It appears that the RNC has been more efficient than the DNC with its funds in the past two election cycles of 2000 and 2004, which lends support to my theory that the Republicans are a more centralized, top-down organization. In other words, staff at the RNC can make executive decisions, which are insulated from the constituency-based politics that often confront officials at the DNC.

To illustrate these points, I focus on the results in the last column of table 12, which was the election of 2004. In a state with the average number of electoral votes (eleven), the model predicts that the RNC transfers an additional $1,156,300 if this state is expected to be a battleground. More important, the RNC provides an increment of $274,500 for each additional electoral vote in the state (see the interactive term Battleground_EV). Similarly, the model predicts that the DNC transfers $1,298,700 to battleground states and an additional $151,200 for each additional electoral vote in these same battleground states. Thus, both parties pursue an Electoral College strategy, with the RNC being slightly more efficient than the DNC. Even though the difference between the RNC and the DNC is not large for just one electoral vote, the substantive effects for states with more electoral votes can be meaningful. In a typical battleground state such as Ohio, with its twenty electoral votes, the model predicts that the RNC would transfer $3,626,800 while the DNC would transfer $2,559,500, a difference of more than $1 million.

The only cycle in which the RNC did not outperform the DNC in its targeting was during the 1996 Clinton-Dole election. In retrospect, there appears to be a good explanation. This was a runaway election for the Democratic nominee, Bill Clinton, and the RNC wisely chose to invest some of its resources in House elections to help Republican congressional candidates, as news articles reported (Apple 1996, 1). A separate analysis for 1996 (not shown here) that includes variables for House races that "lean Republican" or "lean Democrat" demonstrates that the RNC played a defensive strategy in 1996, sending an additional $342,000 to state parties for each House race that was leaning Republican. This seems like a rational response to concerns that a Democratic landslide might jeopardize the election of Republican House candidates, who were slightly favored going into the election. The capacity of the RNC to switch strategies from the Electoral College to House races suggests, as expected, that Republican Party professionals retain the flexibility to revise plans in a way that will maximize party gains.

What to make of the failure by the DNC to allocate resources efficiently in 2000? Given the closeness of this presidential election, there was no comparable incentive for Democrats to channel funds to congressional races as the RNC did in 1996. In that election, the DNC appeared to allocate funds based purely on the amount of money they gave to states in the previous (1996) election. The DNC failure to revise its strategy in 2000 may have contributed to the inability of the Democratic nominee, Al Gore, to win a majority of electoral votes, even though he won the popular vote. The cross-sectional analysis shows that the DNC improved its Electoral College strategy substantially in 2004 in support of its nominee, John Kerry.

There is little evidence from this basic model that national parties use their

TABLE 12. Regression Predicting National Committee Transfers to State Parties (in 2004 real dollars, thousands)

Republicans (RNC)	1992	1996	2000	2004
Electoral College Strategy				
Battleground state	172.7**	435.0	1,848.8*	1,156.3**
	(2.79)	(0.87)	(2.30)	(3.20)
Electoral votes	– 8.0	126.4**	83.9	–14.1
	(1.20)	(5.74)	(1.22)	(0.71)
Battleground_EV	28.4**	– 54.0	434.1**	274.5**
	(3.91)	(– 0.81)	(4.02)	(4.90)
Previous presidential	1.0	– 39.1	41.2	22.2
competition	(0.26)	(– 1.03)	(0.80)	(1.11)
Party Building/Support				
South	10.6	– 123.7	– 1,955.6*	110.7
	(0.16)	(0.27)	(2.18)	(0.30)
Rocky Mountain	– 36.2	– 215.8	– 828.7	336.4
	(0.43)	(0.41)	(0.85)	(0.84)
Previous transfers	1.2**	2.9**	0.6	0.1
(thousand $)	(5.73)	(3.30)	(1.75)	(1.54)
Control Variables				
Senate toss-up	– 105.7	– 94.3	25.6	405.3
	(0.55)	(0.23)	(0.02)	(1.09)
Gubernatorial toss-up	– 127.0	374.5	16.9	162.6
	(0.72)	(0.55)	(0.02)	(0.35)
House toss-up	43.3	342.5	427.8	– 6.3
	(1.07)	(1.68)	(0.78)	(0.03)
Population density	– 0.2	– 1.8*	– 1.1	0.6
	(1.64)	(2.67)	(0.66)	(0.99)
Soft money state	58.7	336.5	– 910.1	– 481.4
	(1.18)	(0.87)	(1.23)	(1.54)
Constant	– 92.3	4,533.3	– 1,170.3	– 1,656.8
Observations	50.0	50.0	50.0	50.0
R-squared	0.8	0.8	0.8	0.8

wealth to exploit long-term opportunities. Neither party, for example, appears to have allocated extra funds to states in the South (where Democrats have fallen behind) or in the Rocky Mountains (where the population is booming) to enhance party prospects in these regions. The DNC invested additional resources in the South only in 1992. In that election, the party believed that Bill Clinton, a southerner, could win southern states, which he did. In the subsequent cycle, however, the party actually sent fewer resources to southern states and has not made any efforts to shore up parties in the South since 1992. Nor

TABLE 12.—Continued

Democrats (DNC)	1992	1996	2000	2004
Electoral College Strategy				
Battleground state	– 71.4	1,146.3	186.3	1,298.7**
	(0.66)	(1.69)	(0.24)	(4.72)
Electoral votes	10.3	91.9	–84.7	–13.5
	(0.73)	(1.91)	(1.56)	(1.05)
Battleground_EV	– 26.0	259.3*	102.8	151.2**
	(2.00)	(2.69)	(0.93)	(3.90)
Previous presidential	6.9	34.1	–8.5	15.0
competition	(0.92)	(0.69)	(0.18)	(1.01)
Party Building/Support				
South	356.1**	–1,485.2*	–1,077.8	– 281.8
	(2.84)	(2.37)	(1.28)	(1.00)
Rocky Mountain	76.8	– 677.6	– 633.4	317.8
	(0.51)	(0.94)	(0.70)	(1.04)
Previous transfers	0.9**	1.1	1.8**	0.2**
(thousand $)	(2.98)	(1.25)	(6.68)	(4.73)
Control Variables				
Senate toss-up	– 87.8	49.0	161.6	44.8
	(0.26)	(0.09)	(0.11)	(0.16)
Gubernatorial toss-up	– 227.9	–1,181.0	–140.6	–172.0
	(0.71)	(1.29)	(0.14)	(0.49)
House toss-up	186.2*	264.0	–544.1	35.1
	(2.26)	(0.97)	(1.07)	(0.25)
Population density	0.0	– 1.8	– 0.6	0.2
	(0.04)	(1.92)	(0.40)	(0.38)
Soft money state	16.7	449.7	–1,236.4	– 38.7
	(0.19)	(0.85)	(1.83)	(0.17)
Constant	– 551.5	–1,588.8	1,670.2	–1,251.5
Observations	50.0	50.0	50.0	50.0
R-squared	0.8	0.7	0.8	0.9

Note: Absolute value of *t*-statistics in parentheses.
*Significant at 5%   **Significant at 1%

have Republicans sent additional dollars to the South, probably because they expect their candidates to fare well in southern states. The Democratic nominee, Al Gore, did not win a single southern state in 2000 even though he hailed from Tennessee.[32] And despite talk from party elites about building the party in the Rocky Mountain states, there is no evidence that the national committees in either party sent additional cash to these states for this purpose. Previous models, which are not shown here, also reveal no systematic strategy to strengthen the party in states with high percentages of immigrants or blacks.

Both parties, however, subsidized their state organizations based on what they gave to them in the previous election cycle. The model predicts, for example, that a Democratic state committee would receive $0.23 in 2004 for every dollar the DNC transferred in 2000. The DNC behaved similarly in previous election cycles. Indeed, they appeared even more generous when they had soft money, giving an additional $1.80 in 2000 for each dollar they gave in 1996. In the 1992 and 1996 elections, Republicans gave funds to state parties based on previous allocations, although this strategy ceased in subsequent elections. Overall, the results suggest that national committees, particularly the DNC, provide ongoing support for state parties regardless of their importance in an Electoral College strategy. Under the BCRA and the soft money ban, however, the national committees are much less generous in doling out funds to state parties.

THE EFFECT OF THE BCRA ON STATE PARTIES

What additional effect did the BCRA have on political parties? To gain a better understanding of the impact of this reform, it is necessary to observe state party activity, which, as shown previously, is supported significantly in federal elections by national committee funds. Changes in state party campaigns reveal clearly the adjustments in response to the BCRA. As table 13 shows, state parties no longer spend money on media in federal elections. The previous strategy of funding issue ads through state parties was completely eliminated in 2004 with the BCRA ban on soft money. Instead, state parties emphasize voter mobiliza-

TABLE 13. State Party Spending, 1992–2004 (in millions of 2004 dollars)

	Media	Mobilization and Grass Roots	Administration	Unidentified	Total Spending
Republicans					
1992	1	10	43	3	57
1996	31	20	64	5	120
2000	106	42	113	7	268
2004	1	71	122	4	198
Democrats					
1992	3	16	49	4	72
1996	90	20	67	8	185
2000	152	55	117	35	359
2004	3	62	108	6	179

Source: Data from the Federal Election Commission, coded by author.

tion, especially Republicans. In 2004, Republican state parties spent $71 million on voter mobilization activities (much in the form of direct mail), almost $30 million more than in the 2000 election. The Democratic increase, however, was less substantial.

Overall, the total spending by state parties in federal elections declined because national parties no longer transfer funds for media spending. The nonmedia portion of the Republican state parties increased from $162 million in 2000 to $197 million in 2004. For Democrats, however, this spending declined from $207 to $176. In this sense, the BCRA was less kind to Democratic state parties than Republican state parties.

Given the previous discussion about Electoral College strategies, we know that differences exist in party spending between battleground and noncompetitive states. To what extent did these differences grow or shrink after campaign finance reform? The answer is that the gap grew significantly between these two kinds of states in the postreform election. More than ever, citizens in battleground states experience political campaigns in ways that those in noncompetitive states can hardly imagine. While voters in places like Michigan and Ohio are inundated with political messages and contacts, those in "easy win" states such as New York, Mississippi, or California may hardly see a campaign commercial or receive a phone call related to the presidential election.

Comparing party spending in battleground and noncompetitive states before the BCRA reveals remarkable parity. Figures 10 and 11 show how much state parties spent per eligible voter in all noncompetitive states versus battleground states. These figures do not include media spending; thus they provide a relatively clean portrait of how the parties invested in broad-based GOTV efforts. In 1996, for example, both parties spent roughly $0.40 per eligible voter, regardless of whether the state was considered competitive or noncompetitive. In 2000, both parties significantly increased the amount they spent per eligible voter across the states. Democrats actually spent slightly more per eligible voter in noncompetitive states than in battleground states (which might explain why Gore won the popular vote but lost the Electoral College). In 2000 Republicans, on the other hand, spent $0.35 more per eligible voter in battleground states than in noncompetitive states, even though spending in the latter increased by 60 percent over the previous election.

After campaign finance reform, both parties in 2004 concentrated even more money in battleground states. Not surprisingly, the ban on soft money under the BCRA did not deter parties from spending in highly competitive states, but it did affect spending in noncompetitive states. Republican parties

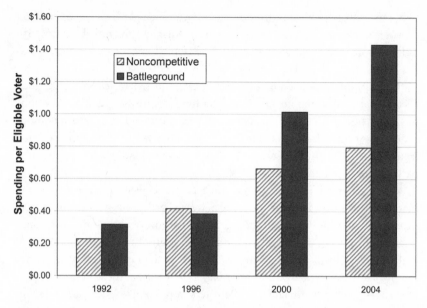

FIG. 10. Republican state party spending (nonmedia), noncompetitive versus battle-ground states

boosted spending in noncompetitive states in 2004 (perhaps to ensure that Bush won the popular vote this time), but the gap with battleground states grew larger. For Democrats the situation was a good deal worse. While party spending leaped in battleground states from $0.92 to $1.54 per eligible voter, it dropped precipitously in noncompetitive states, from $1.02 to $0.60.

The BCRA's impact appeared to hurt parties especially where state campaign finance differed most profoundly with new federal laws. Further analysis shows that the steepest declines in spending among Democratic organizations were in the states with campaign finance laws that differed most from the BCRA.[33] For example, Democratic state parties in soft money states (the fourteen states in which there were no limits on party fund-raising) spent $1.14 per eligible voter in the 2000 elections. In 2004, after the BCRA, this figure declined to $0.46. For similarly situated Republican parties, there was actually a slight increase in spending, from $0.64 to $0.73 per voter. Overall, it appears that the BCRA had its largest effect on Democratic parties in soft money states that lacked a competitive presidential contest. This finding suggests that the federal ban on soft money may have hurt state parties accustomed to using soft money

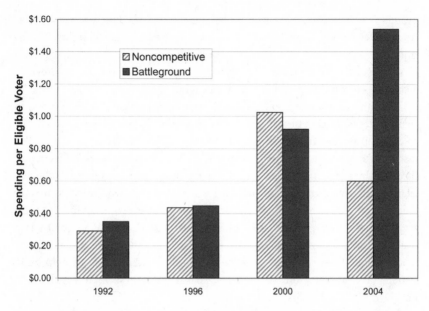

FIG. 11. Democratic state party spending (nonmedia), noncompetitive versus battleground states

under state campaign finance rules. These parties spent considerably less in the presidential elections than previously.

After one election, it is difficult to determine whether the BCRA was the principal engine for enlarging the gap between battleground and noncompetitive states. Three factors, however, make the influence of the reform seem likely. First, as I mentioned earlier, the national parties in the postreform period did not hand out hard money as generously as they distributed soft money during the prereform period. They saved hard money in 2004 primarily for battleground states, since these funds are more difficult to raise than soft money. Second, parties in nonbattleground states may have chosen to avoid federal electioneering because it forced them to spend exclusively hard money. Unlike previously, when they could spend both hard (federal) and soft (state) money for the entire party ticket, the BCRA imposed a definition of federal electioneering that required only hard money for generic party activity if any federal candidate was on the ballot. These state parties simply focused on state election activity to avoid the "penalty" of complying with complex federal laws that restricted their financing. Finally, the new law encouraged the formation of 527 groups, which focused exclusively on battleground states. The lack of coordination between parties, candidates, and 527 groups encouraged all political committees to focus simultaneously in the same obvious places. All of these behaviors conspired to concentrate electioneering—even more than previous elections—in a fraction of the American states.

The implications for political participation seem clear enough. Voters in many states will fail to be mobilized in presidential elections if parties continue to concentrate resources in battleground states. The lack of resources may also discourage partisans in these states from coordinating campaign activities through the state party organization, leaving individual candidates or the legislative caucus to pursue their campaign work independently. The vacuum created by having a resource-poor state party makes it easier for individual incumbents and interest groups to wield influence and discourages broad-based coalition building among activists for candidates up and down the ticket. Some would argue, however, that access to soft money did nothing to help build strong party organizations in the states. That is a fair question, to which I turn next.

DID SOFT MONEY STRENGTHEN POLITICAL PARTIES?

In the aftermath of BCRA reforms, one question that lingers is whether parties will be stronger or weaker without soft money. There are many facets to a strong party, including its ability to win elections, control the legislature, encourage unity in member voting, and create partisan loyalties in the electorate. My discussion here is limited primarily to the capacity of party organizations to influence campaigns. To be sure, strong party organizations can fortify other aspects of the party, particularly if party leaders are able to provide selective benefits to rank-and-file members and voters. As I argued in earlier chapters, resource dependencies matter. Power and influence derive, in part, from unequal interdependencies between political actors, namely, the degree to which one group relies on another for critical resources. For American parties, control over their critical resource—access to the ballot—was eliminated through Progressive-style reforms of the nominating process. Thus, American party organizations lack as much influence over individual candidates as parties in other nations.

Despite the comparative weakness of American parties, it is possible to measure whether they increase their strength to influence campaigns as a result of their wealth. A strong party organization is not simply one that is flush with cash. Conceivably, they could be little more than bank accounts. Rather, wealth must translate into a variety of campaign functions—from recruiting candidates to helping them campaign—that could potentially change the outcome of political contests. To the degree that party activity is potentially decisive in elections across time and across levels of office, it should be considered a strong organization.[34] Demonstrating that the party organization is decisive in a particular race is a difficult task, given that many factors are at work in an election. But one way to begin assessing party strength is to measure whether the organization performs the kind of campaign work that typically brings electoral success. This is what I demonstrate in the following discussion.

In the debates leading up to passage of the BCRA, there was considerable disagreement about what role soft money played in political campaigns. To supporters of the BCRA, the parties were merely conduits to funnel soft money into campaigns of individual candidates—these funds passed through the organization without leaving any lasting benefits for the party. To opponents of the soft money ban, soft money helped strengthen the formal organization, giving it resources to continue functioning in off-election years and augmenting the range of traditional party activities such as recruiting and developing voter lists. In this section I provide evidence for the latter argument, namely, that soft money helped strengthen the party. Whether the loss of soft money under the BCRA will now weaken parties remains to be seen in coming elections. But the argument that parties were merely empty vessels for soft money is simply not true.

In the following analysis I examine the relationship between party soft money spending and the level of party campaign activities—not including television or radio broadcasting. If parties did not use soft money for party-building activities—for example, recruiting candidates, organizing volunteers, gathering voter data, and helping candidates with their campaigns—then there should be no correlation between the amount they spent and the level of activities. If, however, soft money spending is strongly correlated with traditional party activity, then it would appear that soft money had a beneficial effect on party organizations.

The lack of data on national party activity over time makes it difficult to analyze the relationship between soft money and party activity. Instead, I take advantage of state party variation in soft money spending and organizational activity across the one hundred Republican and Democratic state parties. My hypothesis is that state parties that spend more soft money in federal elections are stronger and more active than those that spend less. By *stronger*, I mean these parties exceed others in campaign services, recruitment of candidates, and size and scope of their bureaucracies.[35]

To test this relationship, I combine data about party finances with survey responses about party activity.[36] The financial numbers tell us little about whether party organizations actually perform the work in-house or whether they hire consultants to do it. It is conceivable that parties are simply fronts for candidates. In this scenario, they purchase services that individual candidates request rather than investing strategically for collective party goals. What evidence exists that parties use their wealth to strengthen the organization rather than simply pay for candidate services?

To assess party activity, I sent a fifteen-question survey between December 2000 and June 2001 to the executive directors of the one hundred major state parties.[37] The survey asked questions about party services to candidates, recruitment activities, and basic information about party headquarters.[38] As a framework for analyzing party activity I draw on the work of the Party Transformation Study (PTS) (see Cotter et al. 1984), using its concept of "party organizational strength." In that work, researchers surveyed current and former state party chairs who had served between 1960 and 1980. Based on responses to questions about party activities, they developed measures of party strength.[39] Their factor analysis suggested the three dimensions of party organizational strength: programmatic (breadth of services to candidates), recruitment (breadth of candidate recruitment activity), and bureaucratic (indicators of organizational complexity such as staff, off-election year budgets, and permanent headquarters). Table 14, which provides information on state party activity, is organized along these three dimensions of party organizational strength, used as a conceptual framework for assessing the degree to which parties invest in programs, recruitment, or their bureaucracy.

The results in table 14 demonstrate that party organizations, with their increased wealth, are stronger today than in the past three decades. I compared survey responses for 2000 to party data from 1964–80 collected by the PTS.[40] Given the brevity of the 2000 survey, there are only a few measures to make such comparisons. Nevertheless, across a range of pursuits, both Republican and Democratic organizations are consistently more active in campaigns today than in the past. The findings suggest, as I argued previously, that party organizations have become more important in modern campaigns. Moreover, they exploited the FECA regime, including its allowance for soft money, to build stronger organizations.

Republican parties, in particular, demonstrate remarkably steady progress through the decades across most measures of party strength. In the programmatic area, for example, 70 percent of Republican organizations in 2000 designed and conducted polls, showing a steady increase from 33 percent in 1964.[41] The number of organizations providing campaign research increased from 29 percent in 1964 to 85 percent in 2000. Almost every Republican organization in the 2000 sample claimed to train campaign staff, a significant increase from the 63 percent of organizations doing so in 1964. Similarly, the proportion of organizations that recruit candidates rose steadily from 83 percent in 1964 to nearly 100 percent in 2000.

In terms of bureaucratic capacity, Republican budgets during nonelection years (when the organization is not swelled with temporary staff at the height of a campaign) expanded significantly by 2000, as did staff size.[42] The only measure of strength for which the Republican organizations declined in 2000 is whether they paid their party chair a salary. More GOP party chairs appear to have served as volunteers or simply to have received a stipend than in the past. The decline in salaried chairpersons is unexpected, given that the size of the party staff declined slightly between 1980 and 2000. Executive directors, who

TABLE 14. State Party Activity, 1964–2000

	Republicans					Democrats				
	1964	1969	1974	1980	2000	1964	1969	1974	1980	2000
Programmatic										
Conduct polls (%)	33	59	63	62	70	12	48	52	19	47
Provide campaign training (%)	63	82	92	93	96	47	80	67	82	77
Perform campaign research (%)	29	53	60	78	85	24	52	41	37	77
Recruitment										
Recruit candidates (%)	83	88	90	89	98	82	72	78	44	77
Make contributions to U.S. House challengers (%)	63	65	70	64	55	47	48	56	35	47
Bureaucratic										
Size of staff in off-year	2.1	5.6	5.2	9.0	6.8	2.5	4.2	8.7	5.5	5.2
Size of operating budget in off-year ($ thousands)	185	144	192	492	1,010	49	83	121	182	561
Chair receives salary (%)	29	32	35	37	19	6	44	26	39	38
Permanent headquarters (%)	83	94	98	96	100	77	84	96	85	100
N	24	34	48	27	47	17	25	27	27	47

Source: Data for 1964–80 is from state party organizations, 1960–80: (U.S.) (machine-readable data file) Cornelius P. Cotter (principal investigator). The number of observations for 1960–74 includes interviews of past party chairs in twenty-seven sample states with oversampling in some states.
Data for 2000 from author's survey.

serve party chairs, have assumed a more significant role in party management than in the past, which would allow the chairperson to perform honorific duties and fund-raising part-time.

The development of Democratic organizations is more uneven but still demonstrates maximum activity in 2000. Organizational growth appears to have increased until 1980, when it declined across several areas. In 2000, activity increased to levels that mostly exceeded or equaled the prior maximums achieved in 1974. The reasons for the dip in 1980 are unclear, particularly since there is no similar drop-off for Republicans. One possible explanation is that Democrats felt triumphant during the post-Watergate period, just before the Reagan presidential victory. They controlled both houses of Congress, as well as most state legislatures and governorships. Democrats perceived little need to rebuild state organizations, particularly during an era when candidates seemed completely in control of their campaigns. Democratic incumbents in the majority party could control resources to wage their own reelection campaigns and saw little reason to nurture the next crop of candidates. By this logic, Republicans, as the minority party, had a stronger incentive to build a collective enterprise for gathering resources and recruiting candidates. Indeed, Republicans outpaced Democrats in most categories. In 2000, more Republican organizations engaged in recruiting candidates, training campaign staff, and performing campaign research.

The discrepancy between Republican and Democratic party building in the 1980s also reflects the remarkable partisan changes that took place in the South. In the 1960s, Republicans began party building at a time when conservative Democrats controlled almost all public offices. Although Democrats dominated politics, party structures were weak because there was little genuine partisan competition to spur party organizing (Key 1956). Sensing an opportunity, Republicans began their organizational insurgence in the 1960s. Democrats did not react by building their own organizations until the mid-1980s.

Notably, Democrats have been more involved in recruiting since 1980, probably in reaction to the Republican successes in statehouses across the country. It is also apparent that, in comparison to the past, Democratic organizations are better staffed and have larger budgets in the nonelection years. They are also more active than Republicans in the primary selection process, being more likely to make preprimary endorsements in states where this is permitted, and help preferred candidates with party resources during the primary. These partisan differences are rooted in party traditions and the social bases of their respective constituencies. Since the Democratic Party reflects a more heterogeneous coalition, its primaries are likely to be more adversarial than those of Republicans (Polsby 1983). Democratic leaders might choose to take sides in primaries more frequently than Republicans to ensure that a viable centrist candidate emerges for the general election rather than one that comes forward from an ideological constituency in the party. Republicans appear to sidestep the problem of choosing candidates in the primary because they recruit more heavily. For Republicans, the selection process likely precedes the primary, meaning they encourage favorites to run for office and actively discourage others. Once again, the willingness of potential candidates to step down reflects the deferential culture of Republicans compared to Democrats.

Budget and staff levels suggest that Republicans possess greater organizational capacity than Democrats. Republican parties, on average, operate with budgets that exceed $1 million during the nonelection years, while Democrats make do with approximately $560,000. The average Republican state party has 6.8 staff, compared with 5.2 for Democrats. Almost all parties have permanent headquarters, so there is little to say here except that both parties have a local presence between elections.[43] The only other measure for which Democrats outdistance Republicans is their tendency to pay a salary to the party chair. This finding reflects, once again, the different social bases of the party, with Republicans tending to attract chairs from the business elite and Democrats relying more on people who do not have alternative sources of income when they become party chair.

Consistent with the previous findings, these data show that Republicans stress organization building more than the Democrats (Green 1994; Kayden and Mahe 1985). While the differences between parties are not large, they persist across several measures. Indeed, for the few measures for which Democratic activity exceeds Republican activity—for example, exploiting the use of coordinated campaigns, making preprimary endorsements, and providing primary services to favored candidates—these might be described as strategies to attenuate the divisiveness inherent in the Democratic Party coalition.

To what degree was party activity related to soft money spending? To make general statements about the relationship between spending and organizational vitality, it is helpful to have an overall measure of party organizational strength. To do this, I combine activity scores from survey data into an index of party strength, with some minor adjustments to account for nonresponse for particular survey questions.[44] The index ranges from weak to strong parties, with a minimum score of .125 for the Rhode Island Democratic Party and maximum score of .625 for the Florida Republican Party (see the appendix for a list of parties and their scores). Based on these scores the parties are separated into quartiles of organizational strength: weak, moderately weak, moderately strong, and strong. Then, I compare these quartiles of strength against the average state party expenditures in each quartile, using the amount of soft money that state parties spent between the 1992 and 2000 elections. I did not include spending on broadcast media, which is not a traditional element of party activities, because it simply reflects the use of state parties as conduits through which the national committees sponsor television campaign ads.

Figure 12 shows average soft money expenditures across the party strength quartiles. The results are striking. They demonstrate that soft money spending is highly correlated with the strength of a party. Strong parties spend, on average, five times as much as weak parties. In fact, the relationship between soft money spending and party strength displays a linear relationship. Spending an additional $2 million moves parties from the weak to the moderately weak category; another increment of roughly $1.2 million moves parties into the moderately strong category; an additional $5 million puts them in the rank of strong parties. Note in the appendix that both large and small states can be found at either end of the spectrum, so it is not simply a question of state size. In short, the more soft money parties spend, the more activities they perform.

The findings suggest that money makes a difference in party activity. During the 1990s party spending increased to unprecedented levels, in part because of soft money fund-raising. Although much of this additional spending was devoted to issue ads, a substantial portion was invested in traditional party work that included voter mobilization, grass roots efforts, and general organizational maintenance. This examination of organizational activity at various stages since the 1960s appears to indicate that parties are as strong today as they have been in the previous forty years. Since much of this growth occurred during a period when parties controlled increasing funds, it is more than plausible that soft money helped strengthen party organizations. The highest-spending parties tend to be more active. They recruit and train candidates more regularly and have larger bureaucracies in the off-season than lower-spending parties. The results are mixed for program activities, but this may reflect the fact that many of the high per capita spending states tend to be less professionalized, and, consequently, the candidates require fewer campaign services.

Overall, these patterns suggest that, while party money is often funneled from national organizations through state organizations to help presidential candidates, it has also helped build parties in the states. The observation that money matters is perhaps unsurprising in a campaign environment that relies

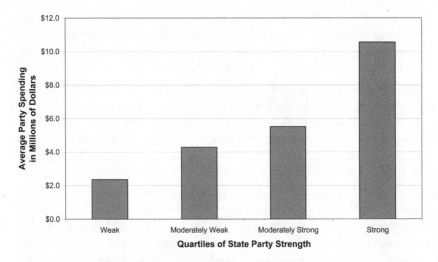

FIG. 12. Party organizational strength and average soft money expenditures (non-media), 1992–2000. (Data from Federal Election Commission, various years, and author survey.)

so heavily on cash rather than labor. But the real significance of this finding is that it makes plain that parties are not simply conduits for candidate committees. They have used their fund-raising prowess to create stable, complex organizations.

SUMMARY

This chapter demonstrated four findings. First, the place of national parties relative to candidates has changed considerably since the 1970s. As the cost and length of presidential campaigns outpaced the ability of a single candidate to manage the process, the party organizations began to assume a larger role. In the past, so long as campaigning remained a short-term affair, candidates could meet the minimal requirements of raising and organizing their own campaigns. But as complexity and uncertainty in campaigns increased, party organizing at the national level became critical. Beginning in the 1970s, the RNC began to build a stronger central operation. The DNC followed this strategy belatedly in the 1980s. Both parties accelerated their party operations by exploiting the campaign finance laws, which permitted them to finance their operations with soft money. Access to soft money notwithstanding, parties benefited simply from having an institutionalized role under the FECA amendments of 1974 and 1979. In 1974, when the FECA forced real contribution limits on candidates and interest groups, the political parties became an important venue for raising and spending money. And in 1979, when the FECA exempted parties from limits imposed on presidential candidates, the parties were encouraged to organize grass roots campaigns in the states. While the FECA was typical of Progressive-style reforms that constrained party activity in many other ways, it inadvertently opened up possibilities for the parties to expand their organizations.

A second finding is that party financing has become centralized at the national level. The increase in organizational wealth and influence by the national party marks an important transformation when viewed historically. For most of American history, the national committees were little more than temporary fund-raising operations. By the 1960s, the old order, based on local and state party influence, was dying and giving birth to one in which candidates would emerge as the central campaign actors. By the 1990s, however, national party committees emerged as co-campaigners for presidential candidates. They have been instrumental in organizing campaigns in the states, using their funds and technical expertise to coordinate voter turnout campaigns.

In particular, they have been highly efficient at targeting resources to key swing states to win the Electoral College. Overall, the RNC appears to pursue an Electoral College strategy better, though the differences are not that large. To be sure, the rational allocation of party campaign dollars does not guarantee electoral success (as the outcomes of presidential contests indicate), though it likely improves the odds of winning key battleground contests (Holbrook and McClurg 2005). These findings confirm some conventional wisdom about party behavior in elections and strengthen support for the party-in-service model. American political parties are clearly electoral organizations that seek to maximize the potential for helping their candidates win rather than use funds for long-term party building. This kind of behavior has been demonstrated previously with congressional campaign committees. These results show that national committees behave the same way in presidential contests. And yet it is also true that national parties remain an important benefactor of state organizations, even in states that are not critical for the Electoral College. While the national committees do not appear to have a long-term strategy for building state parties in high growth states, they nonetheless subsidize every state party to some degree.

A third key finding is that money helps strengthen political parties. In contrast to the conventional wisdom, soft money was not simply tied to individual candidate support. It enabled party organizations to carry out more of their traditional activities. To be sure, parties spent a good deal of money on broadcast communications for candidates. It would be surprising if they did not, given that American parties have always been pragmatic organizations and that broadcast advertising is a critical element of any presidential campaign. Yet parties are not simply bank accounts for candidates. The data shown here illustrate that the majority of funds have been spent on party-based activity. Moreover, the national committees have used their funds to tighten partisan links with parties and candidates in the states. Even post-BCRA, with its ban on party soft money, the incentive to build strong, stable campaign organizations should not diminish, and parties, particularly Republicans, are likely to expand their operations. One question raised here is whether the parties will focus more exclusively on building organizations in battleground states rather than spreading the wealth. Evidence from 2004 suggests that they have concentrated funds more aggressively in these battleground states.

Finally, the parties have adapted to the BCRA in predictable ways that echo party behavior in response to earlier campaign finance reforms (see previous chapter). Under the BCRA, they invested heavily in efforts to raise more money from small donors through direct mail and the Internet. They also decentralized partisan activity—Republicans less so—by encouraging the formation of independent committees outside the formal party structure, which can spend money that parties and candidates cannot. Consistent with the past, Republicans continue to invest more in the formal party infrastructure than Democrats, a pattern that reflects their different political cultures, social bases, and resources.

Importantly, the new law does not appear to alter the amount of money parties spend on broadcast advertising in support of candidates, though it does change how they spend it. Several nonparty 527 groups—a few set up by former party operatives—emerged to sponsor television advertising in support of presidential candidates. One estimate is that federal 527 organizations aired $112 million in ads during the 2004 elections.[45] At the same time, a 527 group called America Coming Together spent at least $85 million to help mobilize Democratic voters in battleground states.[46] Party organizations, especially the DNC, advertised "independently" of their candidates.[47] According to the FEC, the DNC spent roughly $120 million on independent expenditures, while the RNC spent only about $20 million on independent expenditures and an additional

$46 million on generic party advertising intended to help their presidential candidate (Corrado 2005). Thus, the strategic imperatives of contemporary political campaigns appear to influence spending by parties and candidates rather than campaign finance laws. In other words, the real effect of the BCRA—like the Tillman Act of 1907, the FCPA of 1925, the Hatch Act of 1940, and the Smith-Connally Act in 1947—is to shift the locus of political spending within partisan networks from political parties to ideological interest groups, which are less transparent and accountable. The unrealistic party contribution limits and coordination rules also discourage parties from working together— at least openly—with candidates and allied groups.

The BCRA also appears to stimulate different responses from the state parties. In battleground states, the Republicans and Democrats have maintained parity, at least in terms of money spent per voter. But the BCRA appeared to open a significant gap in party spending between battleground states and those states that lack competition for the presidential race. The gap is especially large for Democrat state parties, which suffered a significant decline in spending compared to the previous election. While Democratic parties in the battleground states were flush with resources, parties in noncompetitive states appeared to be neglected by the national party. Indeed, this neglect is one reason why state party chairs pushed strongly for the selection of Howard Dean as DNC chair. In his campaign for the leadership post, Dean promised to help rebuild state parties (Balz 2005b).

After just one election cycle, one cannot determine with certainty the long-term effect of the BCRA on political parties. At the very least, the BCRA appears to have added momentum to some previous trends. On the positive side, the political parties increased their investments in voter mobilization, especially in battleground states. Though this trend predated the BCRA, the new law might encourage parties to focus more on grass roots activity, given that issue ads are banned. On the negative side, a significant amount of money on the Democratic side was pushed outside the system into 527 organizations or spent independently of the presidential candidate rather than in coordination with his campaign committee.

These kinds of independent campaigns existed well before the BCRA, but the mounting use of them makes it more difficult for voters to know who sponsors political ads, especially the highly negative ads (Herrnson 2004, 115–21). Candidates can claim they are not to blame for negative ads against their opponents because they have no control over the independent organizations that sponsor them. Who are the voters to hold accountable if they do not like the tone of political ads? In some instances, parallel campaign organizations may hurt their favored candidate because they cannot coordinate activities with him or her. One consequence is that the candidate's message could get muddied or voters might get angry at the candidate for a political ad or telephone call that the candidate had nothing to do with.

Regardless of whether parallel campaigns hurt or help the candidate, they increase the complexity of the campaign environment, making it more difficult for voters to sort out political information. The dynamic also increases the problems of enforcing campaign finance laws since it is not always clear who is responsible for political activity. Regrettably, unrealistic constraints on party finance under the BCRA can be expected to further institutionalize parallel campaigning, particularly for Democrats. The next chapter takes a closer look at the potential long-term consequences of the BCRA on American political parties.

CHAPTER 7

The Aftermath of the BCRA

The central purpose of this book has been to understand the origins of campaign finance reforms and their consequences for American party organizations. This study broadens the analytical lens by examining an extended history of political reform back to the turn of the twentieth century. In doing so, I sought to illustrate consistent patterns of reform and response by political parties over several decades of American election campaigns. These patterns, I believe, help illuminate motivations and consequences of contemporary efforts to reform the political financing system and illustrate why Americans continue to be dissatisfied with how we pay for the costs of democracy.

One remarkable finding is that the American approach to reform—prohibitionist and antiorganizational—has changed little in the past one hundred years. Regulations typically contain limits on political financing that are unrealistically low and make political organizing difficult for all but the most sophisticated and well-off participants. Forged in a polity that has absorbed the norms of Progressive thought, with its emphasis on candidate-centered politics, the role of political parties as critical intermediary institutions has been degraded. Instead of drawing up rules that encourage partisans to work closely together by forcing them to appeal to a wider coalition of voters, for example, the regulations do the opposite: they encourage campaign fragmentation among partisans and mobilization of ideological factions.

The way the national political parties have responded to various reforms over the decades has changed little as well. Rooted in a constitutional system of strong federalism and separation of powers, the national parties have always been weakly institutionalized and malleable. But as American politics became more nationalized, the political parties did not follow suit. Since the Tillman Act of 1907, each succeeding wave of reform has weakened the capacity of national committees to organize presidential elections, even as the federal government became increasingly important in the lives of Americans.

The political environment in the 1970s—with its lengthening campaign season, burgeoning technical costs, and increasing uncertainties about voter loyalties—gave the parties an opportunity to play a new role in campaigns. Even though the amendments to the FECA in 1974 were crafted as a candidate-centered reform, they left a niche for parties precisely because they imposed enforceable constraints on *other* political actors, including candidates and interest groups. Parties exploited this opportunity, growing in influence in part by taking advantage of much-reviled soft money but still playing a background role to individual candidates, who also relied heavily on interests groups for campaign resources. The BCRA of 2002, which is the most recent reform, fits the mold of previous reforms. With the ban on soft money and restrictions on how the party may coordinate with fellow partisans, it obliges national party organizations to rely more heavily on candidates and outside interest groups for campaign resources and electoral work. This dynamic reduces the transparency of partisan-based activity and reinforces the direct link between political donors and candidates. As I explain in this chapter, however, an alternative approach that places parties at the center of political fund-raising has the potential to attenuate a dynamic in which incumbents, as individual political entrepreneurs, spend inordinate amounts of time seeking political funds directly from interest groups and lobbyists.

A central claim made in this book is that previous explanations of reform provide a thin understanding of the motivations behind these laws. These previous accounts diverge into two camps: the *public interest* and *rational choice* perspectives. Such approaches have failed to explain adequately when and why reform legislation gets passed. The public interest perspective views reform as exogenous: nonpartisan actors insert themselves in the political process to push necessary changes onto unwilling partisans. This argument, however, relies heavily on the role of scandal to induce the recalcitrant to go along with reform. As shown here, the historical record contains scant evidence that scandal has played an important role in passing campaign finance reform.

The rational choice perspective, in contrast, assumes that political actors are self-interested but ignores the tug and pull of factional struggles that give rise to specific reforms. Most accounts have tried to demonstrate that political reforms are motivated to benefit the party in power or to protect incumbents. But I argue that reforms can be instigated by a faction within one party that sees its interests threatened by the flow of electoral resources to other factions within the same party. The threatened faction places campaign reform on the agenda to curtail the resource advantages of other factions.

The role of party leaders is critical at this point. They must determine whether to support the reform faction or risk alienating them from the coalition by rejecting their demands. To hold their party coalition together, party leaders must balance support for reforms favored by a faction against the collective interests of the party. Reform succeeds when party leaders judge that specific reforms will simultaneously satisfy a proreform faction and give their party a competitive edge over the opposing party.

My argument rests on a theory of resource dependency. Various factions influence the party to the degree that they possess vital resources for the party to succeed. These resources include money, of course, but also group membership, expertise, and opinion leadership. Reform factions, which are the inheritors of the Mugwump and Progressive traditions, typically want to devalue the importance of cash, relative to other kinds of resources they possess in greater abundance. In doing so, they elevate their influence within the party.

For this reason, campaign finance rules matter. They augment or diminish the relative value of specific resources depending on how restrictions apply. Rules that clamp down on large donations tend to help groups with large memberships that can provide numerous small contributions or votes. Rules that restrict campaign advertising by candidates and parties tend to help groups that are adept at getting the attention of news media or implementing grass roots strategies on their own.

With regard to consequences of reform, most previous accounts either ignore the impact of money rules on political parties or assert that parties adapt easily to whatever regulations get thrown in their path. In contrast, I argue that reforms have influenced how parties operate, even before the 1974 amendments to the FECA, which most consider the first genuine reforms with any teeth. This study looks backward in time to observe clear patterns of response to reforms that restricted party finance. Most of these laws weakened the capacity of parties to organize elections and gave greater influence to candidates and interest groups.

In exploring causes and consequences, this study gets at broader questions about who may gain or lose influence due to particular kinds of reform. It also helps explain why different parties and interests groups support or oppose particular reforms. In the following section, I use these findings to predict how parties and their allies will adapt to recent and future reforms. I also make recommendations to improve the campaign finance laws in ways that might benefit the electoral system. But first I will summarize the main findings of this book.

KEY FINDINGS

1. The dispersed system of political financing originated in the antipartisan culture of the Mugwump era and the Progressive Era.   Campaign finance reform was secondary to other reform efforts to weaken parties through civil service laws, direct primary elections, and ballot reform, but it was no less a part of a mission to change the culture of partisan politics. Regulatory experiments in the states at the turn of the nineteenth century evolved into a long-lasting regulatory template with a prohibitionist emphasis that minimized the flow of money to political parties. The imposition of contribution caps, spending ceilings, and other restrictions on money made it difficult for political parties at the national and state levels to amass the kind of resources that might enable them to play robust roles in campaigns. Early laws fractured accountability, moving political funds away from broad-based political parties and toward interest groups and candidates.

Campaign finance laws, which grew out of the antipartisan sentiments of reformers, were one reason why national parties were slow to emerge as stable campaign organizations. These statutes reinforced localism and contributed to the weakness of national parties (a finding recognized by the Committee on Political Parties of the American Political Science Association in 1950 when they recommended laws to stimulate the centralization of party funds). To be sure, American parties have always been decentralized organizations, owing primarily to the design of the U.S. Constitution. But regulation of party funds was an additional constraint that hurt national organizations precisely at the time when money was an increasingly important resource and when national politics was becoming more relevant in the lives of Americans.

Progressive reformers focused on anticorruption as a central goal of reform, similar to contemporary reformers who pushed for passage of the BCRA. This goal has fueled a largely successful effort to put "sunshine" laws in place that make political finance transparent to voters. Paradoxically, financial transparency is undermined by the same Progressive-inspired effort to clamp down on campaign spending, a policy that encourages political actors to scatter funds among numerous political committees with vague names.

The assumption that these statutes resulted from a single-minded focus on preventing corruption has obscured a broader agenda of Progressive-led campaign finance reform. The thrust of the statutes has been as much about trying to shape how citizens make choices in politics as about preventing politicians from the quid pro quo. Rather than allow parties and candidates to spend money as they wish, early state laws spelled out in excruciating detail the kinds of expenditures that would be permitted. Some of these statutes were motivated by the desire to prevent the treating and bribing of voters, but others reflected broader schemes to clean up campaigns. By clamping down on party campaigning, Progressives hoped voters would educate themselves through newspapers and government-sponsored brochures about candidates. Negative campaigning was discouraged, as well as emotionally charged strategies that attempted to rouse partisan loyalties. In short, Progressives believed laws that reduced political spending would have a salutary effect on the quality of political participation and discourse.

These early policies surrounding campaign finance law initiated a template that shaped all subsequent reforms—including the BCRA—even when the reformers did not necessarily embrace the antiparty goals of the Progressives. This is a historical institutionalist argument, namely, that the initial policies—and the norms that buttressed them—continue to influence approaches to political reform, even when alternative approaches might be better suited to contemporary politics. As far back as the Tillman Act of 1907, Congress and many governments in the American states set in motion a particular prohibitionist "solution" to the problem of money in politics. To this day, the language of reform, with its emphasis on anticorruption, and the regulatory strategies reflect the first wave of campaign finance policies at the turn of the nineteenth century.

The broader but less transparent goals of early reformers also persist. Beyond the common theme of combating corruption we observe consistencies across political eras in the effort to shape what is said and done in political campaigns. There are strong parallels, for example, between Mugwump and Progressive reformers' attempts to eliminate boisterous, low-brow partisan spectacles and contemporary efforts, under the BCRA, to bar advertisements called issue ads in the weeks prior to an election and to require candidates to say "I approve this ad" in their campaign commercials. Many pro-BCRA supporters believed the restrictions on soft money issue ads would reduce the amount of political advertising and thereby increase grass roots activity. At the same time, the stand-by-your-ad provision by federal candidates would discourage negative advertising since candidates might be reluctant to appear in such ads. Neither of these claims have turned out to be true so far (see Franz, Rivlin, and Goldstein 2006, 141–60).[1]

Campaign finance reform was just one piece of the Progressive project to make democratic government more rational. It was an attempt to thwart Jacksonsian party politics, in part by removing party-based resources. The strategy reflected the middle-class bias of reformers. Laws that undermined political parties enhanced their own position as educated citizens in possession of sufficient resources to engage individually in politics. In the Progressive worldview, the ideal citizen arrives at political judgments independently rather than as a member of a particular social group, be it a party or interest group. The problem with this worldview is that it leaves those with fewer individual resources at a disadvantage. In weakening the capacity of parties to mobilize the passive voter, reforms put the onus on individual American citizens to seek out political information on their own. Then and now, statutes constraining campaign money reveal a poor understanding of the obstacles to collective action. This is no less true of efforts to raise political funds. While Progressives hoped that politics might be funded with the contributions of numerous small donors, it was unrealistic to assume that nonideological and coalitional American parties could survive without the infusion of large donations from wealthy patrons.

2. *Partisanship motivates reform.* Political elites support reform when it will give their party or faction an advantage over rivals. Both Republicans and Democrats have drawn on the Progressive template to invoke prohibitions that favor their side. Given their traditional disadvantages in raising political funds, Democrats typically prefer to invoke financial constraints on parties, such as their enthusiastic support for the Tillman Act and the FCPA in the early part of the century. Republicans, in contrast, prefer to block the in-kind support Democrats receive from outside groups such as labor unions. The Smith-Connally Act of 1943, for example, drew on the precedent of the Tillman Act of 1907 in order to ban labor union political contributions and expenditures. More recently, in the aftermath of BCRA, Republicans have sought to clamp down on 527 organizations, which have been of particular help to Democrats, in spite of the fact that Republicans had championed political spending as free speech in prior efforts to block passage of the BCRA (Edsall 2006c).

This account of reform challenges the reigning view that reformers stand outside the partisan process. Indeed, this nonpartisan frame is itself inspired by a Progressive point of view that some actors are above interest group politics. Reformers, like other groups, stand to gain influence within partisan coalitions from passing laws that constrain sources and uses of political funds. The chief political strength of Progressive—and later "progressive"—reformers is that they possess legal, intellectual, and professional skills that become more valuable to politicians as the role of large party donors diminishes.

Reformers, then, should be conceived as members of a faction in either party who seek to shape rules that give them greater political influence. Southerners, for example, championed the Smith-Connally Act in 1943 because it would curtail labor union influence in the party. More recently, support for BCRA is strongest among ideological liberals in the Democratic Party who want to dislodge the influence of corporate interests and other groups that favor centrist policies. Under the BCRA, corporate soft money no longer flows to the party. Instead, the party is more reliant on both wealthy ideological donors who give to allied 527 organizations and small, highly ideological donors who give hard money to candidates, party committees, and advocacy groups. The handful of moderate Democrats who opposed BCRA did not want the party to be so reliant on ideological membership groups. In this way the BCRA altered the balance of power within the Democratic Party coalition, tilting it toward ideological groups on the left and away from labor unions, minorities, and centrists.

3. Early campaign finance reforms had important and lasting effects on political parties. The argument that early reforms were not enforceable is not the same as saying they did not alter behavior. The laws encouraged experimentation with particular strategies, some of which became institutionalized over time. The Pendleton Act in 1883, for example, made parties turn from dunning government officials for money to relying on corporate sponsors. The Tillman Act in 1907, which banned corporate funds, pushed parties to seek wealthy individual donors. Sunshine laws, such as those embraced in the FCPA of 1910, encouraged parties to find small donors (even though these efforts proved futile for many decades).

When contribution limits were imposed under the Hatch Act in 1940, parties had to redouble their efforts to find small donors. The imperative to fund party operations with small donors led to debilitating strategies such as going into debt (which could only be paid back with large donations) and establishing legally separate entities to accept large donations.[2] The inability of the party to foot the campaign bill fed into the growth of a candidate-centered system that accentuated the role of candidates in funding and organizing their own campaigns. In the 1940s, President Roosevelt, epitomizing the emerging candidate-centered system, became heavily engaged in raising money through "big events" under the auspices of his One Thousand Club. Wealthy donors were wined and dined in the presence of the president. Through the President's Club, FDR built a personal financial constituency outside the party structure, a practice exploited by presidential candidates to this day.

On the spending side, campaign finance laws spurred the development of parallel campaigns run by interest groups. The Hatch Act, for example, imposed an absurdly low $3 million cap on national party expenditures so that both parties established quasi-party committees in the states to raise money as legally separate entities. In response to constraints on party activity, party activists organized donors based on professions and social groups as a way of getting funds to the presidential campaign. On the Democratic side, these groups frequently operated independently from the official party, while Republican-leaning groups were more likely to coordinate activities with party organizations.

Another party-weakening law was the Smith-Connally Act of 1943, which discouraged labor unions from campaigning through the party structure. Under this act, unions could not make donations directly to parties and candidates, nor could they coordinate activities with them. Instead, they operated separate entities called political action committees, which enabled them to spend funds independently from the party and its candidates. Thus, the Smith-Connally Act laid the groundwork for the future explosion of PACs in the 1980s after the FECA was enacted. By spelling out in detail which groups could give money to candidates, campaign finance laws institutionalized emerging campaign practices. And just as the FECA institutionalized the role of PACs, the BCRA will likely institutionalize the role of 527 and 501c organizations, which operate campaigns independently but in parallel with candidates and parties.

4. Parties emphasize different adaptive strategies in response to reform. Under new campaign finance restraints, both parties seek more small donors while simultaneously exploiting new methods to secure large donations through loopholes in the law. These loopholes usually involve setting up fund-raising committees beyond the reach of regulations. This response to campaign finance reform by both parties has been a pattern repeated several times over the century.

In other ways, however, the parties adapt to reform differently depending on the resources available to them from member groups in their coalitions. Republicans tend to centralize organizational activity as much as possible under new laws, while Democrats prefer to allow spin-offs and parallel campaigning by interest groups.

It is easier for Republicans to coordinate and work together because ideological diversity in the party has not been as great as it has been for Democrats. Within the party there is more agreement over means and ends, which reduces the costs associated with trying to maintain organizational cohesion. Culturally, too, Republicans tend to show more deference toward leadership, allowing the party to make decisions centrally. To be sure, Republicans, having been mostly in the minority since the New Deal, have greater incentives to work through a central party organization as a way of regaining the majority. But even before the New Deal, when Republicans controlled majorities and occupied the White House, they exploited centralized hierarchy and raised money centrally much more than the Democrats.

Democrats tend to decentralize campaign activities more than Republicans when faced with new reforms. Democrats find it harder to centralize the party structure, given the looser nature of their coalition. Divisions in the party are tied to strong regionalism, ethnic loyalties, parochial urban machines, and the power of independent labor unions. Given this factional constellation, it makes sense for the Democrats to campaign locally, at least more so than for Republicans.

Campaign finance laws that decentralize or fragment campaign activity suit the Democratic style of organizing. Indeed, members of the Democratic coalition often prefer to have a weak national party so it cannot interfere with local campaigning; the national party image can hurt candidate prospects in the South and Rocky Mountain states. Instead, Democratic candidates rely more than Republicans on personal constituencies and interest groups to support them. While decentralized campaigning is inefficient in terms of resources, it is in many ways more effective for a party with a broader coalition. For this reason, the decentralizing effects of campaign finance laws have become a strategic advantage for the Democratic Party. Tight restrictions on political money impose inefficiencies on Republicans, who have typically lacked an extended partisan infrastructure of interest groups to campaign for their candidates.

The party response to the BCRA fits previous patterns. Both parties sought more small donors and continued to use soft money through quasi-independent groups. The Democrats exploited the latter strategy more than Republicans because they have traditionally been more comfortable campaigning outside the party structure. Republicans, in contrast, continued to invest in party infrastructure more than Democrats. These divergent behaviors illustrate that the costs of collective action have been different across the parties. The parties have relied on the dissimilar resources of their respective constituencies to pursue campaign goals.

5. *Money strengthens the independent role of parties in elections.* This finding challenges a central claim of those who argue that political parties have been simply empty vessels to raise political funds for candidates. According to Senator John McCain, soft money had turned the parties into "conduits" for special interest money. By taking this money, McCain said, the parties had "rendered themselves irrelevant [and] they should go back to motivating their base" (Edsall 2003).

Parties, however, have not been merely extensions of candidates. The majority of party money—including soft money—has been spent internally to maintain robust organizations in Washington and in the states, especially on the Republican side. These funds are spent to strengthen ties with voters through direct mail, telephone solicitations, and canvassing. The national committees have used funds to tighten partisan links with parties and candidates in the states.

The party's push to carve a bigger role for itself—a role that is independent of candidates—has roots in a changing political environment that makes the parties increasingly important in contemporary elections. The new campaign environment favors both a strong organizational approach that mobilizes voters on the ground and a candidate-centered strategy that helps presidential nominees broadcast messages on television, radio, cable, and the Internet. If the electorate in presidential elections continues to be polarized, with the number of undecided remaining small, the parties will emphasize voter mobilization even more in coming years.

The degree of centralization and coordination by the national party marks an important transformation when viewed historically. For most of American history, the national committees were, in fact, little more than temporary fundraising operations, characterized by weak leadership at the top and minimal campaign coordination with the presidential candidates. Early campaign finance laws hampered party efforts to assume a larger role in presidential campaigns. I argue that the national committees might have emerged earlier as stronger players in federal elections had these early campaign finance laws not diverted electoral resources toward candidates and interest groups. Previous laws gave nonparty actors considerable advantages in an electoral environment where television advertising became increasingly important.

In the past decade, however, parties have become critical to presidential campaigns by helping to build a campaign infrastructure in states well before the presidential nominees are selected. While I do not argue that this new party role is a direct result of favorable campaign finance laws under the FECA, these rules certainly helped. The FECA institutionalized an important role for parties by restricting the finances of nonparty actors (candidates and interest groups) and carving out a permanent financing role for parties. As the presidential public funding system collapsed, national parties exploited their unique position. With access to soft money, they were able to help the presidential nominee campaign during the preconvention interregnum with campaign advertising, while simultaneously identifying and mobilizing voters for Election Day.

Under the BCRA, the parties should retain a central, if not dominant, position in presidential elections. The BCRA, however, gives an extraordinary advantage to outside groups, formed as 527 and 501c organizations. While these groups engaged in elections before the BCRA, the new reforms enhance their value as campaign organizations because they can finance campaigns and pay for organizational infrastructure (office space, technology, voter files, etc.) with soft money while parties cannot. The BCRA also discourages these groups from working closely with parties because of tight restrictions on coordination. The BCRA, like previous reforms, thus alters the relationship among partisans. More campaign work will now be done outside the formal party structure.

THE FUTURE FOR POLITICAL PARTIES UNDER THE BCRA

How will the BCRA affect political parties going into future elections? If history is any guide, parties will intensify the search for small donors and simultaneously seek outlets for large donors through nominally independent groups. Interest groups will play a greater role in direct electioneering. Like previous campaign finance reforms, the BCRA has accelerated trends in American political campaigns. Among the most important trends are (1) greater ideological polarization between the political parties, (2) increased outside electioneering, and (3) greater resource asymmetries between established political operations and amateur or novice political groups. Parties will respond to the BCRA in coming elections in several ways.

Parties Will Rely More on Ideological Donors

By removing corporate and union soft money, which is motivated by economic (material) reasons, the BCRA puts pressure on parties to rely more heavily on ideological supporters. These supporters provide both the smaller hard money contributions and the larger soft money contributions to 527 or 501c organizations. For the Democrats, these political contributors are primarily secular liberals who champion pro-choice positions, environmentalism, gay marriage, and other socially liberal causes. For the Republicans, the shift caused by the new law will not be as dramatic. Republicans will continue to receive contributions from probusiness individuals who are moderate on social issues. However, they will rely more heavily on ideological membership groups such as religious conservatives to help organize and mobilize voters.

From a civic participatory perspective, the intensified effort to find small donors is a positive development, though we should not expect too much. After all, even though the 2004 elections set a record for small donors, the percentage of Americans giving money to presidential campaigns remains in the single digits.[3] One goal of the BCRA was to force parties to find additional small donors to replace lost soft money and to broaden the diversity of the contributors (Mann 2002). In this sense, the BCRA was successful; the law certainly facilitated a surge in the number of new small donors, even though the upward trend in small donors preceded the new law. According to the Center for Responsive Politics, the DNC raised roughly $170 million in contributions of less than $250. Those contributions comprised 42 percent of the $404.5 million the party raised from all sources. Four years ago the DNC raised roughly $260 million from *all* sources, including soft money donors (Balz 2005a). This is quite a feat, and many experts and seasoned political professionals were surprised at how well the parties performed.

Overall, however, the individual donor pool remains an elite socioeconomic group: they are well above the national average in education, age, and wealth. One study suggests that the profile of donors in 2004 looks much like those in previous elections (Graf et al. 2006). An important difference in 2004 is that the small donors (those who give in amounts less than $200) who used the Internet included many more young people than in previous campaigns. To be sure, small donors are still wealthy by any standard, but any expansion in the pool of political participants is a healthy sign for democratic politics.

The emphasis on the small donor, however, is not an unalloyed good for political parties. Greater reliance on small contributions means potentially more reliance on ideologically distinct donors. Small donors might be of slightly lower income or age, but like most partisan donors they tend to fall on the ideological extremes of the liberal-conservative spectrum (Francia et al. 2005). Indeed, small donors may prove to be more ideological than large donors. Among contributors to the Republican George W. Bush, for example, 70 percent of small donors who gave less than $100 said they were motivated by the candidate's conservatism or because of social or moral issues, while 57 percent of large donors ($500 or more) made this claim. Among contributors to the Democrat John Kerry, 52 percent of small donors said they gave because of his liberalism, while 50 percent of large donors cited the same reason—a negligible gap. The most common explanation for all Kerry donors was anger toward Bush: 77 percent of small donors and 82 percent of large donors cited this reason (see Graf et al. 2006). With a larger base of ideological or angry donors, parties must hold onto them through alarmist appeals on hot button issues. Unless parties pursue this strategy, they will lose such donors to various interest groups that dedicate themselves solely to particular ideological positions on single issues.

The intense focus by the party on ideological donors creates a mutually reinforcing dynamic. Potential donors respond to ideological appeals, a fact that encourages the party to emphasize strong, noncentrist positions on issues. In making contributions, ideological donors believe they have a strong stake in the party, which means they will hold the party leadership accountable for maintaining its ideological purity. The impersonal nature of solicitations through direct mail and the Internet requires parties to market shrill messages to get the attention of potential donors. This strategy compels the party to be more confrontational since compromise on core ideological issues is seen by supporters as selling out.[4]

The large soft money contributors to 527 committees will also put pressure on the party to conform to ideological litmus tests. These major donors, who formerly gave soft money to political parties, are motivated by policy goals. The BCRA did not lessen their incentive to give money. Instead, they found alternative channels to promote their causes. In many ways, the 527 groups give such donors greater discretion in advertising their causes—they do not have to compromise with other members of the party coalition (Birnbaum 2003). Instead, through their contributions to 527 organizations, major soft money donors have the opportunity to influence the political agenda by financing exclusively the promotion of their chosen issues.

Corporate donors, in contrast, do not give soft money to 527 organizations. Their soft money contributions to the party are given to gain access rather than to pursue electoral goals. Thus, they have little motivation to engage with 527 electioneering groups. To supporters of the BCRA, this is a genuine success story: materially motivated donors no longer write soft money checks. The strong bias of reformers against economic interests reflects a Progressive tradition. In a democracy, it is surely wise to be cautious that wealthy economic interests do not undermine the principles of political equality. And, yet, there are trade-offs to reducing party resources from groups with material incentives. By filtering out economic interests, political parties are more dependent on large donors who are purists. The analogy with James Q. Wilson's amateur versus professional activists is appropriate here (1962). Like other reforms designed to make parties more democratic, the BCRA gives more influence to policy activists over pragmatic interests.

The importance of small and large ideological donors should increase over the long term as the value of PAC donations, which are not adjusted for inflation, diminishes. Under the BCRA, PACs are the only donor group whose contributions are not linked to cost of living increases. PACs, of course, are dominated by business interests. Thus, parties and candidates will rely more heavily over the years on ideologically oriented money.

From a comparative perspective, the changing dynamic among donors in the United States is particularly interesting. American and European parties are converging in terms of their resource dependencies and electioneering behavior. American parties are becoming more ideological, with growing support from like-minded, dues-paying members. At the same time, European parties appear less membership oriented and less ideological, particularly as they rely more on government subsidies to maintain themselves (Ewing and Issacharoff 2006). Moreover, European party campaigns are moving in the direction of American parties as they become more like professional campaign organizations. European party campaigns are centered increasingly around the personality of the party leader rather than around policy-based themes.[5] I would argue that campaign finance laws in both the United States and Europe have abetted the convergence of the party systems. In the United States, limits on the source and size of contributions to parties have made the parties more reliant on ideological factions. In Europe, in contrast, the trend toward giving public subsidies to political parties appears to make party organizations in European nations less beholden to their ideological constituencies (Landfried 1994).

There is a widespread assumption that making the party more reliant on small donors who are "the base" will make it stronger (see John McCain's previous quote, for example) while reliance on large donors will make it weaker. But this interpretation depends considerably on one's definition of *strong* party organization. If one's view of a party is that it should be responsible to its ideologically motivated activists, then it is perhaps true that a campaign finance system that emphasizes small party contributions will encourage this dynamic. But one shortcoming of this version of a strong party is that reliance on true believers makes it more difficult for the party to compete electorally in regions of the country where the national party ideology is well to the left or right of voters in that region. The consequence is one-partyism in many American states.

Another definition of a strong party—the one embraced here—is a party organization that has the resources and agility to compete nationally. This does not mean that the party stands for nothing but that support comes from a sufficiently broad coalition of elite factions that are motivated by a diverse mix of incentives—ideological, material, and solidary. When resources come from elites with diverse motives for supporting the party, this allows the party to sustain diverse support in the electorate and across the nation. As it stands now, more than a third of the electorate now declines to affiliate with either party, in part because of the increasing "purity" of its positions. Paradoxically, a less restrictive campaign finance system might make the two major parties less dependent on supporters on the ideological extremes, potentially reversing the trend that has helped create the growing class of independents in the middle and inhibited either party from competing successfully in regions of the nation (Nye, Zelikow, and King 1997).

Parties Will Rely More on Brokers

Another time-tested strategy to raise money in small increments is to rely on brokers to gather contributions from many individuals within personal and professional networks. Brokers have been around for a long time in politics. In the early part of the twentieth century, they were called "money-diggers" (Pollock 1926). Today, they go by the name of "bundlers." Whatever the sobriquet, these fund-raisers are critical for political campaigns, especially where contribution limits exist. By exploiting their donor networks, brokers deliver funds en masse to candidates and parties. Under the BCRA, with its renewed emphasis on contribution limits, brokers become even more important in financing elections.

Parties rely heavily on two kinds of brokers: lobbyists and candidates themselves. Lobbyists, of course, represent clients with various interests before government. Lobbyists are in a strong position to urge clients to contribute to selected candidates and parties as part of a broader strategy to influence policy. Since the passage of the BCRA, lobbyists have been pressured to attend more fund-raisers than ever. "I'm getting killed with fund-raising requests everywhere," said Robert L. Livingstone, a lobbyist and former chairman of the House Appropriations Committee. Another lobbyist at a prominent law firm said, "There's a lot more pressure to raise hard dollars. Before, you could find a client to kick in soft money. You don't have soft money, so you don't have that outlet" (Justice 2004). Notably, lobbying reform in 2006 did not include restrictions on lobby fund-raising. The reason is clear: lobbyists are a vital part of fund-raising networks for both parties and candidates.

The second kind of broker for parties is the candidate. This is true for both presidential candidates and congressional officeholders. The candidates have a personal constituency of donors—friends and loyal political supporters—whom parties exploit, either by using candidate donor lists or by getting candidate committees to transfer funds to the party committee. Under the BCRA, the brokerage role of candidates has increased substantially, particularly since there are no legal limits on transfers from candidate committees to party accounts. The total amount transferred from candidates to party committees increased by 44 percent in 2004 over 2002 (from $29.3 million to $42.1 million) (Dwyre and Kolodny 2006, 42).

Going into the 2006 elections, congressional party leaders signaled to members that they needed to support the party more than previously. In the past decade, the chairs of congressional campaign committees have asked members to contribute specific amounts, depending on their rank and power in the Congress. In 2004, party "dues" for rank-and-file House Democrats increased from $10,000 to $20,000 and for committee chairs and other leaders from $50,000 to $100,000 (Carney 2004, 2170–71). For House Republicans the jumps were similar. In the Senate, DSCC leader Jon Corzine (D-NJ) asked Senate Democrats to contribute $50,000 from their personal PACs or campaign committees. He also requested another $100,000 on top of that through making phone calls and attending events for the party (leaders are expected to contribute $100,000 and to raise an additional $250,000). Party leaders, meanwhile, traversed the nation, appearing at more fund-raising dinners than ever. House Speaker Dennis Hastert (R-IL) and Nancy Pelosi (D-CA) traveled nonstop for candidates. Rank-and-file House members in both parties credit these two leaders for doing the most to make up for the soft money ban (Carney 2004, 2170–71).

Relying on the candidate to secure party funds has also been critical in presidential elections. When the party nominees participate in the public funding system for the general election, they agree not to spend any funds beyond the grant ($75 million in 2004 dollars). The spending limit encourages the nominees to transfer significant sums of private cash, raised prior to the general election, to both national and state committees. In 2004, for example, the Kerry campaign contributed more than $40 million to Democratic state organizations. The Bush team transferred $11.3 million in October right before the election (Federal Election Commission 2005b). However, if the party nominees opt out of the public funding system in the general election—which it appears they will—the candidates have much less of an incentive to give a portion of their privately raised funds to the party, since candidates would be allowed legally to spend it all themselves. Paradoxically, the BCRA helped seal the demise of the public funding program by making it easier for candidates to raise private money (since individual contribution limits went from $2,000 to $4,000).

In 2008, candidate transfers will be less important to the parties than the network of bundlers who support the presidential campaign committee. Since many donors will be "maxed out" to the presidential campaign, they will be encouraged by the candidate to support the party, which has separate contribution limits. Individual donors may give up to $25,000 to the party each year (if they have not already exceeded giving more than $100,000 in contributions to all federal political committees). Doing double duty for the candidate and the party earns higher status for donors. Bush's Rangers, who raised $200,000 for his committee, were called Super Rangers if they raised an additional $100,000 for the RNC (Kaplan 2004). Similarly, Kerry supporters who collected $100,000 for his committee earned the honorific "Trustee" if they could raise another $250,000 for the DNC. Approaching the 2008 election, the stakes appear even higher. Hillary Clinton's campaign organization has set an early mark of $1 million for bundlers to be considered in the top echelon of supporters (Healy and Zeleny 2007).

There are hidden costs to greater reliance on bundling strategies for the political system. First, members of Congress spend even more time raising money than previously because they must attend more events sponsored by their bundlers. According to Martin Frost, former chair of the DCCC, members were put off by party leaders' pleas to raise additional funds for the party: "I'm not sure they fully understood how heavily the political parties had relied on soft money. I think they now realize that some of us who tried to explain that this would make there lives more difficult were correct" (Carney 2004, 2170). Time spent on fund-raising obviously takes away from legislative activities. It also tends to isolate members from fellow legislators, preventing them from socializing and nurturing personal ties that strengthen Congress as an institution.

As incumbents give more funds to the party, they feel the need to replace this money by raising more for their campaign committees. Indeed, they have turned increasingly to leadership PACs to augment fund-raising. Once the domain of only a few ambitious leaders, these PACS are now becoming standard practice, and leaders often encourage members to start them (Carney 2004, 2170–71). Candidates may receive contributions of up to five thousand dollars. After the BCRA, members loosened restrictions on leadership PACs to allow themselves to have more control over them (Bolton 2003).[6] The number of leadership PACs has almost doubled since 1998, from 120 to 234 in the 2006 cycle.[7] Such PACs will surely remain popular in the future since they can be used to make contributions to parties and candidates, as well as to defray many related campaign expenses, including fund-raising and travel.[8]

The effect of the BCRA is to make individual politicians even more closely tied to donors than previously. These contributors may not be the megadonors of soft money, but they are certainly the wealthy few who can afford to write checks of five thousand dollars or more. Politicians are also brought closer to bundlers, who tend to be political insiders with extensive personal and professional networks to raise money. Finally, the BCRA augments the importance of fund-raising as a leadership skill, giving those politicians with dense donor networks an advantage in competing for high posts in Congress or the party.

The congressional parties, especially, have become more dependent on candidates to raise money. But candidate money comes with strings attached. Incumbents have the power to make claims on the party to finance particular races, including their own. Candidate influence in party decision making may prevent the organization from making long-term investments because candidates tend to focus on the short-term goal of the next election—chiefly their own. A clear example is the struggle confronting DNC chair Howard Dean in his attempt to build party organizations in states where the party is currently weak. He faces the scorn of congressional leaders who dislike the fact that he is not putting all funds into states with upcoming key House elections (Edsall 2006a). To be sure, the DNC and its professional staff are more insulated than the DSCC or the DCCC from pressure by incumbent members of Congress to alter political strategies, since the DNC is supported by a broad constituency of activists in the American states to whom they are responsible. But even leaders at the DNC, like Howard Dean, must sacrifice long-term investments that help state and local candidates or even future presidential candidates when members of Congress care only about the next election.

Party Campaigns Will Be Less Coordinated

The BCRA further fragments the party system by discouraging open collaboration among parties, candidates, and interest groups. Elections in the United States are already among the most decentralized and unthematic of advanced democracies. Our constitutional design of federalism and separation of powers contributes to this, as does a political culture that is ambivalent at best about the role of organized political parties. But parties are our most effective democratic institutions in forging broad-based coalitions and bringing some policy coherence to campaigns across the nation. American-style campaigns tend to be fought mano a mano between two major candidates on local themes and personal characteristics. Campaign finance reforms only foster these entropic tendencies, giving additional leverage to candidates and narrow interest groups at the expense of political parties and a larger mass public.

While American national parties have never been as strong as those in Europe, they are no less vital. In recent decades, national parties have taken unprecedented steps to coordinate partisan efforts with other levels of party by consolidating resources, developing party themes, and working closely with state parties and allied groups. This top-down effort to tighten party links is no small feat in a federal system where a Mississippi Democrat could still run well to the right of a Vermont Republican.

The BCRA's anticircumvention law, designed to prevent soft money from flowing into campaigns, pulls back from this positive development toward partisan cooperation. To prevent circumvention, the law erects fire walls between groups and individuals who might have an interest in working together to pursue partisan goals. Where loopholes *might* appear in the regulatory net, it becomes imperative to plug them to keep the framework airtight. Any group with legal access to, and use of, nonfederal funds (soft money) becomes suspect if it has ties to the national party committees or federal candidates. This is the stern logic of a corruption rationale, which is applied improbably to justify federal regulations on purely local election activities because federal candidates happen to be on the ballot.

Intrapartisan collaboration is now a dicey proposition. Anything classified as federal election activity must be paid for with hard money or with Levin funds (a provision urged by Senator Carl Levin to allow state and local parties to spend a mix of hard and soft funds up to increments of ten thousand dollars for grass roots voter mobilization so long as each unit of the party raises its money independently), even if this activity supports mostly state and local candidates. State parties do have a way out if they do not mention a federal candidate in their campaigns. Otherwise, they must abide by federal campaign finance regulations in raising and spending funds.

The nub of the problem is that four-fifths of the states have laws that exceed some or all of the constraints under the BCRA. Eleven states have no source or size limits on contributions to a party; eighteen have source limits but no limits on contributions from individuals and/or PACs; and twelve have source and size limits, but they are less restrictive than the BCRA. The remaining nine states have source and size limits comparable to the federal law (La Raja 2003, 107). From the perspective of party leaders in this majority of states that rely mainly on nonfederal funds, the most satisfactory solution to the new law is to campaign for a party ticket that does not include federal candidates. As one state leader said, "we're all afraid of spending the 'wrong' kind of money. It's really a problem for the local committees that tend to spend small amounts. They are afraid of falling afoul of the law, with all its requirements, so they choose to just stay out of federal elections or avoid working with groups that might be spending the wrong kind of money" (Phillips 2004).

Conversely, national committees and federal candidates have a diminished incentive to work closely with state and local parties. Instead, national committees now centralize decision making and spending in Washington (Bauer 2006, 105–20). This behavior reflects a fear of breaking laws by working in tandem with state parties that use soft money. In addition, national parties have less of an incentive to send funds to state parties, especially in nonbattleground states. In the past, soft money—which was easier for national parties to raise—was not concentrated as intensively in battleground states but spread more evenly among state parties. The state parties will also suffer from not being able to rely on federal officeholders to help raise money for local political events. Federal candidates are prohibited from actively soliciting nonfederal funds, even though they can appear at party events.[9]

Since nonparty groups may continue to raise and spend soft money under the BCRA, we are likely to see a fracturing and dispersal of partisan activity into separate campaigns run by candidates, interest groups, and different factions of the party. This splintering of campaigns places additional burdens on voters to sort out information and thereby reduces transparency in the electoral process. To be sure, the BCRA requires greater disclosure of political money than previously, but the goal of transparency is undermined by incentives to finance campaigns outside the party campaign structure. Indeed, the BCRA's anticircumvention statutes have encouraged partisans to run operations pseudonymously outside the party structure, with inscrutable names like America Coming Together and Partnership for America's Families. The reforms put enormous faith in the capacity of voters to distinguish between the many different outside groups that will be active in federal elections, making the goal of transparency difficult to achieve. It was easier to track financial activity when control of most soft money contributions resided with political parties.

The BCRA increased the incentives for outside campaigning by giving outside groups a relative advantage over parties in financing political activity. Overhead can be paid for with soft money, even if federal electioneering requires hard money. A typical example of a group that may thrive is MoveOn.org. They can accept soft money donations to finance their core operations, while receiving smaller hard money contributions via the Internet for broadcasting television advertisements in federal races. Business interests, possibly through their trade associations, may try to imitate these strategies as PAC contributions become less valuable. Rather than allow Democratic groups to dominate the airwaves in the 2008 elections, GOP-leaning groups, such as the National Federation of Independent Business and Americans for Tax Reform, may choose to be more active with outside spending.

Regrettably, the party no longer serves as the convening umbrella organization for political campaigns. Any nonparty group that uses soft money cannot coordinate its activities with the parties and candidates. Nor can parties transfer or solicit soft money for allied groups such as the National Association for the Advancement of Colored People or the Christian Coalition. In this way, the BCRA loosens party ties to key mass membership groups that participate in partisan GOTV campaigns.

Instead, partisans will form state-based PACs or federal 527 and 501c organizations in order to conduct separate political campaigns. In anticipation of 2008, party insiders are already developing new for-profit campaign vehicles that give them legal authority to coordinate with fellow partisans (Edsall 2006b). These for-profit entities may become the de facto coordinating mechanism for partisans, usurping the traditional function of formal party organizations. On the Democratic side at least, they will be chiefly responsible for gathering voter information and developing state-by-state campaign plans. To stay within the law, they may "sell" these plans—at relatively cheap rates—to other partisan groups.[10] Based on these plans, partisans will pursue various components of the strategy. In this way, the Democrats partially resolve the coordination obstacles created by the BCRA.

In coming elections, we can expect groups to settle into these new campaign practices. Outside campaigning will become institutionalized as groups find safe havens in the campaign finance laws to pursue their electoral goals. Much like the FECA spawned the growth of PACs (which were only exploited by labor unions prior to the 1970s), the BCRA will make 527 groups, 501c organizations, and electioneering PACs (as opposed to PACs that merely contribute money) more popular as campaign vehicles. These groups will become more important as the influence of traditional PACs wanes. Over time, organizations will move toward bundling operations and direct forms of electoral support. Even business organizations, which are typically risk averse, will find ways to get more involved as they compete with ideological groups over control of the legislative agenda.

Incongruously, the BCRA also drives a bigger wedge between parties and their own candidates. By imposing tighter rules on coordination and eliminating soft money for parties, the BCRA intensifies the party predilection toward independent expenditures. Even before *McConnell vs. Federal Election Commission* (2003), the logic of anticircumvention had fostered a bizarre campaign environment in which parties might choose to spend without consulting with their own candidates. In the Supreme Court decision *Colorado Republican Federal Campaign Committee v. FEC (Colorado I),* the Court argued that there is no special case of corruption when parties act independently of their candidates. Now, parties may spend unlimited amounts of money—just like candidates and interest groups—to influence the election, so long as they do not coordinate with candidates.

The *McConnell* Court, which ruled on the BCRA, struck down a provision that would have compelled parties to choose between making independent expenditures or making coordinated expenditures on behalf of the candidate. In effect, the Court said the parties could do both. But this does not resolve the fundamental problem that the campaign finance system is forcing a split between members of the same organization—even when using hard money—and asking them to behave insincerely. Indeed, the *McConnell* decision maintains the absurd situation in which one set of party officials, who manage an independent campaign, must take a vow of silence with other party officials, who are working with the candidate. In congressional campaigns, the very same candidate who helps raise money for the party can be the beneficiary of party funds that are spent "independently" of his campaign. This state of affairs is hardly putting the campaign finance system on the path toward greater transparency.

WIDER CONSEQUENCES ON THE POLITICAL SYSTEM

Beyond their direct effect on party organizations, campaign finance laws such as the BCRA have wider consequences for the party system. On the positive side, periodic efforts to tighten regulations reinforce important norms against abuses with political funds. Regardless of the specifics of legislation, the fact that Congress is willing to regulate campaigns demonstrates a widely shared understanding that government should ensure that money in politics does not undermine the integrity and legitimacy of the political system. In passing these reforms, a moral standard is reinforced that politicians should not take bribes or be influenced by campaign contributions. Another important norm encouraged by the BCRA is civic participation. This kind of law buttresses the principle that elections should not be financed solely from citizens in the top 1 percent of U.S. earners. At the very least, the rhetoric of reform helps Americans articulate ideals against which they measure the behavior of their political leaders and assess the nation's civic health.

In practical terms, robust campaign finance laws like the BCRA deter widespread abuses in the political system, even if they do not prevent the occasional rogue from violating laws. When laws are backed up by genuine enforcement, politicians are more likely to take them seriously. Avoiding bad publicity from breaking campaign finance laws is often sufficient to keep candidates honest in this process. Laws that limit political contributions may also protect some groups and individuals from shakedowns by politicians interested in getting very large contributions. In this way, the BCRA is reminiscent of the Pendleton Act of 1883, which protected public employees from being pressured into giving contributions to the party. The BCRA, in a similar way, acts to prevent politicians from putting pressure on corporate donors to give millions of dollars to campaigns. Thus, the BCRA has several aspects to commend it, not the least of which is discouraging politicians from extorting political contributions from groups that have an important stake in the outcome of a policy decision.

Overall, however, laws such as the BCRA have deleterious consequences for the political system. Although the BCRA has not caused most of these problems, it has exacerbated them. First, the BCRA reinforces polarization across the two major parties because it favors donors motivated by policy goals over donors motivated by material goals. The latter provide some ballast to the ideological divisions between the parties. Now, parties must mobilize issue factions more than ever to raise money, which is a strategy that will surely push them further from the center.

Second, the BCRA's anticircumvention rules foster message incoherence and inefficiencies in political campaigns. Candidates have little or no control over the content of ads created by groups that support them. Indeed, interest groups have an incentive to set the campaign agenda with their favored issue. The problem of multiple messages and issue themes will be particularly acute in congressional campaigns where outside groups believe they can make a bigger difference with fewer resources.

Even if groups want to coordinate on message and campaign activity they are still hampered by noncoordination rules. The practical result is that groups concentrate their resources in the same places. Paradoxically, elections end up costing more and yet campaigns become more focused on the same set of exclusive voters in battleground states or competitive congressional contests. In the 2004 presidential election, for example, the Democrats did not make an important adjustment with resources. All groups—ACT, state parties, and the presidential campaigns—targeted urban centers with the greatest concentrations of Democratic-leaning voters. While the party won significant margins in these places, they neglected the exurban and rural voters. The Bush campaign won handily in these areas because there was very little Democratic presence. According to ACT organizer Tom Lindenfeld, potential Kerry voters outside the central cities areas were not exposed to radio ads, campaign events, or candidate visits. Moreover, GOTV canvassing efforts were poorly organized. According to Lindenfeld, "we worked under the assumption that if you voted for Gore in 2000, you wouldn't vote for Bush in 2004. We were wrong. In focus groups afterwards we learned that voters in rural and exurban counties didn't like being ignored" (2006).[11] The implication is that these voters might have voted for Kerry if the party and its allied groups had spread their resources into these neglected areas.

The inefficient and imbalanced flow of resources in political campaigns is related to what I perceive as the biggest problem with the BCRA: it simply addresses the wrong problem. That is, it does nothing to address the gap in resources between the haves and the have-nots. In fact, it makes the problem worse. The major problem with the current campaign finance system is not corruption but the *unfair* distribution of resources.

Congressional challengers, for example, rarely have sufficient funds to make elections more competitive. The relative position of challengers has been deteriorating since the 1980s. Figure 13 shows that the fund-raising gap between incumbents and challengers has always been large. Average incumbent receipts are typically three times as much as challengers. The gap grew sharply in 1996, and since then the average gap between funds for incumbents and challengers has exceeded half a million dollars. The BCRA appears to make the problem worse. In 2004, the incumbent-challenger fund-raising ratio exceeded four to one for the first time. On average, incumbents raised $842,000 more than challengers.

The problem with fairness is not limited to individual congressional candidates. Third parties have always experienced great difficulties in raising money to compete with major parties. Occasionally, a third-party candidate emerges to take some votes away from other parties. This happened with Ross Perot in 1992 and 1996. But Perot was a millionaire who could finance his own campaign. In theory, a third-party candidate could have been supported by several wealthy patrons rather than financing the campaign alone. This is no longer possible under the BCRA. Under current rules, even Ross Perot could not give more than sixty thousand dollars per cycle to help finance the Reform Party. The consequence is that third parties will have a tougher time organizing campaigns, even under circumstances in which the public appears receptive to third-party appeals. Only a candidate who can self-finance will have any ability to win a significant number of votes in a presidential election. The other alternative, of course, is public funds. But public funds do little to help build party organizations because the money goes directly to the presidential candidates.

The fairness issue is also about voters. Increasingly, political campaigns focus on just a few states or congressional races, and therefore many Americans are hardly mobilized to vote in elections. As I pointed out in the previous chapter, political parties have not been helpful in this regard. In 2004, for example, the national committees transferred 75 percent of their funds to state parties in just fifteen states! With new technologies that can target voters, the parties have become "too efficient" in focusing their campaign dollars. Rather than spreading their wealth, they tend to pile up money for use only in these toss-up contests. The BCRA has only made matters worse by eliminating soft money, which was easier to raise for nonbattleground states, and making it harder for state parties to get involved in federal elections.

POLICY RECOMMENDATIONS

Since campaign finance reforms are fraught with potential for partisan manipulation, proposals to change the financing system should be modest and incremental. Recent efforts by Republicans in Congress to tighten restrictions on 527

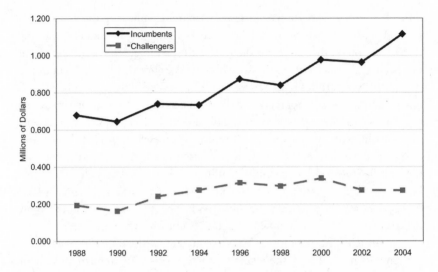

FIG. 13. Average receipts, incumbents versus challengers, U.S. House general elections, 1988–2004 (in 2004 dollars). (Data from Federal Election Commission 2005c.)

groups fit the historical pattern. Republicans want to weaken 527 groups because Democrats have used these groups extensively to campaign. Yet, only a few years ago, Republicans tried to block the BCRA—which was championed by Democrats—because they argued that it infringed on freedom of speech. These back-and-forth skirmishes in pursuit of partisan advantage tend to create instability to which only those with abundant resources can adapt. The smaller, less wealthy groups will find it difficult to navigate rules that are always in flux. More critically, frequent changes to the electoral rules reduce the legitimacy of the system, making it yet another arena for "politics by other means."

Those who desire to change the campaign finance system must also change the rhetoric of reform. Rather than continue the century-long focus on anti-corruption, reformers must make other goals more salient. The logic of anti-corruption is inherently self-defeating in a "porous" political system that values federalism and free speech. With so many access points for citizens to engage in politics, it is wishful thinking that laws will prevent money from getting into politics. The regulatory strategy necessitated by anticorruption rhetoric depends on contribution limits and anticircumvention rules that only provide incentives to create and channel funds through political committees to avoid restrictions.

As money gets pushed away from parties and candidates, it becomes more difficult to track as the process is less transparent. Enforcing the anticircumvention statutes becomes an endless process of plugging loopholes by adding restrictions on fund-raising, coordinating, and spending. From a constitutional perspective, the laws flirt ceaselessly with First Amendment freedoms in trying to navigate the perilous path between election-related activity (regulated) and issue-oriented speech (not regulated). Reason and experience, however, suggest that issues and campaigns are inextricably linked. Citizens pay the most attention to politics and policies in the months preceding elections, yet the law tries to restrict the flow of political messages precisely during this period. In the end, the laws do little to reduce corruption or its appearance, yet they erode the public square by designating certain forms of speech as "electioneering," which triggers a swathe of political regulations. As Justice Antonin Scalia noted in his dissenting opinion in *McConnell*, "the juice is not worth the squeeze."[12]

The anticorruption rationale leads to stinginess with political money that is entirely inconsistent with the reality of election costs. The reform movement has spawned efforts in states such as Vermont to limit contributions to House candidates to as low as $200 per donor. In Massachusetts, where elections are far costlier, the limit is just $500. The Supreme Court, in *Nixon v. Shrink Missouri Government PAC* (2000), upheld a limit of $250 for contributions to candidates for the lower house because this threshold was not "so radical in effect as to render political association ineffective, drive the sound of a candidate's voice below the level of notice, and render contributions pointless."

These excessively low contributions limits, however, force politicians to spend a significant part of their career raising money in increments that experienced observers consider little more than small change. The burden of raising money in small increments all but assures that politicians will also have incentives to be frugal and self-serving in how they spend it. Rarely will political campaigns feel compelled to reach beyond the highly selective core of voters in key districts or swing states who are essential to winning. In a polity in which only half of the electorate votes in presidential elections, electoral laws should be guided by a broader understanding of the role of money in politics. More robust campaigning—not less—will generate greater voter interest in elections.

A major point of this book is that the prohibitionist approach to campaign finance stunts the growth of large mediating organizations—such as political parties—that could play a more active role in recruiting candidates and getting volunteers involved in politics. On the meager fare of relatively small contributions, party organizations will remain fragile entities, dominated by the short-term outlook of individual candidates. Under circumstances in which money is scarce, the central purpose of parties is to raise money and provide low-cost campaign services for candidates.[13] Heavy regulations induce these organizations to become what Sidney Milkis and I have referred to elsewhere as "ossified parties of administration" that are further detached from the grass roots (La Raja and Milkis 2004). The nation's largest civic and voluntary associations, which perform major public tasks—such as the Red Cross, Salvation Army, and Girl Scouts of America—cannot be sustained on small donations. We should not expect American political parties to be effective organizations without major contributions as well.

Rather than organize laws around the goal of anticorruption, there should be greater emphasis on fairness. Campaign finance laws should be designed to improve the balance of political resources among groups. To achieve greater fairness, laws should adhere to two overriding principles. First, "keep it simple." The current laws are extraordinarily complex, creating a chilling effect on political activity among less advantaged groups. One test of simplicity is whether an amateur or volunteer can learn to comply with the regulations without relying on an election lawyer. Getting to this stage should not be difficult, particularly if enforcement agencies develop accounting software similar to the kind that allows many Americans to do their own taxes. But even with the help of software technology, rules should be written so as to minimize the administrative and legal burdens of those with limited experience, time, and expertise.

Second, campaign finance rules should be based on an understanding that groups possess different political resources. Laws, therefore, should maximize opportunities for groups to exploit their unique resources in elections. In contrast to a prohibitionist approach that narrows the scope of legitimate activity, future laws should encourage robust electoral participation with whatever resources groups have available. This strategy would minimize the biases in the system toward groups, such as business corporations, that have sponsoring organizations to defray overhead costs for lobbying and setting up PACs (Gais 1996). A campaign finance system that encourages robust participation with varied kinds of resources should reduce partisan biases in the system. As noted here, Democrats tend to rely more heavily on in-kind support of allied groups, while Republicans prefer to run campaigns through the party organizations. Reforms should allow Democrats to campaign with allied groups while simultaneously permitting Republicans to concentrate their efforts within the party structure. Instead of trying to negate the relative strengths of the parties, the laws should allow them to exploit their respective advantages. This approach would also open up opportunities for third parties. The following party-centered proposals support these principles.

1. Allow soft money donations to national committees up to one hundred thousand dollars.

While many will view the legalization of soft money as backpedaling on reform, there are compelling reasons to view this as an improvement over the current system. First, allowing parties to raise some soft money will reduce incentives for partisans to set up shadow party committees as a way of getting around the current ban. Moreover, allowing party soft money enables them to coordinate more campaign activity with groups that currently use soft money, such as state parties and interest groups. This coordination will make campaigns more cohesive and unified around campaign themes. The one hundred thousand dollar limit also accommodates federalism since it does not compel state-based party organizations to federalize their campaign operations. Instead, they can work across the ticket in support of state and federal candidates.

A cap on soft money donations also gives large donors some protections against pressure from party leaders and candidates to contribute millions of dollars, while reducing the pressure on candidates to raise hard money for the party. It is important to note that the vast majority of soft money donors—more than 90 percent—gave in increments substantially less than one hundred thousand dollars. Many of these donations came from independently owned local businesses that do not have PACs (Apollonio and La Raja 2004, 1134–54). The owners of these businesses made small contributions through their companies simply because it was cheaper than making a political contribution using their personal income.

To address anticorruption concerns, the one hundred thousand dollars might be modified in several ways. First, allow only the national party committees (the DNC and RNC) to raise soft money and not the congressional campaign committees. The latter tend to focus exclusively on individual campaigns rather than generic party activity. Congressional campaign committees used soft money less for party building than for targeted campaign advertising. In fact, congressional members who raised soft money at party fund-raisers often benefited directly from these funds during their reelection campaigns. The appearance of the quid pro quo is certainly more salient when legislators raise party soft money to help their own campaigns. There should be no reason why the law cannot grant more privileges to national party committees, which serve broader interests at the state and local levels. It would encourage organizing and coordination across several constituencies. Of course, the likelihood of Congress establishing different limits for the national and congressional committees is doubtful. The separation of powers provides a strong incentive for members of Congress to have their own well-financed campaign committees (Kolodny 1998). Based on my theory of party differences, congressional Democrats would be especially unwilling to go this route since they are less likely to get along with factions in the DNC. In contrast, the RNC, which often engages in congressional elections, has enjoyed much closer ties with the NRCC and NRSC.

Another variation on the one hundred thousand dollar cap is to permit soft money fund-raising only in off-election years. This should reduce the frenzy to raise large donations during the election season, when politicians appear desperate to pump money into political campaigns. In off-election years, parties are more likely to invest in organization building (for example, expanding voter files, recruiting candidates, and developing long-term campaign plans). Alternatively, the law could prohibit the use of soft money for broadcast activity. To be sure, the availability of soft money frees up hard money for additional broadcasts, but this kind of ban would reduce the value of soft money because these funds would not be completely fungible for all campaign activities.

Finally, any reform should consider ways to stimulate campaign spending in nonbattleground states. Toward this end, the law might allow parties to invest soft money (where state laws permit) in states with wide margins in the previous presidential election (for example, with a gap greater than 10 percentage points). In effect, soft money would be allowed in states that most analysts consider unwinnable. This rule might stimulate greater investment in states that are often ignored by the national parties and encourage long-term party building.

2. Significantly raise caps on party-coordinated spending.

The current rules limiting campaign coordination encourage parties to work independently from their candidates. Parties now establish separate campaign operations apart from the official party committee to make "independent" expenditures. Rather than force these divisions, laws should encourage parties and candidates to work closely together. The law should allow much higher limits on coordinated expenditures for candidates, even for the presidential nominees who accept public funds. Indeed, by allowing parties to support their candidates more generously, they might be more likely to participate in a presidential public funding program. Even under the current outdated public funding system, however, the incentives to participate would increase if candidates knew they could work closely with the party and benefit from party spending.

In congressional elections, higher caps on coordinated spending make even more sense. Given the cost of competitive elections, the current limits are unrealistically low. To encourage parties to support more challengers, the law should be more generous to first-time congressional candidates. The parties, for example, should be able to spend unlimited coordinated money with first-time candidates. This policy would offset some of the formidable advantages possessed by incumbents (although it is unlikely to pass Congress, given that the rule would help challengers). The constitutionality of permitting different limits for different candidates is an open question. However, the logic of doing so is similar to policies that favor first-time home buyers to encourage them to enter the housing market. Our electoral system should provide incentives for potential candidates with fewer resources to take the plunge into electoral politics. Rules that stimulate participation, rather than discourage candidate entry, would help advance political competition and accountability.

3. Let political parties control the release of public funds in the presidential general election.

The current system of presidential public financing is broken. No major candidate wants to take public funds because it is too constraining. After the election, John Kerry averred that taking public funds was the biggest mistake he made in the campaign.[14] His constant fear was that the campaign would run out of funds, so he hesitated to respond to political ads run by the Bush campaign. Kerry could not rely on the DNC to respond on his behalf because the party was limited by coordination spending caps. As long as the current system is in place, there is no incentive for candidates to accept public funds in either the primaries or the general election. Ironically, the BCRA helped reduce the incentives for presidential candidates to take public funds by not including provisions to improve the public financing system and simultaneously increasing hard money contributions to candidates from one thousand dollars to two thousand dollars.

The public funding system needs to be more generous and flexible for candidates. In addition, the parties should be able to help their candidates with private funds, as I have recommended. One problem with the current system has to do with the late release of public money, since candidates do not receive funds until after the conventions. They must languish through the interregnum, which begins several months before the convention. The long interregnum is particularly difficult for the party out of power. The incumbent in the White House typically faces no primary opposition, which allows him to save his campaign resources. The challengers, however, have been through a grueling nomination process and are often trying to replenish their campaign resources precisely at the time when it becomes clear they will win the nomination. The rival party has a golden opportunity to attack the challengers when their defenses are down. In 2004, parties and outside groups tried to defend Kerry by airing broadcast ads during the interregnum. But this response still leaves the challenger at a disadvantage, particularly if the allied groups are barred from coordinating strategy with the candidate. The candidates need the flexibility to draw on resources at critical points in the campaign, but the public funding system forces them to wait until the convention.

There is a relatively easy solution to the timing problem. The law should leave it to the national committees to decide when to release funds to the nominee for the general election. If a candidate has it locked up by March, the party, in consultation with the candidates, may choose to take the public funds at that point rather than wait until the convention. Leaving it to the parties avoids fussing over details of timing and who receives the funds. It forces party members to deliberate over strategies with the candidate and allied groups. The rule should help the challenger party because the nominee would not be starved for funds during the interregnum period before the convention. This is the period when interest groups and shadow parties have come to dominate the airwaves. Instead, the candidate could benefit from an infusion of public funds for the general election *and* the flexibility to work with the party in coordinating campaign strategy. Giving parties decision-making authority over the release of funds also gives them greater leverage in political campaigns, moving the public funding system away slightly from its candidate-centered bias.

Implementing these three proposals would require changing the prevailing mind-set about campaign finance. These recommendations challenge conventional assumptions about the role of money in politics that date back to Mugwumps and Progressives. Campaign reform laws, for better or worse, are imbued with this spirit of Progressivism, with its emphasis on individualism, expertise, and nonpartisan "educational" politics. The difficulty in changing the current approach to reform is that so many Americans have come to accept Progressive-inspired strategies. The choice of reform is circumscribed by powerful norms against the use of money in politics and a deep ambivalence about relying significantly on party organizations in campaigns. While these norms harken back to the founding, they were institutionalized during the Progressive Era through regulations. When the money issue is considered in the context of political parties, voters are not likely to favor generous financing for these organizations. According to a Gallup Poll, just prior to the passage of the BCRA, a strong majority of Americans (69 percent) favored limiting the amount of money that an individual or group could contribute to the national political parties (Jones 2002).

By and large, Progressive-inspired reform can be credited with much that is good about the electoral system. Few nations have as good a system at the national level for disclosing sources of funds. On the other hand, the Progressive approach draws upon faulty and crippling assumptions about the nature of collective action and the role of political parties in the electoral system. The Progressive approach tends to see money in politics as the root of evil when, in fact, the situation is a great deal more complex. A new approach requires that we think more in terms of spreading the wealth rather than keeping it out of politics. One element in spreading the wealth must be a commitment to strengthening the political parties through party-centered campaign finance laws.

The tragedy of the BCRA is that a much simpler set of reforms might have worked to achieve anticorruption goals, without burdening the system with complicated rules that weaken the party system. The current regime simply encourages groups to make end runs around the system and assures that those with abundant resources and expertise can manage their way through the labyrinth of rules. Complicated laws elevate the cost of getting involved in politics and narrow the scope of interests that can petition the government or engage in elections. By keeping laws relatively simple and maximizing diversity of electoral resources, more groups have opportunities to influence the political process and work through the transparent intermediary of the political party. At the same time, the laws should remain sufficiently flexible to allow new kinds of technologies—such as the Internet—to engage Americans in politics. Regrettably, the instinct of many reformers has been to regulate these new forms of electioneering because they are seen as loopholes to get around the

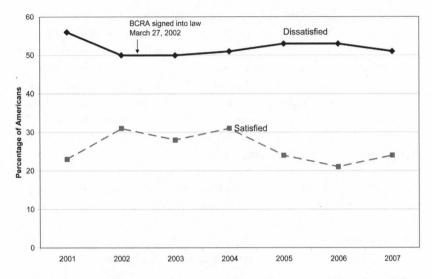

FIG. 14. Satisfaction with nation's campaign finance laws, 2001–7. (Data from Gallup Poll, various years, "Americans Access the State of the Nation.")

system. This prohibitionist approach is not only futile but damaging to robust democratic politics.

This approach has also failed to boost public confidence in the campaign finance system. One telling survey suggests that over time the public has perceived little difference in the campaign finance laws before and after the passage of the BCRA. As figure 14 shows, the percentage of Americans who are dissatisfied with the nation's campaign finance system has barely budged from its prereform level of 56 percent. In 2007, after two federal elections under the BCRA, the majority of Americans still have serious doubts about the system.

It has not been my argument that we should eliminate regulations on political money. Nor should this analysis be considered an effort to delegitimate the enterprise of reforming the political system. Indeed, far from it. By pointing to the partisan nature of reform, I am merely suggesting that the public and its representatives be more clear eyed about the complex motivations behind reform. If it is true that partisanship plays an important role, then we should be wary of grand schemes to reform the "whole system."

More to the point, political reforms should make greater accommodations for the complexity and porousness of the American political system. Since it is not possible to close all the loopholes, we should recognize that "good enough" is sometimes the best policy, particularly when strict controls threaten important democratic values such as liberty, equality, and political competition. A sense of balance and realism should be maintained as reforms ferment at the state level. Many new proposals in the states imitate aspects of the BCRA. Others are focused on providing public funds. It would be wise for policymakers in the states to learn from past experience with campaign finance reforms at the federal level and consider the costs to the party system of burdening political committees with a thicket of complex rules.

The federal campaign finance laws we have today are a long-term product of earlier Progressive-style reforms that induced a clear pattern of party adaptations over the years. Many of these adaptations were not healthy for political parties or the electoral system as a whole. Looking forward, we must be extremely attentive to the potential consequences of new reforms as policy debates continue over how best to shoulder the costs of democracy.

Afterword

Events surrounding the 2008 presidential elections have pushed themselves into the public arena earlier than in previous cycles. The presidential candidates have been trying to make news by touting their success in debates, campaign speeches, and, notably, fund-raising. Several reasons exist for the early public campaigning. An open seat for the White House invites a scramble in both parties for the nomination; the front-loading of primaries to as early as January 2008 means candidates cannot rely on wins in Iowa and New Hampshire to build momentum for later contests; and the unpopularity of the president and the Iraq War encourages political elites and interested citizens to look forward to the next occupant of the White House. All of these combine to make the chase after political contributions especially important for the presidential candidates. The sums that they have raised to this point are extraordinary by historical standards.

However well the candidates do in the 2008 elections, the political parties are relatively disadvantaged in raising and spending money compared to 2004 elections. First, unlike in the past, *none* of the top-tier presidential candidates are likely to participate in the presidential public funding system, which means they will all compete intensely with political parties for campaign dollars. Second, the Supreme Court ruled in *Federal Election Commission v. Wisconsin Right to Life* (2007) that the government may not prohibit corporations or labor unions from broadcasting issue ads with soft money in the days before an election. This ruling makes it even easier than before for wealthy donors to contribute soft money to interest groups that will run issue ads throughout the election in lieu of giving money to the political parties.

Overall, these two decisions—the avoidance of public funding and the Supreme Court ruling—do not alter the arguments made in this book. Indeed, they make them more salient. If anything, the party-weakening effects of BCRA and the futility of trying to ban soft money should become increasingly manifest as the campaigns unfold.

Regrettably, the BCRA precipitated the collapse of the tottering public funding system that, if shored up, might have attenuated the worst features of the campaign finance system. By raising individual contribution limits from $1,000 to $2,000 (and indexing it for inflation), candidates have little incentive to stick with public funds, which are capped, knowing they can raise much more in private contributions. In this way, the money horserace becomes more significant, not less, than previously. The sad irony is that the BCRA was intended to attenuate the money exchange between wealthy donors and candidates. The chase after hard money, however, has reinforced this linkage by making it necessary to spend *more time* conversing with wealthy donors and bundlers who can raise the sums necessary for mounting a candidacy. Scandals that involve bundlers will emerge periodically, as they already have with Norman Hsu, a business executive who turned out to be involved in a fraud case in California, and who raised more than $1 million for Democratic candidates.

Under the BCRA, elections move back toward to the candidate-centered system that reached its zenith in the 1980s. Without access to soft money, the parties will rely heavily on their presidential nominees for money. To be sure, the DNC and RNC have been raising money, but they lag behind their pace in previous elections and fall well short of the remarkable fund-raising success of candidates. Money will flow more easily to the parties once the nominees are selected and the candidates install their own staff at the DNC or RNC. At this point, contributions from donors who are "maxed out" to the candidates will be steered to the party organization, which can begin to make the necessary investments in voter mobilization in the states. But the late surge in campaign infrastructure means that the national and state parties are once again engaged in the triage of putting the short-term needs of the immediate campaign ahead of long-term investments in party operations.

The BCRA, like the Federal Election Campaign Act before it, is vulnerable to court decisions that unravel the interlocking "hole-plugging" statutes aimed at preventing political committees from circumventing the ban on soft money.

The recent Supreme Court decision, *Federal Election Commission v. Wisconsin Right to Life,* sets a new standard for evaluating whether a corporation or union may spend money on political advertising immediately before an election. Under the BCRA, all such advertising was banned thirty days before a primary and sixty days before a general election if the ad mentioned a federal candidate who was on the ballot. The new decision, however, holds that such advertising is banned only if "*the ad is susceptible of no reasonable interpretation other than as an appeal to vote for or against a specific candidate.*" Thus, interest groups have a right to advertise when (a) the ad content appears issue-based, that is, the ads reflect a legislative issue for which the group takes a position and urges the public to do the same; and (b) the ad content lacks typical components of electioneering, that is, the ads do not mention an election, candidacy, political party, or challenger and do not take a position on a candidate's character, qualifications, or fitness for office.

In effect, the *Wisconsin Right to Life* decision makes it far easier to broadcast political advertisements using soft money. To be sure, many groups will choose "independent ads" using hard money to avoid running afoul of the BCRA. However, ideological organizations, with strong ties to partisan, corporate, or labor interests, will take advantage of the court decision to put pressure on candidates to address their issues. These organizations will use their free-speech rights to compete with candidates and political parties for the attention of voters, creating a maelstrom of political messages that are not likely to make it easier for voters to choose candidates.

Overall, political parties are likely to be squeezed from two sides in the 2008 elections. On one side, they compete with candidates more than ever for hard money because candidates have no incentive to participate in the public funding program. On the other, they compete with interest groups that attract wealthy donors willing to fund political ads and other campaign activities with soft money.

In the bigger picture, money tightening campaign finance laws such as the BCRA suggest we have not learned from history. Such laws imply a vast underestimation of what it takes to run political campaigns in the United States, especially for the presidency. Most Americans think sums that politicians raise for campaigns are "obscene" when it is more likely "small change." And since it is difficult to get beyond this illusion that campaigns should not cost much money, the nation continues to put in place laws that produce minor adjustments but not real change in our politics. Thus, the candidates, parties, and interest groups find ways around the laws—and the cycle of cynicism continues. A greater dose of realism is in order about how we pay for the costs of democracy. In the future, campaign finance laws might be crafted with more of an eye toward creating a system that is fair to non-wealthy candidates, supportive of essential democratic institutions such as political parties, and encouraging to greater political competition and participation.

Appendix: PARTY ORGANIZATIONAL STRENGTH SCORES

	Republicans				Democrats		
			100-Party				100-Party
Rank	State Party	Score	Quartile	Rank	State Party	Score	Quartile
1	Florida	0.625	4	1	California	0.575	4
2	Tennessee	0.600	4	2	Michigan	0.575	4
3	Michigan	0.575	4	3	Georgia	0.575	4
4	Washington	0.575	4	4	Washington	0.575	4
5	Minnesota	0.550	4	5	Indiana	0.575	4
6	Pennsylvania	0.550	4	6	Alabama	0.525	4
7	Indiana	0.550	4	7	Pennsylvania	0.525	4
8	California	0.525	4	8	Kentucky	0.525	4
9	Massachusetts	0.525	4	9	Louisiana	0.500	3
10	New Mexico	0.525	4	10	Iowa	0.500	3
11	Hawaii	0.525	4	11	New Mexico	0.500	3
12	Ohio	0.500	4	12	Minnesota	0.500	3
13	Georgia	0.500	4	13	South Carolina	0.500	3
14	Maryland	0.500	4	14	North Carolina	0.475	3
15	Connecticut	0.500	3	15	Ohio	0.475	3
16	Alabama	0.500	3	16	Wisconsin	0.475	3
17	South Carolina	0.500	3	17	Maine	0.475	3
18	Wisconsin	0.475	3	18	Kansas	0.475	3
19	New Jersey	0.475	3	19	Texas	0.450	3
20	Delaware	0.475	3	20	Missouri	0.450	3
21	Oregon	0.475	3	21	New York	0.425	2
22	Alaska	0.475	3	22	Colorado	0.425	2
23	Oklahoma	0.450	3	23	New Jersey	0.425	2
24	Utah	0.450	3	24	Oregon	0.400	2
25	Arizona	0.450	3	25	Oklahoma	0.400	2
26	Mississippi	0.450	2	26	Massachusetts	0.375	2
27	Colorado	0.450	2	27	Montana	0.375	2
28	Nevada	0.450	2	28	Idaho	0.375	2
29	Kentucky	0.450	2	29	Alaska	0.375	1
30	North Dakota	0.450	2	30	Vermont	0.375	1
31	Nebraska	0.425	2	31	Delaware	0.375	1
32	Arkansas	0.425	2	32	West Virginia	0.375	1
33	South Dakota	0.425	2	33	Arizona	0.350	1
34	Rhode Island	0.425	2	34	Wyoming	0.350	1
35	Missouri	0.400	2	35	Illinois	0.350	1
36	North Carolina	0.400	2	36	Virginia	0.325	1
37	Kansas	0.400	2	37	North Dakota	0.325	1
38	Idaho	0.400	2	38	Nebraska	0.300	1
39	New York	0.400	2	39	Connecticut	0.275	1
40	Illinois	0.375	2	40	Tennessee	0.250	1
41	West Virginia	0.375	1	41	Maryland	0.225	1
42	Vermont	0.325	1	42	Nevada	0.225	1
43	Maine	0.325	1	43	Arkansas	0.200	1
44	Louisiana	0.250	1	44	Hawaii	0.175	1
45	Montana	0.200	1	45	Mississippi	0.150	1
				46	Rhode Island	0.125	1

Note: Quartiles: 4 = strong, 3 = moderately strong, 2 = moderately weak, 1 = weak.

Notes

CHAPTER 1

1. The Bipartisan Campaign Reform Act of 2002, also known as the McCain-Feingold Act, after its chief sponsors, Senators John McCain (R-AZ) and Russ Feingold (D-WI), became effective on November 6, 2002. The new legal limits on political contributions went into effect on January 1, 2003.

2. Herrnson (1988) especially makes this point.

3. These were the arguments put forth by the American Political Science Association's Committee on Parties in 1950.

4. For a classic discussion of sources of group inequalities in politics, see Schattschneider 1960.

5. See, for example, Dwyre and Farrar-Myers 2001.

6. The Swift Boat Veterans for Truth, an organization whose members included Vietnam War veterans, was formed during the 2004 presidential election campaign. The organization's chief goal was to thwart John Kerry's candidacy for the presidency through political ads that sharply criticized his leadership as a Navy officer and his stance against the Vietnam War after he left military service. MoveOn.org is a self-described progressive political group with an extensive network of online members. It emerged in 1998 to petition Congress to "move on" past the impeachment hearings of President Clinton. Its founders used this extensive online list of petitioners to create a pressure group to lobby Congress and support favored candidates.

7. In *Colorado Republican Federal Campaign Committee v. FEC* (1996), the Supreme Court held that parties have a constitutional right to spend money on campaigns independent of their candidates. In *Federal Election Commission v. Colorado Republican Federal Campaign Committee* (2000), the Supreme Court held that parties may be limited in the amount they can spend promoting their candidates in coordination with their candidates.

8. For an excellent study that makes this point about legislative campaign committees, which are the congressional campaign committees in the states, see Shea 1995.

9. See, for example, Corrado 1997, 25–60; Sorauf 1992.

10. According to Aldrich (1995) functional orientation of American party elites permits them to use and discard various modes of partisan organizing, depending on the prevailing regulatory and political environment.

11. The assumption that previous campaign finance laws had no impact is reflected in most historical accounts of campaign finance reform, which completely skip over the period between the Tillman Act of 1907 and the FECA in 1971 and its amendments.

12. The Democratic reliance on a broader coalition, for example, has made it difficult

for them to centralize operations nationally, since the national party could not reconcile its disparate factions. They have neglected the kind of party building in the states that might challenge the influence of interest group constituencies such as labor, environment, and pro-choice organizations. For this reason, Democratic national parties have tended to focus on short-term, decentralized strategies that rely heavily on the efforts of individual candidates and allied interest groups to mobilize partisans. In contrast, Republicans have stronger party organizations nationally and at the state level because historically their constituencies—primarily probusiness—have understood the party as the essential vehicle for advancing their interests. These differences are crucial in understanding why the Republicans and Democrats respond to laws differently in elections. I explore these findings in the book.

13. See, for example, Anechiarico and Jacobs 1996. For a discussion of the relatively small importance of business contributions in the campaign finance system, see Milyo, Primo, and Groseclose 2000, 75–88. See also Ansolabehere, de Figueiredo, and Snyder 2003.

CHAPTER 2

1. Progressive strongholds were typically in the northern Midwest.

2. Other Mugwumps included Charles Francis Adams Jr., Josiah Quincy, Leverett Saltonstall, Thomas Wentworth Higginson, and Whitelaw Reid, who was the assistant editor to Horace Greeley at the *New York Tribune* (Sproat 1982).

3. Government control of the ballot created advantages for the major parties relative to minor parties since the former were granted automatic access, while minor parties would have to petition and gather signatures. However, the government ballot diminished the power of the major political parties to mobilize and control votes.

4. See also Sikes 1928.

5. Dahl's *homo politicus* is a citizen who devotes much attention and resources to politics, in contrast to *homo civicus*, who is not preoccupied with politics unless the actions of government threaten his or her pursuit of nonpolitical goals (Dahl 1961, 223–28).

6. According to Owen (1910), the most important laws for extending the people's rule were adequate registration system, direct primary, publicity of campaign contributions, statutes to prevent corrupt practices in campaigns, initiative, referendum and recall, and, finally, the short ballot.

7. After studying the issue, Pollock (1926) acknowledged that many aspects of the problem related to money in politics were misdiagnosed, with far too much emphasis on unenforceable contribution and spending limits. He began a tradition of strong skepticism about campaign finance reform among political scientists that continued through scholars such as Louise Overacker, Alexander Heard, Herbert Alexander, and Frank Sorauf.

8. *Nation* 1888, 428, as quoted in Marcus 1971, 138.

9. The *Congressional Record*, vol. 45, actually reports that Republicans spent $16.5 million, while spending only $1.8 million in 1892. Overacker (1932) believes these estimates are unreliable because they do not agree with testimony given to the Clapp Com-

mittee in 1912–13 during a Senate investigation of campaign finances of the national parties. For comparison with contemporary spending, the Republicans disbursed $715 million in the 2000 elections according the Federal Election Commission.

10. Throughout their history, political parties have been borrowers of practices in the business and nonprofit sectors. Many party fund-raisers had experience as philanthropists raising funds for voluntary and nonprofit institutions.

11. See also McGerr 1986, 144–45. It is likely that Americans were unaccustomed to seeing the likeness of presidential candidates so much during campaigns as during the 1896 elections. As George F. Will observes, "Most of the first 15 presidents—and some after the 16th, Lincoln—could have walked down most American streets virtually unrecognized" (2004, 70).

12. These differences between the major parties will be discussed in chapter 3.

13. As I explain later, it is only recently, at the turn of the twenty-first century, that American parties have been able to sustain themselves with voluntary "member" donors who are attracted to the party for ideological reasons.

14. In the past, local political parties had used an array of selective incentives to attract followers—promises of jobs, services, contracts, and other perks. As these resources diminished under Progressive civil service reforms, the parties needed another form of material benefits to induce followers to help them. Drawing on Duverger's (1954) understanding of the two different kinds of parties, cadre and mass organizations, the American species was certainly the former. As cadre parties, this meant they could not rely on a dues-paying membership to keep the organization afloat, as mass parties did. With fewer jobs to offer they would need to provide material incentives to attract party workers.

15. The difficulty of making campaign finance laws work during this period can hardly be underestimated, given the high cost of information gathering and the rather weak regulatory state at the time.

16. The source of these data is Sikes 1928.

17. The eleven states were Alabama, Arizona, Arkansas, California, Kansas, Montana, Nebraska, North Dakota, Texas, Wisconsin, and Wyoming (Overacker 1932, 306).

18. They quote the sweeping statute from Wisconsin.

19. Among the many theories about the death of Edgar Allen Poe, there is one that claims he died of intoxication from drinks purchased for him by party workers on Election Day (Thomas and Jackson 1987).

20. The five states are California, Massachusetts, Michigan, Minnesota, and Wisconsin (Sikes 1928, 275–78).

21. Ironically, recent studies demonstrate that television ads provide rich sources of information and the emotional tug that engage citizens who are typically uninterested in elections (Freedman, Franz, and Goldstein 2004, 723–41).

22. On the importance of campaign spending in helping voters make decisions, see Coleman and Manna 2000, 757–89. On the importance of negative advertising in informing voters, see Geer 2006.

23. Great Britain, for example, did not require political parties to report political finances under its groundbreaking Corrupt Practices Act of 1883, whose features were otherwise emulated by the American states (Pollock 1926).

24. Progressive efforts to reveal the partisan origins of advertisements in newspapers were part of a broader agenda to cultivate a nonpartisan press. Newspapers in the United States, as elsewhere, had partisan roots at least since the days when Jefferson hired Philip Freneau to edit the *National Gazette*. The Progressives sought to diminish partisan control over newspapers by nurturing a neutral press and giving scope to muckraking journalism as an additional means of keeping politicians accountable. Campaign finance laws were occasionally used to create a fire wall between partisans and the press. In nine states, for example, it was unlawful under campaign finance statutes to purchase editorial support.

25. The expectation is that political committees—and candidates, in particular—will refrain from being negative when they are forced to link themselves closely to the advertisement.

26. Labor unions were not originally prevented from making contributions. At the time, labor unions were far less involved in elections than they are today. The union movement was, in fact, in its infancy and dominated by the American Federation of Labor under Samuel Gompers, who pursued a strategy of nongovernment involvement in bargaining between labor and industry.

27. See, for example, Corrado 1997; Mutch 1988.

28. The state paid for the binding and distribution of the pamphlets, while the printing was paid for by the political parties. Each party was permitted up to twenty-four pages in the pamphlet.

CHAPTER 3

1. See Samples 2006, which argues that the primary goal of political reform is incumbent self-protection by making it more difficult for challengers to mount effective campaigns.

2. See, for example, Abrams and Settle 1978, 245–57; Regens and Gaddie 1995.

3. The investigation looked at how the Mutual, the Equitable, the Prudential, and other firms used policyholder funds for political purposes, particularly by making political contributions to political parties. The chief counsel to the investigating committee was the neo-Mugwump Charles Evan Hughes, who would later become the Republican presidential nominee in 1916. His relentless interrogations of company executives compelled them to acknowledge that they had hoped their payments would secure passage of regulations beneficial to their companies. According to Mutch (1988), at this point public opinion began to mobilize around the issue of campaign finance reform. New York State, however, had already passed the first state corrupt practices act in 1890, which regulated political committee and candidate spending (Pollock 1926).

4. *Congressional Record* 1904, 17.

5. *Congressional Record* 1905, 96.

6. *Congressional Record* 1907, 78. Eventually, all his suggestions would be put into law, except for public subsidies to parties. It would be three-quarters of a century before the federal government would acquiesce to using public funds for campaigns, and this only in presidential elections.

7. Party workers faced the formidable task of persuading citizens to vote the entire

party ticket, even though the design of government-issued ballots allowed a voter to select individual candidates by office rather than party. Reform, such as the secret (Australian) ballot, also made party mobilization more difficult since party poll watchers could no longer identify exactly who was voting for the party.

8. Democrats also received funds from corporate donors, as I show in chapter 5, but these donors were less likely to be from the inner circle of big business. Typically, Democratic donors had businesses that were more local or regional.

9. Root was among the reformist New York Republicans who opposed the state's Republican machine led by Senator Thomas C. Platt. He had been instrumental in establishing the Citizen's Union in New York, which pushed for nonpartisan and off-cycle municipal elections (to detach them from state and national elections), primaries, and other reforms to weaken the grip of the Tammany (Democratic) and Platt (Republican) organizations in New York. While an ardent Progressive, he was strongly opposed to women's suffrage, arguing that "in politics there is struggle, strife, contention, bitterness, heart-burning, excitement, agitation, everything which is adverse to the true character of women" (Jessup 1964, 178).

10. The Seventeenth Amendment, which provided for direct election of U.S. senators, was not in place until 1913. Up to that point, state legislatures chose U.S. senators.

11. His position was a turnaround from his earlier career as a formidable fund-raiser for the Republican Party during the campaigns of 1868 and 1872. Before that he was a longtime lobbyist for corporate interests, including railroad companies.

12. The radical Republicans favored strong federal intervention in the post–Civil War South. Even though Chandler counted himself among the radicals during his youth, he had apparently formed a close friendship with Tillman.

13. Overacker (1932, 157–68) observed that both national committees received contributions from corporate interests (via individual contributions) but that banking and manufacturers supported Republicans more heavily and Democratic contributors were more diverse and tended to give to local parties.

14. The same patterns of fund-raising existed in the 1990s, with Republicans relying increasingly on corporate soft money, while Democrats received funds from wealthy liberals in major cities on the coasts (Pollock 1926).

15. U.S. Congress. Senate. 1906.

16. Mutch (1988, 7) reports that two members in the House raised an objection, on principle, that corporations had the same rights as individuals. The Senate bill that passed, S. 4563, was signed into law January 26, 1907, as Public Law No. 36. While it is often referred to as the Tillman Act, the official title is "An Act to prohibit corporations from making contributions in connection with political elections."

17. It would have a lesser effect on fund-raising for Democratic congressional elections, especially in the South, where primaries—which were the essential elections—would remain untouched. Tillman was distrustful of federal expansion into state affairs, and he ardently opposed Roosevelt's policies to expand national government. He especially disliked Roosevelt's friendliness toward blacks and took offense when the president invited Booker T. Washington to the White House for supper, stating that "the action of President Roosevelt in entertaining that nigger will necessitate our killing a thousand niggers in the South before they will learn their place again" (Morris 2001, 55).

18. Its membership included prominent reformers from both parties, such as Charles Evans Hughes, Seth Low, and William Jennings Bryan (Overacker 1932, 235). Previous to setting up the national organization, Perry Belmont had formed a similar organization in the state of New York, which succeeded using the revelations from investigations into the New York insurance industry to spur the passage of a New York law in 1905 requiring disclosure of party and candidate reports.

19. See also *New York Times* 1910.

20. The financial reports had to include the name and address of each contributor who gave one hundred dollars or more. Before this law passed, the Democrats tried to make a campaign issue of public disclosure. They announced at their Denver convention in 1908 that they would ensure both pre- and postelection publicity of funds. The nominee, Bryan, requested that the DNC publish the names of all contributors of one hundred dollars or more in October. He also said his campaign would limit the size of an individual contribution to ten thousand dollars (almost two hundred thousand dollars in 2004 dollars). The Republican convention rejected a publicity plank, but Taft in his acceptance speech for the nomination said that the RNC treasurers would use the laws of New York State to disclose receipts and expenditures twenty days after the election.

21. The 1911 Publicity Act was remarkable in detailing the kind of candidate expenditures that were exempt from reporting and hence from the imposed spending limits. A candidate did not have to report items for "necessary personal expenses, incurred for himself alone, for travel and subsistence, stationary and postage, writing or printing (other than newspapers) and distributing letter, circulars, and posters, and for telegraph and telephone service, shall not be regarded as an expenditure within the mean of this section" (Pollock 1926, 183). In effect, candidate spending limits did not touch on important aspects of campaigning, namely, advertising the candidate.

22. See also *Congressional Record* 1911, 3005.

23. While *Newberry* was making its way through the courts, the Republicans were able to keep Newberry seated in the Senate for three years until he decided to resign after facing growing public pressure from constituents in Michigan. In the aftermath of the election, the U.S. Senate issued a warning: "The expenditure of such excessive sums in behalf of a candidate, either with or without his knowledge and consent, being contrary to sound public policy, harmful to the honor of the Senate and dangerous to the perpetuity of free government, such excessive expenditures are hereby several condemned and disapproved." See *Congressional Record* 1922.

24. A Senate investigation in 1923 revealed that Harding's secretary of the interior had received bribes to lease government oil reserves to particular oil companies. The resolution of the scandal did not end until 1928, when Albert Fall, the former secretary, was found guilty and given a one-year prison term and a fine of one hundred thousand dollars (*Columbia Electronic Encyclopedia* 2004).

25. According to Overacker (1932, 149), the discovery that Sinclair had made loans to the Republican Party, which were never paid back, did not become public until 1928, well after the 1925 act.

26. According to the *New York Times* (1924c), one week before the election the RNC had raised approximately $3.7 million for the presidential campaign, while the Demo-

crats raised only $550,000. The Republicans claimed, however, that they kept a campaign promise to limit spending to under $3 million in an effort to run an "economical" campaign. The difference was attributed to about $800,000 that the RNC transferred to state parties for campaign operations.

27. The final version of the bill was actually the House version introduced by Congressman Cable (Mutch 1988, 19–21).

28. *Congressional Record* 1925, 2631, 3431, 3487, 3828, 4654, 4707.

29. These reports started in March of an election year. Subsequent reports were due in June, September, ten to fifteen days before Election Day, and then on the fifth day preceding the election. They were required for any committee supporting candidates in two or more states.

30. The law used a per capita method to determine spending levels. For example, Senate candidates could spend ten thousand dollars or three cents for each vote cast at the last general election for senators but not exceeding twenty-five thousand dollars. In the House, candidates could spend twenty-five hundred dollars or three cents for each vote cast in the last general election for representative but not exceeding five thousand dollars. Decades later, the FECA would use similar per capita methods for setting expenditure limits in different states for presidential nominations. This act expanded the disclosure law, requiring all House and Senate candidates and multistate political committees to file quarterly reports that included contributions of one hundred dollars or more, even during nonelection years. Presidential candidates did not have to report receipts or expenditures.

31. Overacker (1932) argues that the law was implemented to clear up confusion emanating from *Newberry*. This is entirely plausible. While previous laws were never genuinely enforced, *Newberry* highlighted the possibility that rivals might use campaign finance statutes to attack them during elections. Members recognized the importance of defining the laws better to provide safe harbors for campaign activity.

32. As I explain in chapters 5 and 6, Republicans would pay a price for pushing many of these reforms because the laws would make it difficult for them to build strong organizations at the national level.

33. Overacker (1946) claims labor unions gave at least $750,000 to the DNC.

34. Most Democratic politicians—including FDR—played down labor's role so as not to offend others in the party coalition. Being the savvy politician, FDR refused to accept the $250,000 check that Lewis brought, but he thanked him, saying, "No John. Just keep it, and I'll call on you if and when any small need arises." Not long after, Lewis received requests for money from Farley, the DNC chair, and several independent Roosevelt groups in the states. Lewis ended up contributing double of what he first offered FDR at the White House. Lewis later ended up supporting Willkie in the 1940 election, but not before he had helped Roosevelt during the 1938 "purge" campaigns to unseat Democrats who were not New Dealers (Shannon 1959, 54).

35. FDR's use of the word *Copperhead* was modified from its original meaning. Originally, it was the designation for a faction of northern Democrats who opposed the Civil War. FDR used it to describe a southern faction of the Democratic Party that opposed his policies. In both senses, the term was applied to indicate disloyalty to the Union.

36. The Works Progress Administration, started by the Roosevelt administration,

lasted from 1935 to 1943 to employ Americans in construction and beautification projects across the nation (Shannon 1959, 55). See also *New York Times* 1939.

37. Hatch was elected and took over his seat following the resignation of Sam Bratton in November 1934. Serving after elections in 1936 and 1942, he did not run for office during the 1948 election.

38. According to Milkis and Young (2003, 51), about half the delegates to the 1936 Democratic convention were federal job holders.

39. The Ramspeck Act (1940), which came after the Hatch Act, extended the civil service merit system to nearly two hundred thousand positions previously exempt under the Civil Service Act. FDR supported this measure, which effectively blanketed in many loyal supporters of the New Deal, granting previously unclassified workers civil service protections (Milkis 1993, 132–33).

40. Democrats loyal to the administration tried to get exemptions for many federal patronage positions but could not. They sought, for example, to exempt appointments for U.S. district attorneys, postmasters, and marshals. These were traditionally rich sources of patronage for the party controlling the executive branch.

41. For example, Kentucky senator Alben Barkley—who was being challenged by Governor "Happy" Chandler for his Senate seat—objected, saying the bill would "politically sterilize" voters just because they worked for the federal government. His immediate concern was that the governor could easily pack the party convention with state employees to win the nomination. Senator Hatch replied, "Is it any reason to say that because there are State political machines we should have a Federal machinery?" (*New York Times* 1938b).

42. As with the previous Corrupt Practices Act the Hatch bill did not affect political committees operating in one state.

43. "I urged that a bill be introduced at this session providing for the financing by the Federal Government of Federal campaigns, with a limitation on the amounts that might be spent. The President said that such a bill could not pass. My rejoinder was that it did not matter whether it passed or not. The introduction of such a bill would open up a discussion of the amount of money that had already been spent by Willkie, and is likely to be spent. In other words, it would get the money issue into the campaign, and this is important" (Ickes 1953–54, 226).

44. This was proposed by Senator John H. Bankhead II (D-AL), a strong supporter of the New Deal, who thought this measure would kill the bill by making it unpalatable for Republicans (Tanenhaus 1954, 441–71). Congressional candidates already had spending limits in place of twenty-five thousand dollars for the Senate and five thousand dollars for the House.

45. *Congressional Record* 1940a.

46. A congressional committee investigating union activity in 1936 had recommended earlier that the FPCA prohibiting corporate political contributions be extended to labor unions (Sousa 1999, 374–401).

47. As quoted in the Supreme Court majority opinion *United States v. Auto Workers* (1957). See also U.S. Congress. House. Committee on Labor. 1945.

48. Unions would challenge these laws unsuccessfully in *United States v. CIO* (1948) and *United States v. Auto Workers* (1957). Yet, the logic of extending a ban on corporate

contributions to labor unions has not been adequately explained in either of these decisions (Mutch 2006). For an analysis based on the argument that campaign finance laws should reflect relative economic power, see Sousa 1999, 374–401.

49. U.S. Congress. House, 1945, 36–37. The report clarified which expenditures would be prohibited, including "salaries to organizers, purchase of radio time, and other expenditures by prohibited organizations in connection with elections . . . with or without the knowledge or consent of the candidates."

50. The Taft-Hartley Act (the National Labor Management Relations Act) touched on many aspects of labor and management practices. The provision regarding campaign finance was one element in a broader strategy to weaken labor unions.

51. Taft stated: "If 'contribution' does not mean 'expenditure,' then a candidate for office could have his corporation friends publish an advertisement for him in the newspapers every day for a month before the election. I do not think the law contemplated such a thing, but it was claimed that it did, at least when it applied to labor organizations. So, all we are doing here is plugging up the hole which developed." See *Congressional Record* 1947:6439.

52. Soon after the Taft-Hartley Act was passed, the CIO endorsed a congressional candidate running for office in a Maryland special election, throwing down a direct challenge to the provision against political expenditures. The courts agreed with the CIO, without directly confronting the constitutionality of the political expenditure limits. See *United States v. CIO* 1948. Later, the Supreme Court overturned a lower court decision allowing the United Auto Workers (UAW) to buy media time to endorse congressional candidates, in *United States v. UAW*. The Supreme Court based its *UAW* decision on Congress's power to prevent corruption or the appearance of corruption in elections. The court, however, did not address the First Amendment issue (Sousa 1999).

53. The committee recommended that financial activity in primaries be required and also that outside groups that spent money in elections be required to obtain candidates' written authorization. A special Senate investigation into spending in the 1952 elections, chaired by Mike Mansfield (D-MT), made similar recommendations and pushed for further clarification of the five thousand dollar contribution limit to candidates and parties, since it encouraged the proliferation of committees. Mansfield's committee also recommended lifting the ceiling on party spending from $3 million to $10 million.

54. According to Johnson's biographer, Robert Caro, he had relied on easy access to campaign cash to make friends in the Senate. Before the Hill committees emerged in the 1980s as key leadership posts from which to dispense cash, Johnson was a pioneer in using campaign money as one resource to win favors and secure loyalty from his Senate colleagues. As revealed by Caro, he routinely sent his aides to Texas to pick up cash in large grocery bags from friends in business, particularly the firm of Brown and Root, which he then deposited in various committees he controlled, including the Democratic campaign committees, to use as his personal campaign account for helping loyal colleagues and getting future commitment from them (Caro 2002). With Johnson's eyes on the presidency, he probably did not want to be constrained by a new set of rules that undermined his ability to raise money.

55. Alexander Heard was the chairman of the commission, and Herbert Alexander was the executive director. Heard had authored *Costs of Democracy* (1960), the most

thorough study of money in politics at the time. Herbert Alexander, as a graduate student, had performed much of the research for this study. Alexander had recently begun his quadrennial series of books on financing elections, sponsored by the Citizens' Research Foundation.

56. The commission also recommended tax deductions for bipartisan activities involving voter registration and fund-raising drives by individuals, businesses, and labor unions. These suggestions led later to a failed experiment with bipartisan fund-raising.

57. As president, Johnson completely ignored any reform proposals for two years. Once Johnson became president he probably did not want to point a spotlight on the campaign finance issue since it could very well turn on him. Certainly, some in the press were already criticizing him for his President's Club, which raised money from wealthy individuals.

58. In a rather controversial move, the commission recommended the temporary suspension before each presidential election of Section 315 of the Federal Communications Act of 1934. This section is typically called the "equal time" provision. What it means in practice is that broadcasters must give equal opportunity to candidates. If they allow one candidate to purchase air time or provide free time, they must allow the same for all rivals, including third-party candidates. The effect was to discourage broadcasters from providing any time at all. The famous Nixon-Kennedy debates were permitted because Congress temporarily suspended Section 315 to allow the two major party candidates to face off rather than open up the forum to third-party candidates (Alexander 1972, 205, 259–64).

59. This was the opinion of the political scientist Alexander Heard, chair of the commission. Heard stated: "The lack of position support from labor leaders for the President's tax incentives may be because contributions to labor political committees would not be eligible for such benefits. And if the money-raising capacity of the parties is improved, the relative importance of labor's help to Democratic candidates could diminish, thus weakening its tactical position" (quoted in Alexander 1972, 208).

60. There was also the fear that only party regulars would get funded if national committees controlled funds, and some incumbents did not like this idea. Herbert Alexander, who served on the commission, believed that members of Congress resisted legislation "that would advantage the party organization with funds which might be denied them as candidates. Congressional reluctance plus labor's opposition resulted in the major reform bills being introduced for the record only, with the understanding that the White House would not push hard for them" (Alexander 1972, 210).

61. The Senate Select Committee, led by Senator Everett Jordan from North Carolina, exonerated Baker from breaking any laws, even though they chastised him for committing "gross improprieties" (Phillips 1966).

62. U.S. Congress, 1967, Senate Finance Committee Hearings, 245–46.

63. Johnson was initially unsure about whether to support the Long measure, but he apparently recognized that the law would benefit him and eventually became a strong supporter. After the Long Act was repealed, Johnson submitted his own legislation in 1967 that resurrected Long's proposal to have public funds allocated directly by congressional appropriation rather than by individual tax checkoff. The president's legislation, however, never made it to the floor for a vote. Instead, Congress considered the House bill, sponsored by Representatives Ashmore and Goodell (Alexander 1972, 217).

64. These included the two senators from Alabama, Lister Hill and John Sparkman (Mann 1992, 250–51).

65. Senator Gore had convinced enough Democrats that the act was sorely deficient. Undoubtedly, there were antiwar liberals in Congress who did not want to strengthen the hand of the president.

66. The bill would not, however, include the antilabor provisions. Nonetheless, it included provisions that increased regulations on PACs, which at that time were mostly labor union PACs. The AFL-CIO strongly opposed the bill because it argued the bill would restrict its political education program (Zelizer 2002, 87).

67. In his 1968 campaign, Richard Nixon spent a record sum of $63 million ($342 million in 2004 dollars); about one-third of it was raised from just 153 donors who gave fifty thousand dollars or more (Alexander 1972, 7).

68. Democrats' debt was so severe in 1971 that AT&T threatened to refuse telephone service for the 1972 Democratic National Convention unless back debts were paid, and a bond was posted to cover prospective telephone costs in Miami (Peabody et al. 1972, 213n12).

69. The meeting was held at the home of Lawrence O'Brien, chairman of the DNC, and included several Democratic contenders for the presidential nomination and the party's congressional leaders.

70. Taxpayers could claim credit against a tax liability for 50 percent of a contribution up to a maximum of fifty dollars for joint returns or a tax deduction for the full amount of the contribution up to one hundred dollars on joint returns.

71. The bill set a ceiling on the amount a candidate could spend on various forms of media—including radio, television, cable television, newspapers, magazines, and automated telephone systems—in any primary, runoff, special, or general election. The spending cap was fifty thousand dollars or ten cents per voting age person in the jurisdiction covered by the election, with the limit set at the greater sum. In addition, the law declared that no more than 60 percent of a candidate's overall media spending could be devoted to radio and television advertising. These limits were to apply separately to primary and general elections and were indexed to reflect increases in the consumer price index.

72. Candidates could receive as much as 70–80 percent off rates offered to other advertisers.

73. The suit charged that the New York–based political parties were encouraging and assisting in the formation of multiple committees to help individual candidates as a strategy to get around the five thousand dollar contribution limits under the FCPA of 1925. The suit also claimed the parties made expenditures in excess of the $3 million cap on political committee spending (Alexander 1972, 228).

74. The act imposed ceilings on personal contributions by candidates and their immediate families of fifty thousand dollars for presidential and vice presidential candidates, thirty-five thousand dollars for Senate candidates, and twenty-five thousand dollars for House candidates.

75. Senator Ted Kennedy intoned on the floor: "Who owns America? Is it the people or a little group of campaign contributors?" (Murray 1974).

76. The House version of the commission requested part-time commissioners and did not give the agency the power to seek civil injunctions in court.

77. Under the 1974 amendments, the president, the Speaker of the House, and the president pro tempore of the Senate each appointed two of the six voting members of the newly created commission. The secretary of the Senate and the clerk of the House were designated as nonvoting, ex officio commissioners. The first commissioners were sworn in on April 14, 1975.

78. Citizens filing tax returns could check a box on their tax returns to confirm their preference for committing two dollars of their tax payments toward a presidential fund.

79. The president's campaign committee laundered funds in Mexico to finance the Watergate break-in. They also raised eye-popping sums from several individuals and organizations. Clement Stone, the insurance tycoon, gave what was considered a record contribution of more than $2 million to the Nixon campaign. Dairy interests contributed as much as $770,000—with more promised—in exchange for raising milk support prices; International Telephone and Telegraph (ITT) offered donations of $100,000–$400,000 for the Republican National Convention in an effort to stop antitrust legislation; and corporate executives from American Airlines and American Ship Building acknowledged they felt the Nixon campaign was extorting them (and others) for political contributions.

80. House candidates could spend no more than seventy thousand dollars. In the Senate, the spending cap was twelve cents per voting age person in the state during the general election (the previous media spending limit was eliminated). These spending limits were declared unconstitutional by the Supreme Court in its decision *Buckley v. Valeo* (1976). See Samples 2006.

81. Mutch notes that business executives commonly made large individual contributions knowing they would be fully reimbursed by the corporation through bonuses. He also notes that Congress passed a bill in 1974 (the "Devine" bill) that lifted the ban on contributions from government contractors, which would likely benefit the majority party (1988, 166).

82. Frenzel had also argued against provisions for public funding of presidential candidates, saying this would displace the role of political parties.

83. The suit was officially against the secretary of the Senate, Francis R. Valeo.

84. The Court affirmed this ruling in *Republican National Committee v. FEC* (1980). The Court also sustained other public funding provisions and upheld disclosure and record-keeping requirements. The Court, however, found that the method of appointing FEC commissioners violated the constitutional principle of separation of powers, since Congress, not the president, appointed four of the commissioners, who exercised executive powers.

85. See Federal Election Commission, 1975, Advisory Opinion 1975–23, related to a request for an opinion from SunPAC, a political committee affiliated with the Sun Oil Corporation.

86. Federal Election Campaign Act, P.L. 96-187, enacted on January 8, 1980.

CHAPTER 4

1. Panebianco (1988) argues parties must have collective goals to maintain loyalty among followers. No party—not even urban machines—can survive without invoking a shared purpose, rooted in ethnicity, nationalism, or some ideology.

2. Few accounts address the puzzle of reform in the absence of scandal. Zelizer's (2002) account emphasizes the role of reform coalitions in Congress, which methodically and persistently pursue reforms. While I agree these reform coalitions are necessary, they are not a sufficient condition of reform. As I argue here, the partisan element drives the passage and shape of reform.

3. See chapter 3. The 1971 laws were not mere window dressing, as some might argue; they enabled the General Accounting Office to investigate President Nixon's campaign and marshal evidence of wrongdoing that led to impeachment hearings (Alexander 1972).

4. Senator Frank Case was offered cash by an oil company in return for his support on legislation. He reported the bribe, and it received national attention (Zelizer 2002, 78).

5. For example, Katz and Mair (1995) introduce a new model of party, the cartel party, in which colluding parties become agents of the state and employ the resources and rules of the state to ensure their own collective survival.

6. On the overriding importance of members pursuing activities that help them get reelected, see Mayhew 1974.

7. Several strands of this theory are found in the political science and economic literature on regulations, including interest group theory, "capture" theory, and cartel theory.

8. Through most of the history of reform, the reforming party avoided this dilemma because campaign finance laws were aimed primarily at national party committees rather than candidate committees. Historically, incumbents have not relied on national party committees for their reelections.

9. This proposition has been put forth by the dependency theorists, most notably, Panebianco (1988) and Pfeffer and Salancik (1978).

10. This characteristic of the Democratic Party has been noted by many others. See, for example, Mayer 1996.

11. As the previous chapter describes, the Hatch Acts in 1940 and 1941 banned electioneering and political contributions by all federal employees and those state workers paid, in part, with federal money. The Smith-Connally and Taft-Hartley Acts attempted to ban labor union contributions and attempted to restrict electioneering by labor organizations.

12. James Q. Wilson (1962) uses these terms to describe two contending elements in the Democratic Party during the 1960s.

13. Wilson (1962) distinguished among three incentives that motivated members to contribute their efforts: *material,* which included access to jobs, contracts, and various forms of financial compensation; *solidary,* which reflected the social enjoyment of working with others and feeling part of a group; and *purposive,* which included ideological motivations and the desire to implement preferred policies.

14. The Club for Growth has been particularly active trying to unseat moderate Republican incumbents (Duran 2006; Whittington 2004).

15. Scholars like James Pollock (1926), Louise Overacker (1932), and Alexander Heard (1960) used these reports and interviews with political leaders to assemble the only data we have about political spending before the Citizens' Research Foundation and the FEC began systematic reporting of financial data. I used national committee data because

these were among the few committees that had to report campaign finance data. Some of the data were collected by congressional committees investigating previous elections.

16. Political party records were submitted regularly to either the clerk of the House or the Senate, which were then used by congressional investigators. In the 1960s, the Citizens' Research Foundation began compiling its presidential series on campaign funds.

17. Since these figures were published in newspapers of record like the *New York Times*, they also created perceptions about which party was stronger financially. Such perceptions are conceivably the basis for action by party leaders.

18. As the chart shows, Democrats achieved these feats in 1892, 1912, 1916, 1948, 1956, and 1992.

19. The one notable exception, of course, was the Long Act, which only called for subsidies for the political parties. Of course, other factors should be considered in some of these elections. For example, in 1912 the Republican Party was split, with Roosevelt running on the Progressive ticket.

20. Democratic leaders began to centralize power in the party during the 1960s, a process that was fraught with high political costs. One example was the McGovern-Fraser reforms preceding the 1972 elections, which created national rules for delegate selection to the convention. These reforms came in response to a legitimacy problem for the party, particularly among younger and middle-class activists, but the rules unsettled the southern faction and traditional party elites.

21. In the 1924 elections, for example, the Progressive presidential candidate, Robert LaFollette, had used campaign money and corruption as an issue against Coolidge (Shannon 1959, 48–49).

22. Harold L. Ickes makes the point in his diaries that it was useful to raise the campaign money issue before presidential elections because it highlighted key Democratic themes that they were the party for the average guy, while Republicans represented the rich (1953–54, 225).

23. The NCEC pushed for the Political Broadcast Act of 1970 and subsequent measures in the FECA to limit expenditures on broadcast spending and compel stations to provide the lowest union rate to candidates for advertising.

24. According to the *New York Times* (1974), political experts at the time agreed the bill would help Democrats and that Republicans could not afford to block legislation so soon after Watergate.

25. In 2000, even before the Enron scandal gave some momentum to reform efforts, the gap between the preferences of strong Democrats and other partisans was greater, with support among strong Democrats at 66 percent versus 52 percent for strong Republicans. Overall support for major reform was 54 percent of the electorate.

26. Support for reform has been shown to be closely tied to one's attitudes toward the groups that would be constrained by reform. Liberals, for example, support reforms that they believe will tighten restrictions on conservative groups they dislike (Grant and Rudolph 2004).

27. Beyond the issue of corruption, then, the BCRA is inextricably linked to a vision of what political campaigns *should* be. Far from being a neutral reform that seeks only to root out corruption, the BCRA reflects an effort to determine how voters should experience elections and what kind of information they should use to make decisions.

Television advertising is bad. Newspapers are good. Hard-hitting direct mail pieces are bad. Face-to-face discussions with campaign volunteers are good. To be sure, there is something qualitatively different among these various means of communication. Perhaps it might be better if campaigns were less shrill and based more on appeals to reason rather than on emotion. But many citizens, particularly those who do not follow politics closely, become interested in political issues when their emotions are aroused through television ads, even those that have a negative tone. It is precisely through these ads that voters begin to pay attention, focus on salient issues, and draw important distinctions between the candidates (Geer 2006).

28. Data from Political Money Line, http://www.politicalmoneyline.com/.

29. Many corporate executives apparently did not like being asked for soft money. The publicity was bad for corporate reputation, and the executives preferred more legitimate and less publicized channels of influence, using PACs and lobbying officeholders without the intermediary of the political party. See Kolb 2000.

30. If Daschle did not run for president, he knew he would face a bitter reelection contest in South Dakota against Representative John Thune. In this populist state, he may have hoped his stance of passing the BCRA would resonate well among voters and also prevent an anticipated barrage of soft money issue ads that would be used against him by the Republican Party and outside groups.

CHAPTER 5

1. Major patrons or entrepreneurs may often choose to bear the heavy costs of organizing. See Walker 1991. Organizing is especially valued to them because they might receive substantial benefits of group action in the form of prestige or influence over policy. Ralph Nader, as a political entrepreneur, organized consumer rights groups in the 1970s. Patrons might include large foundations that provide grants to advocacy organizations.

2. The loosening ties of partisan loyalty increased costs of mobilization since parties had spend more effort persuading the putative independent voter rather than rousing stalwarts to polls through the traditional grass roots canvass.

3. The Publicity Acts of 1910 and 1911 required parties to submit reports to the House clerk about contributions and expenditures. See chapter 3 for details.

4. Parties had begun modest efforts to seek out small donors in the 1908 elections after both presidential candidates promised to disclose their donors.

5. The practice of copying civic models would continue throughout the century. The parties frequently drew upon fund-raising strategies of philanthropic organizations, using dinners, entertainment, and telethons.

6. Data from Overacker 1932, 132–33.

7. *Burroughs v. United States* (1934) upheld provisions of the FPCA requiring political committees operating in two or more states to disclose finances. But the decision did not clarify whether Congress could regulate state and local parties. State parties, which appeared exempt from the FPCA, continued to rely on large donors, contributions from patronage appointees, and assessments on candidates desiring to run for office. See Overacker 1932, 126.

8. The DNC donors included the following (data given in thousand of dollars):

	Preelection Contributions	Postelection Debt Fund	Total
William Kenny	100	175	275
John Raskob	110	250	360
Herbert Lehman	100	160	260
M. J. Meehan	50	100	150
Total	360	685	1,045

(*Source:* Overacker 1932, 155.)

9. The Hatch Act prohibited managers from coercing campaign contributions or political support by promising jobs, promotion, financial assistance, contracts, or any other benefit. Democrats loyal to the administration tried to get exemptions for many federal patronage positions but could not. For example, it had been a long tradition to get electoral support through appointments for U.S. district attorneys, postmasters, and marshals around the nation. The Ramspeck Act, which came later, authorized the extension of the merit system rules, including its prohibitions on political activity, to nearly two hundred thousand positions previously exempted by the law.

10. In the 1990s through 2002, when Congress passed the BCRA, the Pew Charitable Trust helped fund reform organizations committed to preventing wealthy contributors from doing precisely this kind of end run around the system.

11. Ickes 1954, 287–88, 302–3, 306, 309, 313, 323–26, 335, 341, 344–66.

12. The CIO PAC was closely associated with another new PAC that formed at the time by a group of progressives called the National Citizens Political Action Committee. Made up mostly of writers, artists, and academics, they solicited voluntary contributions from their respective groups (Overacker 1956, 58).

13. One example is how interest groups use soft money thirty days before a primary or sixty days before a general election because the BCRA prohibits anything but hard money within these periods. Interest groups may also avoid electioneering terms such as *vote for* that enable them to use soft money rather than hard money.

14. In 2006, for example, labor union–sponsored PACs accounted for 20 percent of total PAC contributions to congressional candidates ($58 million out of $296 million total). The balance overwhelmingly reflects contributions from business interests. Data from the Center for Responsive Politics, http://www.opensecrets.org/pacs/list.asp.

15. Heard (1960), for example, reports on a study of the Massachusetts Democratic Party in 1952 that found many volunteer committees in support of Senate candidate John F. Kennedy and the presidential candidate Adlai Stevenson. These committees did not appear to work closely with the traditional party organizations during the campaign.

16. The party congressional committees now assign quotas to their members to raise money. Members who want greater influence within the party try to meet or exceed these goals as a way to demonstrate their leadership potential. Members also raise money to contribute to colleagues as a way of building personal relationships that might help them gain leadership positions. The national committees (RNC and DNC) cannot

rely on congressional candidates to raise money for presidential elections since these committees have few tangible rewards to give to members of Congress for their help.

17. The fact that he was never asked himself was likely an indicator of his likely failure as finance chair. In the past, DNC finance chairs had been men of immense wealth who had tapped their circle of wealthy friends.

18. Richard Nixon was not supportive of building the RNC. He did not see it as a means of increasing his influence within the party. Indeed, he saw the RNC as a rival base of power.

19. See chapter 3 for details.

20. See chapter 3 for details of a financial scandal involving Bobby Baker. President Johnson also came under scrutiny when the Justice Department dropped antitrust proceedings against Anheuser-Busch of St. Louis. Executives of the beer company were large contributors to the President's Club (see Alexander 1972, 99).

21. P.L. 92-225.

22. P.L. 92-178. Under the Revenue Act—the first of a series of laws implementing federal financing of presidential elections—citizens could check a box on their tax forms authorizing the federal government to use one of their tax dollars to finance presidential campaigns in the general election.

23. See chapter 3 for details.

24. The FEC ruled in November 1975 that Sun Oil Company's PAC could raise funds broadly within the firm from managers. The FEC ruling allowed corporations to solicit widely and to pay for costs of operations from their corporate funds. This decision is widely credited with sparking the expansion of corporate PACs.

25. The situation is different for congressional campaign committees. The leadership in Congress is closely tied to congressional campaign committees. Thus, prospective donors seeking material benefits have a motive to contribute to these committees if they seek legislative favors from the leadership.

26. Two failed experiments in the 1960s with bipartisan fund-raising that appealed to individuals' civic spirit appear to support the conclusion that this incentive, on its own, does little to motivate donors. See Heard et al. 1964.

27. I use a fixed-effect model, with dummy variables for years to control for across-cycle variation.

28. The FEC does not keep records of those who contribute less than two hundred dollars.

29. Mayer (2004) coined the term *interregnum* to describe this period.

30. These observations are based on a random sample of one hundred from a population of twelve thousand groups that gave only soft money. Among these groups, ninety-six were business related. Only four organizations were not business firms: two Native American tribes (Leech Lake Tribal Council and Mashantucket Pequot Tribe) and two educational/research institutions (Sawyer College of Business and Pathology Institute of Middle Georgia). The largest contributor in the sample was the Mashantucket Pequot Tribe, which operates Foxwoods Casino in Connecticut, with a total of $369,000 in soft money contributions (Apollonio and La Raja 2004).

31. It is also noteworthy that the distribution of soft money donor groups has remained remarkably stable over presidential and midterm election cycles since 1992. In

other words, groups from different sectors in business, labor, and advocacy have provided the same percentages of soft money to parties during this period.

CHAPTER 6

1. For an excellent study on congressional campaign committees, see Kolodny 1998.

2. There is a vast literature about congressional campaign committees in political science journals, most of which is concerned with how these organizations allocate their campaign resources to congressional races. See also Kolodny 1998 for a book-length analysis of these committees.

3. For analyses of party resurgence, see Herrnson 1988; Frantzich 1989; Cotter and Bibby 1980, 1–27; Adamany 1984, 72–121; Wekkin 1985, 19–37; and Schlesinger 1985, 1152–169.

4. But see Bernstein and Dominguez 2003.

5. Organizing through the party apparatus is particularly important for the party out of power. The incumbent president has considerable advantages, not the least of which is that the incumbent can raise a lot of money for the party and typically does not have to spend it in a divisive primary. But even incumbent presidents have begun exploiting the benefits of having a year-round campaign operation based at party headquarters. Since Ronald Reagan, presidents have used the party to help advance their policy agenda. The ability of presidents to "go public" is enhanced by having a supportive party organization that can conduct polls, contact voters, and run advertisements.

6. Krasno and Sorauf (2003, 55) argue, in contrast, that candidate-centered spending is incompatible with long-term party building, asserting that "the logic of targeting conflicts with the process of building stronger parties everywhere." They fail to recognize that parties have strong incentives to build their organizations as a means to win elections.

7. Power in the Republican Party, Jo Freeman observes, tends to flow downward: "the Republican party sees itself as an organic whole whose parts are interdependent. Republican activists are expected to be good soldiers who respect leadership and whose only important political commitment is to the Republican Party" (1986, 339).

8. Freeman (1986) also argues, as does Klinkner (1994), that the hierarchical structure can be attributed to the habit of party leaders to borrow management practices from the corporate sector, in which many of them worked previously.

9. To be sure, Republican organizations benefit from having a broader base of wealthy donors, but this wealth is linked directly to a political culture in which activists tend to view the party as the chief instrument through which to achieve their goals, whereas Democratic activists and donors tend to have divided loyalties. Republicans, for example, tend to contribute more exclusively to their party, while Democratic activists, with their divided loyalties, tend to contribute to multiple cause groups (Francia et al. 2003).

10. Indeed, labor unions resisted efforts to make the party stronger in the 1960s when they argued against giving parties public funds. Herbert Alexander (1972) argues that labor unions opposed campaign finance reform that provided public funds to parties because it would diminish candidate reliance on labor union activity.

11. See, for example, Giroux 2005, 2096–98.

12. Each party is required to itemize expenditures that are reported to the FEC.

13. In the general election, political parties are allowed to contribute funds to their nominees based on the following formula: $0.02 × voting age population of U.S. + COLA (with 1976 as the baseline year).

14. These figures do not include the congressional campaign committee expenditures.

15. See Open Secrets, http://www.opensecrets.org/presidential/index.asp?graph= spending.

16. The formal party organization is the party committee. However, as several scholars have documented, there is an extended network of party activists who routinely engage in party-based activity, even if they do not work directly with or for the DNC and other formal party organizations. See Bernstein and Dominguez 2003; Cohen et al. forthcoming; Kroger, Noel, and Musket 2005; Skinner 2005.

17. See Open Secrets, http://www.opensecrets.org/527s/527events.asp?orgid=10.

18. In spite of assertions by Republican operatives that they were able to correlate consumer and political behavior, there is no academic research that I am aware of that would substantiate such claims, particularly at the level of the individual voter.

19. Corrado (2005) coined the term *hybrid* advertising, which is when the presidential candidate and political party jointly fund advertising campaigns that include a message about the party (or the Republican leadership in Congress) *and* the presidential candidate. Because the ads are considered generic party ads, they do not count against the coordinated expenditures the party is allowed to make on behalf of the presidential nominee in the general election. One additional key advantage is that the presidential and party committees have the opportunity to closely coordinate the message. In contrast, "independent" spending by the party allows no direct coordination with the candidates.

20. See information provided by the Center for Responsive Politics, http://www .opensecrets.org/527s/527events.asp?orgid=15.

21. See Magleby, Patterson, and Monson 2005. The reasons for this trend toward mobilization are not entirely clear, but two explanations are likely. First, as the cost of television advertising increases, it increases the incentives to use other forms of political persuasion. Second, new technologies to identify voters through canvassing may be more effective than in the past at getting likely voters to the polls.

22. Data on the number of eligible voters are available from McDonald 2007.

23. The 1992 estimate seems low, but it is possible that Republicans contracted for much of the direct mail in the past while more of the process is now done internally.

24. Those who supported the BCRA also argued that a ban on soft money would spur parties to emphasize grass roots work. To be sure, the party increased its grass roots work, but it is unclear whether the BCRA was a stimulus. Undoubtedly, the BCRA caused parties to increase their efforts to raise money from small donors through direct mail and phone banks.

25. At the time of this writing, the Center for Responsive Politics had not yet finished coding one-third of the expenditures of 527 organizations, which means it is likely that this figure is even higher. See http://www.opensecrets.org/527s/527cmtes.asp?level =E&cycle=2004.

26. National committees would often send soft money to a state party in exchange for

hard money from the state party. The hard money was more valuable in federal elections. State parties usually received a premium on this exchange, getting additional soft dollars for the swap.

27. Several field studies of GOTV operations, for example, show that parties seem to mobilize voters extensively in battleground states (Magleby 2002; Magleby, Patterson, and Monson 2005). There is also evidence that presidential campaign committees pursue the Electoral College strategy through placement of television ads (Goldstein and Freedman 2002) and campaign visits (Shaw 1999, 2003) in marginal swing states that are rich in electoral votes.

28. Van Buren and his fellow Democrats were highly strategic in choosing where to build the party in the states previous to the 1828 elections. They sought to organize first where it was cheapest and where benefits were potentially large (e.g., New England and the middle states with structured and competitive politics). They avoided the South and the West because of their informal politics, which would be costly to organize, and because these states would probably end up voting for Jackson anyway (Aldrich 1995, 116).

29. But see Leyden and Borrelli 1990 for some contrary evidence.

30. I also tried a pooled, fixed-effect model that combined election cycles. The results of the pooled model confirmed the two hypotheses but did not provide insights into how party strategies changed from year to year.

31. All data on party transfers have been collected from the FEC and are adjusted in constant 2004 dollars. These transfers include both hard and soft money, except for 2004, when national parties could no longer use soft money. The RNC and DNC also make transfers in nonpresidential years, typically in support of gubernatorial candidates. But to give clarity to the analysis I focus only on years when the party is campaigning for its presidential candidate.

32. It also appears that neither party does much to strengthen its prospects in states with relatively large numbers of Latinos or blacks. An earlier version of this model tested for whether national committees transfer additional funds to states with a high proportion of voters in these groups. Variables for blacks and Latinos were not significant.

33. This analysis is not presented here, but the results have been presented in La Raja 2006a, 57–74.

34. Thus, a fly-by-night 527 group, such as the Swift Boat Veterans for Truth, which aired television ads that hurt presidential candidate John Kerry, might help generate a one-time victory, but they can hardly be considered a strong organization since they lack an ongoing presence in campaigns. The success of the Swift Boat Veterans for Truth reflects more the influence of a smart strategy in a particular circumstance by a few political entrepreneurs rather than a strong organization that can influence political events over the long term.

35. Of course, several other factors, aside from money, might strengthen party organizations. For instance, Key (1956) argued that political competition spurs party organizing, and he suggested that the anemic development of organizations in the South was tied directly to the dominance of one party. In some states parties flourish because of a political culture tolerant of parties, while in other states an antiparty bias is reflected in restrictive laws on party organizations and efforts to make elections nonpartisan (May-

hew 1986). It is also likely that the contemporary strength of a party is tied to its strength in past years. Former glories endow it with the traditions and resources to exploit new opportunities.

36. Financial data for each of the one hundred state parties were obtained from the FEC, which requires parties at all levels to file reports for any activity related to federal campaigns.

37. The survey was kept short and delivered by e-mail or fax to maximize the response rate. About half of the parties responded to the e-mail, and another fifteen state parties responded to the fax, bringing the total to sixty-five. Follow-up phone calls raised this total to ninety-four out of one hundred major state parties.

38. The method for the survey response was very simple—an e-mail reply or two-page fax that should not have taken more than three to five minutes to complete. The burden of filling out a survey, even for the weakest organizations, was slight.

39. The PTS sent questionnaires to former Republican and Democratic state party chairmen (1960–78) in twenty-seven sample states. They also sent questionnaires to current state party chairmen (1978–80) in fifty-four states, of which twenty-seven were part of the original sample for 1960–78.

40. The PTS data for 1964–74 are based on recollections of past party chairs when the survey was done in 1978–80, so these data must be viewed with some caution. Nonetheless, these data provide a rare empirical baseline for judging the health of parties over time. There are a few caveats about the 2000 data. First, because it was considered important to achieve a high response rate, the 2000 survey asked only fifteen questions and therefore tapped many fewer measures of party activity than those explored by the PTS. These measures, then, provide a rougher approximation of party strength than the index compiled by the PTS. One indication that the 2000 measures are valid, however, is that they are highly correlated (about 0.5) with the party organizational strength scores reported by the PTS in 1980. Apparently, the stronger parties of the past persist as the stronger parties of today.

41. In response to queries about whether the party organization participated in a particular activity, the researchers in the PTS counted a response as "yes" if the party chair simply checked off in the survey that the party engaged in the activity. In my survey I counted a "yes" response if the executive director responded "sometimes" or "often" to a question about performing an activity.

42. These budgets reflect the amounts reported to the FEC. The totals do not include how much state parties spend off-year for state elections.

43. This was not always true. The PTS reports that in the 1950s through 1960s party affairs were sometimes conducted from temporary office space or from the homes of party chairs.

44. I created the index by testing bivariate relationships among all the variables. Within each dimension of party organizational strength, as developed by Cotter et al. (1984), I included correlated variables into an overall measure of party organizational strength. I transformed each variable to a range of 0–1 and took the average of all the scores as a way of minimizing the effect of a nonresponse to a particular question by a party.

45. See the Center for Responsive Politics, http://www.opensecrets.org/527s/527cmtes.asp?level=E&cycle=2004.

46. See the Center for Responsive Politics, http://www.opensecrets.org/527s/527 events.asp?orgid=10.

47. Independent expenditures are campaign activities conducted without coordination with a candidate. The Supreme Court ruling *FEC vs. Colorado Federal Election Campaign Committee* (2000) stated that political parties could not be limited in the amount they spent, so long as they spent their funds independently from their candidates.

CHAPTER 7

1. Proreformers also argue vigorously against allowing issue groups, like the Wisconsin Right to Life Committee, to spend nonfederal funds (soft money) on advertisements within the thirty- to sixty-day window leading up to an election, arguing that these sham ads are intended to influence elections rather than lobby for a policy. See Wertheimer 2006. Such sentiments reveal a belief that advocacy should—and can—be separated neatly from electioneering when, in fact, such political activity is often inextricably entwined. It could be argued, as Justice Clarence Thomas suggested in *McConnell v. Federal Election Commission,* that restrictions on any kind of speech prior to a campaign—be it political advocacy or sharp criticism of politicians—deserve the strictest scrutiny because it is precisely during these heightened moments of electoral accountability and attention that the First Amendment "has its fullest and most urgent application." Thomas is quoting the decision in *Monitor Patriot Co. v. Roy* (1971) in his dissenting opinion in *McConnell v. Federal Election Commission* (2003).

2. Interestingly, parties in the United Kingdom are experiencing the same dilemmas under a recent prohibitionist-inspired reform, the first major campaign finance law in the United Kingdom since the Corrupt and Illegal Practices Act of 1883. After more than 120 years without significant constraints on party finance the major parties face strict limits and disclosure on political financing, which has encouraged them to take on unprecedented election debts. Under the Corrupt and Illegal Practices Act of 1883, limits were placed on candidates but not on political parties, a regulatory strategy that had the opposite effect than in the American system. The parties in the United Kingdom became the main mechanisms for organizing and funding elections, and they depended primarily on large institutional donations from labor unions (for the Labour Party) and corporations (for the Conservative/Tory Party). See Ghaleigh 2006, 35–56; see also BBC News 2006.

3. The NES data usually report a figure of about 10 percent of the U.S. population claiming to make a political contribution. It is very likely this figure is inflated. According to the Center for Responsive Politics, only 0.3 percent of the U.S. population has given a contribution of over two hundred dollars in the 2004 elections. Figures for those making donations below this amount are difficult to assess because these contributions do not have to be reported to the FEC. See www.crp.org.

4. The Scottish philosopher David Hume recognized the importance of the distinction between parties based on interests, principle, or affection. His categories relate directly to the three "incentives" described by Wilson (1962): material, purposive, and solidary. Hume (2007) argued that parties of interest were more likely to be moderate

and willing to compromise, while parties of principle, and even parties of affection, were drawn to "what madness, what fury."

5. According to one study, European parties have been increasingly making intense use of technology, moving from the "selling" of party platforms to American-style "marketing" campaigns, which means finding what particular groups want to hear. They describe three major developments among Western parties that appear strikingly similar to American-style party organizations: (1) more centralized and professionalized campaign apparatus, (2) parties more cognizant of citizen opinion and demands, and (3) party leader's image plays prominent thematic role in campaigns. Accompanying these shifts are citizen preferences to situate themselves with interest groups around single issues as party loyalty wanes and local party organizations decline in importance (Farrell and Webb 2000, 118–223).

6. Lawmakers previously had to limit their contact with their leadership PACs—for example, by serving only as honorary chairmen. The new rules, however, give them more discretion to manage these committees. Roughly 150 members of Congress now have leadership PACs.

7. Data retrieved from the Center for Responsive Politics, http://www.open secrets.org/pacs/industry.asp?txt=Q03&cycle=2006.

8. The new ethics law passed by the 110th Congress in 2007 appears to make leadership PACs even more important to members since lobbyists can no longer pay for travel and events. Instead, lobbyists can make contributions to the leadership PAC, which then pays for the member to do such things.

9. The BCRA severely limits the scope of national party participation in coordinated planning because section 323(a) provides that federal officeholders, candidates, national parties, and their agents may not "solicit, receive, direct, transfer, or spend any soft money in connection with a federal election."

10. Some key aspects of this information is based on an interview on April 11, 2006, with a national campaign strategist who asked to remain anonymous.

11. His conclusion was based on observations from postelection focus groups in Ohio.

12. Justice Scalia concurred with respect to BCRA Titles III and IV, dissented with respect to BCRA Titles I and V, and concurred in the judgment in part and dissenting in part with respect to BCRA Title II.

13. Congressional parties have cut staffs precipitously (the NRCC went from ninety to fifty staff, slashed overhead, and increased telemarketing and direct mail. More than ever, they are narrowly focused on fund-raising. See Carney 2004, 2170.

14. In an April 9, 2006, interview on NBC's *Meet the Press,* the Massachusetts senator said, "I think the biggest mistake was probably not going outside the federal financing so we could have controlled our own message." See *Associated Press* 2006.

References

Abrams, Burton A., and Russell F. Settle. 1978. "The Economic Theory of Regulation and Public Financing of Presidential Elections." *Journal of Political Economy* 86:245–57.

Adamany, David. 1984. "Political Parties in the 1980s." In *Money and Politics in the United States: Financing Elections in the 1980s,* ed. Michael J. Malbin, 72–121. Washington, DC: American Enterprise Institute.

Aldrich, John H. 1995. *Why Parties?* Chicago: University of Chicago Press.

Alexander, Herbert E. 1962. *Financing the 1960 Election.* Princeton: Citizens' Research Foundation.

Alexander, Herbert E. 1966. *Financing the 1964 Election.* Princeton: Citizens' Research Foundation.

Alexander, Herbert E. 1971. *Financing the 1968 Election.* Lexington, MA: Heath Lexington Books.

Alexander, Herbert E. 1972. *Money in Politics.* Washington, DC: Public Affairs Press.

Alexander, Herbert E. 1976. *Financing the 1972 Election.* Lexington, MA: Lexington Books.

Alexander, Herbert E. 1979. *Financing the 1976 Election.* Washington, DC: CQ Press.

Alexander, Herbert E. 1980. *Financing the 1980 Election.* Lexington, MA: Lexington Books.

Alexander, Herbert E. 1992. *Financing Politics: Money, Elections, and Political Reform.* 4th ed. Washington, DC: CQ Press.

Alexander, Herbert E., and Monica Bauer. 1991. *Financing the 1988 Election.* Boulder: Westview.

Alexander, Herbert E., and Anthony Corrado. 1995. *Financing the 1992 Election.* Armonk, NY: M.E. Sharpe.

Alexander, Herbert E., and Brian A. Haggerty. 1987. *Financing the 1984 Election.* Lexington, MA: Lexington Books.

Alsop, Joe, and Robert Kintner. 1939. "Hatch Bill a Trap for President, Devised by Garner, Say Observers." *New York Times,* July 25, 6.

Altschuler, Glenn C., and Stuart M. Blumin. 2000. *Rude Republic: Americans and Their Politics in the Nineteenth Century.* Princeton: Princeton University Press.

The American National Election Studies (www.electionstudies.org). 2000. *The 2000 National Election Study* [dataset]. Ann Arbor: University of Michigan, Center for Political Studies [producer and distributor].

The American National Election Studies (www.electionstudies.org). 2002. *The 2000 National Election Study* [dataset]. Ann Arbor: University of Michigan, Center for Political Studies [producer and distributor].

The American National Election Studies (www.electionstudies.org). 2005. *The 1948–2004 Cumulative Data File* [dataset]. Stanford University and the University of Michigan [producers and distributors].

American Political Science Association. Committee on Political Parties. 1950. "Toward a More Responsible Two-Party System." *American Political Science Review* 44, September, supplement.

Anechiarico, Frank, and James B. Jacobs. 1996. *The Pursuit of Absolute Integrity: How Corruption Control Makes Government Ineffective.* Chicago: University of Chicago Press.

Ansolabehere, Stephen, John M. de Figueiredo, and James M. Snyder Jr. 2003. "Why Is There So Little Money in U.S. Politics?" *Journal of Economic Perspectives* 17 (Winter): 105–30.

Apollonio, D. E., and Raymond J. La Raja. 2004. "Who Gave Soft Money? The Effect of Interest Group Resources on Political Contributions." *Journal of Politics* 66 (4): 1159–79.

Apple, R. W., Jr. 1996. "Focus Shifts to Contests in the House." *New York Times,* October 20, 1.

Associated Press. 2006. "Kerry Says Biggest Mistake May Have Been Taking Federal Money." April 10.

Balz, Dan. 2005a. "Democrats' Grass Roots Shift the Power." *Washington Post,* February 20, A4.

Balz, Dan. 2005b. "Citing Need for Party-Building, Dean to Seek DNC Post." *Washington Post,* January 12, A9.

Balz, Dan, and Thomas B. Edsall. 2004. "Unprecedented Efforts to Mobilize Voters Begin." *Washington Post,* November 1, A1.

Bartels, Larry, and Lynn Vavreck. 2002. *Campaign Reform: Insights and Evidence.* Ann Arbor: University of Michigan Press.

Bauer, Robert F. 2006. "A Report from the Field: Campaign Professionals on the First Election Cycle under the Bipartisan Campaign Reform Act." *Election Law Journal* 5 (2): 105–20.

BBC News. 2006. "Labour Facing Cash Flow Problems." November 28. Available at http://news.bbc.co.uk/go/pr/fr/-/1/hi/uk_politics/6190510.stm.

Bernstein, Jonathan, and Casey B. K. Dominguez. 2003. "Candidates and Candidacies in the Expanded Party." *PS: Political Science and Politics* 36 (2): 165–69.

Berry, Jeffrey M., and Jerry Goldman. 1971. "Congress and Public Policy: A Study of the Federal Election Campaign Act of 1971." *Harvard Journal on Legislation* 10:331–65.

Bibby, John F. 1998. "State Party Organizations: Coping and Adapting to Candidate-Centered Politics and Nationalization." In *The Parties Respond,* ed. L. S. Maisel, 41–46. Boulder: Westview.

Bibby, John F. 2002. "State Party Organizations: Strengthened and Adapting to Candidate-Centered Politics and Nationalization." In *The Parties Respond,* 4th ed., ed L. Sandy Maisel, 19–46. Boulder: Westview.

Birnbaum, Jeffrey H. 2003. "The New Soft Money." *Fortune,* November 10. Available at http://money.cnn.com/magazines/fortune/fortune_archive/2003/11/10/352861/index.htm.

Bolton, Alexander. 2003. "FEC to Loosen PAC Rules for Lawmakers." *The Hill*, November 19, 3.

Brewer, Mark D. 2005. "The Rise of Partisanship and the Expansion of Partisan Conflict within the American Electorate." *Political Research Quarterly* 58 (June): 219–30.

Brown, Clifford W., Lynda W. Powell, and Clyde Wilcox. 1995. *Serious Money: Fundraising and Contributing in Presidential Nomination Campaigns.* Cambridge: Cambridge University Press.

Buckley v. Valeo. 1976. 424 U.S. 1.

Burroughs v. United States. 1934. 290 U.S. 534.

Cantor, David M., and Paul S. Herrnson. 1997. "Party Campaign Activity and Party Unity in the U.S. House of Representatives." *Legislative Studies Quarterly* 22 (3): 393–415.

Carney, Eliza Newlin. 2004. "In the Money." *National Journal*, July 10, 2170–71.

Caro, Robert A. 2002. *Master of the Senate.* New York: Random House.

Clymer, Adam. 2005. "The Donkey's Flush. Will the New DNC Chief Make Hay?" *Washington Post*, February 6, B5.

Cohen, Marty, David Karol, Hans Noel, and John Zaller. Forthcoming. *Beating Reform: The Resurgence of Parties in Presidential Nominations.* Chicago: University of Chicago Press.

Coleman, John J., and Paul F. Manna. 2000. "Congressional Campaign Spending and the Quality of Democracy. *Journal of Politics* 62:757–89.

Colorado Republican Federal Campaign Committee v. FEC. 1996. 518 U.S. 604.

Columbia Electronic Encyclopedia. 2004. 6th ed. New York: Columbia University Press.

Congressional Record. 1904. 58th Cong., 3d sess., December 6, vol. 39.

Congressional Record. 1905. 59th Cong., 1st sess., December 5, vol. 40.

Congressional Record. 1907. 60th Cong., 1st sess., December 3, vol. 42.

Congressional Record. 1911. 62nd Cong., 1st sess., July 17, vol. 47, 3005.

Congressional Record. 1922. 67th Cong., 2d sess., January 12, vol. 62.

Congressional Record. 1925. 68th Cong., 2d sess., February, vol. 66, 2631, 3431, 3487, 3828, 4654, 4707.

Congressional Record. 1940a. 76th Cong., 3d sess., vol. 86, 2852.

Congressional Record. 1940b. 76th Cong., 3d sess., March 13–18, vol. 86.

Congressional Record. 1940c. 76th Cong., 3d sess., July 10, vol. 86, 9463–64.

Congressional Record. 1947. 80th Cong., 1st sess., vol. 93, 6439.

Corrado, Anthony. 1997. "Money and Politics: A History of Federal Campaign Finance Law." In *Campaign Finance Reform: A Sourcebook*, ed. Anthony Corrado, Thomas E. Mann, Daniel R. Ortiz, Trevor Potter, and Frank J. Sorauf, 25–60. Washington, DC: Brookings Institution Press.

Corrado, Anthony. 2005. "Money and Politics: A History of Federal Campaign Finance Law." In *The New Campaign Finance Sourcebook*, ed. Anthony Corrado, Thomas E. Mann, Daniel R. Ortiz, and Trevor Potter. Washington, DC: Brookings Institution Press.

Corrado, Anthony. 2006. "Party Finance in the Wake of BCRA: An Overview." In *The Election after Reform: Money, Politics, and the Bipartisan Campaign Reform Act*, ed. Michael Malbin, 19–37. Lanham, MD: Rowman and Littlefield.

Cotter, Corneliuis P., and John F. Bibby. 1980. "Institutional Development and the Thesis of Party Decline." *Political Science Quarterly* 95:1–27.

Cotter, Cornelius P., and Bernard C. Hennessy. 1964. *Politics Without Power: The National Party Committees.* New York: Atherton.

Cotter, Cornelius, et al. 1984. *Party Organizations in American Politics.* New York: Praeger.

CQ Almanac. 1974. "Congress Clears Campaign Financing Reform." 612.

CQ Weekly. 2002. "For the Record," February 16. 60 (2): 834–40.

Croly, Herbert. 1910. *The Promise of American Life.* New York: Macmillan.

Croly, Herbert. 1965. *Marcus Alonzo Hannah: His Life and Work.* Hamden, CT: Archon Books.

Dahl, Robert A. 1961. *Who Governs?* New Haven: Yale University Press.

Damore, David F., and Thomas G. Hansford. 1999. "The Allocation of Party Controlled Campaign Resources in the House of Representatives, 1989–1996." *Political Research Quarterly* 52 (2): 371–85.

Dorris, Henry. 1939. "House by 242 to 133 Puts Firm Ban on Political Work by Job Holders." *New York Times,* July 21, 1.

Duran, Nicole. 2006. "Club for Growth Airing Anti-Chafee Ads." *Roll Call,* January 30.

Duverger, Maurice. 1954. *Political Parties: Their Organization and Activity in the Modern State.* New York: Wiley.

Dwyre, Diana, and Victoria A. Farrar-Myers. 2001. *Legislative Labyrinth: Congress and Campaign Finance Reform* Washington, DC: CQ Press.

Dwyre, Diana, and Robin Kolodny. 2006. "The Parties' Congressional Campaign Committees in 2004." In *The Election after Reform: Money, Politics, and the Bipartisan Campaign Reform Act,* ed. Michael J. Malbin, 42. Lanham, MD: Rowman and Littlefield.

Edsall, Thomas B. 2002. "Campaign Money Finds New Conduits as Law Takes Effect; Shadow Organizations to Raise 'Soft Money.'" *Washington Post,* November 5, A2.

Edsall, Thomas B. 2003. "Fundraising Specialists, Independent Groups Gain." *Washington Post,* December 11, A29.

Edsall, Thomas B. 2006a. "Democrats Are Fractured over Strategy, Funds." *Washington Post,* May 11, A1.

Edsall, Thomas B. 2006b. "Democrats' Data Mining Stirs an Intraparty Battle." *Washington Post,* March 8, A1.

Edsall, Thomas B. 2006c. "'527' Legislation Would Affect Democrats More." *Washington Post,* March 28, A3.

Edsall, Thomas B., and James V. Grimaldi. 2004. "On Nov. 2, GOP Got More Bang for Its Billion, Analysis Shows." *Washington Post,* December 30, A1.

Eilperin, Juliet. 2002. "After McCain-Feingold, a Bigger Role for PACs; Groups May Be 'Soft Money' Conduits." *Washington Post,* June 1, A1.

Eilperin, Juliet, and Helen Dewar. 2002. "Campaign Bill Heads for a Vote in the House." *Washington Post,* January 25, A1.

Eilperin, Juliet, and Thomas B. Edsall. 2001. "Gephardt Has Large Stake in Bill's Fate; Ambition, Conviction Driving His Efforts." *Washington Post,* July 12, A6.

Ellwood, John W., and Robert J. Spitzer. 1979. "The Democratic National Telethons: Their Successes and Failures." *Journal of Politics* 41:828–64.

Epstein, Edwin M. 1968. *Corporations, Contributions, and Political Campaigns*. Berkeley: Institute of Governmental Studies.

Epstein, Leon. 1958. *Politics in Wisconsin*. Madison: University of Wisconsin Press.

Epstein, Leon. 1986. *Political Parties in the American Mold*. Madison: University of Wisconsin Press.

Erie, Stephen P. 1988. *Rainbow's End: Irish-Americans and the Dilemmas of Urban Machine Politics, 1840–1985*. Berkeley: University of California Press.

Ewing, K. D., and Samuel Issacharoff. 2006. *Party Funding and Campaign Financing in International Perspective*. Portland: Hart Publishing.

Farrell, David M., and Paul Webb. 2000. "Political Parties as Campaign Organizations." In *Parties without Partisans*, ed. Russell J. Dalton and Martin P. Wattenberg, 118–223. Oxford: Oxford University Press.

Federal Election Commission. 1975. Advisory Opinion, AO 1975-23 (the SunPAC opinion).

Federal Election Commission. 2005a. "Party Financial Activity Summarized for the 2004 Election Cycle." Press Release, March 2. Available at http://www.fec.gov/press2005/20050302party/Party2004final.html.

Federal Election Commission. 2005b. "2004 Presidential Campaign Financial Activity Summarized." Press Release, February 3. Available at http://www.fec.gov/press/press2005/20050203pressum/20050203pressum.html.

Federal Election Commission 2005c. "Congressional Candidates Spend $1.16 Billion during 2003–2004." Press Release, June 9, 2005. Available at www.fec.gov/press/press2005/20050609/candidate/20050609candidate.html.

Federal Election Commission v. Colorado Republican Federal Campaign Committee. 2000. 533 U.S. 431.

Finney, John W. 1970. "Senate Approves TV Campaign Curb." *New York Times*, April 15, 1.

Francia, Peter L., John C. Green, Paul S. Herrnson, Lynda W. Powell, and Clyde Wilcox. 2003. *The Financiers of Congressional Elections: Investors, Ideologues, and Intimates*. New York: Columbia University Press.

Francia, Peter L., John C. Green, Paul S. Herrnson, Lynda W. Powell, and Clyde Wilcox. 2005. "Limousine Liberals and Corporate Conservatives: The Financial Constituencies of the Democratic and Republican Parties." *Social Science Quarterly* 86 (4): 761–78.

Franklin, Ben A. 1971. "Democrats' Money Woes Expected to Grow Worse." *New York Times*, November 28, 1.

Frantzich, Stephen E. 1989. *Political Parties in the Technological Age*. New York: Longman.

Franz, Michael M., Joel Rivlin, and Kenneth Goldstein. 2006. "Much More of the Same: Television Advertising Pre- and Post-BCRA." In *The Election after Reform: Money, Politics, and the Bipartisan Campaign Reform Act*, ed. Michael J. Malbin, 141–60. Lanham, MD: Rowman and Littlefield.

Freeman, Jo. 1986. "The Political Culture of the Democratic and Republican Parties." *Political Science Quarterly* 101 (3): 327–56.

Freedman, Paul, Michael Franz, and Kenneth Goldstein. 2004. "Campaign Advertising and Democratic Citizenship." *American Journal of Political Science* 48:723–41.

Gais, Thomas. 1996. *Improper Influence: Campaign Finance Law, Political Interest Groups, and the Problem of Equality.* Ann Arbor: University of Michigan Press.

Gallup Poll. 2001–2007. "Americans Assess the State of the Nation." Available at http://www.galluppoll.com.

Gallup Poll. 1998–2005. "Congress and the Public." Available at http://www.galluppoll .com.

Gallup Poll Editorial Staff. 2002. "Questions and Answers about Enron." *Gallup News Service,* February 14.

Geer, John G. 2006. *In Defense of Negativity: Attack Ads in Presidential Campaigns.* Chicago: University of Chicago Press.

Gerring, John. 1998. *Party Ideologies in America: 1828–1996.* Cambridge: Cambridge University Press.

Ghaleigh, Navraj Singh. 2006. "Expenditure, Donations, and Public Funding under the United Kingdom's Political Parties, Elections, and Referendums Act 2000—And Beyond?" In *Party Funding and Campaign Finance in International Perspective,* ed. K. D. Ewing and Samuel Issacharoff, 33–56. Portland: Hart Publishing.

Giroux, Gregory L. 2005. "Democrats' 2008 Strategy Has a Mountain View." *CQ Weekly,* August 1, 2096–98.

Gitell, Seth. 2003. "The Democratic Party Suicide Bill." *Atlantic Monthly,* July–August. Available at http://www.theatlantic.com/doc/prem/200307/gitell.

Goldstein, Ken, and Paul Freedman. 2002. "Campaign Advertising and Voter Turnout: New Evidence for a Stimulation Effect." *Journal of Politics* 64 (3): 721–40.

Graf, Joseph, Grant Reeher, Michael J. Malbin, and Costas Panagopoulos. 2006. *Small Donors and Online Giving: A Study of Donors to the 2004 Presidential Campaigns.* Washington, DC: George Washington University. Available at http://www.ipdi.org.

Grant, J. Tobin, and Thomas J. Rudolph. 2004. *Expression vs. Equality: The Politics of Campaign Finance Reform.* Columbus: Ohio State University Press.

Green, John C., ed. 1994. *Politics, Professionalism, and Power: Modern Party Organization and the Legacy of Ray C. Bliss.* Lanham, MD: University Press of America.

Green, John C., ed. 1999. *Financing the 1996 Election.* Armonk, NY: M.E. Sharpe.

Grimaldi, James V., and Thomas B. Edsall. 2004. "Super Rich Step into Political Vacuum." *Washington Post,* October 17, A1.

Hall, Richard L., and Frank W. Wayman. 1990. "Buying Time: Moneyed Interests and the Mobilization of Bias in Congressional Committees." *American Political Science Review* 84 (September): 797–820.

Harmel, Robert, and Kenneth Janda. 1982. *Parties and Their Environments: Limits to Reform?* New York: Longman.

Healy, Patrick, and Jeff Zeleny. 2007. "Clinton Setting a $1 Million Goal for Donors." *New York Times,* February 1, A1.

Heard, Alexander. 1960. *Costs of Democracy.* Chapel Hill: University of North Carolina Press.

Heard, Alexander, Julian W. Haydon, Derry F. Daly, and Charles E. Schutz. 1964. *Biparti-*

san Political Fundraising: Two Experiments in 1964. Princeton: Citizens' Research Foundation.

Herbers, John. 1966. "Democrats Plan Gift of $600,000." *New York Times*, March 6, 48.

Herbers, John. 1974. "Bill to Reform Campaign Funds Signed by Ford Despite Doubts." *New York Times*, October 16, 31.

Herrnson, Paul S. 1988. *Party Campaigning in the 1980s*. Cambridge: Harvard University Press.

Herrnson, Paul S. 2004. *Congressional Elections*. 4th ed. Washington, DC: CQ Press.

Hershey, Marjorie Randon. 2007. *Party Politics in America*, 12th ed. New York: Pearson.

Hillman, Sidney. 1944. *Testimony of Sidney Hillman Before U.S. Congress, House of Representatives, Special Committee to Investigate Campaign Expenditures, 1944, Hearings*. 78th Cong., 2d sess., August 31.

Holbrook, Thomas, and Scott D. McClurg. 2005. "Presidential Campaigns and the Mobilization of Core Supporters." *American Journal of Political Science* 49 (4): 689–703.

Hotline. 2004. "Poll Track" [various years]. Washington, DC: National Journal. Available at http://www.nationaljournal.com/members/polltrack/.

Hume, David. 1987. "Of Parties in General." In *Essays, Moral, Political, and Literary*, edited by Eugene F. Miller. Indianapolis: Liberty Fund. First published in 1742. Available at http://www.econlib.org/Library/LFBooks/Hume/hmMPL8.html (accessed August 2007).

Hurd, Charles W. 1940a. "Hatch Backers Win New Senate Fight." *New York Times*, March 8, 1.

Hurd, Charles W. 1940b. "Senate Filibuster by 40 Democrats Blocks Hatch Bill." *New York Times*, March 10, 1.

Ickes, Harold L. 1953–54. *The Secret Diary of Harold L. Ickes*. Vol. 3, *The Lowering Clouds, 1939–1941*. New York: Simon and Schuster.

Jackson, John S., III, Nathan S. Bigelow, and John C. Green. 2007. "The State of the Party Elites: National Convention Delegates, 1992–2004." In *The State of the Parties*, ed. John C. Green and Daniel J. Coffey, 51–74. Lanham, MD: Rowman and Littlefield.

Jaffe, Harry. 1992. "Mr. In-Between." *Washingtonian*, November.

Jessup, Philip C. 1964. *Elihu Root*. Vol. 1. New York: Archon Books.

Jones, Jeffrey M. 2002. "Seven in 10 Support New Campaign Finance Legislation." *Gallup Poll*, February 13. Available at http://www.galluppoll.com.

Joo, Thomas W. 2002. "Corporate Governance and the Constitutionality of Campaign Finance Reform." *Election Law Journal* 1 (3): 361–72.

Josephson, Matthew. 1938. *The Politicos, 1865–1896*. New York: Harcourt Brace.

Judis, John, and Ruy Teixeira. 2002. *The Emerging Democratic Majority*. New York: Simon and Schuster.

Justice, Glen. 2004. "New Rules on Fund-Raising Bring Lobbyists to the Fore." *New York Times*, April 20, A14.

Kaplan, Jonathan E. 2004. "RNC Offers 'Super Ranger' Status." *The Hill*, May 18, 4.

Katz, Richard S., and Peter Mair. 1995. "Changing Models of Party Organization and Party Democracy." *Party Politics* 1 (1): 5–28.

Kayden, Xandra, and Eddie Mahe Jr. 1985. *The Party Goes On: The Persistence of the Two-Party System in the United States*. New York: Basic Books.

Keith, Bruce E., David Magleby, Candice Nelson, Elizabeth Orr, Mark Westlye, and Raymond Wolfinger. 1992. *The Myth of the Independent Voter*. Berkeley: University of California Press.

Kennedy, David M. 1999. *Freedom from Fear: The American People in Depression and War, 1929–1945*. New York: Oxford University Press.

Kent, Frank R. 1940. "Hatch Act Hypocrisy." *Wall Street Journal*, March 21, 4.

Key, V. O., Jr. 1942. *Politics, Parties, and Pressure Groups*. New York: Crowell.

Key, V. O., Jr. 1956. *American State Politics: An Introduction*. New York: Knopf.

Key, V. O., Jr. 1984. *Southern Politics in State and Nation: A New Edition*. Knoxville: University of Tennessee Press.

Kingdon, John W. 1984. *Agendas, Alternatives, and Public Policies*. New York: Little, Brown.

Klinkner, Philip A. 1994. *The Losing Parties: Out-Party National Committees, 1956–1993*. New Haven: Yale University Press.

Koger, Gregory, Hans Noel, and Seth Masket. 2005. "We Appreciate Your Support: Information Exchange and Extended Party Networks." Paper presented at the annual meeting of the American Political Science Association, Washington, DC.

Kolb, Charles E. M. 2000. *Testimony of Charles E. M. Kolb, President of the Committee for Economic Development, Before the Committee on Rules and Administration, United States Senate*. 106th Cong., 2d sess., April 5.

Kolodny, Robin. 1998. *Pursuing Majorities: Congressional Campaign Committees in American Politics*. Norman: University of Oklahoma Press.

Krasno, Jonathan, and Kenneth Goldstein. 2002. "The Facts about Television Advertising and the McCain-Feingold Bill." *PS: Political Science and Politics* 35:207–12.

Krasno, Jonathan S., and Daniel E. Seltz. 2000. *Buying Time: Television Advertising in the 1998 Congressional Elections*. New York: Brennan Center.

Krasno, Jonathan, and Frank Sorauf. 2003. "Why Soft Money Has Not Strengthened Parties." In *Inside the Campaign Finance Battle*, ed. Anthony Corrado, Thomas E. Mann, and Trevor Potter, 54. Washington, DC: Brookings Institution Press.

Krock, Arthur. 1939. "Bi-partisan Majority Checks the New Deal." *New York Times*, July 23, E3

Landauer, Jerry. 1968. "Quiet Burials for Congress Reforms." *Wall Street Journal*, September 6, 8.

Landfried, Christine. 1994. "Political Finance in West Germany." In *Comparative Political Finance among the Democracies*, ed. Herbert E. Alexander and Rei Shiratori. Boulder: Westview.

La Raja, Raymond J. 2003. "State Political Parties after BCRA." In *Life after Reform*, ed. Michael J. Malbin, 107. Lanham, MD: Rowman and Littlefield.

La Raja, Raymond J. 2006a. "State and Local Political Parties." In *The Election after Reform: Money, Politics, and the Bipartisan Campaign Reform Act*, ed. Michael J. Malbin, 57–74. Lanham, MD: Rowman and Littlefield.

La Raja, Raymond J. 2006b. Interview with national campaign strategist who asked to remain anonymous. April 11.

La Raja, Raymond J., and Alana Hoffman. 2000. "Who Benefits from Soft Money Contributions?" Institute of Government Studies Working Paper, University of California, Berkeley.

La Raja, Raymond J., and Sidney M. Milkis. 2004. "For the Plaintiffs: The Honor and Humility of Defending Political Parties in Court." *PS: Political Science and Politics* 37:771–76.

Lawrence, W. H. 1952. "Eisenhower 'Amateurs' Win Separate Role in Campaign." *New York Times*, August 4, 1.

Leyden, Kevin M., and Stephen A. Borelli. 1990. "Party Contributions and Party Unity: Can Loyalty Be Bought?" *Western Political Quarterly* 43 (2): 343–65.

Lindenfeld, Tom. 2006. Telephone interview by Raymond J. La Raja. May 6.

Longley, Kyle. 2004. *Senator Albert Gore, Sr.: Tennessee Maverick*. Baton Rouge: Louisiana State University Press.

Magleby, David, ed. 2002. *Financing the 2000 Election*. Washington, DC: Brookings Institution Press.

Magleby, David B., Kelly D. Patterson, and J. Quin Monson, eds. 2005. *Dancing without Partners: How Candidates, Parties, and Interest Groups Interact in the New Campaign Environment*. Provo, UT: Center for the Study of Elections and Democracy, Brigham Young University.

Malbin, Michael J. 2004. "Political Parties under the Post-*McConnell* Bipartisan Campaign Reform Act." *Election Law Journal* 3 (2): 177–91.

Mann, Robert. 1992. *Legacy to Power: Senator Russell Long of Louisiana*. New York: Paragon House.

Mann, Thomas E. 2002. "Political Parties Now Facing 'Tough Love.'" *Boston Globe*, November 10, E11.

Mann, Thomas E. 2003. "The Rise of Soft Money." In *Inside the Campaign Finance Battle*, ed. Anthony Corrado, Thomas E. Mann, and Trevor Potter. Washington, DC: Brookings Institution Press.

Marcus, Robert D. 1971. *Grand Old Party: Political Structure in the Gilded Age, 1880–1896*. New York: Oxford University Press.

Mayer, William G. 1996. *The Divided Democrats: Ideological Unity, Party Reform, and Presidential Elections*. Boulder: Westview.

Mayer, William G. 2004. "From the End of the Nomination Contest to the Start of the National Conventions: Preliminary Thoughts on a New Period in Presidential Campaign Politics." *Forum* 2 (2): article 1. Available at http://www.bepress.com/forum/vol2/iss2/art1.

Mayhew, David. 1974. *Congress: The Electoral Connection*. New Haven: Yale University Press.

Mayhew, David. 1986. *Placing Parties in American Politics: Organization, Electoral Settings, and Governmental Activity in the Twentieth Century*. Princeton: Princeton University Press.

McConnell v. Federal Election Commission. 2003. 124 S. Ct. 619.

McDonald, Michael. 2007. "United States Election Project," George Mason University, available at http://elections.gmu.edu.

McGerr, Michael. 1986. *The Decline of Popular Politics: The American North, 1865–1928*. Oxford: Oxford University Press.

McSweeney, Dean. 2005. "Reform in a Cold Climate: Change in U.S. Campaign Finance Law." *Government and Opposition* 40 (4): 492–514.

Mileur, Jerome. 1999. "The Legacy of Reform: Progressive Government, Regressive Politics." In *Progressivism and the New Democracy: Political Development of the American Nation,* ed. Sidney M. Milkis and Jerome M. Mileur, 259–88. Amherst: University of Massachusetts Press.

Milkis, Sidney M. 1993. *The President and the Parties.* New York: Oxford University Press.

Milkis, Sidney M. 1999. *Political Parties and Constitutional Government: Remaking American Democracy, Interpreting American Politics.* Baltimore: Johns Hopkins University Press.

Milkis, Sidney M., and McGee Young. 2003. "Parties, Constitutionalism and Reform: The Bipartisan Campaign Reform Act in Historical Perspective." Paper presented at the conference "Reconsidering Campaign Finance Reform," Miller Center of Public Affairs, University of Virginia, September 30.

Miller, Joanne M., Jon A. Krosnick, and Laura Lowe. 2002. "The Impact of Policy Change Threat on Grassroots Activism." Manuscript, University of Minnesota.

Milyo, Jeffrey, David Primo, and Timothy Groseclose. 2001. "Corporate PAC Campaign Contributions in Perspective." *Business and Politics* 2 (1): 75–88.

Monitor Patriot Co. v. Roy. 1971. 401 U.S. 265.

Morris, Edmund. 2001. *Theodore Rex.* New York: Random House.

Morris, John D. 1956. "Senator Reports an Offer of $2500 to Sway Gas Vote." *New York Times,* February 4, 1.

Morris, John D. 1966. "Tax Bill Is Voted by Senate Panel." *New York Times,* March 2, 1.

Morris, John D. 1967. "Labor Lobbies against House Measure Tightening Curbs on the Use of Funds in Political Campaigns." *New York Times,* October 3, 31.

Moscardelli, Vincent G., and Moshe Haspel. 2007. "Campaign Finance Reform as Institutional Choice." *American Politics Research* 35 (January): 79–102.

Moss, J. Jennings. 1992. "DNC's Brown Meets Goals." *Washington Times,* March 22, A1.

Murray, David. 1974. "Who's Who, and Why, in Campaign Reform." *New York Times,* April 14, 162.

Mutch, Robert E. 1988. *Campaigns, Congress, and the Courts: The Making of Federal Campaign Finance Law.* New York: Praeger.

Mutch, Robert E. 2006. "Before and After *Bellotti:* The Corporate Political Contributions Cases." *Election Law Journal* 5 (3): 293–324.

Nelson, Suzanne. 2005. "Mehlman Pushes for 527 Action." *Roll Call,* July 14.

Newberry v. U.S. 1921. 256 U.S. 232.

New York Times. 1910. "Hope for Publicity Law." March 21, 2.

New York Times. 1911. "Letting in the Light." August 3, 6.

New York Times. 1924a. "Campaign Gift Curb Now Seems Certain." June 4, 2.

New York Times. 1924b. "Charges Coolidge Bid for Slush Fund." November 2, 3.

New York Times. 1924c. "Republicans Raised a Total of $3,742,962, Democrats $552,368." November 1, 1.

New York Times. 1938a. "Blow at Laborites Aimed by Hawkins." January 12, 9.

New York Times. 1938b. "Jobholder Politics Upheld by the Senate." April 15, 15.

New York Times. 1939. "Hit at Democrats on 'Political' AAA." July 6, 4.

New York Times. 1940a. "Direct Hatch Test Is Defeated, 47–341." March 13, 19.

New York Times. 1940b. "For Cleaner Politics." July 12, 14.

New York Times. 1940c. "House Body Tables Wider Hatch Act; Sponsors to Fight." May 2, 1.

New York Times. 1966a. "Dodd Inquiry Puts Pressure on Senate." May 1, 70.

New York Times. 1966b. "Ruin of a Tax Bill." October 27, 46.

New York Times. 1974. "Ford Gets a Bill to Finance Races for Presidency." October 11, A1.

New York Times. 1991. "Next, Close the Political Sewer." November 27, A20.

New York Times. 1998. "Plotting against Reform." March 14, A16.

New York Times. 2000. "A Campaign Finance Ruse." June 24, A14.

Nixon v. Shrink Missouri Government PAC. 2000. 528 U.S. 377 161 F.3d 519, reversed and remanded.

Nye, Joseph S., Philip D. Zelikow, and David C. King. 1997. *Why People Don't Trust Government.* Cambridge, MA: Harvard University Press.

Olson, Mancur. 1965. *The Logic of Collective Action.* Cambridge: Harvard University Press.

Overacker, Lousie. 1932. *Money in Elections.* New York: Macmillan.

Overacker, Louise. 1946. *Presidential Campaign Fund.* Boston: Boston University Press.

Owen, Robert Latham. 1910. *The Code of the People's Rule.* Washington, DC: Government Printing Office.

Panebianco, Angelo. 1988. *Political Parties: Organization and Power.* New York: Cambridge University Press.

Peabody, Robert L., Jeffrey M. Berry, William G. Frasure, and Jerry Goldman. 1972. *To Enact a Law: Congress and Campaign Financing.* New York: Praeger.

Pershing, Ben. 2005. "GOP Plans 527 Push." *Roll Call,* December 21.

Persily, Nathaniel, and Kelli Lammie. 2004. "Perceptions of Corruption and Campaign Finance: When Public Opinion Determines Constitutional Law." *University of Pennsylvania Law Review* 153:119–80.

Pfeffer, J. S., and G. Salancik. 1978. *The External Control of Organizations: A Resource Dependence Perspective.* New York: Harper and Row.

Phillips, Gwethalyn. 2004. Telephone interview by Raymond J. La Raja. January 22.

Phillips, Cabell. 1966. "The Baker Case: A Continuing Drama of Many Acts." *New York Times,* January 6, 10.

Pollock, James K., Jr. 1926. *Party Campaign Funds.* New York: Knopf.

Polsby, Nelson W. 1983. *Consequences of Party Reform.* New York: Oxford University Press.

Polsby, Nelson W., and Aaron Wildavsky. 2000. *Presidential Elections.* 10th ed. New York: Chatham House.

Primo, David. 2002. "Public Opinion and Campaign Finance: Reformers versus Reality." *Independent Review* 7 (2): 207–19.

Public Opinion Online. 2002a. Polls conducted by Gallup, January 1–15. Roper Center, University of Connecticut. Available at http://www.ropercenter.uconn.edu.

Public Opinion Online. 2002b. Polls conducted by Gallup, February 8–10. Roper Center, University of Connecticut. Available at http://www.ropercenter.uconn.edu.

Regens, James L., and Ronald Keith Gaddie. 1995. *The Economic Realities of Political Reform: Elections and the U.S. Senate*. New York: Cambridge University Press.

Republican National Committee v. FEC. 1980. 445 U.S. 955.

Roosevelt, Theodore. 1907. Seventh Annual Message to Congress. December 3.

Rosenbaum, David E. 1974. "Ford Gets a Bill to Finance Races for Presidency." *New York Times*, October 11, 81.

Samples, John. 2006. *The Fallacy of Campaign Finance Reform*. Chicago: University of Chicago Press.

Schattschneider, E. E. 1960. *The Semi-Sovereign People: A Realist's View of Democracy in America*. New York: Holt, Rinehart, and Winston.

Schickler, Eric. 2001. *Disjointed Pluralism: Institutional Innovation and the Development of the U.S. Congress*. Princeton: Princeton University Press.

Schlesinger, Joseph A. 1984. "On the Theory of Party Organization." *Journal of Politics* 46:369–400.

Schlesinger, Joseph A. 1985. "The New American Political Party." *American Political Science Review* 79 (4): 1152–69.

Shannon, Jasper B. 1959. *Money and Politics*. New York: Random House.

Shaw, Daron R. 1999. "A Study of Presidential Campaign Event Effects from 1952 to 1992." *Journal of Politics* 61 (2): 387–422.

Shaw, Daron R. 2003. "Erratum for the Methods behind the Madness: Presidential Electoral College Strategies, 1988–96." *Journal of Politics* 61 (4): 893–913.

Shea, Daniel. 1995. *Transforming Democracy: Legislative Campaign Committees and Political Parties*. Albany: State University of New York Press.

Sikes, Earl R. 1928. *State and Federal Corrupt-Practices Legislation*. Durham: Duke University Press.

Silbey, Joel H. 1991. *The American Political Nation, 1838–1893*. Stanford: Stanford University Press.

Simkins, Francis Butler. 1944. *Pitchfork Ben Tillman, South Carolinian*. Baton Rouge: Louisiana State University Press.

Skinner. Richard M. 2005. "Do 527's Add Up to a Party? Thinking about the 'Shadows' of Politics." *Forum* 3 (3): article 5. Available at http://www.bepress.com/forum/vol3/iss3/art5.

Skinner, Richard. 2006. *More Than Money: Interest Group Action in Congressional Elections*. Lanham, MD: Rowman and Littlefield.

Skocpol, Theda. 2003. *Diminished Democracy: From Membership to Management in American Civic Life*. Norman: University of Oklahoma Press.

Sorauf, Frank J. 1992. *Inside Campaign Finance*. New Haven: Yale University Press.

Sousa, David. 1999. "No Balance in the Equities: Union Power in the Making and Unmaking of the Campaign Finance Regime." *Studies in American Political Development* 13 (2): 374–401.

Sproat, John G. 1982. *Best Men: Liberal Reformers in the Gilded Age*. Chicago: University of Chicago Press.

State Party Organizations. 1960–80. Cornelius P. Cotter, principal investigator. Ann Arbor, MI: Inter-university Consortium for Political and Social Research.

Tanenhaus, Joseph. 1954. "Organized Labor's Political Spending: The Law and Its Consequences." *Journal of Politics* 16 (3): 441–71.

Theriault, Sean. 2005. *Power of the People.* Columbus: Ohio State University Press.

Thomas, Dwight, and David K. Jackson. 1987. *The Poe Log.* Boston: G. K. Hall.

United States v. Auto Workers. 1957. 352 U.S. 567.

United States v. CIO. 1948. 335 U.S. 106.

U.S. Congress. House. 1945. *H.R. Report No. 2739.* 79th Cong., 2d sess., 36–37.

U.S. Congress. House. Committee on Labor. 1943. *Hearings before a Subcommittee of the House Committee on Labor on H.R. 804 and H.R. 1483.* 78th Cong., 1st sess., 1, 2, 4.

U.S. Congress. Senate. 1906. *Senate Report No. 3056.* 59th Cong., 1st sess., 2.

U.S. Congress. Senate. 1967. Senate Finance Committee Hearings. *Political Campaign Financing Proposals.* June 1, 2, 6–9.

Verba, Sidney, Kay Lehman Schlozman, and Henry E. Brady. 1995. *Voice and Equality: Civic Voluntarism in American Politics.* Cambridge, MA: Harvard University Press.

Walker, Jack L., Jr. 1991. *Mobilizing Interest Groups in America: Patrons, Professions, and Social Movements.* Ann Arbor: University of Michigan Press.

Ware, Alan. 1985. *The Breakdown of Democratic Party Organization, 1940–1980.* New York: Oxford University Press.

Washington Post/ABC News. 2001. Poll. January 11–15.

Wattenberg, Martin P. 1991. *The Rise of Candidate-Centered Politics: Presidential Elections of the 1980s.* Cambridge, MA: Harvard University Press.

Weaver, Warren, Jr. 1971a. "Anyway, It Was a Good Plan." *New York Times,* December 5, E2.

Weaver, Warren, Jr. 1971b. "Campaign Fund Plan Is Called a Help to Democrats." *New York Times,* November 24, 15.

Weaver, Warren, Jr. 1971c. "Conferees Drop Vote Fund Plan for '72 Campaign." *New York Times,* December 3, 1.

Weaver, Warren, Jr. 1971d. "Senate Approves Federal Tax Aid for Campaigning." *New York Times,* November 23, 1

Weaver, Warren, Jr. 1971e. "Senate, 49 to 46, Backs Fund Plan for '72 Campaign." *New York Times,* November 19, 1.

Wekkin, Gary D. 1985. "Political Parties and Intergovernmental Relations in 1984: The Consequences of Party Renewal for Territorial Constituencies." *Publius* 15 (3): 19–37.

Wertheimer, Fred. 2006. "Democracy 21 Statement on District Court Decision Yesterday Involving Key BCRA Provision, Friday, December 22, 2006." In *Capital Bits and Pieces* 6 (92). Available at http://www.democracy21.org.

White, William Allen. 1910. *The Old Order Changeth.* New York: Macmillan. Quoted in Allen O. Knownlar, *The Progressive Era: Tradition in a Changing Society 1900–1917* (Lexington, MA: D.C. Heath, 1970), 117–21.

Whittington, Lauren W. 2004. "Specter Touting Clout." *Roll Call,* April 19.

Wicker, Tom. 1971. "The Blame Game." *New York Times,* December 3, 47.

Will, George F. 2004. "Events Sprint Past Politics. *Newsweek,* August 2, 70.

Wilson, James Q. 1962. *The Amateur Democrat: Club Politics in Three Cities*. Chicago: University of Chicago Press.

Winkler, Adam. 2004. "Other People's Money": Corporations, Agency Costs, and Campaign Finance Law." *Georgetown Law Journal* 92:871–940.

Woolley, John, and Gerhard Peters. 2006. The American Presidency Project. [online] Santa Barbara: University of California. Available at http://www.presidency.ucsb .edu/ws/?pid=29548.

World Bank. 2006. *World Development Indicators*. July 1. Available at http://www.world bank.org.

Zelizer, Julian E. 2002. "Seeds of Cynicism: The Struggle over Campaign Finance, 1956–1974." *Journal of Policy History* 14:73–111.

Index

W9-BIF-492

Selected Poems

Selected Poems

1957–1987

W.D. Snodgrass

Many of the poems in this volume have been previously published in books, periodicals, broadsides and the like, some in different form. By kind permission, they are reprinted here from:

Heart's Needle, published by Alfred A. Knopf, Inc., 1959.

Remains, Perishable Press, 1970.

Remains: A Sequence of Poems copyright © 1985 by W. D. Snodgrass, reprinted with the permission of BOA Editions, Ltd.

The Boy Made of Meat, published by William Ewert, 1982.

After Experience, Harper & Row, Publishers, Inc., 1967; and Oxford University Press, 1968.

Memphis State Review, in which "Manet: 'The Execution of the Emperor Maximilian'" appeared.

The Fuehrer Bunker: A Cycle of Poems in Progress, copyright © 1977 by W. D. Snodgrass, reprinted with the permission of BOA Editions, Ltd. Poems from "The Fuehrer Bunker" have also appeared in editions published in 1983 by Palaemon Press and Pterodactyl Press, as well as *American Poetry Review* (January–February, 1977), *The Kenyon Review,* New Series, Fall '79 (I.4), and *Salmagundi.*

If Birds Build with Your Hair, published by Nadja Press, 1979, and by Derry Press.

A Locked House published by William Ewert, 1986, and *The Syracuse Scholar,* 1983. "Old Jewelry" was published by Palaemon Press, and by *Stand.* "D. D. Byrde Calling Jennie Wrenne" was published by William Ewert in 1984. "A Valediction," "Silver Poplars," and "The Last Time" appeared in *Ploughshares* (July 1982).

Kinder Capers, three poems published by Nadja Press, 1986. Portions of "The Death of Cock Robin" appeared in *American Poetry Review* (January–February, 1987), *The Kenyon Review,* New Series, Spring '85 (VII:2), *New York Quarterly,* Summer, 1985, *Negative Capability, Salmagundi, Graham House Review, New Virginia Review,* and *Scarab.*

Copyright © 1987 by W. D. Snodgrass
All rights reserved under International and Pan-American Copyright Conventions. Published in the United States of America by Soho Press, Inc., 1 Union Square, New York, NY 10003.

Library of Congress Cataloging-in-Publication Data

Snodgrass, W. D. (William De Witt), 1926–
Selected poems, 1957–1987.

I. Title.
PS3537.N32A6   1987   811'.54   87-9463
ISBN 0-939149-04-4

For Kathy
who puts things together

Contents

Heart's Needle

Ten Days Leave

He steps down from the dark train, blinking; stares
At trees like miracles. He will play games
With boys or sit up all night touching chairs.
Talking with friends, he can recall their names.

Noon burns against his eyelids, but he lies
Hunched in his blankets; he is half awake
But still lacks nerve to open up his eyes;
Supposing it were just his old mistake?

But no; it seems just like it seemed. His folks
Pursue their lives like toy trains on a track.
He can foresee each of his father's jokes
Like words in some old movie that's come back.

He is like days when you've gone some place new
To deal with certain strangers, though you never
Escape the sense in everything you do,
"We've done this all once. Have I been here, ever?"

But no; he thinks it must recall some old film, lit
By lives you want to touch; as if he'd slept
And must have dreamed this setting, peopled it,
And wakened out of it. But someone's kept

His dream asleep here like a small homestead
Preserved long past its time in memory
Of some great man who lived here and is dead.
They have restored his landscape faithfully:

The hills, the little houses, the costumes:
How real it seems! But he comes, wide awake,
A tourist whispering through the priceless rooms
Who must not touch things or his hand might break

Their sleep and black them out. He wonders when
He'll grow into his sleep so sound again.

At the Park Dance

As the melting park
darkens, the firefly winks
to signal loving strangers
from their pavilion
lined with Easter colored
lights, fading out together

until they merge with
weathered huge trees and join
the small frogs, those warm singers;
and they have achieved
love's vanishing point
where all perspectives mingle,

where even the most
close things are indistinct
or lost, where bright worlds shrink,
they will grope to find
blind eyes make all one world;
their unseen arms, horizons.

Beyond, jagged stars
are glinting like jacks hurled
farther than eyes can gather;
on the dancefloor, girls
turn, vague as milkweed floats
bobbing from childish fingers.

Orpheus

Stone lips to the unspoken cave;
Fingering the nervous strings, alone,
I crossed that gray sill, raised my head
To lift my song into the grave
Meanders of unfolding stone,
Following where the echo led
Down blind alleys of our dead.

Down the forbidden, backward street
To the lower town, condemned, asleep
In blank remembering mazes where
Smoke rose, the ashes hid my feet
And slow walls crumpled, settling deep
In rubble of the central square.
All ruin I could sound was there.

At the charred rail and windowsill,
Widows hunched in fusty shawls,
This only once the Furies wept;
The watchdog turned to hear me till
Head by head forgot its howls,
Loosed the torn images it kept,
Let sag its sore jaws and slept.

Then to my singing's radius
Seethed faces like a pauper's crowd
Or flies of an old injury.
The piteous dead who lived on us
Whined in my air, anarchic, loud
Till my soft voice that set them free,
Lost in this grievous enemy,

Rose up and laid them in low slumbers;
I meant to see in them what dark
Powers be, what eminent plotters.
Midmost those hushed, downcast numbers
Starved Tantalus stood upright, stark,
Waistdeep where the declining waters
Swelled their tides, where Danaus' daughters

Dropped in full surf their unfilled tub;
Now leaned against his rolling stone
Slept Sisyphus beneath the hill;
That screaming half-beast, strapped at the hub,
Whom Juno's animal mist had known,
Ixion's wheel creaked and was still.
I held all hell to hear my will.

"Powers of the Underworld, who rule
All higher powers by graft or debt,
Within whose mortgage all men live:
No spy, no shining power's fool,
I think in the unthought worlds to get
The light you only freely give
Who are all bright worlds' negative.

You gave wink in an undue crime
To love—strong even here, they say.
I sing, as the blind beggars sing,
To ask of you this little time
—All lives foreclose in their due day—
That flowered bride cut down in Spring,
Struck by the snake, your underling."

In one long avenue she was
Wandering toward me, vague, uncertain,
Limping a little still, the hair
And garments tenuous as gauze
And drifting loose like a white curtain
Vacillating in black night air
That holds white lilacs, God knows where.

"Close your eyes," said the inner ear;
"As night lookouts learn not to see
Ahead but only off one side,
As the eye's sight is never clear
But blind, dead center, you must be
Content; look not upon your bride
Till day's light lifts her eyelids wide."

I turned my back to her, set out
My own way back and let her follow
Like some curious albino beast
That prowls in areas of drought,
Lured past the town's slack doors, the hollow
Walls, the stream-bed lost in mist,
That breathless long climb, with no least

Doubt she must track me close behind;
As the actual scent of flesh, she must
Trail my voice unquestioning where.
Yet where the dawn first edged my mind
In one white flashing of mistrust
I turned and she, she was not there.
My hands closed on the high, thin air.

It was the nature of the thing:
No moon outlives its leaving night,
No sun its day. And I went on
Rich in the loss of all I sing
To the threshold of waking light,
To larksong and the live, gray dawn.
So night by night, my life has gone.

The Marsh

Swampstrife and spatterdock
   lull in the heavy waters;
some thirty little frogs
   spring with each step you walk;
a fish's belly glitters
   tangled near rotting logs.

Over by the gray rocks
   muskrats dip and circle.
Out of his rim of ooze
   a silt-black pond snail walks
inverted on the surface
   toward what food he may choose.

You look up; while you walk
   the sun bobs and is snarled
in the enclosing weir
   of trees, in their dead stalks.
Stick in the mud, old heart,
   what are you doing here?

September in the Park

For Rita

This pinched face of the moon
   all afternoon
spies through the hanging smoke
that glows where maples, turning,
   recall for one
more hour the tarnished sun
in rust of their last burning.

Still, those who are out walking
   will hear the laughter
of drab, blue-chevroned ducks;
the drunkard echo mocking
   where they carouse
on minnow ponds still flowing.
Beyond the bare oak's
   reach of boughs,
as black as some charred rafter,
are slow and waiting flocks,
   but they are going.

This world is going
to leave the furnitures
of its unsheltering house
   in snow's dustcovers.
This old moon on its rounds
of the estate and grounds
   can well make sure
that no trespasser stirs
the fireplace or uncovers
   the burned out bed
of ashes. The young lovers
will not be coming here
   to give the bear

the offer of their bread.
This watchful face of age
   set pale and stern
over the gray iron cage
where his old habits turn
   and pace again
must mind his days to turn
him back in single, deep,
   cold-blooded sleep.

The hurrying, gray squirrels
   gather together
their hoard of the rich acorns
to their tall, windblown nest.
   And I, dear girl,
remember I have gathered
my hand upon your breast.

The Operation

From stainless steel basins of water
They brought warm cloths and they washed me,
From spun aluminum bowls, cold Zephiran sponges, fuming;
Gripped in the dead yellow glove, a bright straight razor
Inched on my stomach, down my groin,
Paring the brown hair off. They left me
White as a child, not frightened. I was not
Ashamed. They clothed me, then,
In the thin, loose, light, white garments,
The delicate sandals of poor Pierrot,
A schoolgirl first offering her sacrament.

I was drifting, inexorably, on toward sleep.
In skullcaps, masked, in blue-green gowns, attendants
Towed my cart, afloat in its white cloths,
The body with its tributary poisons borne
Down corridors of the diseased, thronging:
The scrofulous faces, contagious grim boys,
The huddled families, weeping, a staring woman
Arched to her gnarled stick,—a child was somewhere
Screaming, screaming—then, blind silence, the elevator rising
To the arena, humming, vast with lights; blank hero,
Shackled and spellbound, to enact my deed.

Into flowers, into women, I have awakened.
Too weak to think of strength, I have thought all day,
Or dozed among standing friends. I lie in night, now,
A small mound under linen like the drifted snow,
Only by nurses visited, in radiance, saying, Rest.
Opposite, ranked office windows glare; headlamps, below,
Trace out our highways; their cargoes under dark tarpaulins,
Trucks climb, thundering, and sirens may
Wail for the fugitive. It is very still. In my brandy bowl
Of sweet peas at the window, the crystal world
Is inverted, slow and gay.

13

Papageno

For Janice

Far in the woods my stealthy flute
Had jailed all gaudy feathered birds
And brought their songs back true to life;
Equipped with lime and quick salt, fruit
And fifty linking nets of words
I went to whistle up a wife.

My mouth was padlocked for a liar.
Losing what old hands never seek
To snare in their most cunning art,
I starved till my rib cage was wire
Under a towel. I could not speak
To hush this chattering, blue heart.

I beat about dead bushes where
No song starts and my cages stand
Bare in the crafty breath of you.
Night's lady, spreading your dark hair,
Come take this rare bird into hand;
In that deft cage, he might sing true.

Song

Sweet beast, I have gone prowling,
   a proud rejected man
who lived along the edges
   catch as catch can;
in darkness and in hedges
   I sang my sour tone
and all my love was howling
   conspicuously alone.

I curled and slept all day
   or nursed my bloodless wounds
until the squares were silent
   where I could make my tunes
singular and violent.
   Then, sure as hearers came
I crept and flinched away.
   And, girl, you've done the same.

A stray from my own type,
   led along by blindness,
my love was near to spoiled
   and curdled all my kindness.
I find no kin, no child;
   only the weasel's ilk.
Sweet beast, cat of my own stripe,
   come and take my milk.

Riddle

So small it is, there must be at least two
Helping each other see it. If each stands
Close enough he may come to be foureyed
And make their sight bifocal, looking through
Each other. If they act as a microscope
Of mounted powers it shall be magnified
Like an airy globe or beach ball that expands
Between them so vast they could never hope
To grasp it without all four of their hands
        Opened wide.

It lengthens, outstretched like a playing field
Where they stand as the two opposing goals
That can't be reached. Or it's a field of force,
Ethereal continuum, whereby they wield
Influence through matter, time and space
(Of all which it's the grave and radiant source),
Yet where attraction drives out their like souls
Across the expansive universe they've built as the poles
That only in circumference embrace
        And by divorce.

You have the damnedest friends and seem to think
You have some right to think. You have kept keen
Our arguments and souls so we have grown
Closely together where most people shrink.
You sleep tonight with threatening relations
In El Dorado; I am here alone
To tell you, *"Vive la difference!"* We have seen
The energetic first stuff of creation
So that today, if there's a world between
        Us, it's our own.

Song

Observe the cautious toadstools
   still on the lawn today
though they grow over-evening;
   sun shrinks them away.
Pale and proper and rootless,
   they righteously extort
their living from the living.
   I have been their sort.

See by our blocked foundation
   the cold, archaic clay,
stiff and clinging and sterile
   as children mold at play
or as the Lord God fashioned
   before He breathed it breath.
The earth we dig and carry
   for flowers, is strong in death.

Woman, we are the rich
   soil, friable and humble,
where all our murders rot,
   where our old deaths crumble
and fortify my reach
   far from you, wide and free,
though I have set my root
   in you and am your tree.

Seeing You Have . . .

Seeing you have a woman
Whose loves grow thick as the weeds
That keep songsparrows through the year,
Why are you envious of boys
Who prowl the streets all night in packs
So they are equal to the proud
Slender girls they fear?

She's like the tall grass, common,
That sends roots, where it needs,
Six feet into the prairies.
Why do you teach yourself the loud
Hankering voices of blue jays
That quarrel branch by branch to peck
And spoil the bitter cherries?

Home Town

I go out like a ghost,
nights, to walk the streets
I walked fifteen years younger—
seeking my old defeats,
devoured by the old hunger;
I had supposed

this longing and upheaval
had left me with my youth.
Fifteen years gone; once more,
the old lies are the truth:
I must prove I dare,
and the world, and love, is evil.

I have had loves, had such
honors as freely came;
it does not seem to matter.
Boys swagger just the same
along the curbs, or mutter
among themselves and watch.

They're out for the same prize.
And, as the evening grows,
the young girls take the street,
hard, in harlequin clothes,
with black shells on their feet
and challenge in their eyes.

Like a young bitch in her season
she walked the carnival
tonight, trailed by boys;
then, stopped at a penny stall
for me; by glittering toys
the pitchman called the reason

to come and take a chance,
try my hand, my skill.
I could not look; bereft
of breath, against my will,
I walked ahead and left
her there without one glance.

Pale soul, consumed by fear
of the living world you haunt,
have you learned what habits lead you
to hunt what you don't want;
learned who does not need you;
learned you are no one here?

A Cardinal

I wake late and leave
the refurbished quonset
where they let me live.
I feel like their leftovers:
they keep me for the onset
of some new war or other.

With half a ream of paper
and fountain pens, equipped
with ink and ink eraser,
a book to hunt up words,
and the same old manuscripts,
I tromp off to the woods,

the little stand of birches
between golf course and campus
where birds flirt through the branches
and the city will be hushed.
Inside this narrow compass
I crash through underbrush,

beer cans and lovers' trash
in search of my horizons
of meadowlark and thrush.
Yet near me, here, it's still.
I carry a scared silence
with me like my smell.

At each of my footsteps
one of the insect noises
in the tall grass, stops.
The weeds sing where I leave.
All the living voices
evade me like beliefs.

Well, let them look *me* up
and take their own sweet time;
I've come to set up shop
under this blue spruce
and tinker at my rhymes.
God knows it's little use;

God knows I have spent ages
peering like a stuffed owl
at these same blank pages
and, though I strained to listen,
the world lay wrapped with wool
far as the ends of distance.

And what do I hear today?
Little that sounds mine—
in town, across the way,
mill whistles squeal;
now, closer by, the whine
of a freight car's wheels;

out on the superturnpike
the cattle trucks and trailers
lumbering toward next week;
beyond, from the county airport,
where golf balls veer like tracers,
great engines thunder their part

in this devil's Mass
of marketable praise.
Oh, they've all found *their* voices.
And now I catch a meter
under this heavy prose
of factories and motors:

the college air cadets
are on their grinder, marching,
counting out their cadence,
one two three four, creating
for the school and market
the ground bass of our credo—

faith in free enterprise
and our unselfish forces
who chant to advertise
the ancient pulse of violence.
Meantime, I fuss with phrases
or clamp my jaws in silence.

Watch out; what's this red
bird, fluttering up to perch
ten feet from my head!
See the green insect wings,
pinched in his beak, twitch.
He swallows it. And sings.

Speak of the bloody devil!
Old sleek satanic cardinal—
you get your bellyful,
maintain the ancient Law,
and celebrate this ordinal
of the red beak and claw.

You natural Jesuit,
sing, in your fine feathers,
Hosannah to Appetite;
announce to the woods and hills
the one god of our fathers
is living in us still;

sing for the flyboys, birdy,
in praise of their profession;
sing for the choirs of pretty
slogans and catch-phrases
that rule us by obsession;
praise what it pays to praise:

praise soap and garbage cans,
join with the majority
in praising man-eat-man,
or praise the young who sell
their minds to retire at forty.
With honor.
                    Go to hell!

Good God! This is absurd!
A veritable scarecrow!
I curse out a poor bird
for daring feed his belly;
now my bird has flown
and left me in this gully.

It is absurd, absurd
Darwinian self-pity!
As if a self-made bird
would sign his days to sergeants,
his soul to a committee,
or call himself a bargain!

As if I'd never heard
what the birds' song means;
as if I'd ask a bird
to mortify his body.
Wait; from the next ravine,
he's singing again, already.

24

And he outspeaks a vital
claim to know his needs;
his song's a squatter's title
on his tree and the half acre
in which he hunts and breeds
and feeds the best he's able.

To enemies and rivals,
to mates and quick beetles,
he sings out for survival:
"I want my meals and loving;
I fight nobody's battles;
don't pardon me for living.

The world's not done to me;
it is what I do;
whom I speak shall be;
I music out my name
and what I tell is who
in all the world I am."

We whistle in the dark
of a region in doubt
where unknown powers work,
as watchmen in the night
ring bells to say, *Watch out,
I am here; I have the right.*

*It should be recognized
I have not come sneaking
and look for no surprises.
Lives are saved this way.*
Each trade has its way of speaking,
each bird its name to say.

We whistle in the dark
to drive the devils off.
Each dog creates his bark.
Even I, in Navy blues,
I whistled *Wachet Auf*
to tell the sailors who.

He's back; obliquely flying
under a trail of vapor,
our sky's white center-line.
A robin goes by, wrestling
a streamer of toiletpaper
his mate might want for nesting.

Selfish, unorthodox,
they live upon our leavings.
Boys or cats or hawks
can scare them out of song.
Still, long as they are living,
they are not still for long.

Each year the city leaves
less of trees or meadows;
they nest in our very eaves
and say what they have to say.
Assertion is their credo;
style tells their policy.

All bugs, now, and the birds
witness once more their voices
though I'm still in their weeds
tracking my specimen words,
replenishing the verses
of nobody else's world.

The Campus on the Hill

Up the reputable walks of old established trees
They stalk, children of the *nouveaux riches;* chimes
Of the tall Clock Tower drench their heads in blessing:
"I don't wanna play at your house;
I don't like you any more."
My house stands opposite, on the other hill,
Among meadows, with the orchard fences down and falling;
Deer come almost to the door.
You cannot see it, even in this clearest morning.
White birds hang in the air between
Over the garbage landfill and those homes thereto adjacent,
Hovering slowly, turning, settling down
Like the flakes sifting imperceptibly onto the little town
In a waterball of glass.
And yet, this morning, beyond this quiet scene,
The floating birds, the backyards of the poor,
Beyond the shopping plaza, the dead canal, the hillside
                          lying tilted in the air,

Tomorrow has broken out today:
Riot in Algeria, in Cyprus, in Alabama;
Aged in wrong, the empires are declining,
And China gathers, soundlessly, like evidence.
What shall I say to the young on such a morning?—
Mind is the one salvation?—also grammar?—
No; my little ones lean not toward revolt. They
Are the Whites, the vaguely furiously driven, who resist
Their souls with such passivity
As would make Quakers swear. All day, dear Lord, all day
They wear their godhead lightly.
They look out from their hill and say,
To themselves, "We have nowhere to go but down;
The great destination is to stay."
Surely the nations will be reasonable;
They look at the world—don't they?—the world's way?
The clock just now has nothing more to say.

April Inventory

The green catalpa tree has turned
All white; the cherry blooms once more.
In one whole year I haven't learned
A blessed thing they pay you for.
The blossoms snow down in my hair;
The trees and I will soon be bare.

The trees have more than I to spare.
The sleek, expensive girls I teach,
Younger and pinker every year,
Bloom gradually out of reach.
The pear tree lets its petals drop
Like dandruff on a tabletop.

The girls have grown so young by now
I have to nudge myself to stare.
This year they smile and mind me how
My teeth are falling with my hair.
In thirty years I may not get
Younger, shrewder, or out of debt.

The tenth time, just a year ago,
I made myself a little list
Of all the things I'd ought to know,
Then told my parents, analyst,
And everyone who's trusted me
I'd be substantial, presently.

I haven't read one book about
A book or memorized one plot.
Or found a mind I did not doubt.
I learned one date. And then forgot.
And one by one the solid scholars
Get the degrees, the jobs, the dollars.

And smile above their starchy collars.
I taught my classes Whitehead's notions;
One lovely girl, a song of Mahler's.
Lacking a source-book or promotions,
I showed one child the colors of
A luna moth and how to love.

I taught myself to name my name,
To bark back, loosen love and crying;
To ease my woman so she came,
To ease an old man who was dying.
I have not learned how often I
Can win, can love, but choose to die.

I have not learned there is a lie
Love shall be blonder, slimmer, younger;
That my equivocating eye
Loves only by my body's hunger;
That I have forces, true to feel,
Or that the lovely world is real.

While scholars speak authority
And wear their ulcers on their sleeves,
My eyes in spectacles shall see
These trees procure and spend their leaves.
There is a value underneath
The gold and silver in my teeth.

Though trees turn bare and girls turn wives,
We shall afford our costly seasons;
There is a gentleness survives
That will outspeak and has its reasons.
There is a loveliness exists,
Preserves us, not for specialists.

These Trees Stand . . .

These trees stand very tall under the heavens.
While *they* stand, if I walk, all stars traverse
This steep celestial gulf their branches chart.
Though lovers stand at sixes and at sevens
While civilizations come down with the curse,
Snodgrass is walking through the universe.

I can't make any world go around *your* house.
But note this moon. Recall how the night nurse
Goes ward-rounds, by the mild, reflective art
Of focusing her flashlight on her blouse.
Your name's safe conduct into love or verse;
Snodgrass is walking through the universe.

Your name's absurd, miraculous as sperm
And as decisive. If you can't coerce
One thing outside yourself, why you're the poet!
What irrefrangible atoms whirl, affirm
Their destiny and form Lucinda's skirts!
She can't make up your mind. Soon as you know it,
Your firmament grows touchable and firm.
If all this world runs battlefield or worse,
Come, let us wipe our glasses on our shirts:
Snodgrass is walking through the universe.

Heart's Needle

For Cynthia

> *When he would not return to fine*
> *garments and good food, to his houses*
> *and his people, Loingseachan told him,*
> *"Your father is dead." "I'm sorry to*
> *hear it," he said. "Your mother is*
> *dead," said the lad. "All pity for me*
> *has gone out of the world." "Your*
> *sister, too, is dead." "The mild sun rests*
> *on every ditch," he said; "a sister loves*
> *even though not loved." "Suibhne, your*
> *daughter is dead." "And an only*
> *daughter is the needle of the heart."*
> *"And Suibhne, your little boy, who*
> *used to call you "Daddy"—he is dead."*
> *"Aye," said Suibhne, "that's the drop*
> *that brings a man to the ground."*
> *He fell out of the yew tree;*
> *Loingseachan closed his arms around*
> *him and placed him in manacles.*

—AFTER THE MIDDLE-IRISH ROMANCE,
THE MADNESS OF SUIBHNE

1

Child of my winter, born
When the new fallen soldiers froze
In Asia's steep ravines and fouled the snows,
When I was torn

By love I could not still,
By fear that silenced my cramped mind
To that cold war where, lost, I could not find
My peace in my will,

31

All those days we could keep
Your mind a landscape of new snow
Where the chilled tenant-farmer finds, below,
His fields asleep

In their smooth covering, white
As quilts to warm the resting bed
Of birth or pain, spotless as paper spread
For me to write,

And thinks: Here lies my land
Unmarked by agony, the lean foot
Of the weasel tracking, the thick trapper's boot;
And I have planned

My chances to restrain
The torments of demented summer or
Increase the deepening harvest here before
It snows again.

2

Late April and you are three; today
    We dug your garden in the yard.
  To curb the damage of your play,
Strange dogs at night and the moles tunneling,
    Four slender sticks of lath stand guard
      Uplifting their thin string.

So you were the first to tramp it down.
And after the earth was sifted close
You brought your watering can to drown
All earth *and* us. But these mixed seeds are pressed
With light loam in their steadfast rows.
Child, we've done our best.

Someone will have to weed and spread
The young sprouts. Sprinkle them in the hour
When shadow falls across their bed.
You should try to look at them every day
Because when they come to full flower
I will be away.

3

The child between them on the street
Comes to a puddle, lifts his feet
And hangs on their hands. They start
At the live weight and lurch together,
Recoil to swing him through the weather,
Stiffen and pull apart.

We read of cold war soldiers that
Never gained ground, gave none, but sat
Tight in their chill trenches.
Pain seeps up from some cavity
Through the ranked teeth in sympathy;
The whole jaw grinds and clenches

33

Till something somewhere has to give.
It's better the poor soldiers live
    In someone else's hands
Than drop where helpless powers fall
On crops and barns, on towns where all
    Will burn. And no man stands.

For good, they sever and divide
Their won and lost land. On each side
    Prisoners are returned
Excepting a few unknown names.
The peasant plods back and reclaims
    His fields that strangers burned

And nobody seems very pleased.
It's best. Still, what must not be seized
    Clenches the empty fist.
I tugged your hand, once, when I hated
Things less: a mere game dislocated
    The radius of your wrist.

Love's wishbone, child, although I've gone
As men must and let you be drawn
    Off to appease another,
It may help that a Chinese play
Or Solomon himself might say
    I am your real mother.

4

No one can tell you why
the season will not wait;
the night I told you I
must leave, you wept a fearful rate
to stay up late.

Now that it's turning Fall,
we go to take our walk
among municipal
flowers, to steal one off its stalk,
to try and talk.

We huff like windy giants
scattering with our breath
gray-headed dandelions;
Spring is the cold wind's aftermath.
The poet saith.

But the asters, too, are gray,
ghost-gray. Last night's cold
is sending on their way
petunias and dwarf marigold,
hunched sick and old.

Like nerves caught in a graph,
the morning-glory vines
frost has erased by half
still scrawl across their rigid twines.
Like broken lines

of verses I can't make.
In its unraveling loom
    we find a flower to take,
with some late buds that might still bloom,
        back to your room.

    Night comes and the stiff dew.
I'm told a friend's child cried
    because a cricket, who
had minstreled every night outside
        her window, died.

5

Winter again and it is snowing;
Although you are still three,
You are already growing
Strange to me.

You chatter about new playmates, sing
Strange songs; you do not know
Hey ding-a-ding-a-ding
Or where I go

Or when I sang for bedtime, *Fox*
Went out on a chilly night,
Before I went for walks
And did not write;

You never mind the squalls and storms
That are renewed long since;
Outside the thick snow swarms
Into my prints

And swirls out by warehouses, sealed,
Dark cowbarns, huddled, still,
Beyond to the blank field,
The fox's hill

Where he backtracks and sees the paw,
Gnawed off, he cannot feel;
Conceded to the jaw
Of toothed, blue steel.

6
Easter has come around
again; the river is rising
over the thawed ground
and the banksides. When you come you bring
an egg dyed lavender.
We shout along our bank to hear
our voices returning from the hills to meet us.
We need the landscape to repeat us.

You lived on this bank first.
While nine months filled your term, we knew
how your lungs, immersed
in the womb, miraculously grew
their useless folds till
the fierce, cold air rushed in to fill
them out like bushes thick with leaves. You took your hour,
caught breath, and cried with your full lung power.

Over the stagnant bight
we see the hungry bank swallow
    flaunting his free flight
still; we sink in mud to follow
    the killdeer from the grass
that hides her nest. That March there was
rain; the rivers rose; you could hear killdeers flying
    all night over the mudflats crying.

You bring back how the red-
winged blackbird shrieked, slapping frail wings,
    diving at my head—
I saw where her tough nest, cradled, swings
    in tall reeds that must sway
with the winds blowing every way.
If you recall much, you recall this place. You still
    live nearby—on the opposite hill.

After the sharp windstorm
of July Fourth, all that summer
    through the gentle, warm
afternoons, we heard great chain saws chirr
    like iron locusts. Crews
of roughneck boys swarmed to cut loose
branches wrenched in the shattering wind, to hack free
    all the torn limbs that could sap the tree.

In the debris lay
starlings, dead. Near the park's birdrun
    we surprised one day
a proud, tan-spatted, buff-brown pigeon.
    In my hands she flapped so
fearfully that I let her go.
Her keeper came. And we helped snarl her in a net.
You bring things I'd as soon forget.

    You raise into my head
a Fall night that I came once more
    to sit on your bed;
sweat beads stood out on your arms and fore-
    head and you wheezed for breath,
for help, like some child caught beneath
its comfortable woolly blankets, drowning there.
Your lungs caught and would not take the air.

    Of all things, only we
have power to choose that we should die;
    nothing else is free
in this world to refuse it. Yet I,
    who say this, could not raise
myself from bed how many days
to the thieving world. Child, I have another wife,
another child. We try to choose our life.

7

Here in the scuffled dust
   is our ground of play.
I lift you on your swing and must
   shove you away,
see you return again,
   drive you off again, then

stand quiet till you come.
   You, though you climb
higher, farther from me, longer,
   will fall back to me stronger.
Bad penny, pendulum,
   you keep my constant time

to bob in blue July
   where fat goldfinches fly
over the glittering, fecund
   reach of our growing lands.
Once more now, this second,
   I hold you in my hands.

8

I thumped on you the best I could
   which was no use;
you would not tolerate your food
until the sweet, fresh milk was soured
   with lemon juice.

That puffed you up like a fine yeast.
    The first June in your yard
like some squat Nero at a feast
you sat and chewed on white, sweet clover.
        That is over.

When you were old enough to walk
        we went to feed
the rabbits in the park milkweed;
saw the paired monkeys, under lock,
    consume each other's salt.

Going home we watched the slow
stars follow us down Heaven's vault.
You said, let's catch one that comes low,
        pull off its skin
    and cook it for our dinner.

    As absentee bread-winner,
I seldom got you such cuisine;
we ate in local restaurants
or bought what lunches we could pack
        in a brown sack

with stale, dry bread to toss for ducks
    on the green-scummed lagoons,
crackers for porcupine and fox,
life-savers for the footpad coons
        to scour and rinse,

snatch after in their muddy pail
    and stare into their paws.
When I moved next door to the jail
    I learned to fry
omelettes and griddlecakes so I

could set you supper at my table.
As I built back from helplessness,
    when I grew able,
the only possible answer was
    you had to come here less.

This Hallowe'en you come one week.
    You masquerade
    as a vermilion, sleek,
fat, crosseyed fox in the parade
or, where grim jackolanterns leer,

go with your bag from door to door
foraging for treats. How queer:
    when you take off your mask
my neighbors must forget and ask
    whose child you are.

Of course you lose your appetite,
    whine and won't touch your plate;
    as local law
I set your place on an orange crate
in your own room for days. At night

you lie asleep there on the bed
and grate your jaw.
Assuredly your father's crimes
are visited
on you. You visit me sometimes.

The time's up. Now our pumpkin sees
me bringing your suitcase.
He holds his grin;
the forehead shrivels, sinking in.
You break this year's first crust of snow

off the runningboard to eat.
We manage, though for days
I crave sweets when you leave and know
they rot my teeth. Indeed our sweet
foods leave us cavities.

9

I get numb and go in
though the dry ground will not hold
the few dry swirls of snow
and it must not be very cold.
A friend asks how you've been
and I don't know

or see much right to ask.
Or what use it could be to know.
In three months since you came
the leaves have fallen and the snow;
your pictures pinned above my desk
seem much the same.

Somehow I come to find
myself upstairs in the third floor
    museum's halls,
walking to kill my time once more
among the enduring and resigned
        stuffed animals,

    where, through a century's
caprice, displacement and
    known treachery between
its wars, they hear some old command
and in their peaceable kingdoms freeze
        to this still scene,

    Nature Morte. Here
by the door, its guardian,
    the patchwork dodo stands
where you and your stepsister ran
laughing and pointing. Here, last year,
        you pulled my hands

    and had your first, worst quarrel,
so toys were put up on your shelves.
    Here in the first glass cage
the little bobcats arch themselves,
still practicing their snarl
        of constant rage.

The bison, here, immense,
shoves at his calf, brow to brow,
      and looks it in the eye
to see what is it thinking now.
I forced you to obedience;
      I don't know why.

      Still the lean lioness
beyond them, on her jutting ledge
      of shale and desert shrub,
stands watching always at the edge,
stands hard and tanned and envious
      above her cub;

      with horns locked in tall heather,
two great Olympian Elk stand bound,
      fixed in their lasting hate
till hunger brings them both to ground.
Whom equal weakness binds together
      none shall separate.

      Yet separate in the ocean
of broken ice, the white bear reels
      beyond the leathery groups
of scattered, drab Arctic seals
arrested here in violent motion
      like Napoleon's troops.

Our states have stood so long
at war, shaken with hate and dread,
   they are paralyzed at bay;
once we were out of reach, we said,
we would grow reasonable and strong.
    Some other day.

   Like the cold men of Rome,
we have won costly fields to sow
   in salt, our only seed.
Nothing but injury will grow.
I write you only the bitter poems
    that you can't read.

   Onan who would not breed
a child to take his brother's bread
   and be his brother's birth,
rose up and left his lawful bed,
went out and spilled his seed
    in the cold earth.

   I stand by the unborn,
by putty-colored children curled
   in jars of alcohol,
that waken to no other world,
unchanging, where no eye shall mourn.
    I see the caul

that wrapped a kitten, dead.
I see the branching, doubled throat
    of a two-headed foal;
I see the hydrocephalic goat;
here is the curled and swollen head,
        there, the burst skull;

    skin of a limbless calf;
a horse's foetus, mummified;
    mounted and joined forever,
the Siamese twin dogs that ride
belly to belly, half and half,
        that none shall sever.

    I walk among the growths,
by gangrenous tissue, goiter, cysts,
    by fistulas and cancers,
where the malignancy man loathes
is held suspended and persists.
        And I don't know the answers.

    The window's turning white.
The world moves like a diseased heart
    packed with ice and snow.
Three months now we have been apart
less than a mile. I cannot fight
        or let you go.

10

The vicious winter finally yields
    the green winter wheat;
the farmer, tired in the tired fields
    he dare not leave, will eat.

Once more the runs come fresh; prevailing
    piglets, stout as jugs,
harry their old sow to the railing
    to ease her swollen dugs

and game colts trail the herded mares
    that circle the pasture courses;
our seasons bring us back once more
    like merry-go-round horses.

With crocus mouths, perennial hungers,
    into the park Spring comes;
we roast hot dogs on old coat hangers
    and feed the swan bread crumbs,

pay our respects to the peacocks, rabbits,
    and leathery Canada goose
who took, last Fall, our tame white habits
    and now will not turn loose.

In full regalia, the pheasant cocks
    march past their dubious hens;
the porcupine and the lean, red fox
    trot around bachelor pens

and the miniature painted train
   wails on its oval track:
you said, I'm going to Pennsylvania!
   and waved. And you've come back.

If I loved you, they said I'd leave
   and find my own affairs.
Well, once again this April, we've
   come around to the bears;

punished and cared for, behind bars,
   the coons on bread and water
stretch thin black fingers after ours.
   And you are still my daughter.

Remains

The Mother

She stands in the dead center like a star;
They form around her like her satellites
Taking her energies, her heat, light
And massive attraction on their paths, however far.

Born of her own flesh; still, she feels them drawn
Into the outer cold by dark forces;
They are in love with suffering and perversion,
With the community of pain. Thinking them gone,

Out of her reach, she is consoled by evil
In neighbors, children, the world she cannot change,
That lightless universe where they range
Out of the comforts of her disapproval.

If evil did not exist, she would create it
To die in righteousness, her martyrdom
To that sweet dominion they have bolted from.
Then, at last, she can think that she is hated

And is content. Things can decay, break,
Spoil themselves; who cares? She'll gather the debris
With loving tenderness to give them; she
Will weave a labyrinth of waste, wreckage

And hocus-pocus; leave free no fault
Or cornerhole outside those lines of force
Where she and only she can thread a course.
All else in her grasp grows clogged and halts.

Till one by one, the areas of her brain
Switch off and she has filled all empty spaces;
Now she hallucinates in their right places
Their after-images, reversed and faint.

And the drawn strands of love, spun in her mind,
Turn dark and cluttered, precariously hung
With the black shapes of her mates, her sapless young,
Where she moves by habit, hungering and blind.

Diplomacy: The Father

Your mission, in any disputed area, is to find
    (as in yourself)
which group, which element among the contending forces
    seems, by nature, most fit to take control.
Stronger perhaps, more driven, gifted with resources—
    no matter: able to bind in a firm goal
the ennervating local passions native to our kind.
    That force, of course, is

your enemy—whom you cannot choose but love.
    As in yourself,
it's this, it's those so loved, that can grow oppressive
    and steal your hard-bought freedom to choose
that you won't love. Act loving, then. Make no aggressive
    move; make friends. Make, though, for future use,
notes on their debts, beliefs, whom they're most fond of—
    their weaknesses. If

anything, appear more loyal—pretend to feel
    as in yourself
you'd truly want to feel: affectionate and admiring.
    Then hate grows, discovering the way such foes enslave
you worst: if you loved them, you'd *feel* free. Conspiring
    to outwit such subtlety, devise and save
good reasons for your hatred; count wounds. Conceal,
    though, this entire ring

of proofs, excuses, wrongs which you maintain
    as in yourself
might harbor some benign, enfeebling growth.
    As for followers, seek those who'll take your aid:
the weak. In doubt who's weaker, finance both.
    Collect the dawdlers, the brilliant but afraid,
the purchasable losers—those who, merely to gain
    some power they can loathe,

would quite as willingly be out of power
        as in. Yourself?—
friend, this is lonely work. Deep cravings will persist
    for true allies, for those you love; you will long
to speak your mind out sometimes, or to assist
    someone who, given that help, might grow strong
and admirable. You've reached your bleakest hour,
        the pitiless test.

But think: why let your own aid diminish you?
        As in yourself,
so in those who take your help, your values or your name,
    you've sought out their best thoughts, their hidden talents
only to buy out, to buy off. Your fixed aim,
    whatever it costs, must still be for a balance
of power in the family, the firm, the whole world through.
        Exactly the same

as a balance of impotence—in any group or nation
        as in yourself.
Suppose some one of them rose up and could succeed
    your foe—he'd *be* your foe. To underlings, dispense
all they can ask, but don't need; give till they need
    your giving. One gift could free them: confidence.
They'd never dare ask. Betray no dedication
        to any creed

or person—talk high ideals; then you'll be known
        as, in yourself,
harmless. Exact no faith from them, no affection;
    suppose they've learned no loyalty to you—
that's one step taken in the right direction.
    Never forbid them. Let no one pay back what's due;
the mere air they breathe should come as a loan
        beyond collection.

56

Like air, you must be everywhere at once, where-
        as, in your self-
defense, make yourself scarce. Your best disguise
        is to turn gray, spreading yourself so thin
you're one with all unknowns—essential. Vaporize
        into the fog all things that happen, happen in
or fail to happen. In the end, you have to appear
        as unworldly in the eyes

of this whole sanctioned world that your care drained
        as in yours. Self-
sacrifice has borne you, then, through that destruction
        programmed into life; you live on in that loving tension
you leave to those who'll still take your instruction.
        You've built their world; an air of soft suspension
which you survive in, as cradled and sustained
        as in yourself.

The Mouse

I remember one evening—we were small—
Playing outdoors, we found a mouse,
A dusty little gray one, lying
By the side steps. Afraid he might be dead,
We carried him all around the house
On a piece of tinfoil, crying.

Ridiculous children; we could bawl
Our eyes out about nothing. Still,
How much violence had we seen?
They teach you—quick—you have to be well-bred
In all events. We can't all win.
Don't whine to get your will.

We live with some things, after all,
Bitterer than dying, cold as hate:
The old insatiable loves,
That vague desire that keeps watch overhead,
Polite, wakeful as a cat,
To tease us with our lives;

That pats at you, wants to see you crawl
Some, then picks you back alive;
That needs you just a little hurt.
The mind goes blank, then the eyes. Weak with dread,
In shock, the breath comes short;
We go about our lives.

And then the little animal
Plays out; the dulled heart year by year
Turns from its own needs, forgets its grief.
Asthmatic, timid, twenty-five, unwed—
The day we left you by your grave,
I wouldn't spare one tear.

Viewing the Body

Flowers like a gangster's funeral;
   Eyeshadow like a whore.
They all say isn't she beautiful.
   She, who never wore

Lipstick or such a dress,
   Never got taken out,
Was scarcely looked at, much less
   Wanted or talked about;

Who, gray as a mouse, crept
   The dark halls at her mother's
Or snuggled, soft, and slept
   Alone in the dim bedcovers.

Today at last she holds
   All eyes and a place of honor
Till the obscene red folds
   Of satin close down on her.

Disposal

The unworn long gown, meant for dances
She would have scarcely dared attend,
Is fobbed off on a friend—
Who can't help wondering if it's spoiled
But thinks, well, she can take her chances.

We roll her spoons up like old plans
Or failed securities, seal their case,
Then lay them back. One lace
Nightthing lies in the chest, unsoiled
By wear, untouched by human hands.

We don't dare burn those canceled patterns
And markdowns that she actually wore,
Yet who do we know so poor
They'd take them? Spared all need, all passion,
Saved from loss, she lies boxed in satins

Like a pair of party shoes
That seemed to never find a taker;
We send back to its maker
A life somehow gone out of fashion
But still too good to use.

Fourth of July

The drifting smoke is gone, today,
From the mill chimneys; the laborers from the great
Iron foundries are on strike. They celebrate
Their Independence her own way.

She stopped a year ago today.
Firecrackers mark the occasion down the street;
I thumb through magazines and keep my seat.
What can anybody say?

In her room, nights, we lie awake
By racks of unworn party dresses, shoes,
Her bedside asthma pipe, the glasses whose
Correction no one else will take.

Stuffed dogs look at us from the shelf
When we sit down together at the table.
You put a face on things the best you're able
And keep your comments to yourself.

It is a hideous mistake.
My young wife, unforgivably alive,
Takes a deep breath and blows out twenty-five
Candles on her birthday cake.

It is agreed she'll get her wish.
The candles smell; smoke settles through the room
Like a cheap stage set for Juliet's tomb.
I leave my meal cold on the dish.

We take the children to the park
To watch the fireworks and the marching band.
For hours a drill team pivots at command.
For hours we sit in the dark

Hearing some politician fume;
Someone leads out a blonde schoolgirl to crown
Queen of this war-contract factory town;
Skyrockets and the last guns boom.

I keep my seat and wonder where,
Into what ingrown nation has she gone
Among a people silent and withdrawn;
I wonder in the stifling air

Of what deprived and smoke-filled town
They brush together and do not feel lust,
Hope, rage, love; within what senseless dust
Is she at home to settle down;

Where do they know her, and the dead
Meet in a vacancy of shared disgrace,
Keep an old holiday of blame and place
Their tinsel wreathe on her dark head?

We tramp home through the sulfurous smoke
That is my father's world. Now we must
Enter my mother's house of lint and dust
She could not breathe; I wheeze and choke.

It is an evil, stupid joke:
My wife is pregnant; my sister's in her grave.
We live in the home of the free and of the brave.
No one would hear me, even if I spoke.

The Survivors

We wondered what might change
Once you were not here;
Tried to guess how they would rearrange
Their life, now you were dead. Oh, it was strange
Coming back this year—

To find the lawn unkept
And the rock gardens dense
With bindweed; the tangling rosebushes crept
And squandered over everything except
The trash by the fence;

The rose trellises blown
Down and still sprawled there;
Broken odd ends of porch furniture thrown
Around the yard; everything overgrown
Or down in disrepair.

On the tree they still protect
From the ungoverned gang
Of neighbor boys—eaten with worms, bird-pecked,
But otherwise uncared-for and unpicked,
The bitter cherries hang,

Brown and soft and botched.
The ground is thick with flies.
Around in front, two white stone lions are crouched
By the front steps; someone has patched
Cement across their eyes.

The Venetian blinds are drawn;
Inside, it is dark and still.
Always upon some errand, one by one,
They go from room to room, vaguely, in the wan
Half-light, deprived of will.

Mostly they hunt for some-
thing they've misplaced; otherwise
They turn the pages of magazines and hum
Tunelessly. At any time they come
To pass, they drop their eyes.

Only at night they meet.
By voiceless summoning
They come to the living room; each repeats
Some words he has memorized; each takes his seat
In the hushed, expectant ring

By the television set.
No one can draw his eyes
From that unnatural, cold light. They wait.
The screen goes dim and they hunch closer yet,
As the image dies.

In the cellar where the sewers
Rise, unseen, the pale white
Ants grow in decaying stacks of old newspapers.
Outside, street lamps appear, and friends of yours
Call children in for the night.

And you have been dead one year.
Nothing is different here.

To a Child

We've taken the dog out for his walk
   To the practice football field;
We sit on a dead branch, concealed
In the scraggly brush and trees
Beside the stale, old spring; we talk our talk
   About the birds and the bees.

How strange we should come here.
In the thick, matted grass, ten feet away,
   Some twenty years ago I lay
     With my first girl. Half-dead
Or half-demented with my fear,
   I left her there and fled.

Still, I guess we often choose
Odd spots: we used to go stone-dapping
On the riverbanks where lovers lay
Abandoned in each others' arms all day
   By their beached, green canoes;
   You asked why were they napping.

We've sat on cemetery
Stones to sing; found a toad
Run over on the graveyard road
That no one had seen fit to bury;
   We've deciphered dark
Names carved in stone, names in the white birch bark.

We've waded up the creek
Over sharp stones and through deep
Slime, toward its source; caught a turtle
And carried the thing home to keep.
   At best, he lived a week.
We said that ought to make the garden fertile.

We learned the animal orders' name-
    tags, posted in the park;
We fed the llamas, fawns and goats that roam
    The childrens' zoo, a sort of Ark
    For the newborn, hurt or tame,
      A home away from home.

We heard a bantie chick there that had wandered
      Into the wrong pen
    Peeping, peeping, scurrying
    After a huge indignant hen
      That fled. You said we'd bring
    Our feather duster to crawl under.

    And I mailed you long letters
    Though you were still too young to read;
    I sent you maple wings that fly,
Linden gliders and torqued ailanthus seeds,
    Pine cones crammed with flyers that flutter
      Like soft moths down the sky;

    Told you how Fall winds bear
    The tree seeds out, like airmailed letters,
To a distant ground so, when they come up later,
    They will find, possibly,
    Rain, sun and the soil they need
      Far from the parent tree.

    They threw my letters out.
    Said I had probably forgotten.
    Well, we have seen the glow of rotten
Wood, the glimmering being that consumes
    The flesh of a dead trout.
    We have walked through living rooms

And seen the way the dodder,
That pale white parasitic love-vine, thrives
    Coiling the zinnias in the ardor
    Of its close embrace.
We have watched grown men debase
Themselves for their embittered wives

And we have seen an old sow that could smother
    The sucklings in her stye,
That could devour her own farrow.
We have seen my sister in her narrow
    Casket. Without love we die;
    With love we kill each other.

You are afraid, now, of dying;
    Sick with change and loss;
You think of your own self lying
Still in the ground while someone takes your room.
    Today, you felt the small life toss
    In your stepmother's womb.

I sit here by you in the summer's lull
Near the lost handkerchiefs of lovers
    To tell you when your brother
    Will be born; how, and why.
    I tell you love is possible.
    We have to try.

The Boy
Made of Meat

A Poem for Children

Why do they make boys out of meat?
Whenever I sit down to eat
They say, "Sit up. Don't swing your feet.
You'll spill that milk. Now have some meat."

I say, "I've heard cupcakes taste good
With marmalade; I'll bet they would."
They say, "You know that's much too sweet
For growing boys. Here; take some meat."

I say, "Or some cream puffs with these
Dill pickles—would you pass that, please?"
They say, "Just sit down in that seat
And drop those cookies. Eat that meat!"

I say, "Ice cream with nuts would do;
But no candy—not till I'm through."
They jump up; they all stamp their feet:
"No! NO!! You need your meat, Meat, MEAT!!!"

"Sweet stuff makes you grow weak and fat—
You're not built out of things like that.
A growing boy's made out of meat;
Meat's the one thing all boys must eat."

What makes them think I can't grow strong
Except with meat? They must be wrong:
Why, right now I feel weak and sick
To see my plate get piled up thick

With meat, Meat, MEAT. I'd tell them so;
They'd say, "Get straight to bed, then," though;
"Bed's where all sick boys belong."
All the same, though, I know they're wrong.

A growing cow finds all he needs
To get strong eating grass and weeds.
I'll say, "Please help yourself and pass
The weeds. Here; have some nice, fresh grass."

Horses don't eat their meat at all;
They grow up strong and fast and tall.
Sometime try feeding meat to one—
You'll see how fast horses can run!

Just take one look at elephants:
They never eat *their* meat—not once.
If I ate peanuts till I got
That big, I'd show them what was what!

Why, they've been mixed up, all along;
Meat isn't how to grow up strong.
Just think of all the ones that do
Eat meat—think what they grow into:

Frogs eat their bugs up—each last bit;
They don't get big or strong from it.
Cats eat their mice—raw mice at that!
I'm bigger *now* than any cat.

And what if boys *are* made of meat:
We don't turn into what we eat—
It turns to us! Each cow I've seen
Ate grass; not one of them was green.

Our cat eats birds—she's got no wings;
Those birds don't help her when she sings!
Mice don't look like cheese and what's
More, squirrels don't look much like nuts.

Then, what if they were right? If we
Ate beefsteak just think what we'd be!
Next time they say, "Beef's good for you,"
I'll swish my tail up and say, "Moo!"

They say, "Eat meat so you'll grow big."
I'll say, "I thought you said, 'Don't be a pig!' "
Or when we've got pork for a meal
I'll just roll in the mud and squeal.

The way they pile meat on my dish,
Why, I could grow scales like a fish,
Horns like a sheep, feet like a hen—
I guess they'd all feel sorry then!

Still, here's what they should feel afraid of:
If we should eat just what we're made of
And growing boys are made of meat—
People are what we'd ought to eat!

Maybe they're right; maybe I'm wrong;
I'll eat my meat and grow up strong
Like good lions or good tigers do—
They won't keep *me* locked in some zoo:

I'd prowl down the main street of town
To see if any meat's around;
All the folks I'd meet I'd say,
"My, but you *do* look good today!"

Wouldn't they pat me on the head
And rub my ears while they all said,
"Good boy! You're so big and well-fed;
That's enough meat—try cake instead."

I'd sniff them over; then I'd roar,
"No sweet stuff! Meat! I want more! MORE!!
Just meat, Meat, MEAT!!! A man-sized steak!
I need some for this stomach-ache!"

I'd eat my meat up till I grew
So big that they'd see who was who;
They'd never say, "Please just get finished";
They'd say, "I like you small and thinnish;

"Why not just dawdle?" since they knew
They'd all be gone if I got through.
I'd eat it all up 'till I'd grown
So whopping, I'd be left alone.

Alone?—just wait now. That could be
Some trouble. Who'd look after me?
Where would I go, then, to get food?
Who'd fix it for me?—no one would!

And who'd fuss at me to get done?
Eating *that* much meat's no darn fun!
I may let meat folks stick around
Just till some better setup's found—

Till the great Topsy Turvy comes
And his voice booms like ten bass drums:
"Let everything around here change;
Let everything be good and strange.

"Kittens will chase big dogs up trees;
Flowers will chase the bumblebees;
Foxes will run from hens and hide;
Rocks will catch cold and come inside;

"Mothers will just love lots of noise;
Fathers will smile at naughty boys;
Grandparents will act strict and mean;
Nothing will be the way it's been.

"And boys? We'll make boys from mince pies—
That ought to grow boys the right size;
We'll make boys out of gum and candy—
That ought to build boys brisk and dandy;

"We'll make boys out of plum preserves
To build strong muscles and quick nerves;
We'll make boys out of cakes and tarts
To give them rich blood and stout hearts;

"Make them from popcorn, pecans, pickles,
Jam, jelly, crackerjack, Popsicles,
Ice cream with toppings sweet and sour;
We'll make those boys just bulge with power!"

Then, then, when I sit down to eat
They'll say, "Slide down in your seat;
Don't sit so tall! Please swing your feet.
And don't just sit there looking sweet!

You finish all that candy! Stop;
Don't eat that meat! Now drink your pop!"

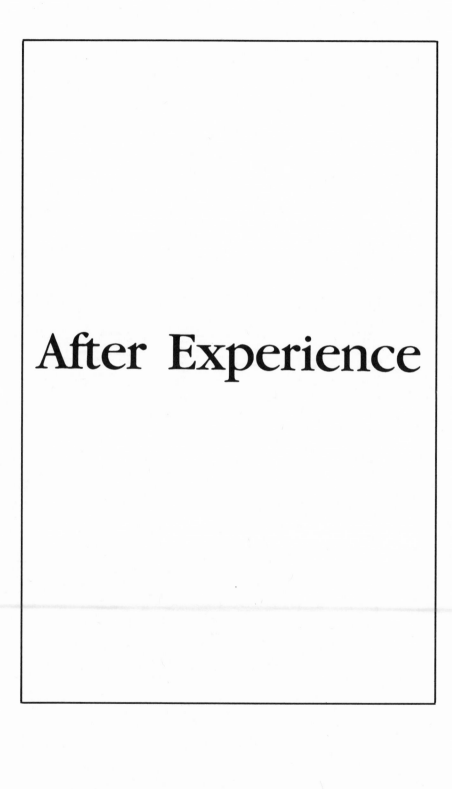

After Experience

Partial Eclipse

*Last night's eclipse, 99 percent
complete, seemed at times to be
total because of light mists
and low-hanging clouds.*

—RADIO NEWS REPORT

Once we'd packed up your clothes
   It was something to talk about:
The full moon, how it rose
   Red, went pale, then went out

As that slow shadow crossed—
   The way Time might erase
Its blackboard: one cheek lost,
   The eyes, most of the face

Hovering dim as a ghost,
   Or the dark print of some light
That seared the eyes, almost,
   Yet lives in the lids, clenched tight.

But still one brilliant sliver
   Stayed, worrying the eye,
Till even that would shiver,
   Go sick and the whole sky—

We wished it all blank, bereft.
   But no; the mists drifted on;
Something, one glint was left.
   Next morning you had gone.

September

In town, your friends play hide-and-seek
   In dead leaves piled by the sidewalk.
Today I hiked along the creek,
   Through dry weeds and the sharp oat stalks,

Carrying my old binoculars;
   I hoped to spot that small Green Heron
We saw together down the marsh
   This August. He'd gone off on an errand.

Then too, of course, this *is* September.
   The newts in the creek had gone, already.
I don't know where. I can't remember
   Your face or anything you said.

Reconstructions

This fall, we left your Grandma's
And had to leave your plant behind;
You said if no one watered it
And it would die, you didn't mind.
You mean to play the zinnia
In some sorry melodrama.

You offered me, one day, your doll
To sing songs to, bubble and nurse,
And said that was her birthday;
You reappeared then, grabbed her away,
Said just don't mess with her at all;
It was your child, yours.

And earlier this summer, how
You would tell the dog he had to "Stay!"
Then always let him sit
There, ears up, tense, all
Shivering to hear you call;
You turned and walked away.

We are like patients who rehearse
Old unbearable scenes
Day after day after day.
I memorize you, bit by bit,
And must restore you in my verses
To sell to magazines.

We keep what our times allow
And turn our grief into play.
We left you at your mother's; now
We've given the dog away.

The First Leaf

The first leaf, as we drive off,
Spins down the windshield, red;
Birds flock near the driveway.
We say what has to be said:

Autumn, winter, spring,
We'll write our usual letter;
One month for each finger.
And this makes you feel better.

We park by a transport trailer
Of bawling, white-faced cattle
That stare between the truck rails
Like men being shipped to battle,

Perhaps, in some other country,
But who will ever know?
From somewhere down the station
I hear a rooster crow.

Next year we'll hardly know you;
Still, all the blame endures.
This year you will live at our expense;
We have a life at yours,

Now I can earn a living
By turning out elegant strophes.
Your six-year teeth lie on my desk
Like a soldier's trophies.

You move off where I send you;
The train pulls down its track.
We go about our business;
I have turned my back.

Mementos, 1

Sorting out letters and piles of my old
   Canceled checks, old clippings, and yellow note cards
That meant something once, I happened to find
   Your picture. *That* picture. I stopped there cold,
Like a man raking piles of dead leaves in his yard
      Who has turned up a severed hand.

Still, that first second, I was glad: you stand
   Just as you stood—shy, delicate, slender,
In that long gown of green lace netting and daisies
   That you wore to our first dance. The sight of you stunned
Us all. Well, our needs were different, then,
      And our ideals came easy.

Then through the war and those two long years
   Overseas, the Japanese dead in their shacks
Among dishes, dolls, and lost shoes; I carried
   This glimpse of you, there, to choke down my fear,
Prove it had been, that it might come back.
      That was before we got married.

—Before we drained out one another's force
   With lies, self-denial, unspoken regret
And the sick eyes that blame; before the divorce
   And the treachery. Say it: before we met. Still,
I put back your picture. Someday, in due course,
      I will find that it's still there.

What We Said

Stunned in that first estrangement,
We went through the turning woods
Where inflamed leaves sick as words
Spun, wondering what the change meant.

Half gone, our road led onwards
By barbed wire, past the ravine
Where a lost couch, snarled in vines,
Spilled its soiled, gray innards

Into a garbage mound.
We came, then, to a yard
Where tarpaper, bottles and charred
Boards lay on the trampled ground.

This had been someone's lawn.
And, closing up like a wound,
The cluttered hole in the ground
A life had been built upon.

In the high grass, cars had been.
On the leafless branches, rags
And condoms fluttered like the flags
Of new orders moving in.

We talked of the last war, when
Houses, cathedral towns, shacks—
Whole continents went into wreckage.
What fools could do that again?

Ruin on every side—
We would set our loves in order,
Surely, we told each other.
Surely. That's what we said.

Lying Awake

This moth caught in the room tonight
Squirmed up, sniper-style, between
The rusty edges of the screen;
Then, long as the room stayed light,

Lay here, content, in some cornerhole.
Now that we've settled into bed
Though, he can't sleep. Overhead,
He hurls himself at the blank wall.

Each night hordes of these flutterers haunt
And climb my study windowpane;
Fired by reflection, their insane
Eyes gleam; they know what they want.

How do the petulant things survive?
Out in the fields they have a place
And proper work, furthering the race;
Why this blind fanatical drive

Indoors? Why rush at every spark,
Cigar, headlamp or railway warning
To knock off your wings and starve by morning?
And what could a moth fear in the dark

Compared with what you meet inside?
Still, he rams the fluorescent face
Of the clock, thinks that's another place
Of light and families, where he'll hide.

We'd ought to trap him in a jar,
Or come, like the white-coats, with a net
And turn him out toward living. Yet
We don't; we take things as they are.

Lobsters in the Window

First, you think they are dead.
Then you are almost sure
One is beginning to stir.
Out of the crushed ice, slow
As the hands of a schoolroom clock,
He lifts his one great claw
And holds it over his head;
Now, he is trying to walk.

But like a run-down toy;
Like the backward crabs we boys
Splashed after in the creek,
Trapped in jars or a net,
And then took home to keep.
Overgrown, retarded, weak,
He is fumbling yet
From the deep chill of his sleep

As if, in a glacial thaw,
Some ancient thing might wake
Sore and cold and stiff
Struggling to raise one claw
Like a defiant fist;
Yet wavering, as if
Starting to swell and ache
With that thick peg in the wrist.

I should wave back, I guess.
But still in his permanent clench
He's fallen back with the mass
Heaped in their common trench
Who stir, but do not look out
Through the rainstreaming glass,
Hear what the newsboys shout,
Or see the raincoats pass.

Looking

What was I looking for today?
All that poking under the rugs,
Peering under the lamps and chairs,
Or going from room to room that way,
Forever up and down the stairs
Like someone stupid with sleep or drugs.

Everywhere I was, was wrong.
I started turning the drawers out, then
I was staring in at the icebox door
Wondering if I'd been there long
Wondering what I was looking for.
Later on, I think I went back again.

Where did the rest of the time go?
Was I down cellar? I can't recall
Finding the light switch, or the last
Place I've had it, or how I'd know
I didn't look at it and go past.
Or whether it's what I want, at all.

A Friend

I walk into your house, a friend.
Your kids swarm up my steep hillsides
Or swing in my branches. Your boy rides
Me for his horsie; we pretend
Some troll threatens our lady fair.
I swing him squealing through the air
And down. Just what could I defend?

I tuck them in, sometimes, at night.
That's one secret we never tell.
Giggling in their dark room, they yell
They love me. Their father, home tonight,
Sees your girl curled up on my knee
And tells her "git"—she's bothering me.
I nod; she'd better think he's right.

Once they're in bed, he calls you "dear."
The boob-tube shows some hokum on
Adultery and loss; we yawn
Over a stale joke book and beer
Till it's your bedtime. I must leave.
I watch that squat toad pluck your sleeve.
As always, you stand shining near

Your window. I stand, Prince of Lies
Who's seen bliss; now I can drive back
Home past wreck and car lot, past shack
Slum and steelmill reddening the skies,
Past drive-ins, the hot pits where our teens
Fingerfuck and that huge screen's
Images fill their vacant eyes.

Leaving the Motel

Outside, the last kids holler
Near the pool: they'll stay the night.
Pick up the towels; fold your collar
Out of sight.

Check: is the second bed
Unrumpled, as agreed?
Landlords have to think ahead
In case of need,

Too. Keep things straight: don't take
The matches, the wrong keyrings—
We've nowhere we could keep a keepsake—
Ashtrays, combs, things

That sooner or later others
Would accidentally find.
Check: take nothing of one another's
And leave behind

Your license number only,
Which they won't care to trace;
We've paid. Still, should such things get lonely,
Leave in their vase

An aspirin to preserve
Our lilacs, the wayside flowers
We've gathered and must leave to serve
A few more hours;

That's all. We can't tell when
We'll come back, can't press claims;
We would no doubt have other rooms then,
Or other names.

The Lovers Go Fly a Kite

What's up, today, with our lovers?
  Only bright tatters—a kite
That plunges and bobs where it hovers
  At no improbable height.

It's shuddery like a hooked fish
  Or a stallion. They reel in string
And sprint, compassing their wish:
  To keep in touch with the thing.

They tear up their shirts for a tail
  In hopes that might steady
It down. Wobbling, frail,
  They think it may now be ready

And balance their hawk aloft—
  Poor moth of twigs and tissue
That would spill if one chill wind coughed,
  Dive down to tear, or to kiss you;

Yet still tugs the line they keep
  Like some exquisite sting ray
Hauled from a poisonous deep
  To explore the bright coasts of day,

Or say it's their weather ear
  Keeping the heart's patrol of
A treacherous, washed-out year,
  Searching for one sprig of olive.

What air they breathe is wrung
　　With twenty subtleties;
Sharp bones of failure, hung
　　In all the parkway trees;

It's enough to make you laugh—
　　In these uncommitted regions
On an invisible staff
　　To run up an allegiance!

Regraduating the Lute

Having gathered power and resonance
   Through two years' playing, the finger board
Replaned to the warp of the living grain, then
   We are ready. Keeping the strings
Tuned and under tension, we gradually
   Pare away, while playing constantly,
All excess from behind the tempered face.
   The way a long grief hollows the cheeks away.
Not so much as might lose
   Endurance to sustain a music,
Yet until the sounding board is parchment-
   thin, and the white bonestructure or a strong
Light would shine nearly through.
   Until it trembles to the least touch,
Trembles to the lightest song.
   By hand we slowly rub away
The preserving brilliant varnish to a soft
   Old silver glow. Its voice now
Is equal to any in the world. We take it
   Home to sing to or lay it on the bed.
In any place, at any time I play,
   Behind this face where nobody can see
I have burned your name. To stay.

The Examination

Under the thick beams of that swirly smoking light,
    The black robes are clustering, huddled in together.
Hunching their shoulders, they spread short, broad sleeves like night-
    Black grackles' wings; then they reach bone-yellow leather-

y fingers, each to each. And are prepared. Each turns
    His single eye—or since one can't discern their eyes,
That reflective, single, moon-pale disc which burns
    Over each brow—to watch this uncouth shape that lies

Strapped to their table. One probes with his ragged nails
    The slate-sharp calf, explores the thigh and the lean thews
Of the groin. Others raise, red as piratic sails,
    His wing, stretching, trying the pectoral sinews.

One runs his finger down the whet of that cruel
    Golden beak, lifts back the horny lids from the eyes,
Peers down in one bright eye malign as a jewel,
    And steps back suddenly. "He is anaesthetized?"

"He is. He is. Yes. Yes." The tallest of them, bent
    Down by the head, rises: "This drug possesses powers
Sufficient to still all gods in this firmament.
    This is Garuda who was fierce. He's yours for hours.

"We shall continue, please." Now, once again, he bends
    To the skull, and its clamped tissues. Into the cran-
ial cavity, he plunges both of his hands
    Like obstetric forceps and lifts out the great brain,

Holds it aloft, then gives it to the next who stands
    Beside him. Each, in turn, accepts it, although loath,
Turns it this way, that way, feels it between his hands
    Like a wasp's nest or some sickening outsized growth.

They must decide what thoughts each part of it must think;
    They tap at, then listen beside, each suspect lobe;
Next, with a crow's quill dipped into India ink,
    Mark on its surface, as if on a map or globe,

Those dangerous areas which need to be excised.
    They rinse it, then apply antiseptics to it;
Now silver saws appear which, inch by inch, slice
    Through its ancient folds and ridges, like thick suet.

It's rinsed, dried, and daubed with thick salves. The smoky saws
    Are scrubbed, resterilized, and polished till they gleam.
The brain is repacked in its case. Pinched in their claws,
    Glimmering needles stitch it up, that leave no seam.

Meantime, one of them has set blinders to the eyes,
    Inserted light packing beneath each of the ears
And caulked the nostrils in. One, with thin twine, ties
    The genitals off. With long wooden-handled shears,

Another chops pinions out of the scarlet wings.
    It's hoped that with disuse he will forget the sky
Or, at least, in time, learn, among other things,
    To fly no higher than his superiors fly.

Well; that's a beginning. The next time, they can split
    His tongue and teach him to talk correctly, can give
Him opinions on fine books and choose clothing fit
    For the integrated area where he'll live.

Their candidate may live to give them thanks one day.
    He will recover and may hope for such success
He might return to join their ranks. Bowing away,
    They nod, whispering, "One of ours; one of ours. Yes. Yes."

Flash Flood

The worst is over; the people
are all glad
to show you where it passed, scattering
paving bricks like handbills, elbowed
STOP
signs into respectful
attitudes, then filched the smug
porch off a house.
They lead you to a black hole where
it broke straight
through one block wall of a basement, then
as if appalled by something found in there,
broke back out through the opposite wall.
They will recite
the history of its progress:
its small beginnings in the hills; down
what gulleys it had gathered mud and power,
gathered rock, stumps, dead trees; gathering body
parts and boulders, engines, armchairs, train wheels, gathering
down into the town.
They argue over who first
spotted it, bubbling out of sewers;
recognized its stench; who heard it, angering
back of the welding shops and car barns; argue, finally,
where had it clambered over the creek banks, rioting
down their stunned streets, irresistibly splintering
the goods they had used their
lives collecting. For years
of skimping, hard work,
jockeying for position; for all
their small, reluctant, timorous swindlings;
for their dedication—this
is their reward. They talk about it
with such pride, you'd think
it was their own.
Think back how the orderlies danced while

bombs crazed their bunker
and the Third Reich died.
Think of the Thirties—of all those
who saw their lives totter and
falter and
go under, finally;
then began to live. Who
would not like to kick
some pretty girl?
The firemen clump around in their boots, now,
on one of the porches, talking
to the young Italian, loud, who owns it,
whom everybody watches;
he has achieved, at last, celebrity of a kind—
his kitchen departed like an excursion steamer;
he clutches his shirtfront like some short-legged Oedipus
and seems, for once, one with his destiny.
Meantime, his neighbors who have not, these many months,
found time to address each other
saunter about with coffee and extra bedding;
surprised as refugees, they may
shake hands; or will walk together, like prisoners
out for exercise. They watch
three tow trucks strain to resurrect the bones
of next year's Chevrolet, junked in the creek.
Isn't it terrible, they ask. Their eyes
are glittering with the flares and searchlights.
Awful, they say. And they may stay up, now,
probably, talking, half the night.

"After Experience Taught Me . . ."

After experience taught me that all the ordinary
Surroundings of social life are futile and vain;

    I'm going to show you something very
    Ugly: someday, it might save your life.

Seeing that none of the things I feared contain
In themselves anything either good or bad

    What if you get caught without a knife;
    Nothing—even a loop of piano wire;

Excepting only in the effect they had
Upon my mind, I resolved to inquire

    Take the first two fingers of this hand;
    Fork them out—kind of a "V for Victory"—

Whether there might be something whose discovery
Would grant me supreme, unending happiness.

    And jam them into the eyes of your enemy.
    You have to do this hard. Very hard. Then press

No virtue can be thought to have priority
Over this endeavor to preserve one's being.

    Both fingers down around the cheekbone
    And setting your foot high into the chest

No man can desire to act rightly, to be blessed,
To live rightly, without simultaneously

    You must call up every strength you own
    And you can rip off the whole facial mask.

Wishing to be, to act, to live. He must ask
First, in other words, to actually exist.

        And you, whiner, who wastes your time
           Dawdling over the remorseless earth,
        What evil, what unspeakable crime
           Have you made your life worth?

Inquest

Under the lamp your hands do not seem red.
What if the vicious histories didn't lie
And, in good time, might cover you with shame?—
You seldom hope to see yourself as dead.

How can you guess what vices on your head
Might shine like dead wood for some distant eye?
Of course you have your faults; you make no claim
To sainthood, but your hands do not look red.

It's no crime to be envied or well fed;
You aimed at no man's life. Who would deny
Yours is the human and the normal aim?
You scarcely want to see yourself as dead.

Only last week the commentators said
Not even foreign generals need die
For circumstantial crimes. You would proclaim
Your own guilt if you saw your own hands red.

If you were hungry, who'd give up his bread
Without a fight? A person has to try
To feed himself; earn his own wealth and fame;
Nobody wants to see himself as dead.

Still, men go back to wars. They're not misled
By the old lies. They know the reasons why.
When you can't praise the world your world became
And see no place where your own hands are red,

It must be someone, then—how have they fled
The justice you had hoped you could apply?
You've hanged your enemies, shown up their game,
So now you don't dare see yourself as dead

And things lose focus. You can lie in bed
Repeating Men do starve. Their children cry.
They really cry. They do not cry your name.
Go back to sleep, your hands do not feel red.

Or sit in some dark newsreel to be led
Through barbed wire and the white dead piled boot-high.
Your palms sweat; you feel just about the same.
Your last hope is to see yourself as dead

And yet you did not bleed when those were bled.
The humans carry knives. "It is not I!"
The screen goes blank, you see no one to blame.
Till you endure to see yourself as dead
Your blood in your own hands would not seem red.

A Flat One

Old Fritz, on this rotating bed
For seven wasted months you lay
Unfit to move, shrunken, gray,
No good to yourself or anyone
But to be babied—changed and bathed and fed.
At long last, that's all done.

Before each meal, twice every night,
We set pads on your bedsores, shut
Your catheter tube off, then brought
The second canvas-and-black-iron
Bedframe and clamped you in between them, tight,
Scared, so we could turn

You over. We washed you, covered you,
Cut up each bite of meat you ate;
We watched your lean jaws masticate
As ravenously your useless food
As thieves at hard labor in their chains chew
Or insects in the wood.

Such pious sacrifice to give
You all you could demand of pain:
Receive this haddock's body, slain
For you, old tyrant; take this blood
Of a tomato, shed that you might live.
You had that costly food.

You seem to be all finished, so
We'll plug your old recalcitrant anus
And tie up your discouraged penis
In a great, snow-white bow of gauze.
We wrap you, pin you, and cart you down below,
Below, below, because

Your credit has finally run out.
On our steel table, trussed and carved,
You'll find this world's hardworking, starved
Teeth working in your precious skin.
The earth turns, in the end, by turn about
And opens to take you in.

Seven months gone down the drain; thank God
That's through. Throw out the four-by-fours,
Swabsticks, the thick salve for bedsores,
Throw out the diaper pads and drug
Containers, pile the bedclothes in a wad,
And rinse the cider jug

Half-filled with the last urine. Then
Empty out the cotton cans,
Autoclave the bowls and spit pans,
Unhook the pumps and all the red
Tubes—catheter, suction, oxygen;
Next, wash the empty bed.

—All this Dark Age machinery
On which we had tormented you
To life. Last, we collect the few
Belongings: snapshots, some odd bills,
Your mail, and half a pack of Luckies we
Won't light you after meals.

Old man, these seven months you've lain
Determined—not that you would live—
Just to not die. No one would give
You one chance you could ever wake
From that first night, much less go well again,
Much less go home and make

Your living; how could you hope to find
A place for yourself in all creation?—
Pain was your only occupation.
And pain that should content and will
A man to give it up, nerved you to grind
       Your clenched teeth, breathing, till

Your skin broke down, your calves went flat
And your legs lost all sensation. Still,
You took enough morphine to kill
A strong man. Finally, nitrogen
Mustard: you could last two months after that;
       It would kill you then.

Even then you wouldn't quit.
Old soldier, yet you must have known
Inside the animal had grown
Sick of the world, made up its mind
To stop. Your mind ground on its separate
       Way, merciless and blind,

Into these last weeks when the breath
Would only come in fits and starts
That puffed out your sections like the parts
Of some enormous, damaged bug.
You waited, not for life, not for your death,
       Just for the deadening drug

That made your life seem bearable.
You still whispered you would not die.
Yet in the nights I heard you cry
Like a whipped child; in fierce old age
You whimpered, tears stood on your gun-metal
       Blue cheeks shaking with rage

And terror. So much pain would fill
Your room that when I left I'd pray
That if I came back the next day
I'd find you gone. You stayed for me-—
Nailed to your own rapacious, stiff self-will.
       You've shook loose, finally.

They'd say this was a worthwhile job
Unless they tried it. It is mad
To throw our good lives after bad;
    Waste time, drugs, and our minds, while strong
Men starve. How many young men did we rob
       To keep you hanging on?

I can't think we did *you* much good.
Well, when you died, none of us wept.
You killed for us, and so we kept
You, because we need to earn our pay.
No. We'd still have to help you try. We would
       Have killed for you today.

Matisse: "The Red Studio"

There is no one here.
But the objects: they are real. It is not
As if he had stepped out or moved away;
There is no other room and no
Returning. Your foot or finger would pass
Through, as into unreflecting water
Red with clay, or into fire.
Still, the objects: they are real. It is
As if he had stood
Still in the bare center of this floor,
His mind turned in in concentrated fury,
Till he sank
Like a great beast sinking into sands
Slowly, and did not look up.
His own room drank him.
What else could generate this
Terra cotta raging through the floor and walls,
Through chests, chairs, the table and the clock,
Till all environments of living are
Transformed to energy—
Crude, definitive and gay.
And so gave birth to objects that are real.
How slowly they took shape, his children, here,
Grew solid and remain:
The crayons; these statues; the clear brandybowl;
The ashtray where a girl sleeps, curling among flowers;
This flask of tall glass, green, where a vine begins
Whose bines circle the other girl brown as a cypress knee.
Then, pictures, emerging on the walls:
Bathers; a landscape; a still life with a vase;
To the left, a golden blonde, lain in magentas with flowers
        scattering like stars;
Opposite, top right, these terra cotta women, living, in
        their world of living's colors;
Between, but yearning toward them, the sailor on his red
        café chair, dark blue, self-absorbed.

These stay, exact,
Within the belly of these walls that burn,
That must hum like the domed electric web
Within which, at the carnival, small cars bump and turn,
Toward which, for strength, they reach their iron hands:
Like the heavens' walls of flame that the old magi could see;
Or those ethereal clouds of energy
From which all constellations form,
Within whose love they turn.
They stand here real and ultimate.
But there is no one here.

Vuillard: "The Mother and Sister of the Artist"

(Instructions for the Visit)

Admire, when you come here, the glimmering hair
Of the girl; praise her pale
Complexion. Think well of her dress
Though that is somewhat out of fashion.
Don't try to take her hand, but smile for
Her hesitant gentleness.
Say the old woman is looking strong
Today; such hardiness. Remark,
Perhaps, how she has dressed herself black
Like a priest, and wears that sufficient air
That does become the righteous.
As you approach, she will push back
Her chair, shove away her plate
And wait,
Sitting squat and direct, before
The red mahogany chest
Massive as some great
Safe; will wait,
By the table and her greasy plate,
The bone half-chewed, her wine half-drained;
She will wait. And fix her steady
Eyes on you—the straight stare
Of an old politician.
Try once to meet her eyes. But fail.
Let your sight
Drift—yet never as if hunting for
The keys (you keep imagining) hung
By her belt. (They are not there.)
Watch, perhaps, that massive chest—the way
It tries to lean
Forward, toward her, till it seems to rest
Its whole household's weight

Of linens and clothing and provisions
All on her stiff back.
It might be strapped there like the monstrous pack
Of some enchanted pedlar. Dense, self-contained,
Like mercury in a ball,
She can support this without strain,
Yet she grows smaller, wrinkling
Like a potato, parched as dung;
It cramps her like a fist.
Ask no one why the chest
Has no knobs. Betray
No least suspicion
The necessities within
Could vanish at her
Will. Try not to think
That as she feeds, gains
Specific gravity,
She shrinks, light-
less as the world's
Hard core
And the per-
spective drains
In her.
Finally, above all,
You must not ever see,
Or let slip one hint you can see,
On the other side, the girl's
Cuffs, like cordovan restraints;
Forget her bony, tentative wrist,
The half-fed, worrying eyes, and how
She backs out, bows, and tries to bow
Out of the scene, grows too ethereal
To make a shape inside her dress

And the dress itself is beginning already
To sublime itself away like a vapor
That merges into the empty twinkling
Of the air and of the bright wallpaper.

Monet: "Les Nymphéas"

The eyelids glowing, some chill morning.
O world half-known through opening, twilit lids
   Before the vague face clenches into light;
O universal waters like a cloud,
   Like those first clouds of half-created matter;
O all things rising, rising like the fumes
   From waters falling, O forever falling;
Infinite, the skeletal shells that fall, relinquished,
   The snowsoft sift of the diatoms, like selves
Downdrifting age upon age through milky oceans;
   O slow downdrifting of the atoms;
O island nebulae and O the nebulous islands
   Wandering these mists like falsefires, which are true,
Bobbing like milkweed, like warm lanterns bobbing
   Through the snowfilled windless air, blinking and passing
As we pass into the memory of women
   Who are passing. Within those depths
What ravening? What devouring rage?
   How shall our living know its ends of yielding?
These things have taken me as the mouth an orange—
   That acrid sweet juice entering every cell;
And I am shared out. I become these things:
   These lilies, if these things are water lilies
Which are dancers growing dim across no floor;
   These mayflies; whirled dust orbiting in the sun;
This blossoming diffused as rushlights; galactic vapors;
   Fluorescence into which we pass and penetrate;
O soft as the thighs of women;
   O radiance, into which I go on dying . . .

Manet: "The Execution of the Emperor Maximilian"

"Aim well, muchachos: aim right
here;" he pointed to his heart.
With face turned upward, he waited
grave but calm.

Dear good God, we've blundered into some musical
   Comedy; here we have the girls' *corps de ballet*
Got up as legionnaires and shooting several
   Supernumeraries. These dainty backs display
No strain lifting up and steadying rifles twice
   The length of those we use. True; their aim's not quite right.
What difference, though; their uniforms look so nice;
   The sabers in their white holsters all gleam so bright;
Their hats and spats and dress gear trim and orderly.
   They've worked hours to crease their pants, to shine buttons for
An event which—if you're a soldier—ought to be
   The peak of your career: to shoot an emperor!
One's shown up late, though—of course; to one side, he stands
   Coolly inspecting his rifle. Who knows, though—he
Maybe just gets bored with politics. Still, his hands
   Have just cocked the fate of nations. Wait, now; his cap's
Red; he doesn't wear spats—is he a sergeant, set
   To render the *coup de grace*? His face alone shows
Dignity and calm; he, above all, seems real. Yet
   Whether he has a name or purpose, no one knows.

A second volley was necessary for
Maximilian who had asked to be shot
in the chest so that his mother
might see his face.

111

The scumbly, half-formed heads of these few peons peak
   Up over the background which is a flat rock wall.
One yawns, one leans on his elbows, one rests his cheek
   On his crossed arms, drowsing. The others, meantime, sprawl
Around every which way like idlers who've gone numb
   With heat and flies watching some would-be matadors.
They look like angels bored with one more martyrdom.
   This one's not yawning, though—he's yelling. Still, of course,
That could mean triumph, hate, outrage or just shock. Who
   Knows? It could well be that he's waving to somebody
He knows—or just wants us to know he's here. We *do*
   Know him, after all: an old friend from Daumier's study
Of a mob rioting. So we can assume he
   Wants a revolt. Or. . . . wait; this face with the mantilla
And the fan—the classic Spanish temptress. What's she
   Doing here?—a high class lady straight out of Goya!
Meantime, along the wall, one hat's sneaking away
   At right, past our sergeant—or turned up late also.
One thing we *do* share with these peons—we can't say
   What they're doing here. This late, who will ever know?

               On the spot where he died, the Haps-
               burgs—whose general downfall was
               prefigured in his—built a chapel
               to further his remembrance on earth
               and his forgiveness in heaven.

As for the victims, they would scarcely seem worth mention—
    Stuck in a corner, their whole world washed with flat light,
Focusless, having no perspective or convention
    To lead us in the way we ought to turn our sight.
At the center where the Emperor ought to stand, just
    This blank space rifles cross; otherwise, shadows thrown
In all directions; you'd think every man here must
    Have his inner light, like Quakers, or his own
Outer darkness. As if each flag flew in some thwart
    Direction, feeling a different wind. All the same,
For Maximilian, all aim and purpose stops short
    In this flat rock wall. Why speak of hints of cypress
Trees, shadowed lanes and cool vistas beyond the wall
    Far off at left? Out there, one white shape like a plaster
Bust drifts through the trees—a sort of neo-classical
    Ideal head floating, ghost-like, over the disaster.
Our hero stands as far from that as from this nameless
    Sergeant's real head, whose feet are well braced in the scene;
Untroubled, purposeless—he won't, for long, go aimless.
    He and stone walls are what men should not come between.

      When Maximilian refused to believe the
      absurd claim that he *had* been elected
      by the peons, Napoleon threatened to
      crown some other candidate. That, of
      course, overcame all doubts.

Still, for Maximilian, he whose widow soon went
    Mad with loss—or with some love disease he'd brought
Her from Brazil—this "Lord of all the Firmament"
    As she always called him—this high-flown head that thought
All life one grand staircase at whose top he might stand
    Bestowing his smile of infinite grace upon
The human beings at its base, cannot command
    The central spot in its own execution.
Or the surest brush-work! This head with its fine dreams
    It could unite, somehow, the Old World with the New,
Bind the Divine Rights of Hapsburgs with half-baked schemes
    And liberal sentiments, could link the True Church to
The freely divisive mind, seems half-way divorced
    From its own body. Perched on a puff of smoke,
It bobs the way a kid's balloon slues back and forth
    At the end of its string. And, as a last bad joke,
Flaunts this broad sombrero—the tasteless parody
    Of a halo that may be fitting to a passion
Undergone between two generals. So we see
    Even gods must keep their heads and take note of fashions.

            It was as if some ne'er-do-well had
            finally found his true vocation: as
            martyr and sacrificial victim, he has
            seldom been surpassed.

Still, for Maximilian, he stands here holding hands
    With these two who chose death with him. And that's about
All he held together. Now, even while he stands
    Showing us the wounds in their palms, we've got our doubts.
He's bleached out like some child's two-penny crucifixion;
    Even the eye wanders from that face where we see
Nothing of interest—not, surely, that firm conviction
    We demand. After all, there's *some* nobility
In this unknown sergeant. Or in this general
    At the rear, although he may seem hesitant to enter
The picture—as well he might. Wait, though; after all,
    Maximilian might well have yielded up the center.
It could be this one, back of the others. Or else him,
    In front, with legs spread, whose hand flaps up like a doll's,
The face nearly lost, yet twisting up in a dim
    Shudder of strain—or, say, pain?—as the rifleballs
Break in and his brain cells, the atoms of his mind
    Untie, all bonds dissolved they hurl free, first rats fleeing
The sinking vessel for some new faith, grasping, blind,
    And he, whoever he was, is all done with being.

    1832: Birth, 6 July.
    1854: Naval adminstrator.
    1857: Viceroy to the Lombardo-Venetian Kingdom.
    1864: Emperor of Mexico.
    1867: Deposition; death.

Van Gogh: "The Starry Night"

        Only the little
                town
    remains   beyond
        all shock and dazzle
    only this little
                    still stands
                    calm.

Row on row, the gray frame cottages, small
Barns and sheds of an old Dutch town;
Plane over plane, the village roofs in order,
One by one, contained and ordered lives;
Aging in place, the weathered walls gone
Gray, grown ancient beyond memory.

            what flowers were blossoming, how the fruit
            trees bore, had the nightingale been heard
            yet, the text of Father's sermon

The squared shapes of doorframes, and bright windows;
Angle above angle, a slate ascent of roofs;
Stone upon stone, like broad stairs or the
Planes of a determined head, convergent
On this still dead center, the village chapel
Tiny as a child's toy

            There is something about Father
            narrow-minded, icy-cold, like iron

The village chapel, tiny as a child's toy
And as far. Pale as quartz crystals,
Its salients and the keen blue spire
Slim as a needle transfixed in the horizon
Firm in the high winds, high breakers, this
Still eye to the hurricane, this lighthouse

>   *How could I possibly be in any way of any*
>   *use to anyone? I am good for something!*

In which no light shines.

Through the high zones uncontained
            the uncontaining heavens
     Metaphysics cannot hold
            hump shove swirling blood rising as
     the nipples too come swollen shuddery
                behind the clenched lids, blind
     tracers   *chaos in a goblet*   opening
         like a zinnia bed   and chancres   swamp mouths
                outspattering eleven
            fixed stars   one sunburst moon
     Midspasm   midheavens   the spiral galaxy
            tumbled in trails of vapor
                Art for Art
            The war still raging while the high gods
         copulate on Garganos
                    the holy ground burst
         into flower and a golden dew fell

Energy for Energy
ethereal first mists   light dusts
            Chaos contains no glass
                of our caliber
gathering into force and matter
    obliterating to be whole again
        be one.

            Giotto and Cimabue live in an obeliscal
            society, solidly framed, architecturally constructed.

Row on row, plane over plane, the reddish brown
Houses with stepped gables and high stoops.
One by one, the thoughtless comfortable lives
Like steps in an argument, pigs at their dam;
Side by side in one another's lee, huddled
Against weather, against doubt, passion, hope

                Every individual a stone and
                the stones clung together

The narrow lanes beneath the eaves-troughs,
Hedgerows between the houses and dark
Trees; behind, and laid out side by side,
The kitchen gardens with their heavy odors
Where dew sits chilly on the cabbage leaves
And a bird might sing.

                And if no actual obelisk of too
                pyramidal a tragedy, no rain of frogs

Down those dark lanes you will never see
A lantern move or any shadow sway,
No dog howl and your ear will never know
The footfall of a prowler or some lover's tread,
Nor any wanderer, long gone,

> *four great crises when I did not know what*
> *I said, what I wanted, even what I did.*

who cannot return.

> *In spring, a caged bird feels strongly*
> *there is something he should be doing.*
> *But what was it? He gets vague ideas.*
> *The children say, but he has everything*
> *he wants.*

Beyond the town, blue mountains rising
    range over range over range
Sometimes just as waves break
    on sullen, hopeless cliffs
          upthrusting
     its salt mass into the sky
  in the public square milling chanting obscenities
       ton on broken ton of stone
    the black earth hovering *I feel a*
     storm of desire to
       embrace something
 great ragged crests lumbering in   murderous
  as the seasons   bluer than the years
    the first rocks rattling
through the windows   scattered gunfire
    all you have always held is a lie

Painting   and much screwing are not
   compatible; man   the crowd
   pounds   on and on   blood battering its walls
the feathery surf   first spies   already
         prowling up around the gray
   outbuildings and the orchards
         the unthinkable is also true
                  becomes ambitious as soon
   as he becomes impotent a spume
of ancient vacuum shuddering to
         reclaim its child
to embrace   something   a woman   a sort
         of domestic hen
               so pale
the gardens of olives   gardens
   of agony   frothing
      about its feet in foam.

               the hollow dreams of revolutionaries . . .
               they would wail in despair if once they
               forgot the easy satisfaction of their
               instincts, raising them to the unappeased
               sufferings of the passions.

Down those dark lanes which you can never see
   Shines only so much light:
Eleven windows and one opened door—crystals
   Under tons of ore, clear garnets, warm;
Through those windows you can never see, and yet
   You always wonder who may waken there,

120

Who sits up late over a pipe, sits to hold
   A pious, worn book between worn hands,
Who sits up late together and will talk, will talk
   The night away, planning the garden for
Next year, the necessary furnitures,
   Who works there, shreds the cabbages,
Darns some coarse fabric by a hanging lamp,
   Who may have gotten out of bed to calm
Their children fitfully sleeping, each
   In his own bed, one by one another,
Who goes to curry and bed down the patient beasts
   Warm in their old pens. But nothing moves
In those dark streets which you can never see,
   No one is walking or will ever walk there
Now, and you will never know

                    One vast tree
                between you and the town:
                one cypress   mocks
            the thin blue spire   licking up
                    like flame
                        the green metabolism
                of this forest sword
            driving you from the town

            I have sown a little garden of poppies,
            sweet peas and mignonette. Now we must
            wait and see what comes of it.

Still, though the little town, how peacefully
It lies under the watchful eyes of that
Fierce heaven.

We take death to reach a star.

Nothing moves there yet, and yet
How separate, how floating like a raft, like
Seaweed drifting outward on the tide, already
Dim, half-gone,

And the poor baby, too, whom I had
cared for as if he were my own

diminishing into
Some middle distance of the past.

some canvases that will retain their
calm even in the catastrophe

and still so calm
and still
so still

Zóó heen kan gaan

The
Fuehrer Bunker

Even if we lose this war, we still win, for our spirit will have penetrated the hearts of our enemies.

—Joseph Goebbels

Mother Theresa, asked when she first began her work of relief and care for abandoned children, replied, "On the day I discovered I had a Hitler inside me."

Dr. Joseph Goebbels
Minister for Propaganda

—1 April 1945, 0230 hours

> *(At a French window of his house on
> Schwanenwerder, he watches the air
> raid over Berlin. He sings snatches of a
> song from the Thirty Years War.)*

By day, American bomb flights
Smash us to ash and brick dust; nights,
The British burn us down. Up there,
Not one of our planes anywhere.
Revive, rise, you Powers of the Air—
It's Easter! Ha!—we haven't got a prayer!

Pray, children, pray;
Swedes are on the way.

So "Red Berlin" burns—turning red
Once more. Those same streets piled with dead
Where we once cracked men's skulls to win
Their hearts and high offices. Once in,
We swore we'd never leave except
Feet first—that's one promise we've kept.
We did neglect to tell them, though:
Let this earth tremble when we go!

Oxenstiern will march this way
Teaching children how to pray.

> *(turns from the window)*

The first time I saw a bombed city—
Dresden—corrupted me with pity.
Some suffocated, others burned
Alive; some, lacking air, turned
Black and hard—their body fats ran
Out of them like grease in a pan.

Then he'll roast the fat, young pullets;
Melt church windows down for bullets.

I clumped through those long stacks of dead
Weeping, weeping. Back here, I said
I wanted power right then for putting
This whole nation on a war footing.
Now the foe's halfway through our gate
The Chief gives me the power. Too late.

Bet, kinder, bet;

So once more, the Chief's wrong proves out
Better than my right. I, no doubt,
Could have curbed slaughter, ruin, terror—
Just my old sentimental error.
Our role is to wipe out a twisted
Life that should never have existed.

Morgen komm der Schwed.

Each Ami bomb, each Russian shell
Helps us to wipe away this hell
Called Europe, Man's age-old, unjust
Network of lies, pandering, lust,
Deformity. This is to be
Young again—idealistic, free.

Morgen komm der Oxenstierne

Once, my newscasters would disguise
Each loss as a triumph. Those lies
Were mere truths *we* misunderstood:
There's no evil we can't find good.

Will der kinder beten lerne.

(turns back to the window)

Let it all fall in, burn and burst;
Blest be who dares act out his worst
Impulses, give way to the thirst
For blood, and show this for the accurst
Inferno we took it for, right from the first.

Bet, kinder, bet.
Pray, children, pray.

(kneels)

Our Father who art in Nihil,
We thank Thee for this day of trial
And for the loss that teaches self-denial.
Amen.

Reichsmarschall Hermann Göring

—1 April 1945

*(Göring, head of the Luftwaffe, once
bragged that if one German city were
bombed, they could call him "Meier."
At his Karinhall estate, he questions
himself and his disgrace.)*

And why, Herr Reichsmarschall, is Italy
Just like schnitzel? *If they're beaten
Either one will just get bigger.
Neither cuts too firm a figure.*
Still, all this humble pie you've eaten
Lately, fills you out quite prettily.

Why then, Herr Göring, how can we
Tell you and Italy apart?
*Italy always wins through losing;
I, just the opposite, by using
High skills and cunning, learned the art
Of flat pratfalls through victory.*

You've led our Flying Circus; how
Could our war ace turn to a clown?
*Both pad out over-extended fronts;
Both keep alive doing slick stunts
And, even so, both get shot down.*
But only one's called "Meier" now.

Pray, could an old, soft football be
Much like a man in deep disgrace?
*They don't kick back; don't even dare
Look up—the British own the air!*
Then, stick a needle in someplace;
Pump yourself full of vacancy.

129

Tell us, dear Minister for Air,
Are warriors, then, like a bad smell?
Neither stays inside its borders;
Either's bound to follow ordures;
They both expand and play the swell
Though something's getting spoiled somewhere.

Then answer one more question, which is
Are politicians like whipped cream?
They both inflate themselves with gas;
Also they both puff up your ass
Till you're exposed like some bad dream
Where you've grown too big for your britches.

Herr President, can't we tell apart
An artful statesman and an ass?
Fat chance! One spouts out high ideals;
One makes low rumblings after meals.
But that's the threat of leaking gas
Which all men fear! *No; that's a fart.*

Last, could you give one simple rule
To tell a medal from a turd?
No. They both come from those above you
Conveying their opinion of you.
Right! Here's your new medal, conferred
For vast achievements: April Fool!

*(Himmler's ruthless extermination
policies were based on fantastic
pseudoscientific experiments and
theories. MM=74.)*

```
ANY · TRULY · MODERN · STUDY · OF · THE ·
BRAIN · MUST · COOLLY · METHODICALLY
CONSIDER · THE · RACES · PROGRESS · & ·
DEVELOPMENT · WE · MUST · MAKE · EVERY
EFFORT · TO · ISOLATE · THE · CRUCIAL ·

FACTORS · THAT · MAKE · SOME · PEOPLES
GREAT · WHILE · OTHERS · DEGENERATE ·
HUMANITY · CANNOT · AFFORD · TO · WAIT
IVE · HAD · MY · MEN · GATHER · 1000S · OF
JEWISH · SKULLS · WE · MEASURE · WEIGH

KEEP · COMPLETE · RECORDS · & · BEFORE
LONG · CAN · HOPE · TO · UNRAVEL · THIS ·
MYSTERY · ABOVE · ALL · ELSE · DEVOTED
NAZIS · MUST · KEEP · A · SCIENTIFIC · &
OBJECTIVE · VIEW · IF · WE · WANT · REAL

PROGRESS · I · HAVE · BEEN · STUDYING ·
QUITE · THOROUGHLY · OUR · DARK · AGES
RECORDS · SHOW · 1000S · WENT · TO · THE
STAKE · PEOPLE · HONESTLY · BELIEVED
THEM · TO · BE · WITCHES · ITS · SIMPLY ·

UNTHINKABLE · MONSTROUS · WASTING ·
VALUABLE · GERMAN · BLOOD · TO · BURN ·
WITCHES · THAT · JUST · GOES · TO · SHOW
YOU · WHAT · FOLLY · & · INSANE · EXCESS
ZEALOTS · & · FANATICS · CAN · FALL · TO
```

ALL·OUR·WORK·IS·ENDANGERED·NOW
BY·THIS·BARBAROUS·ONSLAUGHT·OF
COMMUNISTIC·HORDES·SINCE·SUCH·
DUMB·HALF-CIVILIZED·BRUTES·ARE
ENEMIES·OF·TRUE·CULTURE·&·THE·

FULLY·RATIONAL·MIND·SO·WE·MUST
GATHER·ALL·RECORDS·ALL·REMAINS
HIDE·ANY·EVIDENCE·WHICH·COULD·
INDICATE·WHAT·WEVE·DONE·THATS·
JUST·AS·VITAL·NOW·AS·IT·IS·TO·

KEEP·THE·CAMPS·SWEPT·CLEAN·ALL
LABORATORIES·MUST·BE·TORN·DOWN
MOVED·OR·THOROUGHLY·DISGUISED·
NEW·TITLES·SHOULD·BE·ISSUED·TO
OUR·DOCTORS·AND·TECHNICIANS·I·

PALE·TO·THINK·WHAT·THEY·WOULD·
QUITE·POSSIBLY·IMAGINE·IF·THEY
ROOTED·INTO·OUR·MASS·GRAVES·OR
SOME·OF·OUR·BOLDER·EXPERIMENTS
THEYD·MISUNDERSTAND·IT·CALL·US

UNPRINCIPLED·HOODLUMS·GIVEN·TO
VICIOUS·INSTINCTS·THEYD·CLAIM·
WE·HAD·LOST·ALL·CONSCIENCE·AND
YIELDED·TO·THE·WORSHIP·OF·BAAL
ZOROASTER·SOMETHING·IRRATIONAL

132

Adolf Hitler

—20 April 1945, 1900 hours

> *(After his birthday ceremony, Hitler*
> *has withdrawn to his sitting room*
> *where he sits with one of Blondi's*
> *puppies on his knee. Earlier in the*
> *day he had gone up into the garden*
> *for the last time.)*

Better stuffed in a bag; drowned.
My best bitch pregnant once she can't
Survive.

The man will lie down on his back; his partner crouches over his
head or chest as he prefers.

My Effie's little sister
Knocked up by Fegelein. My luck
Lets me off one humiliation:
I breed no child.

He, of course, is completely naked.

This mockery:
Pisspot generals whining for surrender;
Party maggots bringing presents;
Careful not to wish me a long life—
Their one failure I can share.
Pulling at me, whimpering for
Their cities, populations, lives.

Sometimes, she may remove only her underthings. The private
parts, suddenly exposed, can provide an exquisite shock and
pleasure.

Cub, in Landsberg Prison, after
Our first putsch failed, my flowers
Filled three prison rooms. The faithful
Sang beside me in my cell.
I unwrapped presents, cut my cake. We
Laughed: where was the file inside?

The cake my mother made me . . . No . . .

Usually she will turn her back.

No. That's Edmund's cake. My brother's.
But I ate Edmund's cake. I spit on
What was left.

The Prison Governor brought his family's
Kind regards. His little daughter curled up,
Like this, on my lap asleep.

She must not start at once; he must ask, even beg her, to begin.

Whimpering at me; whining. Oh,
We hear their song:

Only live. Live longer. Lead us
To the mountain fastnesses. Keep us
From the guns, the Russians . . .

"Oh stay! don't leave us here forsaken;
Our men are waiting for their Führer."

In the mountains, could these shitheads be
Worthwhile? Over and over, we've said
They could survive: overcome facts.

Today I climbed two flights to the garden:
Sour smoke. Shelling. Schoolboys lined up.
Lines of graves. Hands I have to touch.

He will grovel on the floor, declaring himself unworthy to touch
her shoes, even to live.

Even the zoo animals, my good old
Neighbors, pacing their stalls till
Their keeper brings the right gift—
One lead pellet. A man who would accept
What is, is criminal, too vile to live.

It is not the mere fact of the urine or the feces that is significant.
The crux is that he be able to watch these emerge into existence.

Suffer that again? The elevator
Locked, lurching up through dead rock
In the mountain side? Come out
Freezing, over the receding plains,
Traitorous cities, nauseous dens
And hovels, lecherous faces with insane
Beliefs, Czechs, Jews with blond hair,
Blue eyes, who would steal our birthright,
Pull us down into putrescence, slime?

135

Edmund died though, my brother,
When I was eleven. His birthday
Would have been some days ago.

She must now show disgust; may revile him, even kick at him.

She lost three others. She, only
She, was glad I had survived.

Only when he is fully excited by his own demands, may she
release her urine, open her bowels. The danger of taking this
matter in his mouth heightens the excitement.

Only live; live longer. Don't
Leave us to the loneliness,
The spoiling of affections.

He kept me in. But she,
She made a special cake for me—
Only the two of us together.

Now he will probably achieve his climax, alone and without
assistance.

Namesake, cub, you've done your month
In this filth. My cake; I'll eat it, too.

The First War soldiers; our Old Fighters—
That was comradeship. You have Blondi's
Underside; my diet cook, the drivers,
Secretaries—they know how to listen.

"I stay too long; the Grail has sent for me."

I can eat nothing now—only cake.
Pills and Morrell's injections.
My cake, chairs, rugs—without them,
There's the bare concrete. Like any
Jew degenerate at Auschwitz.

When he has washed and begged forgiveness, she may embrace
and comfort him.

My birthday present, my file: my
Cartridge of pure cyanide. Crawl back
In the cave, work down in dry leaves,
An old dog deciding to lie down.

Or she may curl up by his side.

Eva Braun

—22 April 1945

*(Hitler's mistress received no public
recognition and often felt badly
neglected. Her small revenges included
singing American songs, her favorite
being "Tea for Two." Having chosen
to die with him in the bunker, she
appeared quite serene during the
last days.)*

*Tea for two
And two for tea*

I ought to feel ashamed
Feeling such joy. Behaving like a spoiled child!
So fulfilled. This is a very serious matter.
All of them have come here to die. And they grieve.
I have come here to die. If this is dying,
Why else did I ever live?

*Me for you
And you for me*

We ought never to flaunt our good luck
In the face of anyone less fortunate—
These live fools mourning already
For their own deaths; these dead fools
Who believe they can go on living . . ,

*And you for me
Alone.*

Who out of all of them, officers, ministers,
These liars that despise me, these empty
Women that envy me—so they hate me—
Who else of them dares to disobey Him
As I dared? I have defied Him to His face
And He has honored me.

We will raise
A family

They sneer at me—at my worrying about
Frau Goebbels' children, that I make fairytales
For them, that we play at war. Is our war
More lost if I console these poor trapped rabbits?
These children He would not give me . . .

A boy for you
A girl for me

They sneer that I should bring
Fine furniture down this dank hole. Speer
Built this bed for me. Where I have slept
Beside our Chief. Who else should have it?
My furs, my best dress to my little sister—
They would sneer even at this; yet
What else can I give her?

Can't you see
How happy we would be?

Or to the baby
She will bear Fegelein? Lechering dolt!
Well, I have given her her wedding
As if it was my own. And she will have
My diamonds, my watch. The little things you
Count on, things that see you through your
Missing life, the life that stood you up.

Nobody near us
To see us or hear us

I have it all. They are all gone, the others—
The Valkyrie, and the old rich bitch Bechstein;
Geli above all. No, the screaming mobs above all.
They are all gone now; He has left them all.
No one but me and the love-struck secretaries—
Traudl, Daran—who gave up years ago.

No friends or relations
On weekend vacations

That I, I above all, am chosen—even I
Must find that strange. I who was always
Disobedient, rebellious—smoked in the dining car,
Wore rouge whenever he said I shouldn't.
When he ordered that poor Chancellor Schuschnigg
Was to starve, I sent in food.

We won't have it known, dear,
That we own a telephone, dear.

I who joined the Party, I who took Him
For my lover just to spite my old stiff father—
Den Alten Fritz—and those stupid nuns.
I ran my teachers crazy, and my mother—I
Held out even when she stuck my head in water.
He shall have none but me.

> *Day will break*
> *And you will wake*

We cannot make it through another month;
We follow the battles now on a subway map.
Even if the Russians pulled back—
His hand trembles, the whole left side
Staggers. His marvelous eyes are failing.
We go out to the sunlight less each day. We live
Like flies sucked up in a sweeper bag.

And start to bake
  A sugar cake

He forbade me to leave Berchtesgaden,
Forbade me to come here. I tricked
My keepers, stole my own car, my driver Jung.
He tried to scold me; He was too
Proud of me. Today He ordered me to leave,
To go back to the mountain. I refused.
I have refused to save my own life and He,
In public, He kissed me on the mouth.

For me to take
For all the boys to see.

Once more I have won, won out over Him
Who spoke one word and whole populations vanished.
Until today, in public, we were good friends.
He is mine. No doubt
I did only what He wanted; no doubt
I should resent that. In the face
Of such fulfillment? In the face
Of so much joy?

Picture you
Upon my knee;
Tea for two
And two for tea . . .

Dr. Joseph Goebbels

—22 April 1945

*(On this date, Goebbels moved into the
lowest level of the bunker, taking a
room opposite Hitler's.)*

Stand back, make way, you mindless scum,
Squire Voland the Seducer's come—
Old Bock from Babelsberg whose tower
Falls silent now, whose shrunken power
For lies or lays comes hobbling home
Into this concrete catacomb.

Here's Runty Joe, the cunt collector
Who grew to greatness, first erector
Of myths and missions, fibs and fables,
Who pulled the wool then turned the tables:
He piped the tunes and called the dance
Where shirtless countries lost their pants.

Goatfooted Pan, the nation's gander
To whom Pan-Germans all played pander,
The jovial cob-swan quick to cover
Lida Baarova, his check-list lover;
Swellfoot the Tyrant, he could riddle
Men's minds away, hi-diddle-diddle.

Our little Doctor, Joe the Gimp
Comes back to limpness and his limp:
Hephaistos, Vulcan the lame smith
Whose net of lies caught one true myth:
His wife, the famous beauty, whored
By numbskull Mars, the dull warlord.

What if I took my little fling
At conquest, at adventuring.
Pried the lid of Pandora's box off—
There's nothing there to bring your rocks off.
I never saw one fucking day
So fine I courted it to stay.

If I got snarled in my own mesh
Of thighs and bellies, who wants flesh?
I never hankered after matter.
Let Hermann swell up, grosser, fatter,
Weighed down by medals, houses, clothing;
They leave me lean, secured in loathing.

As a young man, I pricked the bubble
Of every creed; I saw that rubble
And offered myself the realms of earth
Just to say Yes. But what's it worth?
No thank you, Ma'am. Behold the Ram
Of God: I doubt, therefore I am.

Here I forsake that long pricktease
Of histories, hopes, lusts, luxuries.
I come back to my first Ideal—
The vacancy that's always real.
I sniffed out all life's openings:
I loved only the holes in things.

So strip down one bare cell for this
Lay Brother of the last abyss.
To me, still, all abstractions smell;
My head and nose clear in this cell
Of concrete, this confession booth
Where liars face up to blank truth.

My tongue lashed millions to the knife;
Here, I'll hold hands with my soiled wife.
My lies piped men out, hot to slaughter;
Here, I'll read stories to my daughter
Then hack off all relations, choose
Only the Nothing you can't lose,

Send back this body, fixed in its
Infantile paralysis.
I was born small; I shall grow less
Till I burst into Nothingness,
That slot in time where only pure
Spirit extends, absent and sure.

I am that spirit that denies,
High Priest of Laymen, Prince of Lies.
Your house is founded on my rock;
Truth crows; now I deny my cock.
Jock of this walk, I turn down all,
Robbing my Peter to play Paul.

I give up all goods I possess
To build my faith on faithlessness.
Black Peter, I belie my Lord—
You've got to die to spread the Word.
Now the last act; there's no sequel.
Soon, once more, all things shall be equal.

Magda Goebbels

—22 April 1945

(On this date, Magda and her six children by Goebbels moved into the upper level of the bunker.)

i

How could you dare stay constant to
The kind that kept their faith to me?
   They hang on; they need help from you.
How could you dare stay constant to
   Those who can't help you struggle through;
   What use could such poor weaklings be?
How could you dare stay constant to
The kind that kept their faith to me?

ii

Who could you give devotion to?
Those that treat you faithlessly.
   On all sides, this world threatens you;
Who could you give devotion to?
   The strong; they don't care what they do;
   They tramp down all bounds, then go free.
Who could you give devotion to?
Those that treat you faithlessly.

iii

You raise your child devotedly;
He grows strong, then goes his own way.
   How helpless you must seem to be.
You raise your child devotedly
   And that tells him you need him; he
   Sees no real reason not to stray.
You raise your child devotedly;
He grows strong, then goes his own way.

iv

What can you do but turn away?
They'll see you're strong, then; they'll stay true.
    We've seen what loyalties would pay.
What can you do but turn away
      So that they'll need you. *Now* they'll stay
      Too scared to break their ties with you.
What can you do but turn away?
They'll see you're strong, then; they'll stay true.

Reichsmarschall Hermann Göring

—23 April 1945

*(After the conference of April 20,
Hitler's birthday, Göring drove south to
Berchtesgaden with a convoy of forty
vehicles. Having set up headquarters
there, he imagines the splendors of his
erstwhile parties.)*

Dear friends, the moment's come to ask
What lies beneath the glittering gear
And costumes radiantly displayed
At the Reichsmarschall's masquerade;
Find who romanced and danced us here,
To face the face behind the mask.

Who can adapt to each new role
And change costumes so cunningly
With each day's new conditions that
He wears a lantern on his hat
When he must run downstairs to see
The man who comes delivering coal?

Whose self-made uniform asserts
Clear blue, horizon to horizon,
Like azure skies no enemy
Dares invade; where instead we see
Medals like close-drilled stars bedizen
An ever-expanding universe?

Who wears this tent-sized dressing gown
All day, bought forty business suits
So he could change each hour or two
For fear his sour sweat might soak through?
Is this our famous Puss-in-Boots
Or just some knock-down, drag-out clown?

Who steps up now to the forefront
Wearing this pair of lederhosen,
A dagger tucked in his wide belt
And rough-cut vest from a deer's pelt
To signify himself the chosen
Chief of Reich Forests and the Hunt.

Who flaunts this frilly satin blouse,
These velvet knickerbockers, that
Alluring jacket of green suede
And in such fluff and frou-frou played
The true effete aristocrat,
The idle lord of an old house?

Who wears this modern well-ironed version
Of a toga he must hope dangles
Over his circular abdomen
Like an Athenian lord or Roman,
But with his nail paint, rouge and bangles
Looks more like some debauched Persian?

Who, at the Fuehrer's staff confab,
Accused of crimes just short of treason,
Got Hitler's leave to flee Berlin
And drive south, while he stood there in
The smartest fashion note this season:
Garb of American olive-drab?

Who wears this thick flesh, layer on layer—
Loose outposts of a weakening heart?
Who seems a one-man population
Explosion, or expanding nation,
Then, at the showdown, gives you a start:
He lifts his mask and no one's there.

HEINRICH · HIMMLER
FORMER · REICHSFUEHRER · SS
—29 · APRIL · 1945 ·

(After his secret negotiations for surrender to the West were revealed, Himmler was declared a traitor and expelled from the party by Hitler. MM=80.)

```
A · WISE · MAN · ALWAYS · KNOWS · HE · MAY
BE · MISUNDERSTOOD · REVILED · TO · BE
CALLED · A · TRAITOR · WHEN · I · MERELY
DID · MY · BEST · TO · SAVE · OUR · TROOPS
EVEN · SAVE · HIS · OWN · LIFE · WITH · MY

FOREIGN · CONTACTS · ALSO · USING · MY
GOOD · NAME · AFTER · LONG · YEARS · OF ·
HONORABLE · SERVICE · & · HARDSHIPS ·
I · BORE · FOR · HIM · GETTING · RID · OF ·
JEWS · GYPSIES · YOUD · THINK · I · LIKE

KILLING · ALL · THOSE · PEOPLE · O · ITS
LITTLE · THANKS · YOU · GET · BESIDES ·
MY · STOMACH · CRAMPS · TRULY · THERES
NO · JUSTICE · TRUE · I · DIDNT · DO · IT ·
ORIGINALLY · JUST · FOR · IDEALISTIC

PURPOSES · I · COULD · HAVE · MADE · IT ·
QUITE · IDEALISTIC · LATER · ON · AND ·
REALLY · NOW · TO · KILL · THAT · MANY · &
STAY · DECENT · UPRIGHT · IDEALISTIC
THAT · DESERVES · SOMETHING · I · GAVE

UP · MY · HAPPY · CHICKEN · FARM · & · THE
VICIOUS · THINGS · THEY · CALLED · ME ·
WHY · I · FAINT · JUST · SEEING · BLOOD ·
YET · HARD · AS · IT · IS · WE · MUST · KEEP
ZEAL · MORALITY · & · SELF-SACRIFICE
```

Eva Ḃ Hitler, geb. Braun

—30 April 1945

*(After her improvised civil wedding
and the brief reception, Eva sits on the
bed in her room alone. Hitler has gone
with Traudl Junge, his secretary, to
dictate his will before their mutual
deaths in a few hours. Fragments of
the Mass and the formal Catholic
marriage service run through her
mind.)*

Consummatum est.

It is accomplishèd.
   My mother's will be done.
                  Is done.

         The Dodd Girl, the Valkyrie,
      Ley's wife, Geli above all—
         how many died
   so I could carry her
      His name. When we were kids
      we looked at the eclipse
through snapshot negatives. They held
   their longing up to Him; their sight
      flashed out. Twice
   I tried to kill myself.

*To Thee do we cry, poor banished
children of Eve.*

At the photographer's I called Him
"Herr Wolf"; we met
disguised. Later,
He'd slip me an envelope
with enough to live on. Never
a love note; never a word
in public. I sat at my dresser
kissing His picture through glass;
in April weather, the sun
outside my windows
sneered at me. We drove
to the Munich Station; His train
had gone; all we saw
was tail lights. He
was never there. Only my first "suicide"
brought Him in. Tonight
the third. This one
for dead sure.

What God hath joined together
let no man put asunder.

A boy, He wouldn't listen
to the priest; they'd find Him
catching sunlight
in a pocket mirror, playing it
around the trees, the courtyard. Even now
He has gone off with Traudl
to dictate His will. Since He cannot
have His will. He leaves me
this concession
I once was:
my crossed-out name, my
new name on a piece of paper:
Eva ẞ Hitler, geb. Braun.

*Therefore shall a man leave father
and mother and cleave to his wife.
They shall be one flesh.*

And even if He came, He
would be missing; He
would not hear me. I
could look through Him
like a worn-out lantern slide. The priest
held up the monstrance
they said held the Host
before the people, right and left,
while we cast down our eyes. But one day I
crept up in the empty chapel,
to the holy case. There
the sacred vestments, the gold
chains, the monstrance
rayed out gleaming
like the May sun. And in the
center, the tiny glass bead,
I could see nothing.
Nothing.

And yet I have these albums, these
pictures proving it all so.
We danced together; we
sat together over tea; even
the wedding ceremony . . .
My grandmother's brocade—
I left it at the mountain;
I had to wear my long black taffeta.
This ring delivered for me
by the Gestapo . . .
I am black but beautiful
ye daughters of Jerusalem.

With this ring I thee wed;
This gold and silver I thee bring.

. . . this ring torn off some Jew's hand.

in templo sancto tuo in Jerusalem.

I am the Black Bride that will be
devoured, that will pass
down into Him like used water
down a drain, a film stuck,
burning through, or reeling
back into itself.
Like all the women, all
the foreigners, our beautiful
young men—all small
as red ants under
the magnifying glass
He reads His maps by.

Consummatum est.

To be so soon consumed and
never consummated.

O Thou who hast created
all things out of nothing . . .

Now each one has the nothing
they fought for. We have earned
                our deaths. And yet,
my mother, not even she
would will me this. She only wants
            it all to mean
        her meaning. Something instead
of life. To tell the neighbors.
And that I give her. She
            can rest.

Ite. Missa est.

My mother's will be mine.
                            Is
    mine.

        It is accomplishèd.

Adolf Hitler

—30 April 1945, 1520 hours

> *(Russian troops are in Voss and*
> *Wilhelm Strasse. Hitler and Eva have*
> *withdrawn to his sitting room; she has*
> *already committed suicide.)*

More than fifty millions. More.
Who killed that much; who else?

    Russian: twenty million.
    Jew: seven million, five hundred thousand.

        "Casualties can never be high enough.
        They are the seeds of future heroism."

All that and what good: what does
That save you? On and on and on . . .

Traitors on every side! Lies! Lies!

    One gift, finally, to my faithful:
    At Attila's bier. Last night,
    My secretaries, cook, the short-wave girls.
    More potent than bull-sperm; one cartridge
    Each. A helping hand, to save you
    From these Mongolians' greasy hands,
    Pricks, the stink of jism. What then?
    Some will sneak off West; some
    Wait till the Russian tanks . . . overcome
    By their own lust . . .

"𝔅etrayed! 𝔅etrayed! 𝔖hamefully betrayed!
𝔇eceit! 𝔇eceit! 𝔏ying past all revenge!"

Pole: three million.

> "Casualties? But that's what
> the young men are there for."

And seven at one blow.

Again last night, our movie:
Witzleben. General Joke Life. Choke Alive.
Shriveled-up rat, hauled up, wriggling
On the meat-hook, handcuffed, naked,
Six times to choke and strangle. Five times
Hauled down. Brought back. Couldn't
Beg even to die. Not even. Scrawny
Pizzle wouldn't come again. Not dust.
He couldn't even . . .

> I bring you not peace but
> a sword. This death in honor.

> Gypsy: four hundred . . . four . . .
> four hundred thousand.

> Not one truly grateful.

> French: five hundred thousand.

Shoveling lime in a latrine. Oh,
It's dragon seed. We played it three times;
No satisfaction. Not even . . .

160

Jugoslav: five hundred . . .

What use are facts, statistics?
The Impossible always succeeds.
Will enough and the lie turns true.

German: spineless worms. Only four . . .
four hundred . . . only four . . .

(turns to Eva's body)

Not even this one. Not even then.
She chose. Not watching her. Even
To come here was insulting. Mortal.

"𝔒nce recognized, the 𝔊rail 𝔎night must be gone."

Betrayed to! Lies! Betrayed to!

Never to need anyone alive. Whose
Death gets you through? Whose death
Shows you more fit to live? Whose . . .

Who's afraid of the big bad wolf,
Ha-ha-ha-ha-ha!

Tell me I have to die, then. Tell me.
What have I counted on? Tell me
The odds against me. You can't be
Sure enough. My name. My name on
Every calendar. Relentless, each year,
Your birth comes around. My death:
My lackey; my lickass general. My Will
Scrubs it all out, all of you, all gone . . .

                              "I go with the precision and
                              security of a sleepwalker."

I pick my time, my place. I take
This capsule tight between my teeth . . .
Set this steel cold against my jaw . . .
Clench, clench . . . and once more I
Am winning,
              winning,
                       winning . . .

162

Magda Goebbels

—30 April 1945

> *(After Dr. Haase gave them shots of*
> *morphine, Magda gave each child an*
> *ampule of potassium cyanide from a*
> *spoon.)*

This is the needle that we give
Soldiers and children when they live
Near the front in primitive
   Conditions or real dangers;
This is the spoon we use to feed
Men trapped in trouble or in need,
When weakness or bad luck might lead
   Them to the hands of strangers.

This is the room where you can sleep
Your sleep out, curled up under deep
Layers of covering that will keep
   You safe till all harm's past.
This is the bed where you can rest
In perfect silence, undistressed
By noise or nightmares, as my breast
   Once held you soft but fast.

This is the Doctor who has brought
Your needle with your special shot
To quiet you; you won't get caught
   Off guard or unprepared.
I am your nurse who'll comfort you;
I nursed you, fed you till you grew
Too big to feed; now you're all through
   Fretting or feeling scared.

This is the glass tube that contains
Calm that will spread down through your veins
To free you finally from all pains
   Of going on in error.
This tiny pinprick sets the germ
Inside you that fills out its term
Till you can feel yourself grow firm
   Against all doubt, all terror.

Into this spoon I break the pill
That stiffens the unsteady will
And hardens you against the chill
   Voice of a world of lies.
This amber medicine implants
Steadfastness in your blood; this grants
Immunity from greed and chance,
   And from all compromise.

This is the serum that can cure
Weak hearts; these pure, clear drops insure
You'll face what comes and can endure
   The test; you'll never falter.
This is the potion that preserves
You in a faith that never swerves;
This sets the pattern of your nerves
   Too firm for you to alter.

I set this spoon between your tight
Teeth, as I gave you your first bite;
This satisfies your appetite
   For other nourishment.
Take this on your tongue; this do
Remembering your mother who
So loved her Leader she stayed true
   When all the others went,

When every friend proved false, in the
Delirium of treachery
On every hand, when even He
   Had turned His face aside.
He shut himself in with His whore;
Then, though I screamed outside His door,
Said He'd not see me anymore.
   They both took cyanide.

Open wide, now, little bird;
I who sang you your first word
Soothe away every sound you've heard
   Except your Leader's voice.
Close your eyes, now; take your death.
Once we slapped you to take breath.
Vengeance is mine, the Lord God saith
   And cancels each last choice.

Once, my first words marked out your mind;
Just as our Leader's phrases bind
All hearts to Him, building a blind
   Loyalty through the nation,
We shape you into a pure form.
Trapped, our best soldiers tricked the storm,
The Reds: those last hours, they felt warm
   Who stood fast to their station.

You needn't fear what your life meant;
You won't curse how your hours were spent;
You'll grow like your own monument
   To all things sure and good,
Fixed like a frieze in high relief
Of granite figures that our Chief
Accepts into His true belief,
   His true blood-brotherhood.

You'll never bite the hand that fed you,
Won't turn away from those that bred you,
Comforted your nights and led you
   Into the thought of virtue;
You won't be turned from your own bed;
Won't turn into that thing you dread;
No new betrayal lies ahead;
   Now no one else can hurt you.

Hermann Göring,
Former Reichsmarschall

—30 April 1945

*(Disowned by Hitler, arrested by S.S.
troops, Göring does not know whether
he will be executed or fall into
American hands. In his castle at
Mauterndorf—left him by his mother's
lover—he stands, naked, before a
full-length bedroom mirror.)*

When I speak to you, you stand to attention.
Straighten that back up. Lift up your damn head.
You'd featherbed your life out on some pension?
Fat chance of that, Fat Man! You're here to die.
You can't haul that much pork up in the sky
And if you go down and you fry instead
You'll spit like bacon. You lost your nerve
To face the life you once had; why not try
Making your exit with some style, some verve?

Disowned and disinherited? Poor baby!
We'll make a man of you, you slab of blubber.
We'll teach you where your toes are, your spine—maybe
Work you back down to fighting weight again.
Go turn in your silk robes, your diamonds, then
Give back all the paintings, cash in your rubber
Medals for the tub. From those big loose dugs
You'll get no warm milk. Join the world of men
Where pain and death live. And check in your drugs.

You might just as well know just what you've done
Though that's not what they'll hang you for.
You took a fine officer's wife and son;
When you came to power you supplied
Facts that got your friend, Roehm, killed. Then you lied
About Blomberg and Fritsch. To start this war,
You threatened to bomb Prague; and your lies scared
Poor old Hacha who gasped, fell, almost died.
Speak up to your Chief, though—you never dared.

No; one more time, you let yourself be mastered
By someone you sucked up to—who used your blind
Faith, used your worst impulses, then the bastard
Took your honor. You bought your consequences.
Let Speer or Funk whimper and whine repentance
Merely to piss in front and crap behind
A few days more. You can't keep all *that* skin;
Keep some honor. You signed on for your sentence;
You're in so deep, there's no out left but in.

Your father lost the good name he'd once owned
By trying to fink out on his own past—
Your mother played whore; he'd ignored, condoned
That, years, to keep his soft life as a vassal
To Dr. Epenstein, lord of this castle
He left you. Well, nice guys finish last
And you're about to finish. Own your own
Decisions; own your men. And if some asshole
Stands to face you down, you stand alone.

HEINRICH·HIMMLER
FORMER·REICHSFUEHRER·SS
—1·MAY·1945·

(Learning that Hitler's will names
Doenitz as successor, Himmler ponders
his alternatives. MM=104.)

AN·EYE-PATCH·THATS·THE·ANSWER·
BESIDES·ILL·SHAVE·MY·MOUSTACHE
CUT·MY·HAIR·ALL·WRONG·THERE·MY
DISGUISE·IS·COMPLETE·ILL·WEAR·
EYEGLASSES·NOT·THIS·PINCE-NEZ·

FALL·INTO·THE·MOBS·OF·REFUGEES
GOING·WEST·IVE·BECOME·HEINRICH
HITZINGER·WITH·THE·LEGITIMATE·
IDENTITY·CARD·OF·A·SOLDIER·WE·
JUST·SHOT·AS·A·DESERTER·STILL·

KROSIG·SAYS·THE·ONLY·HONORABLE
LINE·IS·JUST·DRIVE·STRAIGHT·TO
MONTGOMERYS·H·Q·&·TELL·THEM·MY
NAME·IS·HEINRICH·HIMMLER·I·CAN
OFFER·MY·FORCES·SURRENDER·I·AM

PERSONALLY·RESPONSIBLE·WITHOUT
QUALIFICATION·FOR·ALL·S·S·ACTS
REALLY·NOW·WHY·NOT·JUST·SIMPLY
SHOOT·MYSELF·COULD·WE·GO·NORTH
TO·SCHLESWIG-HOLSTEIN·THEN·SET

UP·AN·S·S·GOVT·WE·MIGHT·OBTAIN
VERY·FAVORABLE·TERMS·FROM·THE·
WEST·SO·THEN·AT·THE·VERY·WORST
YOUD·KEEP·OUT·OF·THE·HANDS·OF·
ZHUKOV·AND·THE·RED·TROOPS·THE·

AMERICANS • OBVIOUSLY • THEY • WOULD
BE • BEST • BUT • WE • HAVE • NO • JEWS • WE
CAN • TRADE • NO • PRISONERS • WE • MUST
DO • WHAT • WE • CAN • TO • CONVINCE • OUR
ENEMIES • THESE • ARE • SUBSTANTIAL •

FORCES • BETTER • YET • WHY • CANT • WE •
GO • TO • FLENSBURG • WITH • DOENITZ • &
HIS • CABINET • HITLERS • WILL • FLUNG
INTO • POWER • LINE • UP • OUR • CARS • &
JOIN • HIS • ENTOURAGE • WHOLL • DARE •

KEEP • US • OUT • BESIDES • NOW • THEYRE
LIKE • ANY • GOVT • THEY • NEED • ARMED •
MEN • TO • STAY • IN • POWER • SO • THEYLL
NEED • US • EVEN • TO • SURRENDER • ILL •
OFFER • MY • SERVICES • AND • DEMAND • A

POST • SAY • HEAD • OF • POLICE • WE • CAN
QUASH • THIS • SO - CALLED • LAST • WILL
REALLY • HES • NOT • BEEN • HIMSELF • MY
STARS • STILL • SAY • I • MUST • SUCCEED
THE • CHIEF • ALTHOUGH • ITS • HARD • TO

UNDERSTAND • HOW • THAT • CAN • BE • SO •
VERY • PUZZLING • STILL • FLENSBURGS
WHERE • YOUR • CHANCE • MAY • COME • OR •
YOU • CAN • ALWAYS • BITE • INTO • THIS •
ZINC • CAPSULE • & • WHAT • WHAT • WHAT •

Dr. Joseph Goebbels

—1 May 1945, 1800 hours

> *(The day after Hitler's death, Goebbels
> and his wife climbed the steps into the
> garden where both committed suicide.)*

Say goodbye to the help, the ranks
Of Stalin-bait. Give too much thanks
To Naumann—Magda's lover: we
Thank him for *all* his loyalty.
Schwaegermann; Rach. After a while
Turn back to them with a sad smile:
We'll save them trouble—no one cares
Just now to carry us upstairs.

Turn away; check your manicure;
Pull on your gloves. Take time; make sure
The hat brim curves though the hat's straight.
Give her your arm. Let the fools wait;
They act like they've someplace to go.
Take the stairs, now. Self-control. Slow.
A slight limp; just enough to see,
Pass on, and infect history.

The rest is silence. Left like sperm
In a stranger's gut, waiting its term,
Each thought, each step lies; the roots spread.
They'll believe in us when we're dead.
When we took "Red Berlin" we found
We always worked best underground.
So; the vile body turns to spirit
That speaks soundlessly. They'll hear it.

If Birds Build
with Your Hair

A Phoebe's Nest

This green is the green of live moss;
This gray is the breast-feathers' down;
This tan, tough vine-roots;
This brown, dead needles of longleaf pine;

And this, this coppery fine filament
That glints like the light-weight wire
Boys wind off a motor core,
This is my own love's hair.

It's 7% and escrow;
It's Mary Jane and despair;
The ancient aunts say: headaches if
Birds build with your hair.

Near our hedgerow, in a nest snarled
Like a fright-wig, young hawks shriek;
Great red-tails sail our winds all day
While small birds peck at their heads.

But under our kitchen floorboards
Where live wires wind through the dark
Our crewcut phoebe plaited this nest
Like a jetset high pompadour.

Will the birds get dandruff?
Or pubic lice?
Will we go bald as an egg?

They'll knit a fine pucket
To warm up their brats;
You'll find out what'll ache.

This oriole's basket is woven white
Hair of our wolfhound, gone for years;
Our walls are rough plaster, laced with
The oxen's manes that worked this place.

Up under our roofpeak, birds slip
Through the roughcut cherry and beech;
Bare yards over the head of our bed
Strange bills squabble and screech.

It's Starlings stuck down the chimney;
It's where did you go? Nowhere.
It's peckerholes in the siding
And why did you park there?
It's swallows barnstorming the garage.
Things get in your hair.

Sometimes you find the young birds
Gone; other times they're dead;
Ones that stay faithfulest to their nest
Just somehow never got fed. Yet

Nerve ends circuit a memory;
Phone calls lattice the night;
That phoebe shuttled our cellardoor
All day every day of her life.

Some say better not get involved;
   Send Hallmark if you care;
Some say they've come a long way
   And haven't got much to spare;
Some say they're gonna have some fun;
   Too bad you don't dare;
Some say it just isn't fair;
   It stretches but it well might tear;
Get nylon or get wash-and-wear;
   They want their fair share.

Polish ciocias, toothless flirts
   Whose breasts dangle down to there,
Triple sea-hags say: headaches if
   Birds build with your hair.

Still, my lady's brushing-in sunlight
Near our silver maples where,
Like Christmas strings or bright beadwork
We loop loose strands of her hair.

Old Apple Trees

Like battered old millhands, they stand in the orchard—
Like drunk legionnaires, heaving themselves up,
Lurching to attention. Not one of them wobbles
The same way as another. Uniforms won't fit them—
All those cramps, humps, bulges. Here, a limb's gone;
There, rain and corruption have eaten the whole core.
They've all grown too tall, too thick, or too something.
Like men bent too long over desks, engines, benches,
Or bent under mailsacks, under loss.
They've seen too much history and bad weather, grown
Around rocks, into high winds, diseases, grown
Too long to be willful, too long to be changed.

Oh, I could replant, bulldoze the lot,
Get nursery stock, all the latest ornamentals,
Make the whole place look like a suburb,
Each limb sleek as a teeny bopper's—pink
To the very crotch—each trunk smoothed, ideal
As the fantasy life of an adman.
We might just own the Arboreal Muscle Beach:
Each tree disguised as its neighbor. Or each disguised
As if not its neighbor—each doing its own thing
Like executives' children.

                                    At least I could prune,
At least I should trim the dead wood; fill holes
Where rain collects and decay starts. Well, I should;
I should. There's a red squirrel nests here someplace.
I live in the hope of hearing one saw-whet owl.
Then, too, they're right about Spring. Bees hum
Through these branches like lascivious intentions. The white
Petals drift down, sift across the ground; this air's so rich
No man should come here except on a working pass;
No man should leave here without going to confession.
All Fall, apples nearly crack the boughs;
They hang here red as candles in the
White oncoming snow.

Tonight we'll drive down to the bad part of town
To the New Hungarian Bar or the Klub Polski,
To the Old Hellas where we'll eat the new spring lamb;
Drink good *mavrodaphne*, say, at the Laikon Bar,
Send drinks to the dancers, those meatcutters and laborers
Who move in their native dances, the archaic forms.
Maybe we'll still find our old crone selling chestnuts,
Whose toothless gums can spit out fifteen languages,
Who turns, there, late at night, in the center of the floor,
Her ancient dry hips wheeling their slow, slow *tsamikos*;
We'll stomp under the tables, whistle, we'll all hiss
Till even the belly dancer leaves, disgraced.

We'll drive back, lushed and vacant, in the first dawn;
Out of the light gray mists may rise our flowering
Orchard, the rough trunks holding their formations
Like elders of Colonus, the old men of Thebes
Tossing their white hair, almost whispering,

179

Soon, each one of us will be taken
By dark powers under this ground
That drove us here, that warped us.
Not one of us got it his own way.
Nothing like any one of us
Will be seen again, forever.
Each of us held some noble shape in mind.
It seemed better that we kept alive.

Cherry Saplings

—for Russ

You turn your back on them no more
   Than for ten seconds—somebody's got to them.
Weed trees crop up, shadowing them under,
   Tent worms or aphids waste the leaves,
Rot leaches down from a torn branch,
   Woodrats gnaw them, girdle them around.
Take the whole Fall setting them in
   Sunlight, shaping, firming in their soil,
Come Springtime, find some Skidoo
   Snapped them clean off, back to the root.

When white men came to the continent
   First, they grew four feet through the trunk.
Try buying some new cherry, say,
   Six inches wide. Oh, you can find
The old boards still—whole table tops—
   The way you'll still see chestnut cupboards
Or find cross-grained elm chairs for some
   Years yet. We're good and done, though, with
Those broadest old trees, with the tallest.
   Cherries; these are merely the loveliest.

You'd think it was hard for them to take.
   They used it up in horse stalls, barn planks;
That curving tough grain went to roof in
   Dry lives, got buried in the walls
That fixed their hungers, their old wounds, their pride.
   That long-hardened heartwood with its clear
Rays quartering, spreading from the core,
   The ways they stained it—dried milk, dried blood,
Tobacco juice—until it gave way
   To the numbed image ruling their desires.

You'd think they thought it had grown too fine.
  They *never* thought of it. They had their dream.
The saplings stay, though, small stands of them,
  Or alone, there, under other trees,
The satiny red bark, the blown white flowers,
  Their thin trunks leaning outward, outward,
Feeling toward some memory of sun. It is
  Too late to cable them back upright,
Too late to cut down anything around.
  We have no right but to our own grounds.
What will we leave here still worth our hate?

Owls

—for Camille

Wait; the great horned owls
Calling from the wood's edge; listen.
There: the dark male, low
And booming, tremoring the whole valley.
There: the female, resolving, answering
High and clear, restoring silence.
The chilly woods draw in
Their breath, slow, waiting, and now both
Sound out together, close to harmony.

These are the year's worst nights.
Ice glazed on the top boughs,
Old snow deep on the ground,
Snow in the red-tailed hawks'
Nests they take for their own.
Nothing crosses the crusted ground.
No squirrels, no rabbits, the mice gone,
No crow has young yet they can steal.
These nights the iron air clangs
Like the gates of a cell block, blank
And black as the inside of your chest.

Now, the great owls take
The air, the male's calls take
Depth on and resonance, they take
A rough nest, take their mate
And, opening out long wings, take
Flight, unguided and apart, to caliper
The blind synapse their voices cross
Over the dead white fields,
The dead black woods, where they take
Soundings on nothing fast, take
Soundings on each other, each alone.

An Elm Tree

—in memory of Albert Herrick

The winter birds have come;
One of them knows my name:
    Chick-a-dee-dee-dee-dee-dee.
Now, a whole pack of them

Skinning past like hoods;
Up in the maples, hidden,
    One shuffles his deck of wings
And deals me a word, a word;

Then, like a struck spark, gone.
Yet, there's my sentence again
    From an oak branch overhead;
Another one, farther on

Jeers me behind the barn
Where the old path turns
    Past the smoldering mound
Where years of rubbish burn,

And out beyond to the grove
Of pine trees, chill as the grave,
    Where the sun's light never falls
But needles, steady as grief,

Sift up, muffling and soft,
The lower limbs crack off,
    And you sink halfway to the knee
In what shone green, aloft,

What will seep down and in
Before it sees light again.
    You *could* stop, but the bird
Says your name, then

You come out into the whole
Light of day on the hill
    Where, on the high cleared brow
Strongly arching still

Stands that blighted elm,
Rawboned, overwhelmed,
    Stripped like the old mad king
Of this vegetable realm.

This was your great-uncle's tree
That he watered every day—
    30 buckets and the spring
Half a mile away.

The leaves gone and the bark.
As if a man stood, stark,
    Till all had fallen away
But the nerves' field thrown on the dark

Woods behind his back.
A small boy, you came to the shack
    Where he lived alone on his land;
You felt ashamed and sick

At the dark, heavy stain
On your thin wrist all day
    After he shook your hand.
May that not wash away.

Coming Down from the Acropolis

We bent our backs, the two of us, climbing
    That stony yellow hillside, together, to the
Cleared high ground. Already we had climbed
    Castle hills, climbed *schloss, grad* and *var,*
The Kehlstein above Berchtesgaden, Rakoczi's Bastion,
    Traced bullet-pocked walls, the charred siege-gates,
The low, sodden death-camps, gray with horror.
    Here we had arrived at the ancient, sacred ring
Where the West turned from its wars to raise
    White marble, ordinate and clean as
Nursery furniture. Here, every line, every measure
    Led the eye to its security, to its calm.
And this had nourished the thinking of all Europe.
    Of course the temple roof is gone; its stone images
Stripped. The altar ground lies open to rain; it cannot
    Be visited. At random, some unbearing columns stand
Like an elm grove, blighted. Cigar butts underfoot,
    Used Kodak wrappers, orange peels, old drums of marble
Each-which-way like a Scrabble set somebody dropped.
    Below us, the new Athens smoked and clattered, living
Off this dead trunk to support its tourists' light shows,
    Its miles of huckster shops, its bouzoukee joints.
In those public squares where excellence defined itself,
    Impotent crowds brag of their freedom, argue policy;
They cringe under a tyrant-clown propped up in place
    By our own CIA. How quick, how easy the decline,
How quickly they forgot, hot for a different vision.
    They chose and, choosing, took the thief, the liar,
And felt at home with that. Phidias, whose hand carved it,
    Died in their jails. They turned from Pericles, turned
On their own; Greek fought with Greek or sold
    His skill to strangers, to his enemies. And all that time,
We both knew that our own state would choose the same.
    When we came back down to the foot, we sat, together,
On a fallen stone. We said some few, some ugly words
    Then turned our backs; each took his separate way.

Setting Out

Staying here, we turn inflexible,
Stiffening under laws that drive
Sap through the tight stems,
Roots to break down rock;
Relentless as the fall
Of rhymes in a folk ballad.
You are called toward someone free
To come or go as the wind's whim,
Casual as the air whistles,
Trembling all that stands with
Mortal touch, while your hand
Slips through every which way.

Here, we find ourselves unstable
As our fields: crops, cloud-
shadows wash across us;
The various weed-flowers fade
To flat snow; dogs tear
Our deer; streams flow again . . .
You are drawn to someone constant
As a room where the costly wallpaper
Blooms in half-light,
Where at last somebody dearly
Loved is always almost
Ready to appear.

We know we turn exacting,
Monotonous as the hours
Wheel, as the seasons
Wheel, as the arrogant
Stars turn wheeling on their
Cold, determined track.
Go, then, find someone tender
As a child's eyelid closing
In his first sleep, shy
As the warm scent we all seek,
That mild and absent voice
Numbing the sense away.

Perhaps, who knows, in so much
Searching you may not be lost;
Paths you take may take you
Into comfort past our thought;
It may be the finding
Won't enervate your grasp.
You can find us here, still
Going about our rounds,
Fingering out the beat
Of old songs, fixed on ways
Worn out as a star chart,
Unimaginably far.

Seasoning Barn

—for Roy Sheldon

Here in the darkness of these dry, bird-sounding lofts,
The rough thick boards, sawn and stacked up, lie
Under the dusts that sift down over them
                fifteen, maybe twenty years.
It's echoing here, as cool as a catacombs and,
Truly, they are one company of the elect—
Their generation gone into firewood and to rot.
The tides that have broken over them, coursed through them,
Which they were made to carry, gradually go out;
They keep some movement still, a reverberation:
They shrink a little, draw into themselves
Till they turn harder, more virtual, so lighter,
Till they reach their balance with the air.

They are like mirrors reflecting on themselves all night,
As if we thought about our dreams until our dreams
Had dreams about their dreaming.

They lie here, though, as dull as gray old ledgerbooks
Someone's forgotten in a back angle of some attic,
Dull as old *Life*s, bound, laid up in a library,
Dull as mud samplings, as another language.
                Yet, to the right eye, closed
On the accounts, extortions, strategies lives are built by:
Here are the crimes and follies, the beliefs and lies;
Here, the old injuries, the wretchedness when young, forced growth,
Diseases, aims and accidents, the reachings out that
Failed and were buried, live, in the living knots;
Here, in the dark, these change toward changelessness.

Until the right eye and the right hand comes,
The old man with his cat,
                              and lifts them out of here.
He is not looking for the clear, straight grain—
The single consistent color. Leave that to the factories;
It might as well be stained. He's searching
For the sworls and twists, for those deep flaws that mean
Character in the finished work—pithmarks and ingrowings.
He cuts down through the surface; his radio fills the barn with,
Strangely, Brahms. His sure abrasive touch
Will open out, irregular as high-tide marks, telling
As a thumbprint, the topographies of growth: here
Are the open rings of Springtime and the solid summers;
Here the light sapwood, here the heavier, dark heartwood;
Under his hand the darkest knots take on a deeper burnish.
And in some few he can hope to find that luminous figuring
Of the rays that stored and carried sustenance out to the growing edge,
Inward to the core.
                       When he has shaped and planed these, he will sand
And rub by hand, building a finish, hour after hour.

And the old man sits down, rubbing the cat's ears,
Or hikes up his suspenders and walks home.

A
Locked House

Silver Poplars

That winking, glimmering like the wings
    of starlings in their dark flock, wheeling
        into the last light, into the light breeze;
that shivering like lake ripples, like sequins
    on a black lace veil that half reveals
        some face which, loveliest, lies beneath;
that soft shade we once sat to read in
    afternoons, and on then, on through evenings
        one with that tremulous, steady breath;
that giving, true to each slightest wind's
    least impulse, caught where the leaf
        yields up its pale down, underneath:—

done for, gone, down in one night's storm
    to close out twenty-five years' growing,
        gone, that we had meant to stand
watch at our dooryard, to stand firm
    through even its own changing—green,
        yellow, bare, then green again—to stand
for us. For what stands. What rainfall then turned
    stiff that bitter midnight, all unseen,
        glazed and enameled every stunned
numb leaf and twig? By dawn, the whole frame burned
    rigid with enchantment. Each sinew strained,
        shuddering, determined, but the charged tree bent
and shattered. In full daylight, one, torn
    out like a mind from its own ground
        of understanding, sprawled its full length;
split down the main trunk, skewed like some deformed
    drunk lurching through the park, the second
        wears out a sort of half-life to its end.

Not much you can do with it; tends to splinter
    on you, check or twist, suppose it's been left
        years to season. Chainsaw; stack the leavings
against chill mornings, what with winter
    coming on. For all that figured grain, too soft
        to last long; too soft for much real heating.

Mutability

It was all different; that, at least, seemed sure.
We still agreed—but only that she'd changed.
Some things that you still loved might still endure.

You woke in your own, big, dove-tailed bed, secure
And warm—but the whole room felt rearranged.
It was all different; that, at least, seemed sure.

The lamp stood four-square—like your furniture;
The air'd gone tinged, though, or the light deranged.
Some things that you still loved might still endure

Outside. Your fields stretched, a parched upland moor
Where shadows paired and split, where lean shapes ranged.
It was all different; that, at least, seemed sure

And that, from here on in, you could count on fewer
Second chances. Some rules might be arranged;
Some things that you still loved might still endure,

Though some old friends would close, soon, for the pure
Joy of the kill—no prisoners exchanged.
It was all different; that, at least, seemed sure.

Maybe the injuries weren't past all cure.
No luck lasts; yours might not, too long, stay estranged;
Some things that you still loved might still endure.
It was all different; that, at least, seemed sure.

The Last Time

Three years ago, one last time, you forgot
Yourself and let your hand, all gentleness,
Move to my hair, then slip down to caress
My cheek, my neck. My breath failed me; I thought

It might all come back yet, believed you might
Turn back. You turned, then, once more to your own
Talk with that tall young man in whom you'd shown,
In front of all our friends, such clear delight

All afternoon. You recalled, then, the long
Love you had held for me was changed. You threw
Both arms around him, kissed him, and then you
Said you were ready and we went along.

A Locked House

As we drove back, crossing the hill,
The house still
Hidden in the trees, I always thought—
A fool's fear—that it might have caught
Fire, someone could have broken in.
As if things must have been
Too good here. Still, we always found
It locked tight, safe and sound.

I mentioned that, once, as a joke;
No doubt we spoke
Of the absurdity
To fear some dour god's jealousy
Of our good fortune. From the farm
Next door, our neighbors saw no harm
Came to the things we cared for here.
What did we have to fear?

Maybe I should have thought: all
Such things rot, fall—
Barns, houses, furniture.
We two are stronger than we were
Apart; we've grown
Together. Everything we own
Can burn; we know what counts—some such
Idea. We said as much.

We'd watched friends driven to betray;
Felt that love drained away
Some self they need.
We'd said love, like a growth, can feed
On hate we turn in and disguise;
We warned ourselves. That you might despise
Me—hate all we both loved best—
None of us ever guessed.

The house still stands, locked, as it stood
Untouched a good
Two years after you went.
Some things passed in the settlement;
Some things slipped away. Enough's left
That I come back sometimes. The theft
And vandalism were our own.
Maybe we should have known.

A Seashell

Say that inside this shell, some live
Thing hungered, trembled to survive,
Mated, died. Lift this to your ear
The way the young, on tape decks, hear
What to become, or on the phone,
The old evoke a dial tone
To what they had. Your blood will pound
Down those bare chambers, then resound
Your own ear's caverns as a ground

Bass swells, the depths of some salt tide
Still tuned to our salt blood. Outside,
The woods, nights, still ring back each word.
Our young owl, though, that always heard
My hoot, then veered down through the dark,
Our fox that barked back when we'd bark,
Won't answer, though. Small loss, now, when
Friends ask that I not call again.
Our pulse homed in on each other's, then.

Last night, I heard your voice—caught on
Streets we once taped in Isfahan;
Then, in a mosque near Joppa, blent
With hushed devotions and lament.
Now, put the shell back down, at rest
Near this brain coral, this wren's nest,
These photographs that will stand here
On their shelf in the silent, dear,
Locked, empty house another year.

Old Jewelry

This Gypsy bodice of old coins
    From seven countries, woven fast
So that a silver braidwork joins
    The years and places their tribe passed;

This crown-shaped belt, cast in Soufli—
    Jeweled, enameling on silver-gilt—
A trothplight, then that surety
    On which a family would be built;

This Roman fibula, intact
    From the fourth century though bent;
This Berber fibula, once blacked
    With layers of thick tar to prevent

Theft but that, scoured and polished, shone
    As luminous as it ever was;
This lapis, Persian, the unfading stone
    Gold-flecked and implicate with flaws;

Brass arm bands, rings, pins, bracelets, earrings—
    Something from nearly every place
We'd been. Once more to see these dear things
    Laid out for buyers in a glass showcase.

I'd known them, each one—weighed in hand,
    Rubbed, bargained, and then with my love,
Pinned each one on for her, to stand
    In fickle times for emblems of

What lasts—just as they must have once
    For someone long dead. Love that dies
Can still be wrung out for quick funds;
    No doubt someone would pay the price.

A Valediction

Since his sharp sight has taught you
To think your own thoughts and to see
What cramped horizons my arms brought you,
    Turn then and go free,

Unlimited, your own
Forever. Let your vision be
In your own interests; you've outgrown
    All need for tyranny.

May his clear views save you
From those shrewd, undermining powers
That hold you close just to enslave you
    In some such love as ours.

May this new love leave you
Your own being; may your bright rebirth
Prove treacherous, change then and deceive you
    Never on this earth.

Now that you've seen how mindless
Our long ties were, I pray you never
Find, all your life through, such a blindness
    As we two shared together.

My dark design's exposed
Since his tongue opened up your eyelids;
May no one ever lip them closed
    So cunningly as I did.

D. D. Byrde
Callyng
Jennie Wrenn

—for K. T. Browne

Deare wee Browne Byrdie, dare wee too
    Hazzerd an aire togeather?—
A perkie Maytime chickke like yew,
    Me in my frosstie feather?

I bee noe Admirabl Byrde
    Yet sailed the Polar Blizzerd,
Frose all my tose upp and incurred
    Muche miserie in my gizzerd.

Above those icie glares these goggels
    Dimmed thru winters fiftie;
Now mine eye dazzels, my sight boggels:—
    Yea, Byrdie, thou art niftie!

Thy spruce bright eye and bubbelie tonge
    Like gin upspike my tonick,
Surcharginge my Septembre Songe
    To pulse fowrth supersonick.

Thy pert bobtaile and sundrie pritties
    Brim this olde craw to flowe
With Springtime's light, lassivius ditties
    That state: "Byrdes mate, you noe?"

Com sing beside me; fetche thy bottel
    Of joye's best anti-freese;
Torch upp my pipes; pull out my throttel;
    Sparke these darke synapsees.

These shivverie drye bones yearn to test
  A cosy brest of browne
Where deep limb-tangel snugs thy nest
  And feathers are alle downe.

Ginnie Jen, Ginnie Jen, come juice upp these joints;
  De-ice these rime-tipt wings;
Race my pace-maker, gapp my points—
  We'll try som cuppel sings.

O ginnie Jennie, June's long passt
  For stiff olde joints like these;
Still, olde stiff joints could learn to lasst
  Wert thou a chickke-a-dee's.

What iff lean, hawkish sharp-shinnd Age
  Fixxeth me in his sights?
This olde pump's rattelinge its cage
  Too try yewnited flights.

Tho I, in my Lone Rangyr Masque,
  Soon soloe into som sunsett,
Dare famelie, frends or strangyrs ask
  Uss not to duet oncet?

Since soleful witt must needs bee briefe,
  Let me noe more waxxe wordie:
If *yew* don't mind, I'd just as lief;
  Ten-fowr to thee, Browne Byrdie.

Kinder Capers

The poems in Kinder Capers
are related to paintings
by DeLoss McGraw

Through the Nursery Window

—for Dylan Taylor McGraw

There, there, sir. You have every cause
For tears; which of us blames your grief?
Knowing what high estate you've lost,
What powers, what opulence you leave,

That you must give up absolute
Dominion, sole rule of a spot
Where all desires, even your slightest
Wish before that wish was thought

Was satisfied, where you commanded
All breathing things in pashadom
And empiry safe and sure, a land
Which was, in brief, the paradigm

Of every human heart's least earthly
Paradise—how this could be torn
By gross upheaval against your worthy
Person and sweet governance, could turn

You out of doors, roughly . . . dear sir,
To banish you, unknown, abandoned
By followers, washed up on this shore
With no funds, not a leg to stand on,

Helpless to feed and clothe your poor
Small self—truly, it would be best
To think of other matters. Spare
Your eyes, your breath. Try; try to rest.

Have patience with your temporary
Poor berth; we've filled out all your papers
To leave this general dormitory
For what suits with your rank and nature.

A lovely woman, a brilliant man
Will shelter and guard you, help you learn
Your new name, learn our tongue and manners,
Learn that a living can be earned.

If this is not, dear sir, Illyria,
It has its range of choices, freedom
To follow whatever calls might lure you
Into the bounties rude coasts can afford.

You may find, soon, that old life bland,
Short on challenge, too confining for you.
We need your wits, charm, ambition, and
The wilderness lies all before you . . .

True, things may never seem so lovely
From now on. Still, a sort of life
Exists; things can get somewhat lively
Picnicking with our half a loaf

And chipped wine jug. Some have felt glad
They'd set foot over this dark sill.
May your new family have a good
Baby; you have a good exile.

Part I
The Death
of
Cock Robin

The Charges Against Cock Robin

Speaker: His Honor James T. "Just
call me Jim" Crowe.

Chorus: Titmouse and Dormouse, Eagle
and Seagull, Cuckoo and Water Shrew.

It is charged he's been known to warble
(Deplorable!)
An aria, a love song, or recitatif
(Good Grief!)
When he goes walking, long after curfew
(God preserve you!)
Waking both town and country.
(What effrontery!)

We find it far more injurious
(We're just furious!)
That he sings beyond other birds' range
(He's strange!)
Though they practice and pay the best teachers
(Poor creatures!)
While his tunes baffle us and defeat us.
(Elitist!)

Moreover, he dresses in a fashion
(Far too dashing!)
Neither generic nor respectable—
(Get expectable!)
All sorts of bright shreds and patches
(Nothing matches!)
That make no more sense than cuneiform.
(Get a uniform!)

If one wishes to sound operatic
                    (We're emphatic!)
Or to break forth with a cantata
                    (All birds oughta)
Always be careful to bring along
                    (Like a singalong)
Fitting clothes and a high-sounding moral.
                    (Get oral; get choral; wax floral!)

He is urged by us birds of one stripe
                    (Be our type!)
And enjoined by us cats of one color
                    (Get duller!)
Be a horse of one congruous feather.
                    (All together.)
Cease these lyrics of lust, rum and riot
                    (Keep it quiet!)
And incitements to profligate violence.
                    (Silence!)

W. D., Don't Fear That Animal

My hat leaps up when I behold
  A rhino in the sky;
When crocodiles upon the wing
Perch on my windowsill to sing
All my loose ends turn blue and cold;
      I don't know why.

My knuckles whiten should I hark
  Some lonely python's cry;
Should a migrating wedge of moose
Honk, it can shake my molars loose—
Or when, at heaven's gate, the shark
      Doth pine and sigh.

My socks may slide off at the sight
  Of giant squids on high
Or baby scorpions bubbling up
Inside my morning coffee cup—
Somehow, it spoils my appetite;
      My throat gets dry.

At dawn, I lift my gaze in air
  Cock Robin to espy
And mark instead some bright-eyed grizzly;
The hairs back of my neck turn bristly.
That's foolish since it's clear that they're
      More scared than I.

Such innocent creatures mean no harm;
  They wouldn't hurt a fly.
Still, when I find myself between a
Playful assembly of hyena,
I can't help feeling some alarm;
  I've got to try.

W. D. Lifts Ten Times
the Weight of
His Own Body

1.

These Russian heavies are all wrong
On force and form. No doubt they're strong
But if you turn into a hulk
Of mass and muscle, your own bulk
Can drop you into a deep oxtrap:
You lift yourself by your own jockstrap
Besides those weights you jerk and press;
So it's essential to weigh less,
Embodying uplift and *ballon*.
The way these Russians put weight on
You'd think it's going out of style. It's gone.

One lad I knew hefted a heifer
Daily; it grew light as a zephyr
Even when swollen to its full
Beefy bloatitude as a bull.
Myself, I uphold every day
The self-same load, but meanwhile weigh
Less than I did the day before.
Like ants, I now tote ten times more
Than my own tonnage. At the gym
I pare myself down, airier, slim,
Till I become a 98-
Pound Charles, at last, of underweight.
An auto-hoist, combating gravity,
I rise up in high spirits and levity,
Unbending my irreverent knee
To overcome brute force and mightiness;
Getting things off the ground takes flightiness.

2.

Snodgrass's Second Theorem states: You're
Stronger when bending to things' nature.
Don't lift; release things toward the skies—
Release what's meant, or means, to rise.
Raise jackstraws, piles of pickup sticks,
Spokes, pikes and pickets, spikes, toothpicks;
Raise kite sticks, stalks, struts, Roman candles,
Rays of bright sunlight, hafts, helves, handles;
Raise vaulters' poles, Olympic javelin
Shafts, sword strokes, streaks of starlight traveling
Through black wastes; raise up jet trails, tracers;
Raise fish rods, bike spokes, lances, lasers.
Be one with all things light and luminous
Like a Zen sage or some old Humanist
Whose drive to transport and to heighten meant
Shouldering a general Enlightenment.
Now, like a Chinese waiter, scoop
This universal mare's nest soup
To shoulder level, all the while
A fat moon peering through the pile
And cosmic tangle has to smile
To see Cock Robin, calm, at rest
And sleeping sound in that vast nest
Or twiggy burden, borne along
The steady airstream on a strong
Dream's wingbeat or on springs of song.

W. D. Is Concerned About the
Character Assassination of Cock Robin

Yo no quiero verla;
Yo no lo se.

Come, Rosie Angel, clasp
   Over each eye, each ear,
Your gauze-soft hands that grasp
   What not to see or hear.

     Don't care to,
     Won't dare to,
     Can't bear to
       See.

Should the secret inspectors
   Knock once at your locked door,
Not even bill collectors
   Know your name any more.

     Don't choose to,
     Refuse to,
     No use to
       Hear.

As your stock falls, old friends
   Fall off. Fall into danger—
If you survive depends
   On some total stranger.

Past all thought;
Best forgot.
Surely not
Here.

Small wonder dear friends turn
  Acrimonious and cruel
When Love's most fierce fires burn
  Denatured hate for fuel.

Never more,
Neither nor,
Not friend or
Foe.

All you once knew goes strange.
  Some you've known all their lives
Outside your window range,
  Tongues flashing slick as knives

Numb, deaf, blind;
May we find
No man's mind
So.

Where Cock Robin's once-loved name
  Sank like fat in the sands
And his good neighbors came
  Licking their snouts and hands.

I'd deceive
All who'd grieve.
Come; believe
Me.

A face, now, fixed with wide
Open eyes, constantly
Loitering near outside,
Keeps close watch over me.

No, never;
Nerves, sever;
Don't ever
Know.

Yo no quiero verla;
Yo no lo se.

Lullaby:
The Comforting of Cock Robin

Smooth quill and bristle down;
Soothe day's shrill whistle down;
Bestow the head
To its own bed
Of soft moss and thistledown.

May the insatiable powers,
The vast cravings of the dark,
Spend their forces and their hours
Each on each, or miss their mark;

May the raccoon and the agile
Long-tailed, long-toothed squirrel pass,
Find the fox and miss the fragile
Clutch of eggs in the long grass.

May the weasel, the lithe snake,
May the housecat on the prowl,
Creeping up the limbs all night,
Meet and satisfy the owl.

Let the shivering eyelid close,
The down-surrounded egg, turn in
On the steady urge that grows
What might be from what has been

Till beneath the illusory lamps,
Burned out, the hankering moth miller
Sprawls, and toward fresh new green leaves tramps
The lockstep, workday caterpillar

While, fresh, the sprinkler on the lawn
    Lures the young, nutritious worm
To loll and sunbathe in the dawn,
    Plump, seductive, pink and firm.

Then shall your well-supported song,
    Drafting the full breath's thermal currents,
Carry the mastered woodlands, strong
    With portamento, with endurance.

        Smooth quill and bristle down;
        Soothe day's shrill whistle down;
           Bestow the head
            To its own bed
        Of soft moss and thistledown.

W. D. Tries to
Warn Cock Robin

The Brutish are coming; the Brutish;
The Rude-Coats with snares and bum-drumming!
> The Skittish and Prudish
> The Brattish and Crude
> Who'll check on your morals
> And find your song's lewd
Then strip off the bay leaves and laurels
That garnished your brows and your food,
All tongues and all tastebuds benumbing.
> They'll dull all your senses
> Then lull your defenses
And rule you through blue-nosed and tasteless pretenses;
> The Brutish!

The Ruffians are coming; the Ruffians!
Those rowdies with mandolins strumming!
> They'll stomp out your stuffings
> And all you've been taught;
> Pan-Slobs from Vulgaria
> Will come; if you're caught
Knowing more than your own name, they'll bury you.
Inter your own brain, so they'll not
Take more than your watch and your plumbing.
> Those red-necked invaders,
> Those radical raiders
Who'll root out free thinkers, free lovers, free traders!
> The Ruffians!

The Merkans are coming; the Merkans!
Those jingoes whose jingles keep gumming
      Your intimate workings
      With terms periphrastic;
      The fare that they offer
      Will ruin your gastric
Intestinal tract; then they'll cover
Your country with asphalt and plastic
To hide what keeps oozing and scumming.
      They'll plug up your juices,
      Slipcover your sluices,
Then turn your equipment to mercantile uses,
      The Merkans!

The Krishans are coming; the Krishans!
Hear the chants, psalms and hymns they keep humming!
      They'll offer you visions
      Of undying blisses
      With premises, promises,
      And crucifixes
To prop up all Questioning Thomases.
They'll double criss-cross you with kisses
And blessings. With grim mimes and mumming,
      The hairy one omming,
      The balded ones psalming,
      With rituals and riddles
      And charity victuals,
You'll jump into hellfire to get off their griddle;
      The Krishans!

The Youmans are coming; the Youmans!
Hear the backslapping rascals, the chumming
      Of Masculs and Woomans
      Who built up this Babel
      Of Atoms and Evils
      And hope that they're able
To raise further cain and upheavals.
That Garden foreclosed in the fable
Foretold how this world's going slumming:
      In cold greed, the cowards
      Still split and unite
      For unneeded powers,
      While backbiting spite
      Pulls down all their towers;
      With air, sea and soil
      And their own minds to spoil
And spin their bright cosmos to unending night;
      The Youmans!

W. D. Meets Mr. Evil
while Removing
the Record of Bartok
and Replacing It with
a Recent Recording
by the Everly Brothers
in Order to Create a Mood
Conducive to Searching
for Cock Robin

So; caught you in, my fine young fellow?
Thought I'd just drop past to say Hello,
Dish out some hot poop—how to find
The outlawed Redbreast on your mind:
His Cockiness whose Robinhood
Echoes the Forest of Sure Would.

I know *you*, though. Just call me Mystery
Bill, B.S., M.S. in doctored History,
Onetime Sheriff of Nothing Am,
Ambassador of Havasham,
Last Past Master of Hoke Lodge,
High Priest and Medium for Mirage.

First off, we've got to change the record—
Such grim sounds evidence a checkered
Past—then concoct an atmosphere full
Of hopeful tunes, loving and cheerful.
Dump these sour tones, this cleverly infernal
Dissonance; we'll choir forth an Everly eternal

Psalm of unchanging Brotherhood,
Fake chords real folks would like real good,
Cut platters of pattering platitudes
To impart the politic, pat attitudes
Taught by our founder, Dr. Garbles,
Who struck dumb multitudes with marbles

Held in mouthfuls of popular melody.
Or better still, this high fidelity
Digital of an eighteen minute
Gap: you'll feel, each time you spin it,
Pure as a Quaker, freed from violence
And expletives by blissful silence.

To lure down this bird you desire
We'll mute our loot, moot every liar,
Ban all Anacreonisms or Sapphics
Then chart this on our phoni-Graphics,
Banish gloom, gravity and art talk.
Besides, we'll lie about the Bartok.

W. D. Attempts
to Save Cock Robin

no sir i would not like to sell
this bird for soup yes sonnie i have heard
the polish joke and yes i know
the bird says get this joker
off my ass and indeed professor i have
seen that rembrandt with the small dog
shitting in the foreground so if you
could just inform me señor who
might own this bird or where it lives
or merely point me toward a
doctor and no fraulein kindly not
to a psychiatrist the bird
is real and heavy and the blood
gets down my neck mon capitaine but no
i am not familiar with the
napoleonic code so would you
please remove those handcuffs and
believe me no i do not have
a songbird license since quamlibet i
shot not this bird is there a
real need you behind the mask there
to lock me in this cage you see
WELL
i was practicing for
oberammergau and in this country
wood is too expensive for a cross

Coroner's Inquest

Who killed Cock Robin?
Don't you blyme me, says the sparrow;
I gone strictly straight-and-narrow,
Reformed, true-blue, a real straight arrow.
I never done that slob in.

Who saw him die?
Not I, certainly, says the fly;
My dear, this polyhedral eye
Can only make things out nearby.
I mind my own bee's wax; that's my
Alibi.

Who'll wash the body?
We know too well, says the raccoon,
He sang low songs, played the buffoon
In many a road house or saloon
From bawdy midnight to high noon.
It's only fitting that so soon
He's left lowdown and cruddy.

Who'll weave his shroud?
Our local folkarts, says the spider,
Are unbecoming an outsider
Or untraditional fore-slider
Who's rejected every guide or
Guideline, led by spiritual pride or
Sensual passion through a wider
World than we're allowed.

Who'll dig his grave?
I'm committed, says the mole,
To exploring my own hole
Liberated from control
Of any social, prefixed role;
I keep my deep molehood whole
Seeking my true self and soul.
My blind eye's fixed on this goal;
Go find a cave.

Who'll bear his casket?
Count me out there, says the ant.
I'm too small; I simply can't.
With my legion friends, I grant
We might, yet we're all adamant
That unless he should recant
Each lewd song and surreal chant
With their sly, anarchic slant,
Even if we could we shan't
So don't ask it.

Who'll say the last words?
Of course I'd like to, says the parrot;
I'm aware that all his merit
Was so rare we can't compare it,
Yet my grief and great despair at
This sad loss, if I should share it,
Is so vast, I couldn't bear it.
Then besides, my friends don't care at
All for anyone who'd dare it.
Those that sing strange songs inherit
Faint praise—few and fast words.

All the beasts of earth and air
   Fell a-weaselin' and a-bobbin'
When they heard of the death
   Of poor Cock Robin.

Call for Clues

Okay, you leaves up there, come clean;
Your turn to sing out: whattaya seen?
You can't just perch there high and mighty
Whispering, rubbing your palms politely.
Speak up; someday you gotta tumble
Down in the dirt, red-faced and humble
Just like him. Now, who done this bird?
Whattaya seen and whattaya heard?

Cough it up, clouds; you're on the hook.
Don't give me no vague, wandering look.
Maybe you're short on shape and "It-ness";
We know damn well you was a witness.
You took in loads; you been aroun';
It weighs on you; it's a bringdown
Holding back. Spill it all, posthaste:
Who brung that bird out here to waste?

Okay, you stars, you sun and moon,
Pipe up; we're here to cop your tune.
You gone past here, so come acrost.
You gonna let his tunes get lost,
Buried in self-important sounds
Or dead air, then just go your rounds?
Ain't no tight-lipped, black hat can frighten us.
You high-flown, radiant types, enlighten us.

Listen, you hunks of sky, blank spaces
Absent-minded above our faces,
Between all stars, all small-time particles:
Man, beast, bird, tree, all living articles
That slump down groundward, dead and rotten,
Fly off in you and get forgotten.
Save something wunst. Get this thing solved.
Vast tracts of nothing, get involved!

W. D. Sits in Kafka's Chair
and Is Interrogated Concerning
the Assumed Death of Cock Robin

Now "W"—we'll call you "W,"
    Okay? We like the friendly touch.
Just a few questions that won't trouble you
    For long; this won't hurt much.

First: name, age, sex, race, genus,
    Specific gravity and species;
Hat size, color of hair and penis;
    Texture and frequency of feces?

Republican? No? Then a Baptist.
    If not, why not? If so, explain
Why you switched sides. Did your last Pap test
    Turn pink or blue? Are you insane?

When did you halt, cease or desist
    Beating your wife? Was she friends
With this Cock Robin long? Please list
    Payments from foreign governments.

Have you changed sperm count or IQ
    Within six months? Signed a confession?
Why are we holding you? If you
    Don't know, then why ask you this question?

A simple yes or no is all
    We want; the truth always shines through.
Thank you. Please wait out in the hall
    Until somebody comes for you.

W. D. Creates
a Device for Escaping

After one first green step ahead,
I brake down on this foot of red;
        A stop foot, then a go foot.

One arm, one leg in my own spokes,
A balance wheel of counterstrokes,
        A to foot, then a fro foot.

These blood-red hands before my face,
Carrots that keep me at my pace,
        A fast foot, then a slow foot,

As a pit pony cranks a winch,
Ixion axles, inch by inch,
        A start foot, then a whoa foot,

Beneath the circling stars and seasons,
Time's roulette game of rhymes and reasons,
        A con foot, then a pro foot,

Plodding, wing-burdened like a pack,
This dead-weight Robin on my back,
        A heel foot, then a toe foot.

He wears my stripes, he rides my wheel;
How shall my galls and blisters heal?—
        A high foot, then a low foot—

And where do ten-ton Robins sleep?
On my back still while I still creep,
              A quid foot, then a quo foot.

I could cut loose, leaving him bound
To ride this giddy Fun-Go-Round,
              A joy foot, then a woe foot,

Or turn weak like old Sisyface,
Letting him roll back to the base;
              A yes foot, then a no foot.

Disguised as Cock Robin,
W. D. Escapes

Come, Rosie Angel, faced with blues,
   Join hands and we'll be piped together
      Pilots of our own quarter, decked
In multiplicity's fast hues—
   This Joseph's cloak that many a feather
      Weaves—in fact, a factory reject

That is becoming without seems.
   Fortuna's game wheel be our helm;
      We'll shoot the jazzy straits of I-Am,
Flee all Utopia's bonded schemes
   Of ideal bondage for a live realm
      Where I'll lush up my lute like Khayyam

While you beside me, blushing warm,
   Sing out like Saki. At this wheel
      We'll steer, veer, chart what course we shipped,
Skipped, slipped out, then rode out the storm
   Reeling our catch of all that *is* real
      Out of this land of Gyp and Be Gypped.

Assuming Fine Feathers,
W. D. Takes Flight

Over these cheekbones,
  Streaked thick with bristle,
Draw down the soft down
  Sleek as a whistle.
    See feedle, seedle, tweedle tree.

My slimy nostrils,
  My slithery lips
Turn to a beak, blunt
  As dry facts or tinsnips.
    Homo nonsapiens conturbat me.

These split lids fit
  My eye like a filter;
The dim world clicks
  To a new green kilter.
    Earclay, eanseclay ymay ightsay.

Scapular, spellbound,
  These feathers drape
My shoulderblades
  Like an opera cape
    Cheggange meggee; freggee meggee.

Or a Sioux priest's vestments;
  Dare to assume
The adept's full mantle
  And the long tail-plume.
    Sing-a-ling, wing-wary-way.

Through clouds of unknowing
  I veer and sail;
Below, men's heads
  And dogs' heads wail—
    In nubibus, ignotum per ignotius—

Hot on my track still,
  But I tricked 'em;
Now who's your criminal;
  Where's your victim?
    Dee-flee-a-beadle-tweedle-free!

W. D. Disguised as Cock Robin and Hidden Deep in Crimson

They'll never find me hidden
So close to them, inside
Switched-on electric wires
Or nerve ends, in forbidden
Urges, rage, lust, pride,
Sweet murderous desires,
The medulla of old fires.

I go cloaked in the charged rag
That matadors must wave
To keep them out of sight;
Protected by the flag
They run up in the brave
Country of Dynamite;
I lurk in the Geistzeit.

I ride the pulse that swells
Lips, nails, all feverish parts;
I wear the blushing scarlet
Alphabet that spells
The blazing braille of hearts,
The shorted shorts of the harlot,
Virgin, housewife, starlet.

I doppelgang some grander
Land that schizophrenics
Colonize from earth,
One with the salamander,
With that flaming phoenix
Or lodgepole pine whose clenched cones need
The forest fire to cast their seed.

Auction

For the gay tailfeathers, say, what'll you pay?—
Red, blue and purple plumes—a bouquet
Of heather-spume, or a lit fountain's spray. Hey!
Shave a fine penpoint, whisk dust away
Or trim sharp the virginals' quills when you play.

Who'll buy an eye—aye, buy an eye!
This ringset onyx jet, black tack for your tie
Or oldtimer's photocell, spy in the sky,
Laserbeam click-ticking off who's slipped by
Or to glow soft by the cribside till dawntide draws nigh.

What am I bid for this swift wing?—
A deft wing, an arched-out lifting thing
To nail fast on your hallwalls or set fling
The soul's boomerang, the young shepherd's sling
That brings huge despair down, crowns the new king.

How much for the bones?—built-light-for-flight bones,
Leached, bleached out, scaled to high kite zones—
Buoyance that scoured out, scored, then bored right, loans
Range to a flute floating our warm and bright tones
Over the vast frozen waste no man owns.

How far will you go for his hard, sharp toenails?—
For harp picks, guitar picks, to pick locks, open jails,
Thumb tacks, phononeedles, needles to sew sails,
To turn toward true North in high snowthrown trails
Or seek the soft South when winter winds blow gales.

For this heart, smart and artful, hey, where will you start?—
A life's thump pump, formed to pyrite love's feverchart!
Let's throw in lights, liver, lungs, each left, torn apart,
Worn out part. Who'll start out—shebang and applecart
Go along; so what's wrong? Who'll buy a heart?

> I, said the fly, I go for the eye.
> Me, said the beetle, I'll buy me a bone.
> Mine, said the earthworm, I take the heart.

Part II
Darkling

A Darkling Alphabet

A is for Atom, the source
of the matter. Within it,
childlike, primal forces
meet, pivoting their courses
as unlike poles attract, submit
to power's laws, commit
themselves to form and limit.
For good or evil, it,
like humans, can be split.

B is for Brain, which helps us cope,
sometimes, with theories, art,
math, cataclysms, styles,
passions and affections.
Its networked scope
and tally of connections
exceed the sum of all
particles in this universe.
There *are* imperfections:
all fall
short; some, apart;
its core is still a reptile's
and we don't know
what that rules. Still, it's the one hope
of human being. And the curse.
At birth, you *did* have one
with all its nerve cells, though
if you start
using it, new circuitries can grow.
With luck, that's scarcely just begun;
if it's done, we're done.

C is for Cow; when little, you
were told that she said, Moo,
and had a crumpled horn.
She could get in the corn
but breathed sweet timothy and clover.
Maybe she *has* jumped over
the moon only to reappear
in strange new guises here:
in plastic cartons, wax-
lined boxes, thin-sliced stacks
of cheese, ranked steaks or chops
lining cool butcher shops,
as catchers' mitts, chairs, shoes,
purses, things we use
each day. Still, it's curious how
you never see one now.

D is for Demand, which is
normally for power, riches,
privilege and freedom
(most likely freedom from,
not to). Also,
for some outward show
of earned respect and love
that other people know
lies far above
our merit, so
keep to themselves. Be mindful of
what rank, insatiable itches
fester in the britches
of those *other* lustful, greedy sons of bitches.

E is for Earth, the Earth
that each man gains at birth,
at death. He thinks his mirth
or grief, her wealth or dearth,
implicit with his worth.
She, meantime, spreads his berth.

F is for Family where
we first learn we must share
a world with others, bear
their being, spare, or care
for, what we want to drive
away. In its snug hive
we also learn to lie, connive,
blame, betray, and to survive.

G is for Glamour; once, that meant
a diabolical enchantment
gypsies or sorcerers could lay
over one's eyes; this took away
all common sense, all will to fight
their will, all care for wrong or right
until their power grew absolute.
Now'days, we'll take no substitute.

H is for Hitler, the great
purveyor of Glamour and of Hate
who promised heaven on earth, then tossed
us all to hell and holocaust
and fifty millions dead—a cost
that might seem small, suppose we'd lost.
Some who survived suspect
he hides among us still. Correct.
Their post-war histories
prove his victorious enemies
harbor him, in whole or part,
locked in the heart
of every living man or woman.
Hate this: he still is human.

I is for I, since we
are the only creatures whose Identity
concerns them. Most are content
to live; we must live with Intent.
We Invent Images, Ideas,
Ideals, are Impelled to be as
Important as our thought.
In time, we think we're what we're not.
Philosopher, teacher, poet
say you get one self: know it.
You just might grow it.

J is for Jay, whose splash
of gorgeousness transforms
middle class lawns—a slash
of blue-black plumes that clash
with business suits and sober norms
like school band uniforms.
Its music, sadly, is a brash,
rude jeer that well might waken
the dead—waken even critics, jurists—
pure poetry to purists
of the factory horn. Mistaken,
often, for American tourists.

K is for Key; we use
it to shut out a world that's rife
with possibilities we choose
to miss—murder, rape and theft,
e.g.   Jailed up inside our life,
we try to make terms with what's left:
three chairs that match, one wife.
It confers mastery of space
by setting bounds, is sovereign mace
and scepter to the exclusive place
where we think we belong.
It does as much for Song.

L is for Love, another
paradox. When we were born,
apparently our mother
fed us and so chose
to save our lives. Still, such care shows
our frailty. All our lives, we are torn
by our relentless needs
and our conspicuous scorn
for anything that feeds

and so betrays our weakness.
If that sounds like sickness,
think: we also admire and emulate
those we hate.

M is for Mystery that's never
scarce in this life. It will endure:
men are stone-blind; meantime, it winks
out everywhere. Yet each man thinks
there must be ways he can secure
its glance in favor of some clever
scheme or self-concerned endeavor.

Then these dolts boggle at our hurry
to find out what this world's about.
You've heard the Mystery-mongers say:
Wait! Wait! Mystery's being driven away!
Have faith: Mystery can look out
for itself—from all sides. Mystery
reads all the papers. Not to worry.

N is for Nest, that's hidden
far in the arched and bending limbs.
There, young boys are forbidden
to get too curious and molest
songbirds where they take their rest
or come together in unsuppressed
vaults of elation—as the blest
congregation of seraphim's
spanned cathedral groins attest
to exalted impulse and, possessed,
choir forth lascivious hymns.

O is for Others, the one
thing one can't abide. Comparison
is odious. We can't endure
that others seem stronger, more secure,
more gifted; self-preservation
and pride
drive out uncommon sense,
brilliance or power, try to dispense
with genius and its cruel pretense
to difference.
Lonely, bored, you take a bride
only in due time to learn
she has more concern
with some strange life of hers
than yours.
All men may be brothers;
brothers are known
for treachery. If you had your druthers
you'd just as lief be left alone
with your own
looking glass or clone.

P is for Power, whose name
has fallen into ill repute
since it corrupts—absolute
power, absolutely. Yet the same
thing must be said, also,
for weakness. All things can
corrupt those born corruptible: Man.
If you're gonna go, you're gonna go.
Further, we'd have to say
rich chances for increased fertility
lie, often, in impurity,
corruption and decay.
Rapists say if you can see
no possibility to escape
suffering or committing rape,
why not . . .? I don't think I'd agree.
It *might* pay to avoid hysterics
and broad theories. Offered powers,
free time, funds, you could manure flowers
or write yourself some deathless lyrics.

Q is for Quiet,
a deep calm in the ear
whose qualities allow the spirit
to seek out its own voice. You just might try it;
Quakers love it. Most others fear it
worse than the news they hear
of plague and riot.
Lord, won't you buy
us eight-tracks, horns for cars;
give us our daily fix of violence
from ghetto blasters, pitchmen; keep us high
while waiting for restoring silence
to settle among the stars
by and by.

R is for Rhythm, for the deep
push and pull of tides, the thud
of pulse and impulse in our blood
to rise and fall, wake and sleep,
the rhyme that beats time for the tune
and moves the circling sun and moon
waltzing around again to bring
summer, autumn, winter, spring
and renaissance to each green thing.
It's like a chime, the echoing sound
of heartbeat from our mothers' wombs
so all our lives we must surround
ourselves with music in our rooms.
We're like a relocated puppy
alone at night; if he wakes up, he
takes solace in the tick and talk
of an old, fur-wrapped alarm clock.
Failed musicians learn one fact:
true rhythms seldom are exact—
lovers, also, whose wild rhythm
propels them through a bestial dance
that moves their loins to take the chance
and unexpected children with them.

S is for Success
which we flee like a curse
and so dispossess
ourselves; some malediction which
we swore against the rich
could fall on our own head.
Then, too, one who succeeds
can't act abused or frail;
instead,
he must face others' needs.
We'd rather fail.
Yet this can make sense, too:
conquerors do well to do
with less
than everything. Choose
to win too much
too soon and you lose touch
with your wrongheadedness.
Lose
early and avoid the rush
at the war's end. Look up, perhaps,
the Avars or the Alans who
gained ground till they seemed ready to
swallow up all the maps;
now, nobody knows their name.
Species can do the same.

T is for Tyrant, one
who rules by force and terror,
deathsquad, noose and gun.
With no trial, no pity,
he'll rase field, farm and city
to sniff out every bearer
of bad news, all whose error
is thinking their own thoughts. If cursed
by those who live elsewhere
and can afford
such talk—who think their lord
more bountiful, much fairer,
tenderhearted—he should care.
By those who see him at his worst,
sweat cold beneath his sword,
he'll be adored.

U is for Urge
which we try to control;
still, even on the verge
of some long-sought goal,
we learn we've paid a toll:
we've had to purge
the surge
and voltage of our whole
self and soul.

V is for Vote. You do?
Supposing Whatchamacallit
And Whosis want to pick my wallet,
I don't pick who.

W is for Wrong which we,
however good or bright,
must be.
Dictators, hedged in might,
can wallow in one rare delight:
infallibility.
So, they prolong
the time before humanity
proves what mortal fools we be.
Achilles, strong,
self-righteous, racked with spite,
brought friend and foe alike to flight
and slaughter, yet in that great song,
bent his head, too, along
with the vast throng
of those who'd been, and who'd done, wrong.

X is for X-ray
that pries and pokes into
things set in its way.
Taking a broad view
of the body's blue-
prints, it can lay
out balance sheets
and schedules where it meets
our record of transactions, true
outlays and false receipts,
areas of decay
we're loath
to ponder, that dark growth
we hide away.
It discerns both
hairline splits in bone
and open, spikey
fractures. None is known
that witnesses the psyche.

Y is for Yes and that's
the poet's word. He must affirm
what makes ideacrats
and joiners itchy. He can't squirm

out by trying to deny
what doesn't fit his definition
of the Good and True. His mission
is to believe only his eye,

the burning witness of his senses,
his emotions, passions—
a private mandate that dispenses
with theories and fashions.

The rest all know how to create
a world they think would suit
them better, how to set life straight
by their lights, their law. He'd not dispute

one word, but sees the blind child starving
on the doorstep, bodies in the street
the rich drive down, lovers carving
each other's guts out, defeat

wrung from our greatest triumphs by
our greed and cowardice. He may
ask what and how and why;
he can't ask things to go away

unsaid. What he'd prefer
cuts no ice here. He knows his place is
breadth and his appetite embraces
victim and executioner.

His job's to celebrate
what IS—now, while it's not too late.
If all the groupies hate him,
he's doing *something* right; congratulate him.

Z is for Zero, the last
numeral and, in a blast,
the last place to be on the ground.
It's infinite, since round,
and devoid of any contrast.
All things on earth have passed,
or will, through this small, profound
hole to enter the vast
and the vacuum. It closes fast.

Disguised as Humpty-Dumpty,
W. D. Practices Tumbling

What is more odious than all
Fence-sitting, straddling a wall?
Why should we back away and stall
    Teetering here all day afraid of
    Showing the world the stuff we're made of?

We know a man by what he'll tumble
To; pride goes before a stumble.
It's falling keeps a body humble.
    Some fall to work, some to their meal;
    All life must fall with Fortune's wheel.

Some use their training and their talents
To walk up wires and keep their balance;
Some leap, all buoyancy and valiance,
    In broad air; still we judge their worth
    When they've come back in touch with earth.

Into the nest of twig and feather
The egg must fall; the question's whether
You bounce back keeping things together.
    Some fall to tumbling in the hay;
    Some fall in love and crack that way.

Let others practice wings and Springs;
The falling leaf, the fall of kings
Rings out the old—the downward swing
    Of clocks and stocks, the Fall of Man,
    Fall is where everything began.

We hope to build this to a smash
Hit sport just like the Fender Bash,
The Fall from Grace, the Market Crash.
    The real point isn't winning; what's
    Important is to show some guts.

The House the Poet Built

This is the house the poet built.

This is the silence everyone heard
Inside the house the poet built.

Here is the high goal out in the yard;
This is the silence everyone heard
Inside the house the poet built.

Here is a hummingbird on guard
Perched on the high goal out in the yard;
This is the silence everyone heard
Inside the house the poet built.

Here is the lady of his regard
Who watched the hummingbird standing guard
Next to the high goal in the yard;
This is the silence everyone heard
Inside the house the poet built.

Here are the heavens, many-starred,
Over the lady of his regard
Who saw the hummingbird on guard
Near to the high goal out in the yard;
This is the silence everyone heard
Inside the house the poet built.

Here is the hawk whose screams were heard
Throughout the heavens, many-starred,
Over the lady of his regard
Who saw the hummingbird stand guard
Near to the high goal out in the yard;
This is the silence everyone heard
Inside the house the poet built.

Here is the flitter-bat that whirred
At night when the hawk was no more heard
Under the heavens, many-starred,
Over the lady of his regard
Who knew where the hummingbird stood on guard
Beside the high goal out in the yard;
This is the silence everyone heard
Inside the house the poet built.

Here is the poet, the daft, old bard
Who watched the flitter-bats that whirred
At night when the hawk was no more heard
Under the heavens, radiant-starred,
Over the lady of his regard
Who fed the hummingbird standing guard
Beside the high goal out in the yard;
This is the silence everyone heard
Inside the house the poet built.

These are the lips that uttered the word
That rang in the ears of the dotty old bard
While watching the flitter-bats that whirred
At night when the hawk was no more heard
Under the heavens, radiant-starred,
That lit the lady of his regard
Who spoke to the hummingbird on guard
Beside the high goal in the yard;
This is the silence everyone heard
Clasped in the house the poet built.

Dostoievsky Warns W. D.
about Wearing Raskolnikov's Hat

*(Dostoievsky, a large blue rabbit,
addresses a startled child.)*

To step out sporting such a topper
Seems highfalutin' and improper
To men of average ability;
You catch their eyes, then their hostility.
They'll brand you uppity and vain,
Acting as if you had more brain
To cover up. You'll hear it said:
There's more inside this than his head—
What if he's smuggling contraband,
Cocaine or concealed weapons? *And*
There's room in such a tall hatband
For worse: a pair of rabbit ears!
He could be one of those that hears
Lost voices, taps top-secret thought
Whose meaning even we forgot,
That scans, like supersonic bats,
The blips we keep beneath our hats,
Decodes brain waves, bugs dreams of ours,
Broadcasting them to foreign powers!
Why else would he need such antennae?
Good honest folks sure don't have any.
Let's get rid quick of this high-hatted dude;
Besides, we just don't like his attitude.

W. D. Attempts to Swallow the Symbol‘ ‘ ‘ ‘ ‘ ‘ ‘ ‘ ‘ ‘ ‘ ‘ ‘ ‘ ‘

*—The poet, assisted by a small
blue angel, tries to swallow a large
pyramidal object.*

Never put anything, they tell you,
inside your ear
that's smaller than your elbow.
Then hand you THIS.
It is like swallowing your head
with corners. And, like a good deed
or an ill-intended oyster,
revisits you. It's
like a dumb love
song, this aftertaste
of doubt, of questioning
that says: too much yet not enough.
Here is this
triangle of equal sides and
Cajun dances, alarms
clanging, calls to prayer;
this trinitarian delta where
all waters ought
to flow; this pyramid
supposed to sharpen razors,
preserve our steaks and sanity,
restore time and your timepiece,
frame the God's eye and
my I.
With all the good will and with all
the orange juice in the world,
                                        it
won't
          go
down.

The Poet Ridiculed
by
Hysterical Academics

Is it, then, your opinion
    Women are putty in your hands?
Is this the face to launch upon
    A thousand one night stands?

First, please, would you be so kind
    As to define your contribution
To modern verse, the Western mind
    And human institutions?

        Where, where is the long, flowing hair,
            The velvet suit, the broad bow tie;
        Where is the other-worldly air,
            Where the abstracted eye?

Describe the influence on your verse
    Of Oscar Mudwarp's mighty line,
The theories of Susan Schmersch
    Or the spondee's decline.

    You've labored to present us with
        This mouse-sized volume; shall this equal
    The epic glories of Joe Smith?
        He's just brought out a sequel.

Where are the beard, the bongo drums,
Tattered T-shirt and grubby sandals,
As who, released from Iowa, comes
To tell of wondrous scandals?

Have you subversive, out of date,
Or controversial ideas?
And can you really pull your weight
Among such minds as these?

Ah, what avails the tenure race,
Ah, what the Ph.D.,
When all departments have a place
For nincompoops like thee?

Notes on Publication

I. *Heart's Needle* was first published by Alfred A. Knopf, Inc. in 1959. The following year the Marvell Press published an English edition which included a prose essay entitled "Finding a Poem". Of the original thirty poems, I here include seventeen.

II. *Remains* was first published in a small, letterpress edition under the pseudonym S. S. Gardons by the Perishable Press in 1970. After the death of my parents, a new edition was issued by BOA Editions, Ltd. under my own name. In that edition, as here, a single poem, "The Father", has been substantially revised.

III. *The Boy Made of Meat* was first written in 1962 for a series of children's books edited by Louis Untermeyer; it was accepted but never published since the series was discontinued. After Untermeyer's death William Ewert found the manuscript among Untermeyer's papers and asked if he could make a small, fine press edition. After substantial revisions in 1981 and 1982 it appeared in the latter year under his imprint.

IV. *After Experience* was first published by Harper & Row, Inc. in 1967; the following year, Oxford University Press issued an English edition. Of the forty poems I here include twenty-four. Of these, "Manet: 'The Execution of the Emperor Maximilian'" and "Van Gogh: 'The Starry Night'" have been substantially revised.

V. *The Fuehrer Bunker* was published as a "poem-in-progress" by BOA Editions, Ltd. in 1977. Two further selections from the cycle appeared in small, fine press edition: "Magda Goebbels" was published by Palaemon Press in 1983 and "Heinrich Himmler" by Pterodactyl Press in 1983. The cycle now consists of some seventy poems not including the choruses from the performance staged at The American Place Theatre in 1981 and from the performances at the University of Eastern Michigan at Ypsilanti, Michigan in 1987; I hope to finish it shortly. Of the sixteen poems included here, all but two appeared in the volumes listed above.

VI. *If Birds Build with Your Hair* was published in a small letterpress edition by Nadja Press in 1979. I reprint here poems from that volume as well as one other poem written in the same period and never collected in a volume, "Coming Down from the Acropolis", which appeared as a separate broadside issued by the Derry Press.

VII. *A Locked House* was published by William Ewert in 1986. I include here all poems from that volume as well as "D. D. Byrde Calling Jennie Wrenne", which was published by William Ewert in 1984.

VIII. *Kinder Capers* is the title of a cycle of poems which includes as Part I "The Death of Cock Robin" and as Part II "Darkling". *The Kinder Capers,* published by Nadja Press in 1986, consisted of three poems included in this volume. A volume to be entitled *The Death of Cock Robin* will be published by The University of Delaware Press in 1987. That volume will contain thirty-three poems and reproductions of thirty-four paintings by DeLoss McGraw which often bear the same titles and to which the poems are intimately related. All the poems in *Kinder Capers* are closely related to paintings by DeLoss McGraw except "Through the Nursery Window". "Through the Nursery Window", which is dedicated to McGraw's son, is previously uncollected.

Copyedited by Margaret Wolf.
Designed by Frank Lamacchia.
Production by H. Dean Ragland,
Cobb/Dunlop Publishers Services, Inc.
Set in Garamond by Kachina Typesetting, Inc.
Printed by the Maple-Vail Company on acid-free laid paper,
and manufactured with sewn bindings.